SMALL WORLD

International Readings in Sociology

EDITED BY

Lorne Tepperman

James Curtis

Susannah J. Wilson

AND

Alan Wain

PRENTICE HALL CANADA INC.,
SCARBOROUGH, ONTARIO

Canadian Cataloguing in Publication Data

Main entry under title:
Small world: international readings in sociology

ISBN 0-13-099268-2

1. Sociology.   I. Tepperman, Lorne, 1943-

HM51.S63   1994   301   C93-094294-9

Prentice-Hall, Inc., Englewood Cliffs, New Jersey
Prentice-Hall International (UK) Limited, London
Prentice-Hall of Australia, Pty. Limited, Sydney
Prentice-Hall Hispanoamericana, S.A., Mexico City
Prentice-Hall of India Private Limited, New Delhi
Prentice-Hall of Japan, Inc., Tokyo
Simon & Schuster Asia Private Limited, Singapore
Editora Prentice-Hall do Brasil, Ltda., Rio de Janeiro

ISBN 0-13-099268-2

Acquisitions Editor: Michael Bickerstaff
Developmental Editor: Lisa Penttilä
Production Editor: Mary Ann Field
Permissions/Photo Research: Robyn Craig
Interior and Cover Design: Monica Kompter
Cover Image: Masterfile/Damir Frkovic
Page Layout: Arlene Edgar

1 2 3 4 5   BG   98 97 96 95 94

Printed and bound in Canada

Every reasonable effort has been made to obtain permissions for all articles
and data used in this edition. If errors or omissions have occurred, they will
be corrected in future editions provided written notification has been received
by the publisher.

Portions of the articles have been deleted. Some footnotes have been removed;
those remaining have been renumbered.

TABLE OF CONTENTS

SECTION 2: Socialization

SECTION 3: Deviance and Control

SECTION 4: Class, Inequality, and Stratification

SECTION 5: Race and Ethnic Relations

SECTION 6: Gender Relations

SECTION 7: Family

SECTION 8: Work and Organizations

SECTION 9: Population

SECTION 10: The State and Government

SECTION 11: Ideology and Protest

SECTION 12: Social Change

PREFACE

A rapidly changing world calls for new kinds of textbooks. Instructors in sociology need textbooks that talk about social life in ways their undergraduate students can relate to this fluid, changeable world. Students need books that will teach them about the world and its variety while introducing the topics and traditions of sociology.

With this in mind, we have examined other textbooks on sociology, reviewed our own experiences in teaching undergraduates, spoken to other sociology instructors and, finally, recalled our own first years in sociology. *Small World* reflects our sense of what we as instructors can tell undergraduate students of sociology that is true, important, clear, and interesting.

In this book, we use materials from around the world to illustrate basic sociological concepts and theories. *Small World* is designed to supplement the historical and cross cultural materials in any introductory text in sociology, and to augment the typical sociology-as-science approach with other, competing approaches. The effect is a richer and hopefully tastier slice of sociology.

We believe that the best way for students to learn about the various influences on social life in a modern world and the kinds of institutional arrangements that support them is to study sociology from an international perspective. Material for this type of study is what this book aims to provide. Some of the excerpts are cross-nationally comparative, while others are case studies of a single country. Our goal is to include excerpts from as many countries and sociological perspectives as possible.

Professional social scientists have written all of the excerpts in this book. Since professional writing is often telegraphic and sometimes obscure, we introduce each excerpt in *Small World* with a few paragraphs describing the purpose and setting the context of the piece. As well, each section of the book is introduced by a brief essay that foreshadows and integrates the excerpts that follow.

Because of the great diversity of materials and approaches, learning aids play a critical role in making this book a success. Each section ends with discussion questions and exercises that help the student understand and review the pieces. These questions will stimulate classroom discussion by suggesting unresolved issues and recalling earlier readings. A glossary at the end of the book defines the key concepts.

Again, the purpose of this review material is to help students unpack the case studies they are reading and find relevance in them for their own lives. In this way we guide the student to seeing meaningful patterns in what is, admittedly, a world's worth of material.

This book departs from the usual textbook in at least one more respect: its constant concern with relating sociology to everyday life. In particular, the readings reflect two main kinds of everyday experience: on the one hand, the routines of family and work; on the other hand, the structures of social inequality (i.e., gender, class, and racial) which influence family, work and other everyday experiences.

As for the articles we have chosen to excerpt, there are certainly many other topics we might have covered. The issues we *do* cover are all (1) important and (2) timely. We could not cover *all* of the important issues a reader can think of. In the next edition, we will cover some other topics, depending on the availability of good articles on those topics. Let us know what you want to see!

We have had a lot of fun and excitement putting this book together. We hope you enjoy it too.

ACKNOWLEDGEMENTS

Lorne, Jim, Sue and Al have worked together as editors in pairs and trios several times before, always with good effect; and most of us have worked with Prentice Hall Canada before too. So, not surprisingly, our work on *Small World* went very smoothly.

Our thanks go to Prentice Hall Canada and first of all to acquisitions editor Mike Bickerstaff for seeing the merit in this book and supporting it fully. Thanks, also, go to Prentice Hall's anonymous reviewers who gave us good advice on things we ought to modify in our final plan. Then, Lisa Penttilä, the developmental editor, Elizabeth Long, the initial production editor, and Robyn Craig, the permissions editor, quickly jumped our manuscript through the usual hoops, obtaining permissions to reprint these excerpts and otherwise seeing that everything went smoothly. Jean Ferrier made sure that all the pieces fitted together in a sensible, understandable way, and Mary Ann Field edited the copy with great thoroughness. In fact, the entire Prentice Hall staff worked with dedication, professionalism, and good humour to get this book out on time. Thanks, all of you.

Other thanks go to the authors whose articles we have excerpted here, and who have allowed us to reprint them in a shortened (sometimes *drastically* shortened) form. This book could not have existed without their insight and effort.

Finally, we are grateful for support from the University of Toronto. A grant from the Provost's Ethno-Cultural Academic Initiatives Fund helped Lorne to collect international materials for his Sociology 101 (Introduction to Sociology) course. This book is a byproduct of that activity.

Our experience as teachers tells us Canadian undergraduate students are struggling mightily to understand this rapidly changing, exciting, and sometimes terrifying world. We hope they will find this book helps them in their struggle.

CULTURE

Introduction

"Culture" includes all the ways people regularly think and act, the material objects they use in daily life, and the ideas that guide them. In fact, "culture" is a humanly created environment for all our thoughts and actions.

By having a culture, every social group — whether a society, community, or an ethnic or religious group — also gains a memory of its past. Many groups even have "bibles" in which they record their legends, parables, and ideas. For example, the Jewish and Christian bibles both contain histories of the famous and the infamous, the wise and the wicked. In the Judeo-Christian tradition, the Old and New Testaments provide us with a "great code" — a set of heroes and villains, legends, and parables — that shapes our ways of seeing the world.

"Civil religions" have the same effect. For example, in the United States, people learn legends and parables about Washington, Lincoln, Roosevelt, Kennedy, and Martin Luther King. Their words and deeds are often invoked to mobilize patriotic sentiment and set an example for the younger generation.

Even social sciences like sociology are culturally shaped ways of understanding and remembering our history. This point is developed further in excerpt 1.1, which explores variations in sociology around the world.

Although culture is a means of remembering the past, it is often a poor way of thinking about the future. And since it is about a particular tradition or set of experiences, a culture rarely helps people tolerate other cultures very well. Many people tend to think their own culture is better than any other. As a result, they have difficulty understanding and appreciating the traditions of another culture.

How Culture Shapes Behaviour

Culture influences people's behaviour in three main ways: (a) through values; (b) through norms; and (c) through language and perception.

All behaviour is an interplay of our personal experience, the social order that surrounds us, and the culture in which we live. Whether we are painting a picture, getting married, starting a business, practising medicine or raising children, we do this under the influence of personal history, current social conditions, and the received cultural tradition.

As we mix these elements together in new combinations that reflect current social conditions and personal experiences, we change the cultural tradition. We form somewhat new kinds of families, make somewhat new kinds of businesses, paint somewhat new kinds of pictures. So we are, all of us, always creating our own culture while using the culture that other generations have left behind.

Values

As a set of values, culture changes more slowly than the social rules, or norms, which define our institutions. Consider this example. In his classic work, *The Protestant Ethic and the Spirit of Capitalism*, Max Weber argued that the sixteenth century rise of Calvinism, a type of protestant Christian belief, was essential to the development of capitalism.

Today it is hard to believe that people once thought life on earth was less important than life after death, or that they saw hard work, thrift, and saving as unimportant or even wicked. Yet people in the medieval, Catholic societies of Europe *did* think a concern with worldly activities, wealth, and profit-making through the investment of money was immoral. They were much more communally oriented, like the Nigerians described in excerpt 1.2 below, and the pre-industrial English described in excerpt 1.3.

By contrast, Calvinism urged people to conduct their lives in ascetic, inner-worldly ways. It encouraged them to save, rather than spend, their money, and to work very hard. They worked hard, Weber said, not because good works or success would guarantee them a place in heaven, but because success in this world would show whether they were among the "Elect," those chosen to go to heaven after death. And since people wanted to know if they were "saved," they worked very hard and looked for signs of God's grace.

Weber argued that these habits of thrift and hard work were crucial to the rise of capitalism. Calvinism did not invent the ideas of capitalism, private ownership, or free enterprise: people had already thought about these things at many times and places. But it did supply a religious and emotional basis for the flowering of capitalist practices.

What's more, Calvinism justified and encouraged activities that the Catholic Church had frowned on. By doing so, it offered a moral justification for the economic behaviour we call capitalism. This, says Weber, is why capitalism developed in Protestant Europe, rather than in Catholic southern Europe, or in India, China, or ancient Israel — other societies Weber studied.

This link between the rise of protestantism and capitalism shows how changes in one cultural domain (in this case, religion) may unintentionally bring about changes in another (in this case, the economy). And, as you can see, these cultural changes can survive for many centuries.

Norms

However, few of our everyday life activities are directed by basic values: they are more likely to be directed by the norms (or rules) that grow out of these basic values. *Norms* serve as guidelines for our everyday behaviour. They tell us what is appropriate or inappropriate, normal or abnormal, in everyday situations.

In every society most people follow the appropriate norms of behaviour most of the time. We have internalized these rules, making them part of our personalities. And because we are social creatures, we need the approval of others in order to feel worthwhile. Conformity to the rules of our culture is thus largely self-imposed and unconscious.

Like values, norms change over time and as they change they give rise to changes in material culture. Take nasal hygiene: it has only been a Western cultural concern for three or four centuries. Today, most of us know the rules of nose-blowing: e.g., carry a tissue, use it discreetly, and dispose of it neatly, without inspecting the contents. Personal hygiene is very important in our culture: although we may pollute the air and water with smoke and chemicals, we are careful not to wipe our noses on our sleeves.

As we shall see in a later section, norms do not determine our behaviour automatically. Deviation from these norms is always possible and all of us deviate from some norms some of the time. So we should view norms as rules which most people accept and follow most of the time, but they are always being modified, always gaining and losing acceptance. People are often uncertain about the social norms: that's why there are books of etiquette.

Language

Each culture has its own set of assumptions about reality that influences behaviour and that is often betrayed in the use of language. Language is one aspect of culture Canadians are particularly sensitive about, because Canada is a multicultural, multilingual society.

Language is a system of sounds (speech), signs (written characters), and gestures (non-verbal communication) by which the members of a society express their thoughts, feelings, ideas, and desires. Language provides ready-made categories through which speakers deal with the world. When children learn to speak the language of their culture, they also adopt the assumptions that pervade their language.

It is useful to think of language in the same way we think of a computer operating system like DOS: it allows us to share a way of structuring information and to run a cultural "program" (e.g., learn the rules of nasal hygiene to be socially acceptable). From this standpoint, we can think of Calvinist religion as a system modification that allowed Western culture to run the program titled "capitalism" smoothly and quickly.

The "computing language" that works in our society will not, necessarily, work in another one; indeed, many concepts and commands would be incomprehensible. That is because cultures make words to describe what a society cares about. No wonder then that the Inuit have dozens of words for "snow" of different kinds, while English speakers may have only a half dozen. On the other hand, the English language has dozens and possibly hundreds of words that describe machines of various kinds. Inuit and other pre-industrial languages have very few such words.

In general, languages differ in their ability to name and talk about certain kinds of things, and this makes communication across cultures very difficult. It also makes rapid cultural change very difficult. A person from a pre-industrial culture who wishes to assimilate into an industrial society will have to learn new speaking and thinking patterns which may differ considerably from those of his or her own culture.

Words communicate ideas to us both directly and indirectly. They are a way of expressing what we want to say; but they are also a way of organizing what we may not even realize we think. Other cultural "category systems" have a similar effect: for example, the tendency to categorize and evaluate people according to their skin colour. As we see in excerpt 1.4, there is a nearly universal tendency to rate light-skinned people above dark-skinned people. But this turns out to tell us more about cultural imperialism than it does about a "natural" tendency in human beings.

In short, "culture" encompasses a wide variety of patterns of thought and action. The few excerpts that follow can only hint at the richness of this topic for sociologists and other social scientists. Appropriately, we begin with an excerpt on the ways culture has influenced the development of sociology itself.

1.1 Neil J. Smelser

Cultural Influences on Sociology

INTRODUCTION

As we have said, sociology includes the study of culture. But sociology itself is a culturally defined style of thinking. It has a particular history and varies from one society to another. In the West, sociology only emerged in its present form a little over a century ago. In other societies, the development of sociology is even more recent and incomplete.

Wherever we find it, and however old or recent it may be, sociology reflects its social and cultural environment. As the next excerpt by Smelser shows, North American sociology is very much a product of North American culture. For example, it focuses on the values and motives of individuals, making the assumption that freely acting individuals are the basis of any sociological explanation.

In other societies, sociologists may put less emphasis on individuals and more emphasis on social classes, ethnic groups, and regions of a country. In Canada, for example, sociologists pay far more attention to political and economic forces, acting in a historical context, than one normally finds in American sociology. In this respect, Canadian sociology is an interesting mixture of American and European traditions.

Throughout this book we will see a wide variation in the kinds of questions sociologists ask and the ways they go about answering them.

There is a multiplicity of cultural, economic, political and organisational influences in the evolution of a field of knowledge as large and complex as sociology. To speak of cultural influences is to suggest that major motifs and emphases in any national sociological tradition will reflect the implications of the major value and ideological components of the larger culture that harbours it. Several examples come readily to mind:

- In Latin American sociology, there is a special emphasis on the political and class dimensions. It has been declared that even though the starting point of inquiry may be work, health, or social protest, all sociological analysis in Latin America ends up as political analysis. This is clearly an exaggeration, but any review of theoretical writings and empirical research in these countries reveals the salience of that theme.

Smelser, Neil J. (1989). "External Influences on Sociology," *International Sociology*, 4(4), December, 419–429. Reprinted by permission.

- In Great Britain is found a special scholarly fascination with social stratificatio and social classes, and the manifestation of these in all other areas of social life, such as education, culture and family.

- Sociological theory in the Soviet Union and the socialist countries of Eastern Europe was for a long time under the ideological shadow of often orthodox Marxist-Leninist doctrines that proscribed official interpretations of capitalist and socialist societies that left little room for the development of alternative lines of thought; as that shadow has lifted sociological theory is becoming increasingly variegated.

- American research on social stratification has stressed individual mobility more than collective mobility, and upward mobility more than downward mobility. These emphases can be seen as manifesting a special preoccupation with the American cultural value of individual achievement. That research also has focussed on rates of individual mobility over time and above all with blockages to mobility (e.g., racial discrimination) which no doubt reveals a sensitivity to the degree to which the American cultural value of equality of opportunity is or is not being realised (Blau and Duncan, 1967).

Turning to the American value system more generally, it is possible to cull from the insights of various observers and analysts (Tocqueville, 1841; Parsons, 1951; Williams, 1963) a number of recurrent themes:

- individualism, with an assumption of responsibility for one's conduct;

- mastery of nature and of one's fate;

- voluntary cooperation as the basis of interaction;

- social order based on moral consensus, as contrasted with hierarchical ordering, class or authority (consistent with the early Republican rejection of European patterns of monarchy and aristocracy);

- pragmatism, incrementalism, and reform as principles of social changes;

- a resultant optimism.

It would be a serious oversimplification to argue that these themes have dominated American sociology, and, more broadly, the behavioural and social sciences in general, but it would also be a mistake to ignore them.

Similar continuities might be observed in many schools of thought that have had indigenous American origins. It can be argued, for example, that role theory is based on the assumption of socialisation into, and more or less voluntary compliance with, the "expectations" of others, and the mechanisms of social control associated with role theory stress conformity rather than obedience to authority or submission to coercion. The school of symbolic interaction, rooted in the pragmatic philosophies of Dewey, Mead and Blumer conceive of the actor as an agent, an active user and manipulator of his or her symbolic environment, and not in any way enslaved by the structural forces of society, by instinct, or by mechanical principles such as behavioural conditioning; in this sense the tenets of symbolic interactionism can be regarded as a kind of celebration of individual mastery and freedom, in contrast to the more deterministic theories against which it is counterpoised. Much of exchange theory, too, while it has origins in economic theories of competition, shares with these the underlying assumption that exchange is a matter of freely supplying and demanding resources and rewards to and from others. And, finally, the central features of Parsonian sociology, and functionalism in general, are voluntarism and consensus around a moral order.

To point out these continuities, of course, is to simplify matters greatly. American sociology has been characterised also by theoretical formulations that stand in critical dialogue with these strands and stress themes of inequality, domination and coercion. Many of these theories are of European origin, and have found their way into American sociology through the works of those who came from Europe (for example, Sorokin, 1927) or studied in Europe (e.g., Parsons, 1937), or who were otherwise inspired by the European masters (e.g., Mills, 1956).

These system/collectivist/critical/radical perspectives have themselves come to constitute a major part of sociology in the United States, and continue to be nourished by the more contemporary contributions of European scholars, such as Habermas, Touraine, Bourdieu, Giddens, and others. The field can be regarded as a kind of continuous dialogue and ferment among these strands of thought, some consonant with and some in critical opposition to the dominant themes of the American cultural tradition.

This notion of a continuous cultural dialogue within the discipline is closely connected with an observable but not very well understood phenomenon of the periodic rise and fall of the great historic figures of the field in sociological research and explanation. Durkheim and Freud held great sway in the two post-war decades in American sociology and social science generally, but the fortunes of both, especially the latter, have now faded somewhat and the neo-Marxian and neo-Weberian themes have risen in salience. European sociology has witnessed an ebbing of Marxian sociology as such, but continues to generate and nurture theories which cannot be described as Marxian but which retain some distinctive thread of Marxian thought, such as the ideas of domination and protest (new critical theory and the new social movements school, for example). As indicated, we do not understand the vicissitudes of the masters very well. Some of these might be a generational matter; one cohort of sociologists may embrace and make productive use of the insights of a Tocqueville or a Freud, while the next, facing new intellectual problems, and perhaps eager to distance itself from the work of its teachers, will forsake those figures and resurrect others; still another cohort will call up the heroes of their teachers' teachers. In any event, this invocation of the notion of a kind of myriad of cultural dialogues within sociology that mirror large cultural themes brings into question the strict distinction between internal and external influences on the evolution of a field of inquiry.

Keeping Up with Society

One of the key influences in the development of sociology is the fact that much of its subject-matter is dictated by real and perceived social trends in the larger society. If one examines the rise of new areas of interest in the past several decades, one will find the family and unemployment emerging in the years of the Great Depression, propaganda and public opinion and rumour in World War II, a burst of new interests in the sociology of poverty, sociology of education, sociology of youth and feminist sociology in the 1960s and immediately thereafter, and environmental sociology, the sociology of energy, and the sociology of risk more recently. All these are evident reactions to social problematics.

The rise and fall of major figures, mentioned before, might also be explained in part by the changing historical circumstances of any given society. The evident rise of interest in Marx and Weber in the United States in the 1960s and 1970s can be regarded as a kind of intellectual mirror of the group conflict and political turmoil of those decades. It also makes sense in that, as colonial countries are struggling under the yoke of the colonial powers and subsequently are fighting to consolidate their own independence, they may turn to the Marxian notions of exploitation and dominance to enlighten their understanding; when they move actively into the phase of building institutions and promoting economic growth, the theories of a Joseph Schumpeter might appear more attractive.

A closely related tendency to these is for our subject-matter to run ahead of the conceptual frameworks under which we study it. The most important illustration of this concerns the study of international relations and international interdependencies. If we examine our major sociological heritage, it is apparent that most of our theories are based on the postulate that most of what transpires in social life does so within single societies and, indeed, intra-societal forces are the main operative determinants. Put another way, sociologists have tended to regard the single society, nation or culture as the principal unit of analysis for their studies. When we look around the contemporary world, however, it is apparent that the relevance of this kind of approach grows less and less. Nations grow more dependent on one another; the major forces affecting the decisions of national governments are not within the hands of national decision-makers but outside their control; in short, it is systems of societies, not single societies, that constitute the most important level of analysis. Accordingly, analyses built on the idea of single societies, states, nation-based ideologies, and the like, are less powerful. But, with few exceptions, the corpus of our inherited traditions does not provide very many theories and frameworks for moving to the higher systemic levels.

Influences From Science

One of the remarkable features of human history during the past several hundred years is the extent to which science as a culture has come to be such a dominant feature of Western culture in general.

It is important to recognise, moreover, that as the scientific impulse emerged in one intellectual area after another, it arose in a unique historical context, and its character was influenced by that context. Here the contrast between the histories of European and American sociology are instructive. The emergence of the field in continental Europe — associated above all with the efforts of Emile Durkheim and Max Weber — occurred in two principal contexts: first, the distinctive emphases in European social thought, and second, the simultaneous emergence of the scientific impulse in economics and psychology. With respect to the first, European sociology oriented itself above all to the intellectual traditions of European thought as represented in the study of history, philosophy, law, and the classics in the academy and in the critical intellectual traditions focussing on the state, social classes and the economy, to be found both in the academy and in the more general intellectual life of those countries. It also oriented itself to the emerging social-scientific emphases of the day, as Durkheim's negative polemic toward psychology and Weber's suspicion of the assumptions of formal economics reveal this second stress. The current preoccupations of European sociology with macroscopic and critical issues — phenomenology excepted — of the state, classes and the economy, and the critical treatment of each bears witness to the power of these traditions.

America is something of an exception. Just as its nation arose without the necessity to fight off the burdens of European feudalism, so its sociology arose in a context that did not include (with exceptions to be noted presently) the peculiar intellectual history of European nations. Our sociology grew up in two major intellectual and social contexts. First, it made its appearance in the public institutions of higher education in this country several decades after the passage of the Morell Act of 1862, which solidly established the scientific and applied impulses (mechanical and agricultural) in American higher education; a related part of this development was that economics and psychology preceded sociology, and had fully adopted the scientific "definition" of their own fields. Second, in the 1890s, the reform theme was in the air and sociology picked up that theme from both the social gospel and the progressivist movements. It is not surprising that sociology, struggling to establish its legitimacy in those days, picked up the twin themes of scientific respectability and social reform as its motifs to broadcast to the academy and to the larger society. Those themes persist to the present day. These themes also fit comfortably into American cultural emphases on pragmatism, reform and optimism identified in the previous section.

Political Influences

We know enough about the systemic character of societies to be able to assert with confidence that sociology — or any other field of inquiry, for that matter — never exists in isolation from the polity, but is embedded in its complex ways. In particular, sociology's general relations with national governments and its many publics are always fraught with uncertainty and ambivalence. These relations may be likened to a troubled marriage. The two partners may constantly irritate one another as governments and publics raise ideological concerns and pressures that threaten to compromise the freedom of thinkers and researchers in the discipline, and sociologists forever generate information and ways to describe social events and situations that have an unsettling, needling, and even debunking effect. At the same time the two may find that they cannot live without one another, governments and publics being dependent on data, information and perspectives for their policies and their interpretations of the social world, and sociology requiring autonomy as well as financial and institutional support. This inevitable ambivalence can be resolved in a variety of ways. Sociology may be afforded a free and happy welcome as part of the academy; it may be given only low status and a bad press in the public eye; or it may be constantly hounded to be something that it is not or driven underground altogether by oppressive measures.

One of the remarkable features of American sociology is that it has been housed in academic departments in universities, which have as a matter of historical fact been institutionally removed from the political winds, despite periodic forays of interested legislators and usually right-wing political groups that have imperiled academic freedom in universities. This is a relative statement, of course, but if one compares the American case with others — including those of Eastern European societies — the field has emerged as one which is, by and large, non-politicised from the standpoint of its environment.

As the functions of the state have grown, and the welfare state in particular, sociology and the other social sciences have taken on a different kind of political significance. Government agencies, pursuing their various missions, are inevitably called upon to justify both their concerns with societal problems and their policies relating to these problems in terms of some kind of factual base. In establishing this kind of empirical scope, various political agencies have borrowed both methods (mainly survey) and findings from sociology and the other social sciences, giving them applied or political significance, if you will. In many respects the research carried out by agencies is very similar to social science research in general.

Where sociology has come under greater political influence is not in its significance as an academic discipline in the university setting, but in its significance as a science based on research, with the support for that research coming from the science establishment (and ultimately from the Congress and the Executive branch); it is the case, furthermore, that the phenomenon of research has a political dimension.

REFERENCES

Blau, P. and O. D. Duncan (1967). *The American Occupational Structure.* New York: Wiley.

Mills, C. W. (1956). *The Power Elite.* New York: Oxford University Press.

Parsons, T. (1937). *The Structure of Social Action.* New York: Macmillan.

Parsons, T. (1951). *The Social System.* Glencoe, Ill.: The Free Press.

Sorokin, P. (1928). *Contemporary Sociological Theories.* New York: Harper.

Tocqueville, A. de (1841). *Democracy in America.* New York: J. & H.G. Langley.

Williams, R. (1963). *American Society: A Sociological Interpretation.* New York: Knopf.

1.2 Veena Sharma

Leisure in a Traditional West African Society

INTRODUCTION

A central element in any culture is the way people organize their time. The next excerpt, which describes leisure activity in nineteenth century Nigeria, illustrates the importance of leisure for Africans and, particularly, the communal focus of leisure there.

In North America, leisure time is often a period of inactivity enjoyed in private. As such, leisure is little more than an escape from work. But in much of the agricultural and non-Western world, leisure is intensely active and sociable: a celebration of group life and family life.

The description of leisure in Nigeria (below) is based on an analysis of the Nigerian writer Chinua Achebe's famous novel Things Fall Apart. *Though fictional, the novel illustrates certain basic ideas of West African culture, put forward elsewhere by the African sociologist Akiwowo. (See the suggested readings below for a reference.) They include the idea that individual lives may be the building blocks of a society, but these individual lives are empty and meaningless without the fellowship provided by a community.*

The importance of community is a defining feature of non-Western agricultural societies. Industrialism, capitalism, colonialism, and Christianity all play a part in shifting the culture from a focus on communal goals to narrowly individual goals. That's when "things fall apart," at least by traditional standards. Even the meaning and practice of leisure changes.

In trying to see leisure as done in a traditional West African society (through a work of fiction) the aim is not to impose a foreign concept on a self-subsistent society in which such a concept does not exist. Nor is the idea to judge it by some linear norms of development. By using the idea of leisure as I understand it, I found that it was possible to use it to get an insight into the world-view of the society and to learn something about its social ethic and aspirations and expectations from life. In this way leisure became a tool for looking at a culture and in the process its own varied dimensions also emerged.

Sharma, Veena (1988). "Leisure in a Traditional West African Society as Seen Through a Work of Fiction," *Africa Quarterly*, XXVIII(1–2), 67–74. Reprinted by permission of the Indian Council for Cultural Relations.

With this end in view Chinua Achebe's *Things Fall Apart* has been chosen to explore the concept of leisure. Through this novel leisure can be perceived at two levels — the communal and the individual. At the communal level it coincides with what Joseph Pieper has called the fulfilling of the ritual of public sacrifice. At the individual level it is seen as a state of mind and is reflected in the attitude to the environment and to interpersonal relationships.

Leisure and Celebration

At the heart of celebration lies a recognition and an acceptance of the wonder and the mystery of the world. Feasts and festivals, with their plentiful offerings freely given, are as much a human need as the desire to acquire. They express the very human feeling of gratitude, a gratitude for the wonder that is life.

Feasting and celebrations also become a forum for the coming together of the tribe, and of the affirmation of kinship bonds. Celebrations are not made for any specific and given material ends. They are an expression in themselves of the joy of existence, of life, and in that affirmation the whole group becomes bound. A sense of plenty is generated from the element of sacrifice that is embedded into it — every one contributes that which he is capable of.

Before Okonkwo leaves his mother's village to which he was banished for the violation of custom committed accidentally by him, he says, "It is not to pay you back for all you did for me in these seven years. A child cannot pay for its mother's milk. I have only called you together because it is good for kinsmen to meet" (p. 117).

An older member of the community thanks Okonkwo by saying, "A man who calls his kinsmen to a feast does not do so to save them from starving. They all have food in their own homes. When we gather together in the moonlit village ground it is not because of the moon. Every man can see it in his own compound. (p. 118). "We come together because it is good for kinsmen do to so." Had there been a utilitarian objective attached to the act, it could not serve the purpose of bringing people together, just for the sake of being together.

Ibo society of the 19th century is permeated with a sense of magic and spirits which weave their way in and out of the daily life of living beings providing a connection with a world beyond, allowing space for the fulfillment of the human yearning of making contact with a beyond which is as much a part of the human psyche as the yearning to achieve and excel in the utilitarian world of work.

Harmony with Nature

As work in traditional society is not governed by machines, but by the seasons, there remains an inbuilt possibility for rest and rejuvenation which is in harmony with nature. A sense of plenitude and of inner joy that arises from this experience is that during the harvest season when nature is bountiful and the human heart communes with the freely yielding earth. "Every child loved the harvest season.

Those who were big enough to carry a few yams in a tiny basket went with grown-ups to the farm. And if they could not help in digging up the yams, they could gather firewood together for roasting the ones that would be eaten there on the farm. This roasted yam soaked in red palm-oil and eaten in the open farm was sweeter than any meal at home" (p. 43). This may be work but the attitude that goes with it is one of sheer joy and of opening out to mother Earth. The dividing line between work and leisure gets obliterated.

The harvest is preceded by a feast in the New Year which was "an occasion for giving thanks to Ani, the earth goddess and the source of all fertility. Ani played a greater part in the life of the people than any other deity. She was the ultimate judge of morality and conduct. And what was more, she was in close communion with the departed fathers of the clan whose bodies had been committed to earth" (p. 26). The sacrifice to Ani, the earth goddess, was an offering from the heart to this personified unknown spirit. As she governs the codes of morality and conduct the rules of behaviour that bind the group together are learnt and imbibed in an atmosphere of joy.

The offering freely given generates a sense of abundance even in societies that are comparatively poor. "Men and women, young and old, looked forward to the New Yam Festival because it began the season of plenty — the new year. On the last night before the festival, yams of the old year were all disposed of by those who still had them. The new year must begin with tasty, fresh yams and not the shrivelled and fibrous crop of the previous year. All cooking-pots, calabashes and wooden bowls were thoroughly washed, especially the wooden mortar in which yam was pounded. Yam foo-foo and vegetables soup was the chief food in the celebration. So much of it was cooked that, no matter how heavily the family ate or how many friends and relations they invited from neighbouring villages, there was always a huge quantity of food left over at the end of the day" (p. 26).

It is not only a temporary sense of abundance that is generated here. The generosity and comradeship that is evoked has a long lasting impact on interpersonal relationships.

The absence of the feeling of toil for fulfillment of utilitarian ends brings out the creative, the generative talents of men and women. And this constitutes the essence of leisure — an activity that is not functional and is undertaken for its own sake. It is an end in itself and is its own fulfillment. It is here that men and women commune with their inner beings within the social framework. Before the festival, "Okonkwo's wives had scrubbed the walls and the huts with red earth until they reflected light. They had then drawn patterns on them in white, yellow and dark green. They then set about painting themselves with cam wood and drawing beautiful black patterns on their stomachs and on their hair, which was shaved in beautiful patterns. The three women talked excitedly about the relations who had been invited, and the children revelled in the thought of being spoilt by these visitors from their motherland" (p. 27).

This period of abundance gives way to a period of pause till the earth is ready to receive further planting through human activity and toil. This harmony with the rhythms of nature allows for a leisurely pace of life where there is enough time to spend on lively conversation. So much so that among the Ibo conversation has been refined to the level of a fine art. The book is replete with scintillating proverbs that encapsulate, in a charming and elegant way, the wisdom developed through generations. Captivating use of proverbs itself has become, as Achebe says, the palm oil with which words are eaten.

The Role of Sports

Feasting is followed by wrestling matches. All activity surrounding this season is rooted in the inherent propensity of human beings to excel themselves, to transcend their ordinary mortal limitation. These matches also become the occasion for the choice of marriage partners, while at the same time serving to bind the tribe together as these are often held as contests between different villages. Achebe writes, "It was difficult to say which the people enjoyed more — the feasting and fellowship of the first day or the wrestling contest of the second" (p. 28). It was through his wrestling skill that Okonkwo had won his second wife Ekwefi. "There was no festival in all the seasons of the year which gave her as much pleasure as the wrestling match. Many years ago when she was the village beauty Okonkwo had won her heart by throwing the Cat in the greatest contest within living memory. She did not marry him because he was too poor to pay her bride-price. But a few years later she ran away from her husband and came to live with Okonkwo. All this happened many years ago. Now Ekwefi was a woman of forty-five who had suffered a great deal in her time. But her love of wrestling contests was still as strong as it was thirty years ago" (p. 28).

Sigrid Paul (*Sport in Africa*, William J. Baker and James A. Mangon (ed) Africana Publishing Company, 1987) has written about the importance of wrestling. "Wrestling in Black Africa traditionally served several social functions for individuals and groups." Salamone has pointed to the fact that, at least among the Gungawa, intravillage wrestling helped to establish a male rank order. Intragroup wrestling may often have been mere children's play without any serious connotations, but what has sometimes been called "children's rolling about" or "wrestling in a haphazard fashion" might in reality have been a struggle of children belonging to rival maternal or paternal households to attain or confirm their own rank and that of their family unit. Similarly, remarks about wrestling to settle disputes, either between men or women or adults of the opposite sex, may refer to such attempts to underline rank relationship, for instance between wives of one common husband, or adult sons of one father but different mothers (p. 40).

Wrestling reflected not only physical powers but also other qualities such as a keen sense of justice and socially appropriate behaviour. To quote the Fulani teacher Traore from the same book, "The best wrestler, who was leader of the formal boys' society, would exhort his followers to observe fairness in the game, to be ambitious for leadership, and to emulate his social skills. But he also organized a big meal for them at the end of the wrestling season, thereby establishing his role as a host. This behavior exemplifies a widespread African practice: namely, that the one being honored because of his social qualities has to support and entertain his followers" (p. 40).

The Role of Magic

The other public ceremony in the novel is the Egwugwu in which there is the impersonation of the ancestral spirits of the clan. A non-technological, non-textual oral society draws its laws and codes of conduct from oral and visual manifestations of the spirits of the elders of the clan. Deeply embedded in the psyche of its members, who are conditioned to accept magico-religious rites as real, (and to not expressing their doubts even if they have any) these ceremonies provide a fear-inducing link with the world beyond. Justice is dispensed through an elaborate ceremony that relies as much on magic and superstition as on basic common sense. Such a society, which bases its relation with the environment not on an idea of conquering or taming it, but through a belief in its mystery is also superstition ridden. Ceremonies, even as they release them from work, become awesome happenings also during which justice is given out as a divine dispensation. Twins are relegated to die in the evil forest, human sacrifices are made to avoid evil forces. It is the rigid and cruel customs attached to these happenings that cause some thinking ones to question them and seek other ways of expressing their worship or devotion. Worship that led to such cruel results lacked something. It did not fulfil. It is significant that Nwoye felt a "snapping inside him" the day after the harvest. The modes of communion with the divine are held in question. The questioning spirit has to wait until an alternative mode of worship is devised. Christianity with its message of love and forgiveness provides this alternative.

Evil spirits and magic pervade the air throughout the book like a concrete reality. Nature in its varied moods appears to heighten this prospect.

Leisure at the Individual Level

It is interesting to note, that at the individual level Ibo society (with all its "non-productive" rituals and ceremonies rooted in a culture that believed in magic and superstition) is a highly materialistic society which reveres a man of achievement more than anything else. It has no place for a man of contemplation or one who spends his life in "non-useful" pursuits such as magic. Unoka, Okonkwo's father was a good flutist and very much in harmony with his surroundings. "He was tall but very thin and had a slight stoop. He wore a haggard and mournful look except when he was drinking or playing on his flute. He was very good on his flute, and his happiest moments were the two or three moons after the harvest when the village musicians brought down their instruments, hung above the fireplace. Unoka would play with them, his face beaming with blessedness and peace. Sometimes another village would ask Unoka's band and their dancing Egwugwu to come and stay with them and teach them their tunes. They would go to such hosts for as long as three or four markets, making music and feasting. Unoka loved the good fare and the good fellowship, and he loved this season of the year, when the rains had stopped and the sun rose every morning with dazzling beauty. Unoka loved it all, and he loved the first kites that returned with the dry season, and the children who sang songs of welcome to them. He would remember his own child-hood, how he had often wandered around looking for a kite sailing leisurely against the blue sky. As soon as he found one he would sing with his whole being, welcoming it back from its long, long journey, and asking if it had brought home any lengths of cloth" (p. 4). He is introduced as man who is happy to share. "If any money came his way, and it seldom did, he immediately bought gourds of palm-wine, called round his neighbours and made merry" (p. 3).

His inability to think about the future or to make good materially is looked down upon by the society and by Achebe. Yet he has a personality that makes him much loved by the people. He is able to continue borrowing despite the fact that people do not wish to lend. This is because of his capacity to relate to the outside world from a central position of self-reliance. Man lives in a range of external rela-tionships and being the centre of that field of relationships, he is the coordinator of those relations. The higher the order of being, or the degree of inwardness, the more embracing and wider are its power of establishing relationships. With all his debts he is loved and no one can feel annoyed with him as with Okonkwo (p. 5). Seen to be weak and lazy, even "idle" by his society and son, Unoka is peaceloving and gentle and could not stand talk of war. Yet he is shown to have a courage that comes from an inner harmony. When he dies due to a disease which his society looked down upon and he had to be left in the Evil Forest to die alone, Unoke "took with him his flute." With all his inability to cope with the utilitarian world he does not contravene any laws of the land as his "successful" son does time and again.

1.3 Peter Laslett

English Society Before and After the Coming of Industry

INTRODUCTION

As we hinted in the introduction to the last excerpt, the "industrial revolution" brings with it a fundamental change in people's social relations and cultures. We see this clearly in the next excerpt by Peter Laslett.

In pre-industrial, agricultural England, everyone had a place and everyone knew his or her place. The national society, if it existed at all, was a collection of small and slightly larger communities. Within these communities lived small and slightly larger families. People drew their identity from the family and community to which they belonged. Though they may have had secondary identities — for example, as members of a particular guild or occupational group — their primary loyalty was to the family and community.

In those days before the industrial revolution, there was little movement around the country and little information coming in from outside the local community. In general, people stayed where they were born and knew little — either firsthand or by word of mouth — about the world that existed more than 50 kilometres away. This meant that local languages, superstititions, and customs flourished in relative isolation from one another.

What a far cry this is from the global culture of the late twentieth century. Today, even rural English people know a lot about life outside their own family, community, and nation. In a great many ways, lives around the world have become the same.

In the year 1619 the bakers of London applied to the authorities for an increase in the price of bread. They sent in support of their claim a complete description of a bakery. There were thirteen or fourteen people in such an undertaking: the baker and his wife, four paid employees who were called journeymen, two apprentices, two maidservants and the three or four children of the master baker himself.

A London bakery was undoubtedly what we should call a commercial or even an industrial undertaking, turning out loaves by the thousand. Yet the business was carried on in the house of the baker himself. There was probably a *shop* as part of the house, *shop* as in *workshop* and not as meaning a retail establishment. Most of the house was taken up with the living-quarters of the dozen people who worked there.

It is obvious that all these people ate in the house since the cost of their food helped to determine the production cost of the bread. Except for the journeymen they were all obliged to sleep in the house at night and live together as a family.

The Family Setting

The only word used at that time to describe such a group was "family." The man at the head of the group, the employer, or the manager, was then known as the master or head of the family. He was father to some of its members and in place of father to the rest. There was no sharp distinction between his domestic and his economic functions. His wife was both his partner and his subordinate, a partner because she ran the family, took charge of the food and managed the women-servants, a subordinate because she was woman and wife, mother and in place of mother to the rest.

Laslett, Peter (1979). "English Society Before and After the Coming of Industry," Chapter 1 in *The World We Have Lost*. London: Methuen and Company. Reprinted by permission.

The paid servants of both sexes had their specified and familiar position in the family, as much part of it as the children but not quite in the same position. At that time the family was not one society only but three societies fused together; the society of man and wife, of parents and children and of master and servant. But when they were young, and servants were, for the most part, young, unmarried people, they were very close to children in their status and their function. Here is the agreement made between the parents of a boy about to become an apprentice and his future master. The boy covenants to dwell with his master for seven years, to keep his secrets and to obey his commandments.

> *Taverns and alehouses he shall not haunt, dice, cards or any other unlawful games he shall not use, fornication with any woman he shall not commit, matrimony with any woman he shall not contract. He shall not absent himself by night or by day without his master's leave but be a true and faithful servant.*

On his side, the master undertakes to teach his apprentice his *"art, science or occupation with moderate correction."*

> *Finding and allowing unto his said servant meat, drink, apparel, washing, lodging and all other things during the said term of seven years, and to give unto his said apprentice at the end of the said term double apparel, to wit, one suit for holydays and one suit for worken days.*

Apprentices, therefore, and many other servants, were workers who were also children, extra sons or extra daughters (for girls could be apprenticed too), clothed and educated as well as fed, obliged to obedience and forbidden to marry, often unpaid and dependent until after the age of twenty-one. If such servants were workers in the position of sons and daughters, the sons and daughters of the house were workers too. John Locke laid it down in 1697 that the children of the poor must work for some part of the day when they reached the age of three. The children of a London baker were not free to go to school for many years of their young lives, or even to play as they wished when they came back home. Soon they would find themselves doing what they could in bolting, that is sieving flour, or in helping the maidservant with her panniers of loaves on the way to the market stall, or in playing their small parts in preparing the never-ending succession of meals for the whole household.

The patriarchal arrangements which we have begun to explore were not new in the England of Shakespeare and Elizabeth. They were as old as the Greeks, as old as European history, and not confined to Europe. And it may well be that they abused and enslaved people quite as remorselessly as the economic arrangements which had replaced them in the England of Blake and Victoria. When people could expect to live for so short a time, how must a man have felt when he realized that so much of his adult life must go in working for his keep and very little more in someone else's family?

But people very seldom recognize facts of this sort, and no one is content to expect to live as long as the majority in fact will live. Every servant in the old social world was probably quite confident that he or she would some day get married and be at the head of a new family, keeping others in subordination.

It will be noticed that the roles we have allotted to all the members of the ca-pacious family of the master-baker of London in the year 1619 are, emotionally, all highly symbolic and highly satisfying. We may feel that in a whole society or-ganized like this, in spite of all the subordination, the exploitation and the obliter-ation of those who were young, or feminine, or in service, everyone belonged in a group, a family group. Everyone had his circle of affection: every relationship could be seen as a love-relationship.

Not so with us. Who could love the name of a limited company or of a gov-ernment department as an apprentice could love his superbly satisfactory father-figure master, even if he were a bully and a beater, a usurer and a hypocrite? But if a family is a circle of affection, it can also be the scene of hatred. The worst tyrants among human beings, the murderers and the villains, are jealous husbands and resentful wives, possessive parents and deprived children. In the traditional, patriarchal society of Europe, where practically everyone lived out his whole life within the family, though not usually within one family, tension like this must have been incessant and unrelieved, incapable of release except in crisis. Men, women and children have to be very close together for a very long time to gener-ate the emotional power which can give rise to a tragedy of Sophocles, or Shakespeare, or Racine.

The Size of Society

All this is true to history only if the little knot of people making bread in Stuart London was indeed the typical social unit of the old world in its size, composition and scale. There are reasons why a baker's household might have been a little out of the ordinary, for baking was a highly traditional occupation in a society increas-ingly subject to economic change. A family of thirteen people, which was also a unit of production of thirteen, less the children still incapable of work, was quite large for English society at that time. Only the families of the really important, the nobility and the gentry, the aldermen and the successful merchants, were ordinar-ily as large as this. In fact, we can take the bakery to represent the upper limit in size and scale of the group in which ordinary people lived and worked. Among the great mass of society which cultivated the land, the family group was smaller than a substantial London craftsman's entourage.

In the baking household sex and age were mingled together. Fortunate chil-dren might go out to school, but adults did not usually go out to work. There was nothing to correspond to the thousands of young men on the assembly line, the hundreds of young women in the offices, the lonely lives of housekeeping wives, which we now know only too well. Those who survived to old age in the much less favourable conditions for survival which then were prevalent, were surpris-ingly often left to live and die alone, in their tiny cottages or sometimes in the almshouses which were being built so widely in the England of the Tudors and the Stuarts. Poor-law establishments, parochial in purpose and in size, had begun their melancholy chapter in the history of the English people. But institutional life was otherwise almost unknown. There were no hotels, hostels, or blocks of flats for single persons, very few hospitals and none of the kind we are familiar with, almost no young men and women living on their own. The family unit where so great a majority lived was what we should undoubtedly call a "balanced" and "healthy" group.

To every farm there was a family, which spread itself over its portion of the village lands as the family of the master-craftsman filled out his manufactory. When a holding was small, and most were small as are the tiny holdings of European peasants today, a man tilled it with the help of his wife and his children. No single man, we must remember, would usually take charge of the land, any more than a single man would often be found at the head of a workshop in the city. The master of a family was expected to be a householder, whether he was a butcher, a baker, a candlestick maker or simply a husbandman, which was the universal name for one whose skill was in working the land. Marriage we must insist, and it is one of the rules which gave its character to the society of our ancestors, was the entry to full membership, in the enfolding countryside, as well as in the scattered urban centres.

Some peasants did well: their crops were heavier and they had more land to till. To provide the extra labour needed then, the farming householder, like the successful craftsman, would extend his working family by taking on young men and women as servants to live with him and work the fields. This he would have to do, even if the land which he was farming was not his own but rented from the great family in the manor house. Sometimes, he would prefer to send out his own children as servants and bring in other children and young men to do the work. This is one of the few glimpses we can get into the quality of the emotional life of the family at this time, for it shows that parents may have been unwilling to submit children of their own to the discipline of work at home. It meant, too, that servants were not simply the perquisites of wealth and position. A quarter, or a third, of all the families in the country contained servants in Stuart times, and this meant that very humble people had them as well as the titled and the wealthy. Most of the servants, moreover, male or female, in the great house and in the small, were engaged in working the land.

A boy, or a girl, born in a cottage, would leave home for service at any time after the age of ten. A servant-in-husbandry, as he might be called if he were a boy, would usually stay in the position of servant, though very rarely in the same household, until he or she got married. Marriage, when and if it came, would quite often take place with another servant. All this while, and it might be twelve, fifteen or even twenty years, the servant would be kept by the succession of employers in whose houses he dwelt. He was in no danger of poverty or hunger, even if the modest husbandman with whom he lived was worse housed than his landlord's horses, and worse clothed than his landlords servants.

But poverty awaited the husbandman's servant when he got married, and went himself to live in just such a labourer's cottage as the one in which he had been born. Whoever had been his former master, the labourer, late servant in husbandry, would be liable to fall into want directly when his wife began to have children and he lost the earnings of his companion. Once he found himself outside the farming household his living had to come from his wages, and he, with every member of his family, was subject for his labour to the local vagaries in the market.

The Creation of Mass Society

The removal of the economic functions from the patriarchal family at the point of industrialization created a mass society. It turned the people who worked into a mass of undifferentiated equals, working in a factory or scattered between the factories and mines, bereft for ever of the feeling that work was a family affair, done within the family. Marxist historical sociology presents this as the growth of class consciousness amongst the proletariat, and this is an important historical truth. But because it belongs with the large-scale class model for all social change it can also be misleading. Moreover it has tended to divert attention from the structural function of the family in the pre-industrial world, and has impeded a proper, informed contrast between our world and the lost world we have to analyse.

With the "capitalism changed the world" way of thinking goes a division of history into the ancient, feudal and bourgeois eras or stages. But the facts of the contrast which has to be drawn between the world we have lost and the world we now inhabit tends to make all such divisions as these into subdivisions. The time has now come to divide our European past in a simpler way with industrialization as the point of critical change.

The word, alienation, is part of the cant of the mid-twentieth century and it began as an attempt to describe the separation of the worker from his world of work. We need not accept all that this expression has come to convey in order to recognize that it does point to something vital to us all in relation to our past. Time was when the whole of life went forward in the family, in a circle of loved, familiar faces, known and fondled objects, all to human size. That time has gone for ever. It makes us very different from our ancestors.

1.4 Robert E. Washington

Imperialism and the World System of Racial Stratification

INTRODUCTION

Imperialism was one of the reasons "things fell apart" in many parts of the pre-industrial world, including Africa. Western culture brought new ways of thinking and behaving. For example, it brought an almost universal tendency to rank white people above brown people and brown people above black people. (For an illustration of this tendency in Haiti, see excerpt 10.1 below.) That is the topic of the next excerpt by Robert Washington.

To put the matter bluntly, Western culture is a source of worldwide racism. The author explains this pattern in terms of the European dominance of other countries during the colonial period, and the resulting views of colonists. Europeans viewed the whites as supreme and the blacks as unworthy. Browns — who include racially mixed peoples — came to be seen as somewhere in between. In time, non-whites adopted these views too.

For many decades (and even centuries), these views influenced people around the world because of continued Western economic and cultural penetration. People who aspired to Western cultural behaviour unconsciously accepted Western ideas about race. Thus, the influence of Western culture upon other cultures has included transmitting the idea that evaluations of people should be based on skin colour.

This study implies that we will not abolish racism until we have eliminated Eurocentric thinking throughout the world. More will be said about this in Section 5.

P robably no problem of race relations in the contemporary world has been more free from critical scrutiny than brown racism. I use "brown" here in the figurative sense, as a reference to the neither white nor black but colored peoples of the third world (the Chinese, East Indians, Filipinos, Mestizos, etc.). These peoples occupy an intermediate position along the black-white spectrum of color classification. By brown racism, I refer to the prevalence of prejudice among these fair complexioned colored groups and societies toward blacks, especially those of African ancestry.

Brown racism is commonplace throughout the third world. In what follows I shall contend that the current form of brown racism, and the global system of racial stratification through which it is manifested, are post-colonial adaptions of white Western imperialism and are effected through the latter's cultural hegemony in third world societies.

The Emergence of Brown Racism

European colonial expansion into Asia, Africa, and the Americas was legitimated by beliefs in white racial superiority. As one author has noted:

> *The dilemma of the imperialist democracy was much more happily solved if "the native" was permanently and genetically inferior.... It seemed manifest that evolution had culminated in the people of North-Western Europe and North America, who dominated the world and, in their own eyes, surpassed all others in skill, intelligence, beauty and moral standards. (Mason, 1970a:31–33)*

Washington, Robert E. (1990). "Brown Racism and the Formation of a World System of Racial Stratification," *International Journal of Politics, Culture and Society*, 4(2), 209–227. Reprinted by permission of Human Sciences Press, Inc.

Often European colonial conquests were viewed as religiously mandated obligations to spread Western civilization and assume control over the backward people of color throughout the world.

The effect of early European colonial conquests was the emergence of localized dual layered systems of racial stratification comprised of white Europeans at the top and "natives" at the bottom. "In European colonies all natives were treated alike, regardless of the numerous distinctions they made among themselves" (Shibutani, 1969, 1969:201). These localized dual layered systems of racial stratification, however, were seldom of long duration. Either because of a shortage of European women or the importation of nonwhite laborers from other regions or both, they evolved into multi-layered stratification systems which were maintained by direct European colonial domination (Ballhatchet, 1980; Mason, 1970a; Schermerhorn, 1970).

In one type of situation, where sexual relations between European men and native females resulted in offspring, a status distinction was established between those of mixed race and those born of the native population. The dominant European groups drew boundaries of the color line, placing the mixed race group into a separate and intermediate racial category.

The appearance of these mixed race European-native groups in colonies and their identification with the Europeans resulted in the first pattern of brown racism: the antipathy of mixed race groups toward the native groups.[1] The antipathy of these mixed race groups resulted from their having internalized the color valuations of the European colonials and from the superior status privileges granted them — such as separate schools, better employment opportunities, and in some cases, the right to emigrate to the mother country. These privileges were denied to the darker skinned native groups.

Early manifestations of brown racism were also evidenced in situations where there was importation of groups from one colonial region to another for the purpose of providing labor. Such policies often resulted in the co-presence of brown skinned and black African groups.

What is significant about the above patterns is the formation of localized multi-layered stratification systems comprised of white Europeans at the top, mixed race and/or brown groups in the middle, and Africans at the bottom (Morner, 1970). Interestingly, the status distinction between browns and blacks originated by European colonials became so ingrained that the moral objections to the abuse of browns were seldom extended to blacks (Mason, 1970a; Rout, 1976). As one British student of racial relations notes in reference to Brazil,

> It is pertinent to recall that many of the liberal Portuguese who ... championed the cause of the South American Indians at this time, did not regard the enslavement of Negroes as wrongful or protest so strongly about their ill treatment. (Banton, 1967:259)

It is also noteworthy that Mahatma Ghandi, who began his resistance movement against the racial policies of British colonialism in South Africa, restricted his protest to the treatments of Indians. He ignored the plight of the much larger and more severely oppressed African group. The pariah status imposed on Africans was deliberately contrived to prevent integration of brown and black communities and thereby fragment opposition to white European colonial domination.

During the colonial era, to briefly recapitulate, brown racism arose out of European administrative and military domination and the status gradations the latter created through elaborating a racially based ideology.

The Transitional Anti-Colonial Phase and the Illusion of Unity

Throughout much of the third world, the post World War Two era was character-ized by national independence movements oriented to both anti-colonial and anti-racist ideology. Among third world intellectuals and political elites of color a feeling of unity evolved based on the view that racism was the prejudice of white Westerners toward nonwhites.

The high point in this movement of solidarity among third world leaders of color was the conference in Bandung, Indonesia in 1955. In the words of a *Newsweek Magazine* article:

> The Columbo Powers (India, Pakistan, Ceylon, Burma, and Indonesia) convoked an unprecedented conference of officials from 30 Asian and African nations, representing more than half of the world's people.... The sponsoring powers seemed to be aiming vaguely at a sort of Monroe Doctrine against colonialism. Their basic philosophy was that Asian and African nations have some common destiny, freeing them from the power politics of the white race and setting them aside from the Atlantic and Soviet blocs. (Newsweek, 1955:32)

The effects of a number of world shaking events led up to this movement of third world unity. First, there were Marxist influences. As one author has noted, "Lenin's dicta ... that 'colonialism is the worst and the most extreme form of capitalism, but also its last' could not fail to impress anti-imperialists from Asia and Africa" (Kimble, 1973:3).

Second, there was the feeling of a bond among non-white peoples influenced by the shared experiences of racial oppression. In fact, as early as the beginning of the century, we can see an assertion of this view of a simple white/nonwhite divi-sion of the world in the declaration of W. E. B. DuBois, the black American pan-Africanist leader, that, "the problem of the twentieth century is the problem of the color line" (Tuttle, 1973:65). This sentiment was echoed by Richard Wright, the exiled black American writer, who attended the Bandung Conference and characterized that gathering as a meeting of "the despised, the insulted, the hurt, the dispossessed — in short — the underdogs of the human race" (Wright, 1956:12).

The spirit of Bandung fueled the anti-colonial movement and gave it a new impetus.

Significantly, however, no one mentioned the color prejudice of brown groups toward Africans. Apparently that prejudice was deemed insignificant in the face of the overwhelming force of European colonial domination and the deep-rootedness of white racism. No doubt some were motivated not to mention the brown racism issue because of its potentially disruptive effect on the solidarity of the anti-colonial struggle.

A World System of Racial Stratification Emerges

Western imperialism during the post World War Two era shifted from a colonial to a neo-colonial form of domination. White Western capitalism forged ties of economic dependency between itself and the former colonies as well as those third world regions that had escaped colonialism.

While much has been written about the economics of neo-colonialism, too little attention had been paid to its cultural process. What had been previously achieved through direct administrative and military control was achieved during the post war era through cultural hegemony — the propagation of Western values through which third world peoples are conditioned to acceptance of a world view that facilitates Western economic domination. Two crucial preconditions lay behind this development: the political displacement of direct European colonial control and the transformation of the technology of cultural communication. Under the control of white Western nations, this new technology of cultural communication facilitated the diffusion of Western popular culture — via films, radio, television, etc. — throughout the third world.

Among the values diffused by Western culture are color valuations based on ideological assumptions of white superiority. This is evidenced in the consistency of race/color rankings throughout the contemporary world.

The valuations underlying this global stratification system are perceived not as racial but modern because white Western films, magazines, television and news publications project such values in a subliminal form. Thus, the images of white superiority propagated by these cultural products largely escape the notice of the recipient societies. Indeed, the same cultural influences that create attractions to hamburgers, Western music, Western clothing fashions and Western style home furnishings also create attractions to Western categories of color valuation. Third world societies, subjected to this cultural hegemony, soon began to evidence clear tendencies toward brown racism — manifested in positive valuations of whiteness and negative valuations of blackness.

Whereas the colonial form of brown racism was the result of contacts between browns and blacks, the neo-colonial form often exists independent of such contact. Thus, when we find these negative valuations of blackness in an ideological form (that is, expressed in terms of beliefs about the biological inferiority of blacks) in societies that have had no contact with blacks except that derived from white Western cultural media, we must conclude these are products of white Western culture.

The Manifestations of Brown Racism

What is most striking is the extent of antipathy toward blacks among brown groups throughout the world. This antipathy, based on beliefs about the innate inferiority of Africans — beliefs which typically precede contacts with the latter, is the result of the assimilation of white Western culture in the post colonial era. An illustration of how these negative race/color categories are formed is provided by the experience of black American soldiers when first stationed in Oahu, Hawaii, during World War Two.

> The presence of a large number of white soldiers from the mainland had much to do with the importation of stereotyped conceptions. At first, many Hawaiian girls treated the Negroes like all other soldiers, but they soon found themselves under pressure to make distinctions. Girls who danced with Negroes at the U.S.O. were ostracized; in time most hostesses refused to dance with Negroes, even though they had initially assumed that they were to entertain all servicemen. (Shibutani, 1969:205)

Parallel problems are encountered by blacks in China. In May 1986 at Tianjin University, a skirmish between African and Chinese students occurred. It was a five hour long rock and bottle throwing brawl between 300–500 Chinese students and approximately 18 foreign (mostly African) students (Scott, 23 June, 1986:51). Shortly afterwards, in June 1986, as a result of the incident, there was a mass demonstration of 200 African students in Beijing to highlight racism in China. Complained one African student from Togo, "The Chinese do not consider us human" (Scott, 19 June, 1986:20)

According to the African Student Union (which monitors cases of racism against African students), "most cases of trouble with university or government authorities involve Africans who dated Chinese women" (Scott, 23 June, 1986:51)

Brazil — another society that evidences a pervasive brown racism — is often mistakenly thought to be free of racial prejudice, because the few blacks who attain upper class status are socially defined as whites. However, this token exemption in no way obviates the negative categorization of blackness. As one scholar has pointed out:

> The Brazilian outlook assumes that everyone would like to be white and that the whiter a person is the higher he is likely to be in the social status scale ... The psychological effects upon dark skinned people of a wholesale desire for whitening are also unfavorable. They entail acceptance by dark people of the belief that whites are justified in discriminating against them. (Banton, 1967:280)

This pattern is hardly restricted to societies where blacks constitute a minority. We see a similar hierarchy of race/color in the West Indies where the majority populations are black. Referring to Jamaica, Henriques notes: "The important point is that all the different groups, from the black to the white, accept that the European is the ideal and the Negro inferior" (Henriques, 1964:128).

Hundreds of illustrations of brown racism could be cited.[2] Its prevalence in such countries as Mexico, Saudi Arabia, Sudan, Dominican Republic, Thailand, Morocco, and Venezuela is documentable.

The Social Psychological Dynamics Behind Brown Racism

Like any other racism, brown racism is based on a culturally embedded categorical system of classification. In this instance, the system is absorbed concomitant with Westernization. This process facilitates the largely unconscious assignment of negative valuations to blacks based solely on their physical appearance. However, it does not explain the social psychological functions of those valuations. To explain this, it is necessary to understand the psychological implications of the Western white oriented racial stratification system from which brown racism derives. That stratification system is distinguished by the following characteristics:

1. It is based on the ideal of white racial features.

2. It consists of a continuum of color valuation — that is, the further away one's group is from the ideal, the lower its status.

3. Because the system has a positive and a negative node, it possesses only two unambiguously defined statuses: whiteness at the top and blackness at the bottom.

For individuals and groups who fit neither the positive or negative ideal, the consequences for their color/racial identity of acculturating the white Western world view (i.e., Westernization) are marginalization and psychological anxiety. Because they occupy an ambiguously defined position, browns fear being categorically identified with blacks. Their preoccupation with segregating themselves from blacks reflects their desire to avoid the stigma associated with blackness. This helps to explain why there is considerably more fraternization between whites and blacks and whites and browns than between browns and blacks. Whites, who possess the clearly defined superior status in the racial hierarchy, need not fear being subsumed under the same category as blacks. Whereas browns, lacking such a clearly defined superior status, are plagued by this fear. And for this reason, they exert strenuous energy to segregate themselves from blacks.

It is not only brown groups' repulsion from blacks but also their attraction to whites — indeed in many cases their aspirations for whiteness — that are produced by marginalization and the attendant psychological anxiety. This helps us to understand another curious fact. Among brown/white, black/white and brown/black rates of intermarriage, the latter are always — and by a considerable degree — the lowest. And in those few instances where members of a brown group marry a black person, they will tend to be ostracized by their community.

It might be argued that these low intermarriage rates between browns and blacks are merely the effect of ethnic differences, i.e., of the desires of brown groups to retain their distinctive ethnic cultures. However, this thesis fails to account for the consistently higher rates of intermarriage of browns to whites and to members of other brown groups who have different ethnic backgrounds.

Insofar as brown groups internalize the Western world view, they will experience a psychological need to distance themselves from blacks in order to validate their claims to superior racial status within the hierarchy of Western white color valuations. Thus, their anxiety about their racial status has the paradoxical effect of causing them to inadvertently support the principle of white superiority and the hierarchy of color stratification. That is, it causes them to support the system which also defines them as inferior.

ENDNOTES

[1] This incipient pattern of brown racism differs from the modal pattern in that it was not characterized by Afrophobia. Nevertheless, it shared the basic characteristics of the modal pattern — identification with whites and antipathy toward the darker skinned native population.

[2] Actually, symptoms of brown racism can be found among groups with African ancestry. For instance, until relatively recently, fair complexioned African Americans (e.g., often those of mixed racial backgrounds) tended to express prejudice against darker skinned African Americans. (see Urdy *et al.,* 1971:722–733).

REFERENCES

Ballhatchet, K. (1980). *Race, Sex and Class Under the Raj.* New York: St. Martin Press.

Banton, M. (1967). *Race Relations.* New York: Basic Books.

Henriques, F. (1964). *Jamaica.* New York: London and Maxwell.

———— (1975). *Children of Conflict.* New York: E. P. Dutton.

Kimble, D. (1973). The *Afro-Asian Movement.* Jerusalem: Israel Universities Press.

Mason, P. (1970). *Patterns of Dominance.* Oxford, England: Oxford University Press. *Race Relations,* Oxford, England: Oxford University Press.

Morner, M. (1967). *Race Mixture in the History of Latin America.* New York: Little Brown.

———— (1970). *Race and Class in Latin America.* New York: Columbia University Press.

Newsweek (1955). "Asia — A Place in the Sun," 17 January.

Schermerhorn, R. A. (1976). Comparative *Ethnic Relations.* New York: Random House,

Schiller, H. I. (1976). *Communication and Cultural Domination.* White Plains, N.Y.: International Arts and Sciences Press.

Scott, M. (1986). "Blacks and Red Faces," *Far Eastern Economic Review,* 132, 19 June.

———— (1986). "Black Students and the Tide of Prejudice," *Far Eastern Economic Review,* 132, 23 June.

Shibutani, T. and K. Kwan (1969). *Ethnic Stratification.* New York: McMillan.

Tuttle, W. M. (ed.) (1973). *W. E. B. DuBois.* Englewood Cliffs, N.J.: Prentice Hall.

Urdy, J. R., K. E. Bauman, and C. Chase (1971). "Skin Color, Status, and Mate Selection," *American Journal of Sociology,* 76 (Jan.).

Wright, R. (1956). *The Color Curtain.* Cleveland and New York: The World Publishing Co.

QUESTIONS

DISCUSSION QUESTIONS

1. In your experience, how do cultural differences make communication between people difficult?

2. What kinds of assumptions do people from your own cultural background tend to make about life and the way society works?

3. Is it likely that a society that is industrializing today will go through all the same stages of cultural change, at the same rate, as a society like England, which started industrializing two centuries ago?

4. Can you usually identify a person's cultural biases? For example, are you able to tell if someone is a snob? a racist? a jock? What signs do you look for?

DATA COLLECTION EXERCISES

1. By means of a survey, collect some data on people's use of leisure time. Examine the data to determine how similar to, or different from, these people are from the West Africans described in an excerpt in this Section.

2. Read at least two short stories on village life in Asia or Latin America. Do these villages sound similar, culturally, to the village in West Africa Achebe describes; and if not, how do they differ?

3. What difficulties, if any, do African societies have accepting and integrating other racial groups: for example, people from India, the Arabian peninsula, or China? Collect some data on this question from one or more African countries. (An interesting way to begin is by viewing the movie *Mississippi Masala,* about the migration of a Southeast Asian family from Uganda to Mississippi.)

4. In the "world we have lost," people made little distinction between home and the workplace. Collect some data that will reveal whether there is a trend in Canada back to working at home. Interview someone who actually works at home for pay.

WRITING EXERCISES

1. Write a brief essay on changes in the meaning of the word "leisure" over the past two centuries, indicating what those changes tell us about our society and culture.

2. "It is inevitable that modern life will mean a loss of leisure as well as a loss of individuality. In fact, the two go hand in hand." Write a brief essay in which you evaluate this statement.

3. Write a brief essay showing how Washington's analysis of racial imperialism is very "unAmerican" in the sense that Smelser would mean.

4. Write a brief essay explaining why sociology, as we know it today, could not have existed in the "world we have lost."

SUGGESTED READINGS

1. Archer, Margaret (1991). "Sociology for one world: Unity and diversity," *International Sociology*, 6(2), June, 131–147. An interesting essay on the challenges and problems of creating a world sociology. It deals with some of the issues Smelser has highlighted; in particular, Archer warns us away from the notion of "modernization," because of its hidden assumptions.

2. Buss, Andreas (1989). "The economic ethics of Russian–Orthodox Christianity," Parts I and II, *International Sociology*, 4(3), September, 235–258, and 4(4), December, 447–472 respectively. An extended essay that follows in the tradition of Max Weber's attempt to explain social and economic change in terms of religious beliefs that help and hinder such change. This is applied to the Russian case.

3. Jianxiong, Pan (1990). "The dual structure of Chinese culture and its influence on Modern Chinese society," *International Sociology*, 5(1), March, 75–88. Another attempt to apply Weber's cultural analysis to the explanation of economic and political change. This article finds the Chinese traditionally caught in a bind between religiosity and secularism, collectivism and individualism.

4. Akiwowo, A. A. (1986). "Contributions to the sociology of knowledge from an African oral poetry," *International Sociology*, 1(4), 343–358. See also this author's response to critics in *International Sociology*, 6(2), 243–251. Akiwowo shows that we can learn a lot about the basic beliefs of Yoruba (West African) people by studying their traditional poetry.

SOCIALIZATION

Introduction

Primary and Secondary Socialization

The introduction to Section One described culture as "all of the ways people regularly think and act, the material objects they use in daily life, and the ideas that guide them." Socialization is the process of learning cultural values and norms. To some extent, observed differences between groups reflect differences in the ways people have been socialized. People *learn* to be different (or the same).

People who grow up in a particular culture internalize a similar "package" of norms, beliefs and values. The more generally people accept this package, the more smoothly the group will function. Sociologists call this smooth functioning "social integration."

Socialization begins when we are born and continues throughout our lives. The most intense learning occurs when we are young, so we call this "primary socialization." Children have less power than adults, so primary socialization is more or less imposed. Through socialization children learn to conform to adult expectations about the right ways of managing physical needs, and about manners and morals. For example, young children learn to be hungry at meal-time, sleep when it is dark, and so on.

By contrast, "secondary socialization" is an ongoing process of learning throughout the life cycle. It occurs as we anticipate and adjust to new experiences and new situations.

How does the more basic process of primary socialization occur? Symbolic interactionism, an important theoretical approach in sociology, has provided us with insight into this process. It argues that people actively participate in their own socialization. George H. Mead (1863–1931) and Charles H. Cooley (1864–1929), two American sociologists, were key influences in developing this symbolic interactionist perspective. In fact, they influenced the way *most* sociologists think about socialization.

Cooley and Mead were interested in how people develop a sense of self. Cooley believed children are born with an instinctive capacity for self development that unfolds through social interaction. A key element in the development of the self is the perception of others' reactions to us. Cooley's concept of "the looking-glass self" captures this idea: "*I feel about me the way I think you think about me.*"

Mead was interested in the ways we learn to present ourselves in different social situations. According to Mead, we learn symbolically through role-taking. As children, our behaviour comes to combine instinctive reaction and imitation. This Mead called the "pre-play" stage. Later, during the "play" stage, children learn to take on the roles of others. They objectify their experience by seeing themselves from other people's point of view. In the next, "game" stage children learn to handle several roles at once. In this way, they learn to anticipate the behaviour of others.

Finally children learn to internalize general social expectations by imagining how others will act and react. At this "generalized other" stage, the child has a sense of self and can react in a socially approved way.

Social meanings are based on assumptions about other people's understandings and intentions, so they are always more or less ambiguous. In this sense, they are subject to ongoing interpretation and negotiation. In most situations, previous experience helps us to imagine new experiences, so we become good at what sociologists call "anticipatory socialization." Many social arrangements make anticipatory socialization easier. Some examples include university initiation weeks, new employee orientation programs, parenting support groups, and pre-retirement courses.

Sometimes new situations are so strange that we cannot rely on previous experience to tell us how to act. Then we may enter a period of resocialization. An extreme example of resocialization is military "boot camp." Similarly, whenever we change important roles — as we do in divorce, relocation, or career change — we may need a period of disengagement before we can establish new relationships.

Nature Versus Nurture

Socialization is not something that "happens to us" so much as something we actively engage in. Because of their individual differences, people experience socialization differently. And inevitably, our socialization experience depends on a combination of personality and social experiences. For example, the same family may socialize sons differently than daughters, first-born children differently than later children, and so on.

One of the big questions in social science — a question that puzzles sociologists and psychologists alike — is how much of "what we are" is determined by socialization and how much is inborn? This question is sometimes called "the Nature versus Nurture debate." The assumption that nature dominates us is called "biological determinism." The opposite of biological determinism is "social determinism," which at its extreme gives us an "oversocialized" view of human nature (Wrong, 1961:183–193).

In the past people believed that behavioral differences were (for the most part) genetically determined. That is, people are born with certain aptitudes and dispositions, including an aptitude for good or evil. People even applied this point of view to explaining differences between races and differences between men and women.

Today, we are more conscious of weakness in this line of reasoning. It is one thing to say that nature helps explain *individual* differences and quite another to say it explains *group* differences. Some recent evidence indicates that many differences once thought to be innate are really the result of socialization. However the question remains unresolved. The relative weights of nature and nurture continue to interest researchers.

Consider the focus of current attention on male–female differences. Some argue that gender differences develop because parents react to innate differences in their children. In other words, girls become more verbal than boys because they are more receptive to verbal interactions with their parents. Boys become more physically aggressive because they respond more positively to aggressive play.

Others argue that parents reinforce behaviour in a way that is consistent with their (cultural) expectations and stereotypes. In fact, parents begin to think differently about male and female children even before birth! For example, they assume a large and active fetus will turn out to be a baby boy.

It seems likely that sex differences in adults are the result of gender-based socialization interacting with some innate biological differences. To draw attention to this interplay, sociologists distinguish between sex (the *biological* fact of maleness or femaleness) and gender (the *social distinction* between maleness and femaleness). Then they rephrase traditional assumptions about sex differences as research questions about gender learning.

The second excerpt in this Section is a study of gender socialization in Singapore. The author of this study argues that girls are socialized to expect that they will be supported economically after marriage. Because they have not anticipated or trained for well-paid jobs, women in Singapore end up working at the lowest wage levels.

The Context of Socialization

For most young children thoughout the world, the family is the most significant "agent of socialization." Other "agents of socialization" include friends, school. church, volunteer organizations, and the media.

How children are socialized depends on their sex, ethnicity, birth order, and so on. But one thing is common to all: socialization always occurs in *a social* context. What's more, most cultures, including our own, put a high value on children and care for them within family settings. But the first excerpt in this Section describes an exception to this rule. The children ot Oneida were raised in an intentionally non-family communal setting.

Adult values and childrearing techniques change over the course of time. In western countries it is only within the last century that we have come to see childhood as a special period, or to think of children as having special emotional or psychological needs.

Another important context within which socialization occurs is social class. The kinds of work adults perform and the strategies they use to cope with their work influence the ways they socialize children. Consider the work of Kohn (1977), who pioneered research on the relationship between social class and socialization practices. Kohn's research has certainly helped us understand cross-cultural variations in childrearing

Kohn argued that attitudes to childrearing vary by social class because of important class differences in job experience. According to Kohn, the key job variables are closeness of supervision, routinization, and the complexity of work. Blue collar workers are more closely supervised, perform more routine tasks, and work primarily with physical objects, rather than with people or ideas. Parents with these kinds of jobs are likely to demand conformity, neatness, and orderliness of their children.

By contrast, middle-class, white-collar work is more autonomous, more creative, and less predictable. For this reason, middle-class parents are more permissive with their children and put a greater emphasis on self-reliance. So, for example, Lee's (1987) cross-cultural research finds a universal relationship between adult autonomy and the demand for self-reliance in children.

Along similar lines, Remley (1988) argues that there has been a general shift in North American parental values over the past few decades. Parents used to want their children to be obedient and conforming. Today they are more likely to want their children to be independent. In fact, socialization values seem to be converging around the world. Studies in Germany, Italy, England, and Japan all show a similar desire, among parents, to develop independence in children (Remley, 1988).

Summary

Socialization is a reciprocal process that continues throughout life. How we are socialized depends on our sex, our social class, and our ethnicity, among other things. Finally, for most of us the family is the most significant influence, but we are shaped by all of our social interactions, formal and informal, in childhood and adulthood, whether we consciously perceive this or not.

REFERENCES

Elkin, Frederick and Gerald Handel (1989). *The Child and Society: The Process of Socialization, Fifth Edition.* New York: Random House.

Kohn, M. L. (1977). *Class and Conformity: A Study of Values, Second Edition.* Chicago: University of Chicago Press.

Lee, Gary R. (1987). "Comparative perspectives," pp. 59–80 in M. B. Sussman and S. K. Steinmetz, eds. *Handbook of Marriage and the Family.* New York: Plenum Press.

Remley, Anne (1988). "From Obedience to Independence," *Psychology Today*, October.

Wrong, Dennis (1961). "The oversocialized concept of man in modern sociology," *American Sociological Review,* 26:183–193.

2.1 S. Matarese and P. G. Salmon

The Children of Oneida

INTRODUCTION

For most people, the family is the most important influence on early development. But the next excerpt describes how a group of children were socialized outside the context of family living, by the community as a whole. (Remember the importance of "community" we discussed in earlier excerpts!)

The Oneida community was started by a religious leader named John Noyes in the mid-1800s in New York State. Reverend Noyes' followers agreed not to marry or form attachments to one particular partner but, rather, to define themselves as part of a community-wide "complex" marriage.

Children born into the community remained with their mothers until they were weaned. After that, the whole community raised them. Noyes strongly discouraged close relationships between mothers and their children. Indeed he thought any close bonds, even friendship, would disrupt the group, so he devised ways of preventing their formation.

Noyes may have disregarded the emotional needs of his followers; but materially, he provided for them very well. At a time when few American children received a formal education, children in the Oneida community received both day care and schooling. They learned to read and write, and later they integrated their school work with useful labour: a kind of nineteenth century "work-study program." Whatever we may think of Noyes' views about marriage and sexuality, he and his group created a "modern" and inventive way of socializing children.

One of history's most remarkable experiments in family organization is found in the Oneida Community, a religious utopia which flourished in northwestern New York State during the nineteenth century. Its social structure and child-rearing practices represented a radical alternative to patterns of community organization based upon the nuclear family. Some of the community's children were the result of one of the earliest experiments in human eugenics. All were raised communally according to religious ideals which stressed cooperation and non-exclusive attachments among community members. The purpose of this essay is to provide a broad overview of the community's unique social organization and resultant child-rearing practices.

Matarese, S. and P. G. Salmon (1983). "Heirs to the Promised Land: the Children of Oneida," *International Journal of Sociology of the Family*, 13(2), Autumn, 35–43. Reprinted by permission.

Founded in 1848 by radical theologian John Humphrey Noyes, the Oneida Community was based upon the doctrine of "Perfectionism" which held that through union with God, persons could live lives free from sin.[1] Noyes and his three hundred followers sought to emulate the primitive apostolic church in which "believers possessed one heart and one soul and held all things in common."[2] These principles gave Oneida some of its most distinctive features: economic communism, communal sleeping and dining arrangements, government by mutual criticism and collective labour in agriculture, manufacturing and light industry.

The communal ideal extended even to sexual relations and resulted in the controversial practice: "complex marriage."[3] Under this systems, monogamous relationships were forbidden and adults were encouraged to have sexual relations with a wide variety of partners. Central to the institution was the practice of "male continence," a method of birth control which allowed the community to separate the propagative from the social functions of sex.[4]

During the first twenty years of the community's history, the number of births was intentionally limited, averaging fewer than two a year.[5] By 1868, however, Noyes had become mindful of the need to develop a new generation of Oneidans to carry out his ideals. He initiated an experiment in human breeding which he called "stirpiculture." [6] During the next ten years, fifty-eight children were born as a result of these selected pairings.

According to "Perfectionist" doctrine, children belonged to the entire community, and the women were exhorted to understand they produced children not for their own satisfaction, but for God and communism. Noyes maintained the love of the community was superior to the "special love" engendered by exclusive child-parent bonding. The community's newspaper, the Oneida *Circular,* emphasized the need to "communize the children as completely as we have all other possessions."[7]

In keeping with this doctrine, the community assumed primary responsibility for child-rearing. There were several reasons for this. First, Noyes wanted to ensure that socialization was standardized as far as possible. To this end, he appointed as caretakers a small group of his most loyal and trusted followers. Second, Noyes feared that an intense attachment between parents and children would threaten the system of complex marriage by encouraging exclusionary loyalties.[8]

Separating parents and children took place in stages. During the first year of life, children were cared for by their mothers, much as in any traditional family. At the age of weaning, however, the community began to take a more active and intrusive role. At this time, children were placed in the community's nursery during the day. This nursery was located in a special wing of the Mansion House, the main residence of the community's members. Here they encountered for the first time not only new caretakers, but other children of comparable age. The intent was to wean the child not only physically, but psychologically. This process was virtually completed when at age three they were moved into communal sleeping quarters which further curtailed the amount of maternal-child contact. Although parents and children were allowed time together during the day, this marks the point at which parental — especially maternal — influence ceased to have a decisive impact on the child's day-to-day behaviour.

Since Noyes opposed what he termed "philoprogenitiveness," that is, special loyalty or love for one's own progeny,[9] it is surprising that he permitted mothers and children virtually unrestricted access to each other during the infant's first fourteen months. Sustained contact of this duration allowed ample time for the formation of strong maternal-child attachment. This resulted in powerful emotional ties that ran counter to the spirit of communal love. The subsequent separation of mother and child was apparently quite traumatic, especially for the mother.

Although the advantages of communal care were publicly supported by women's testimonials in the Oneida *Circular*, memoirs of the community's children reveal considerably more ambivalence on the part of their mothers. For example, Pierrepont Noyes' autobiography poignantly describes weekly meetings in his mother's room in which she lavished affection upon him as though trying to make up for lost opportunity. He recalled she frequently interrupted his play to ask, "Darling, do you love me?"[10] Yet toward the end of their visits, she became aloof if it appeared he would resist returning to the Children's House. To a young child, this abrupt change in demeanor must have been confusing. For the mothers, it created strong feelings of conflict. They needed an outlet for the love that had developed during the child's first year. On the other hand, they were aware of the community's practice of temporarily suspending visiting privileges between parents and children for displays of "special love."[11] This is illustrated in Corinna Ackley Noyes' recollection of a chance encounter with her mother during a two-week enforced separation:

> I caught a glimpse of (my mother) passing through a hallway near the Children's House and rushed after her screaming. She knew — what I was too young to know — that if she stopped to talk to me another week might be added to our sentence. Hoping, I suppose, to escape, she stepped quickly into a nearby room. But I was as quick as she. I rushed after her, flung myself upon her, clutching her around the knees, crying and begging her not to leave me, until some Children's House mother, hearing the commotion, came and carried me away.[12]

Between the ages of three and six, the children spent their days in the East Room, appointed much like modern-day nurseries. Toys and playthings were provided, which the children were expected to share in a non-possessive fashion.[13]

Although play was encouraged, Oneida's philosophy of child-rearing emphasized constant instruction and training. As a result, even young children's schedules were planned to allow ample time for many activities which were explicitly instructional. The young children arose at 5:35 every morning. After washing and dressing, they had a brief exercise period, breakfast and a session of Bible reading. At this point children participated in work, recreation and religious training that filled most of the day. By seven o'clock, the youngest children were in bed; the older ones retired an hour later.[14]

Education

At age six, children were moved to the South Room and formal education began. Formal education was required of all children, and encompassed primary and secondary grades. Instruction was provided in a range of subjects, including reading, spelling, grammar, composition, arithmetic, algebra and Latin.[15] Although books and other instructional aids were available, students were encouraged to master these subjects through discussion and class reports rather than by memorization.[16]

A community University was planned but never materialized. Several young men received college educations subsidized by the community. They received training in applied areas, such as medicine, which they were then expected to practice within the community.[17]

In addition to their schoolwork, the older children were required to work in the community's agricultural and manufacturing activities. On an average day, children devoted approximately equal time to work and formal studies. In addition to farming, carpentry, and housekeeping, children's jobs included the production of traps, boxes, and traveling bags.[18] Despite the community's stated belief in sexual equality, young women were most often channeled into traditional women's work including laundry, sewing and housekeeping services.

An important aspect of socialization concerns the manner in which a community responds to transgressions. At Oneida, people other than biological parents played a significant role in socializing and disciplinary activities. Children were accountable not only to the community's adult members, but to God and their peers. Accountability to adults took the form of frequent "criticisms," a practice in which even young children were apprised of their flaws by a group of adults and provided with guidelines for rectifying their mistakes. These criticisms had religious overtones as well, for children were encouraged to "confess Christ" and thereby restore themselves to good standing in the spiritual realm. Children were also encouraged to monitor one another's behaviour, and to report transgressions to appropriate adults.[19]

Discipline

Noyes had a liberal attitude toward discipline and discouraged corporal punishment.[20] Instead, efforts were made to talk and reason with young offenders. Adults were encouraged to use positive rewards and incentives to encourage behavior consistent with community norms. For example, one Children's House worker initiated a club known as the "Order of the O and F" (Obedient and Faithful), giving badges for good behaviour.[21]

Descriptions of the children generally portray them as cheerful, energetic and well-behaved. Compared with children outside the community, they were perceived as highly cooperative and mutually supportive.[22] They were also physically robust: a medical report by Dr. Theodore Noyes revealed they were taller and heavier then a sample of children taken from a Boston school.[23]

Among the most controversial features of the community's child-rearing practices was sexual initiation. This occurred at a young age, in some cases predating puberty.[24] At the age of 10 to 12, children were considered to be adults and moved into individual rooms in the Mansion House. There their sexual initiation took place. Young boys were paired with women past child-bearing age; girls were initiated primarily by Noyes himself.

The practice of sexually pairing young and old members of the community was based upon the doctrine of "ascending fellowship," a reflection of Noyes' belief that community members ranged in ascending order from those who were the least to those who were the most nearly perfect. He argued persons who were at lower levels of spiritual development should associate with their superiors; hence the term, "ascending fellowship."[25] In general, it was felt older persons were spiritually more advanced than their younger counterparts. When applied to complex marriage, this principle dictated younger persons should be paired with older persons of the opposite sex. This arrangement was buttressed by systematic segregation of young men and women between the ages of 12 through 25 to curb what Noyes termed "horizontal fellowship." This referred to the natural attractions of young people for one another.[26] Noyes believed children experienced "amative desires" when quite young, and apparently thought it best to channel such sexual energies in ways which promoted community solidarity.[27] Specifically, he wished to avoid the intergenerational conflict responsible for the demise of earlier communal efforts.

The Dissolution of the Community

Despite his best efforts, many of the offspring grew dissatisfied with community life and thereby contributed to its dissolution.

Several reasons explain this unanticipated outcome. First, though raised under conditions that promoted social homogeneity, children of the Oneida community were not preselected for specific spiritual or moral values as their forebears had been. This is true even of the stirpicults, who were presumed by Noyes to have inherited their parents' moral and spiritual commitment.[28] There is implied in this a perhaps unfounded faith both in the powers of environmental control and the mechanisms of heritability.

Educational factors contributed as well. Children sent to college developed a perspective on life that transcended the community's boundaries. Those who returned often did so with criticisms of the existing social order.[29] Even those whose education took place within the community grew dissatisfied. For one thing, Noyes encouraged a spirit of scientific inquiry in the educational process that undoubtedly undermined the faith and obedience which had been fundamental to the Perfectionist creed.[30] Second, the children's teachers lacked the charismatic qualities that had aided Noyes in converting people to Perfectionism. Moreover, aside from his role in sexually initiating young women, Noyes appears to have been remote from the day-to-day activities of the children.

Finally, despite Noyes' emphasis on "ascending fellowship," children developed strong peer attachments. They ate, slept, studied, worked and played together beginning at a very early age. This fostered solidarity vis-a-vis adults. They founded secret societies, resisted pressures to report on one another, and proved to be mutually supportive in the face of adult intrusions.[31] Despite frequent contact with older community members in sexual encounters, they retained a loyalty to their own cohort.

The Oneida experiment came remarkably close to achieving a system of child-rearing in which environmental factors and heritability were successfully controlled. Under such highly regulated conditions, it may come as a surprise that the community was racked by internal dissent and ultimately dissolved. This outcome attests to the difficulties in reshaping traditional family structure and insuring the continuity of the resultant changes from one generation to the next.

ENDNOTES

[1] Noyes (1849).

[2] Oneida (1867:11).

[3] Carden (1969:49–61).

[4] Noyes (1866).

[5] Oneida (1875:19).

[6] Noyes (1875).

[7] Oneida *Circular,* June 5, 1868.

[8] Barren and Miller, eds. (1875:282). An early community statement of "general principles" regarding the relationship of parents to children also declared that love between adult men and women was a "superior passion" to love between adults and children. Oneida *Circular,* January 29, 1863.

[9] Oneida *Circular,* October 5, 1868.

[10] Noyes (1937:65–67).

[11] Carden (1969:63–66).

[12] Corinna Ackley Noyes (1960:16).

[13] Oneida *Circular,* June 15, 1868.

[14] Oneida *Circular,* October 29, 1857.

[15] Robertson (1970:182–185).

[16] Oneida (1850:15).

[17] Robertson (1970:178).

[18] Noyes (1937:101).

[19] Pierrepont Noyes (1937:51).

[20] Oneida (1850:13–14).

[21] Kanter (1972:14)

[22] Noyes (1937:148).

[23] Theodore Noyes (1878:2).

[24] Van de Warker (1884:789).

[25] Carden (1969:52–53).

[26] Oneida *Circular,* April 4, 1864.

[27] Van de Warker (1884:789).

[28] Parker (1935:264). Parker quotes Noyes as follows:

I can tell just when all this repeating of troubles is going to end. It will be when wisdom and righteousness are fixed in the blood, so that the lessons which the parents have learned by experience, the children will have in them when they are born.... Educating (children) is not going to do it, only as it helps the process of breeding. It is breeding that is going to finish the work.

[29] Noyes' eldest son. Theodore, for example, was an avowed agnostic. See Carden (1969:96).

[30] Oneida *Circular,* January 4, 1869.

[31] Pierrepont Noyes (1937:49,112).

REFERENCES

Carden, Maren Lockwood (1969). *Oneida: Utopian Community to Modern Corporation.* Baltimore: Johns Hopkins Press.

Kanter, Rosabeth (1972). *Commitment and Community.* Massachusetts: Harvard University Press.

Noyes, Corinna Ackley (1960). *The Days of My Youth.* Utica, New York: Widtman Press.

Noyes, John Humphrey (1849). *Confessions of John Humphrey Noyes, Part 1: Confessions of Religious Experience: Including a History of Modern Perfectionism.* Oneida, New York.

——— (1866). *Male Continence.* Oneida, New York: Office of the *Circular.*

——— (1875). Essay on Scientific Propagation. Oneida, New York: Oneida Community.

——— (1875). *Home Talks.* Edited by Alfred Barron and George Noyes Miller. Oneida, New York: Oneida Community.

Noyes, Pierrepont (1937). *My Father's House: An Oneida Boyhood.* New York: Farrar and Rinehart.

Noyes, Theodore (1878). Report on the Health of Children in the Oneida Community. Oneida, New York: Oneida Community.

Oneida (1850). *Second Annual Report of the Oneida Association.* Oneida, New York: Leonard and Co., Printers.

——— (1864–1879). The *Circular.* Oneida, New York: Oneida Community: Thirteen Volumes.

——— (1867). Handbook of the Oneida Community. Wallingford, Connecticut: Office of the Circular

——— (1875). Handbook of the Oneida Community 1875. Oneida, New York: Office of the Circular.

Parker, Robert Allerton (1935). *A Yankee Saint.* New York: G. P. Putnam's Sons.

Robertson, Constance Noyes (1970). *Oneida Community: An Autobiography.* New York: Syracuse University Press.

Van de Warker, Ely (1884). "A Gynecological Study of the Oneida Community," *The American Journal of Obstetrics and Diseases of Women and Children,* XVIII:785–810.

2.2 Stella R. Quah

Sex-Role Socialization in Singapore

INTRODUCTION

In North America much of the focus of the women's movement in the 1960s was on the long-term effects of "traditional" socialization. Betty Friedan's book The Feminine Mystique *was instrumental in drawing attention to the issue of media stereotypes. Study after study followed, finding consistently stereotyped behaviour and underrepresented female characters.*

Magazines, television drama, cartoons, and educational texts all portrayed young girls and women as passive actors whose activities and interests centred on home and the family. By contrast, men and boys were active, decisive, and involved in public (often outdoor) activities.

The next excerpt is a study of school readers used by children in the first to fifth grades in Singapore. As researchers found in North America, Quah finds these books represent women primarily as housewives, men as wage-earners. At issue for Quah is the long-term impact on girls of accepting the traditional view that home and employment are incompatible.

Typically young women in Singapore do not anticipate working for pay, yet an increasing number end up doing just that. They work in "female" jobs, with low rewards and little job security. As long as young girls expect that they will be wives and mothers exclusively, they will fail to train for jobs that can give them economic security. As a result, the role conflict (between paid work and housewife roles) Quah describes will continue.

The purpose of this paper is twofold: firstly, to discuss the sex-role stereotypes children encounter in school textbooks. Secondly, to contend that the influence received during the first years of school, which emphasize traditional sex-roles, contradicts the latter social call faced by young women to join the labour force and may give rise to role conflict particularly among female workers who are wives and mothers.

The typical example of a social situation where females face role conflict and role strain due to contradictory-role demands, is a society with the "two-role ideology" described by Bernard (1972:235–46). The two-role ideology exists when women are expected to "combine motherhood and the care of home with outside activities" (1972:237), particularly a formal job. Bernard uses the concept to describe

Quah, S. R. (1980). "Sex-Role Socialization in a Transitional Society," *International Journal of Sociology of the Family*, 10(2), July–December, 213–231. Reprinted by permission.

the United States, Britain and some other European countries in the 1960s. The next development which Bernard already sees in those countries albeit in an incipient stage, is the "shared-role ideology" whereby both family and occupational roles are shared by men and women (1972:242).

The "two-role ideology" concept is useful in understanding sex-role stereotypes in nations of the Third World which are currently in advanced stages of industrialization. Singapore is one such nation. Two important characteristics come to light when the two-role ideology lens is used for analysis. Firstly, industrialization in the Third World does not necessarily bring a change in traditional values. On the contrary, one may observe the coexistence of traditional values and beliefs together with modern ideas; the former are likely to predominate in family and primary group behaviour while the latter are implemented mostly in formal interactions including technology issues and transactions dealing with the production and distribution of goods and services.

Secondly, the two-role ideology may not give way to the shared-role ideology in Third World nations. It is not uncommon to find people who contend that women are called to take jobs — the two-role ideology — only as a temporary measure while the national economy stabilizes; once this is accomplished, legislators, the common man, or both, hope "to return things to normal," to put females back at home.

The preceding concepts lead the way for the twofold objective of this paper: namely, (a) to test the assumption that schools contribute to the legitimization of sex-role stereotypes through textbooks thus providing formal anticipatory socialization for traditional female roles; and (b) to probe the proposition that young women socialized under this process face role conflict and role strain as the two-role ideology demands from them performance of two mutually exclusive — from a traditional viewpoint — sets of roles, family and job.

Formalizing Anticipatory Socialization on Traditional Roles

One common finding appears in several analyses of children's books and sex-roles in the United States: the books systematically emphasize the male roles and play down or neglect the role of females.

A content analysis of six reading textbooks[1] used in the first to fifth grades of elementary school in Singapore reveals similarities as well as differences with the above studies. The most important similarity is the emphasis given to traditional male and female roles. The most important difference rests on the fact that female roles are portrayed in higher proportions than male roles.

The textbooks analysed here concentrate on a few sex-role stereotypes for males and females conveyed through written expressions, stories, exercises and/or through sketches or pictures. The most frequently mentioned sex-role for females is that of housewife. Children learn to put letters and sounds together by reading sentences such as "mother cleans table," "the lady sweeps the floor," "mother does not want the boy in the kitchen," but "girls help mother in the kitchen."

On the other hand, the Husband Economic Provider Role or HEPR, the label introduced by Gronseth (1972) for the traditional sex-role assigned to males, is not neglected in these textbooks. Another example is this story found in a third grade's textbook:

> Mr Lee gets up early, he goes to his shop in his car, (and after working all day) at six o'clock (he goes) home. Every evening he has dinner at home and plays with his children. The children go to bed at eight o'clock. Then Mr Lee talks with his wife. (Cobb and Cheong, 1970:3)

This story is a typical example of the characterization of men in these textbooks. As said earlier, housewife is the most frequently found sex-role for females, followed by teacher and nurse and activities dealing with child care, buying clothes and personal care. Moreover, girls are portrayed as naturally more interested in dolls than in sports and even afraid of mice. Conversely, the typical sex-roles for males in addition to HEPR are that of mechanic, repairman, driver, fireman, policeman, doctor, dentist, sportsman and businessman among others.

Sex-role stereotypes go beyond determination of occupations. They involve norms on appropriate behaviour. Girls are expected to wear dresses while "boys wear shirts and shorts." Recreational activities should be differentiated too; for example, "girls play with dolls, but boys don't. Do girls play football? No they don't" (Cobb and Cheong, 1970:2). Girls in fact undergo anticipatory socialization through stories and phrases depicting girls playing with dolls and caring for their little brothers.

In sum, there is a striking similarity in the use of sex-role stereotypes between elementary school textbooks in Singapore and those in some industrialized western countries.

With reference to the major difference presented by school materials in Singapore, females far from being neglected are given more "coverage" than males. In the six elementary school textbooks analysed here, the average proportion of references to females is 65 percent, while only an average of 35 percent deal with males.

A tentative interpretation of the above finding may be given based on cultural values and traditions. Traditionally, the Chinese, Malays and Indians — the three major ethnic groups in Singapore — perceive the main goal of women as wives and mothers (cf. Ryan, 1971). Consequently, it is understandable that the purpose of schooling for girls be seen by textbook writers as a means to enhance these roles and provide further, more "formal" preparation for their implementation. On the same line of thought, the strong emphasis on traditional sex-roles for girls may counteract any harmful, modernizing effects of education.

Basically, the first assumption probed in this paper is supported by the data. School materials do present stereotypes that reinforce the anticipatory socialization of girls for the roles of housewife and mother.

Female Workers and Role Conflict

The percentage of Singapore's total female population aged 15–64 years in the labour force has increased from 31.5 percent in 1971 to 42.3 percent in 1978 (Department of Statistics, 1979b).

This increase however, is not evenly distributed in all sectors of the economy. The nature of economic development in Singapore is reflected in the concentration of the labour force into three major sectors i.e., manufacturing, commerce, and services including community, social and personal services. The distribution of male and female workers in the latter two sectors became almost equal in 1977. But there are higher proportions of females than males in the manufacturing sector.

Singapore's female workers usually work for the bottom wage levels in the labour force. This situation is typical in Third World nations. Another common feature in these nations is the systematic disparity in salaries given to males and females holding the same jobs. This occurs in Singapore throughout the occupational system but particularly in the lower ranks and among the daily-rated workers (Ministry of Labour, 1979: 45–53; Ong, 1979:14–15; Nain, 1979:6).

The preceding supports Gronseth's (1972) argument on the negative effects of the husband economic provider role (HEPR). Gronseth observes that the HEPR is conducive to discrimination against working women. Their salaries are perceived as "extra" income for the family and thus expendable while men, considered by employers to be main breadwinners, are given preference in job allocation, promotion and higher salary.

The picture before us presents two key characteristics: (a) women are needed and called into the labour force out of national economic necessity and personal financial need; (b) concurrently, social values favouring traditional sex-role stereotypes remain highly influential. This picture may be completed by yet another trend of female labour in Third World nations. This is the female withdrawal from the labour force upon marriage or childbearing. The peak of female labour force participation in Singapore is reached between 20 to 24 years of age. A sharp and steady decline takes over from there on. This decline coincides with the average age of marriage for Singaporean females: namely 24.2 years (Ministry of Finance, 1979: Quah, 1979).

The most likely interpretation of the withdrawal experienced in the female labour force in Singapore rests on the concepts of role conflict and role strain. Female workers face incompatible role demands and expectations in their daily lives. The degree of incompatibility may be lowest for single female workers; it increases for married female workers, and may be highest for working mothers as the latter are likely to have more of their time demanded by concurrent job, marital, child care and housework commitments. The role expectations generated from the role of worker or employee are incompatible with those from the housewife and mother roles in that the latter two are traditionally perceived as the major if not the only goals of women in society. The priorities are clear for females who have fully internalized the sex-role stereotypes transmitted through anticipatory socialization. They simply leave their jobs, if any, when one or both of these two roles are attained. For those who can afford to leave the withdrawal from their jobs is a "solution" to the problems of role conflict and role strain.

The proportion of females over 25 years old who remain in the labour force suggests there is a small but steadily increasing number of women who either cannot leave their jobs due to financial need, have not solved their role priorities and/or are convinced that self-fulfillment goes well beyond marriage and motherhood.

This group of women has the highest probability of undergoing stress trying to comply with contradictory role demands. The most important reason for the incompatibility of role expectations is the preponderance of a version of the two-role ideology.

In Singapore there is a common belief that home and work are incompatible spheres of activity for females. If one role is attained, the other will be neglected. The absence of comprehensive institutional arrangements to support working wives and mothers lends credibility to this belief in incompatibility.

The Director of Manpower Planning of the Economic Development Board perceives problems of role conflict and role strain when he states that among married women, "those who continue working suffer through considerable difficulties and divided loyalties. Those who leave do so with considerable regret" (Ong, 1979:19). Indeed, even some educated working women have expressed their belief in traditional values and the stress generated by incompatible demands.

At the national level, the call for solutions solve the problems faced by working wives and mothers, is becoming stronger. Suggestions have been made by community leaders, private citizens and government bodies but the solutions do not come easily in a free-enterprise economy. Three major suggestions can be identified. The most popular appears to be "split-work shifts" or part-time jobs for married female workers (Loh, 1979:36; NTUC, 1979:57), which the Ministry of Labour has recommended to employers (*New Nation*, 1979a). A few factories have already established flexible working hours for women (*New Nation*, 1979b).

Another idea is the provision of prolonged unpaid maternity leave of one year (*Sunday Times*, 1979b; *Straits Times*, 1979b) or three years as suggested by a male pediatrician.

The third major suggestion is the expansion of child day-care services (Loh, 1979:36) and the establishment of full-day school (*Straits Times*, 1979d). The trade unions and the People's Association are expanding their day-care service (*Straits Times*, 1979e). However, there are indications of prejudice against institutional child-care. Working women seem to prefer the personalized care provided by relatives and friends (Quah, 1979).

In conclusion, the beliefs that the woman's main goal is family and motherhood, that she is unable to handle housekeeping and a paid job simultaneously, and that she should participate fully in the national economy, are all part of the Singaporean version of the two-role ideology.

This paper has presented evidence which supports two propositions. Firstly, school textbooks give legitimization to traditional sex-role stereotypes of males as providers and females as housewives and mothers. These ideas reinforce what children learn through socialization and home. The traditional sex-role stereotypes are thus carried into adult life as part of anticipatory socialization.

Secondly, real-life economic pressures require women to play alternative roles in the labour force. Yet, the social and cultural environment does not provide women with the means for a congruent working life. Family and children are still emphasized as the ideal goal of women; the husband's sharing of household chores is a little known idea or if known, it is poorly accepted; discrimination in wages still exist. The two-role ideology is strongly embedded in the minds of Singaporeans of both sexes. Some voices have been recently calling for a more equitable deal for working women. The changes may come but not before the two-role ideology has been left behind.

ENDNOTES

[1] The procedure of selection of these six reading textbooks involved two steps. The first step was listing the ten most widely used reading textbooks in elementary school during the past three years. A preliminary analysis of these textbooks showed a great similarity in presentation and emphasis of sex-role stereotypes. Such similarity allowed the second step, the random selection of six of the ten textbooks using a table of random numbers. The smaller number of textbooks facilitated the content analysis. No textbook was found portraying equal roles for males and females.

REFERENCES

Bernard, J. (1972). "Changing family life styles: one role, two roles, shared roles," in L. K. Hoke (ed.), *The Future of Family,* pp. 235–46. New York: Simon & Schuster.

Cobb, D. and W. S. Cheong (1970). *Looking Ahead with English 3.* Singapore: Longmans.

Department of Statistics (Singapore) (1979b). *Singapore Annual Key Indicators.* Singapore: Department of Statistics.

Gronseth, E. (1972). "The breadwinner trap," in L. K. Hoke (ed.), *The Future of the Family,* pp. 175–91. New York: Simon & Schuster.

Hobbs, J. (1973). *New Primary English Book 5.* Singapore: Longmans.

Loh, M. (1979). "The social responsibilities of working women in the home and in society," in NTUC, *The Responsibilities and the Aspirations of Working Women in Singapore,* pp. 34–39. Singapore: NTUC.

Ministry of Finance (Singapore) (1979). *Economic Survey of Singapore* 1978. Singapore: SNP.

Nair, C. V. D. (1979). "Opening address," in NTUC, *The Responsibilities and Aspirations of Working Women in Singapore,* pp. 6–7. Singapore: NTUC.

New Nation (1979a). "Call for split shifts to lure housewives," 6 March, p. 5.

New Nation (1979b). "The new breed factory workers," 6 March, p. 3.

NTUC (National Trade Union Congress) (1979). Seminar on the Responsibilities and Aspirations of Working Women in Singapore. Singapore: NTUC.

Ong, W. H. (1979). "The problems and prospects of working women in Singapore," in NTUC, *The Responsibilities and Aspirations of Working Women in Singapore.* Singapore: NTUC.

Quah, S. R. (1979). "Child welfare and socioeconomic development: the Singapore experience," *Indian Journal of Public Administration,* 25:815–27.

Ryan, N. J. (1971). *The Cultural Heritage of Malaya.* Singapore: Longman.

Straits Times (1979a). "Religious class helps them face moral dangers," 22 Oct., p. 7.

Straits Times (1979b). "Priority now," Editorial, 15 Oct., p. 16.

Straits Times (1979d). "Full-day school: only 25 pc mums will seek jobs," 2 Oct., p. 1.

Straits Times (1979e). "Plan to expand PA's child day-care service," 23 Oct., p. 15.

Sunday Times (1979b). "Call to allow a year's unpaid maternity leave for women," 14 Oct., p. 6.

The New Syllabus n. d. *The New Syllabus English Book 4.*

2.3 Donald E. Miller and Lorna Touryan Miller

Memory and Identity Among Armenian Survivors and Their Children

INTRODUCTION

We have already noted that social context affects the nature of socialization practices. For example, children raised during an economic depression (e.g., the 1930s and 1980s) will grow up worried about financial security. By contrast, children raised during prosperous times (e.g., the 1950s and 1960s) will grow up optimistic and obsessed with the need to express themselves.

The next excerpt shows the effect of a catastrophic event on the survivors of that catastrophe, and even on their children and grandchildren. Between 1915 and 1923, the Turks massacred about one and a half million Armenians. This tragedy affected the lives of children and grandchildren of survivors through stories told, first, by grandparents and, later, by the next generation. These stories kept the bitter memory alive and strengthened feelings of Armenian nationalism. Strong national pride and sense of community survived even among families emigrating to the United States.

Miller, Donald E. and Lorna Touryan Miller (1991). "Memory and Identity Across the Generations: A Case Study of Armenian Survivors and Their Progeny," *Qualitative Sociology,* 14(1), 13–38. Reprinted by permission of Human Sciences Press, Inc.

These stories had a very great impact on some members of the third generation who later became involved in terrorist activity aimed at drawing world attention to the Armenian genocide. (Typically, ethnic and religious groups tend to remember the misdeeds of their enemies; on this, see excerpt 5.2 below, on religion in the former USSR.) Although the actions of these terrorists were extreme, "they embody many issues and conflicts present more generally in the Armenian population."

From 1915–23, approximately 1.5 million Armenians died in Ottoman Turkey in what has been called the first genocide of the twentieth century. This article examines the ways in which the trauma of this genocide has affected the identity of survivors, their children and grandchildren. To approach the topic, we have borrowed a methodological principle from one of America's most eminent philosophers and psychologists, William James.

In *Varieties of Religious Experience*, James (1961:24–25) asserts he will map the terrain of the religious life, by studying those for whom religion has been a passion: the saints, mystics and, as he calls them, the "geniuses" of religion. From these extreme cases, James believes one can better understand persons for whom religion may be a much blander commitment.

We have adopted a similar methodological principle. In this article we will elaborate the case histories of several Armenian terrorists for whom the Armenian cause, and the genocide in particular, has been a commitment for which they were willing to die. Although their commitment may be extreme, they embody many issues and conflicts present more generally in the Armenian population.

The Armenian Terrorist Movement

Between 1973 and 1985 the terrorist movement claimed the lives of 30 Turkish diplomats or members of their immediate families; in addition, 34 non-Turks were killed and over 300 persons were wounded (Gunter, 1986:1). These assassinations occurred in the Middle East, Western Europe, and North America. Their objective was to focus world attention on Armenian claims, and to counter the continuing denial of the genocide by the Turkish government.

Two groups masterminded the attacks. The Justice Commandos of the Armenian Genocide (JCAG) were relatively discrete in their tactics, killing only political representatives of the Turkish government. The Armenian Secret Army for the Liberation of Armenia (ASALA), on the other hand, claimed credit for attacks that involved the deaths of non-Turks as well as Turkish civilians and diplomats.

Methodology

There are three sources of data for this study. First, between 1974 and 1986 we interviewed more than one hundred survivors of the 1915 genocide. These interviews lasted a minimum of two hours. Survivors were at least seventy years old when interviewed, and averaged between 11 and 12 years of age at the time of the genocide.

Second, in 1990 we interviewed four Armenians who were arrested in 1982 for terrorist activities against Turkish targets, and are currently serving prison sentences or else are on parole. At the time of their arrests, they ranged in age from their late teens to middle twenties. All are grandsons of survivors, and all indicated the Armenian genocide played an important role in motivating them to pursue the political actions which resulted in their arrests and convictions.

A third source of data is the personal experience of the authors. Lorna Touryan Miller is the daughter of two survivors. Seven of her father's nine family members died in the genocide. Half of her mother's family lost their lives. For almost twenty years the authors have lived in Pasadena, California, which has an Armenian population of 12–15,000.

Summary of Our Interviews

Grandparents and Grandsons

Because of the extended family network among Armenians, the bond between grandparents and grandchildren has been extremely strong. In the case of the terrorist Levon, his primary education regarding the genocide came from his grandparents.

This was not exceptional. For example, Shaunt (not his real name), another terrorist, was born in Lebanon. In Beirut he lived in an extended family setting in which his uncle's house — where his maternal grandfather also lived — adjoined his own. Shaunt described his relationship with his grandfather:

> He loved us tremendously, both of us [referring to his older brother]. I remember him kissing my forehead every morning. I think my personality was developed when my grandfather was carrying me around talking to his survivor friends about the horrible times. I think my responsibility started to be conveyed to me even that early as he walked through parks ... he holding my hand and talking to me. These conversations about the genocide were ubiquitous.

When Shaunt was 12, the family moved to the United States. This move was preceded, however, by the deaths of his grandfather, and uncle. These losses saddened him greatly, and when reflecting on his commitment to the Armenian cause, he commented his involvement was in direct response to a felt obligation to the vision of his uncle and grandfather.

> I was so immersed and committed to this belief of making my grandparents proud, my uncle proud, and giving them the message, "See, I did what you expected me to do. I died for the cause."

This statement by Shaunt parallels Levon's comment that his involvement in a terrorist plot was a way of fulfilling his grandfather's desires.

Vahe (not his real name) said he did not know much about his grandparents. At the time, we took this at face value. However, several weeks after he wrote to us saying he had talked to his mother about his grandparents, and she had said, that as a child he had been obsessed with their stories. He reported he was surprised at how he had "filtered out the 'tragic' and converted the 'memory' of suffering into political phenomena." His mother told him his paternal grandfather had been killed in the deportations, along with his brother. Also, his great grandfather, on his mother's side, had been killed in the 1895 massacres, and his mother's father had escaped death by being sent to hide among friendly Kurds. At some level these stories, or the anger surrounding them, had been communicated to Vahe, and had contributed greatly to his political consciousness.

Turning from terrorists to our sample of survivors (i.e., grandparents), the pattern becomes more complex. Survivors varied remarkably in their response to the tragedy of their childhood. A substantial number said they never spoke with their children about the genocide. Often they would say something like, "My story is too sad; I didn't want to burden my children with it." A majority, however, had told their children at least pieces of their story and many said their grandchildren frequently asked them about their experiences.

A small, but significant, group of survivors appeared reconciled to their past. They seemingly have forgiven the perpetrators of the violence against them, sometimes drawing on religious imagery, and even religious conversion experiences, to explain their attitude. Other survivors seemed resigned about the past; indeed, many might be labelled clinically depressed. Other survivors were vocal about the injustices of the past, with some limiting their rage to verbal expression, while others suggested specific political goals related to reclaiming their homeland in Turkey. The latter group tended to affirm assassinations of Turkish diplomats as legitimate political expression.

Some survivors, who objected to political violence, instead put the responsibility on God, saying God would avenge the Turks. And other survivors struggled with what they felt should be their *Christian* response to the genocide, as opposed to what they said their *human* feelings were.

On the other hand, survivors who have been vocal with their children and grandchildren about the genocide sometimes expressed ambivalence about the effect of these conversations, as is expressed in this statement:

> We don't want to fill our children with revenge. Also, we don't want to trouble or hurt their hearts. But we feel that our children should know what kind of people their ancestors were and that obviously includes how they were killed.

Another survivor said she used to tell her husband not to tell their children about his experiences in the genocide: "But nothing would stop him. Now my sons are filled with revenge. Even my grandchild comes and asks him questions."

Nearly universal among the one hundred survivors we interviewed was the desire for their grandchildren to maintain their Armenian identity. For many, Armenian identity is tied to the Armenian language. They also commented on the importance of knowing the history of the Armenians and maintaining a commitment to the Armenian church.

Parents and Children

Some Armenian parents isolate their children from non-Armenians because assimilation is a threat to any ethnic minority.

The terrorists we interviewed all came from homes where assimilation was very low. We attribute the depth of their feelings not only to the influence of grandparents, but to the significant role played by parents.

Raffi (not his real name) told us that when he was growing up his grandmother used to tell stories of her childhood to his older sisters. He would overhear these stories and wonder at his grandmother who wept as she talked. Raffi's father would say to the grandmother, "It's no use to talk about the past." But Raffi said he noticed his father's own eyes would water as he listened to his mother's stories.

His father's communication about the genocide was always indirect. To offer a further example, he repeatedly told Raffi to "be good," meaning not to be influenced by revolutionary rhetoric, but then he would teach his son the revolutionary songs from the 19th century which *his* father had taught him. Raffi said there was one song his father could never complete:

> Every time my father sang [this song] he would never finish because he would cry. He always cried as he sang that song and choked. And whenever I sing that song today, I also cannot finish it. (paraphrase)

When he was arrested, Raffi said his father never asked "Why did you do it?" Deep inside, said Raffi, he must have felt that what his son had done was right.

Indirect communication between fathers and sons may be one of the most powerful forms of communication.

The Role of Socializing Institutions

In Levon and Shaunt's experience, school functioned to reinforce as well as to universalize the stories they had heard at home. At school they came to realize all Armenians had been touched by this tragedy.

Vahe believes his primary political education came from Armenian political organizations [such as] the Scouts which he joined at age 7 or 8, and the Junior Organization of the ARF, which he joined at 13.

In Lebanon, as a member of the Junior Organization, Vahe received informal military training to serve as an armed guard at the gates of his own school. The Armenian community made heroes of these young men who were willing to defend Armenian institutions.

When he came to the United States with his family at age 16, he was upset at leaving the Armenian community that had been so affirming of him.

Psychosocial Development

Shaunt believes his radical commitment to "the cause" was a way of filling a deep personal void occasioned by the death of his grandfather and uncle, as well as a profound sense of rootlessness that he felt upon coming to the United States at 12 years of age. In high school he felt abused because of his foreignness and accent. This pushed him further into the Armenian subculture and he started to read voraciously in Armenian literature. In college, his accent actually got worse; in his view, this was symbolic of his rejection of American culture and his attempt to root himself in Armenian history and culture.

In reflecting on the terrorist activity in which he was involved, he said [that] "as the opportunity developed to do something that would make me feel more anchored as an Armenian, I think I grabbed it." As quoted earlier, his commitment to "the cause" was also a symbolic way of telling his grandfather and uncle that he had lived up to their expectations.

Two individuals raised another issue that we believe has developmental implications. Both Vahe and Raffi said that as children what bothered them greatly was the image of large groups of Armenians being deported by a handful of gendarmes. How could the Armenians have been so weak, they wondered. This feeling was compounded by a perception Armenians are always on the losing side.

Vahe said that when he first heard of the assassinations, he could not believe it for two reasons: First, Armenians don't kill; and secondly *Armenians are not capable* of killing. Vahe said he became fascinated with Armenian terrorism, and at first he did not include in his analysis the fact that people were losing their lives. It was the *capacity* to kill, the counter to Armenian impotence, that interested him.

In a somewhat different interpretation, Levon said the assassinations were something the Armenian community "needed" in the 1970s and early 1980s to counter the *powerlessness* they were feeling.

Theoretical Extrapolations

Can one generalize from the Armenian experience of memory transmission among generations to a more expansive theory of identity of descent? We offer the following points for consideration.

First, traumatic events such as genocides potentially serve as the axial point for group and generational self-understanding. Conversations that link generations radiate around these events. These traumatic events become the template through which generations relate to each other and through which group self-understanding evolves. These events define the parameters of communal conversations, thus providing the components from which collective identity is built.

Second, grandparents are primary carriers and transmitters of collective group memories. Grandparents symbolize the past to grandchildren, and embody the collective memory of the family or group. For all of their protests, grandchildren hunger for roots that define from whence they have come.

Third, when our stories of origin include moral contradictions, we may reject them because they paralyze and threaten us, or we may seek to correct our past in an effort to achieve personal wholeness and healing. What may appear to be fanatical behavior, may be based in battles with demons rooted in the injustices (and failures) which surround the stories of our predecessors.

Fourth, parents establish the context for mediation between grandparents and grandchildren. Parents communicate in direct and indirect ways whether the stories told by grandparents are to be valued.

Fifth, parents and grandparents together bear primary responsibility for creating and maintaining the institutions that preserve cultural and group values.

Sixth, there is nothing mechanical about the transmission of memory from one generation to another. Children exercise considerable control in what they accept and reject, which is another way of saying individuals exercise considerable freedom in constructing their personal sense of meaning.

REFERENCES

Gunter, M. (1986). *"Pursuing the Just Cause of Their People," A Study of Contemporary Armenian Terrorism.* New York: Greenwood Press.

James, W. (1961). *The Varieties of Religious Experience.* New York: Collier.

Jacoby, S. (1983). *Wild Justice: The Evolution of Revenge.* New York: Harper and Row.

2.4 Nao Oyama

Japanese Values in the Younger Generation

INTRODUCTION

Each generation learns, and lives by, somewhat different values than the generation that came before it. And, within any complex industrial society, we are likely to find a variety of different outlooks on life ranging from very "traditional" to very "modern."

That's largely why generational conflict occurs; indeed, the conflict between generations

Oyama, Nao (1990). "Some Recent Trends in Japanese Values: Beyond the Individual-Collective Dimension," *International Sociology*, 5(4), December, 445–459. Reprinted by permission.

has been a persistent feature of industrial societies for at least a century. A related problem is what Durkheim called "anomie" — a conflict between moral systems that arises out of the fact that people lead a wide variety of lives in a highly specialized industrial society.

The next excerpt studies values to document the shift in Japanese culture from a community orientation to increased individualism. (On this shift, see also excerpt 12.4 on the values associated with Europe's second demographic transition.) The author, Oyama, explains that the shift is due to the influence of Western culture, increased prosperity, city living, and changes in the family — changes we often find associated with industrialization.

But she also finds that in Japan, individualism is being tempered by a sentiment of "universalism," which gives priority to general human happiness over individual happiness when the two are in conflict. She speculates on the likely continued growth of such values. But it is too soon to tell whether one value-system will prevail or many systems will continue to co-exist.

Here I propose a three-fold classification of value orientations: individual-collective-universal. Collectivism, which means behaviour patterns dependent on a group or a society, has been emphasised as a special feature of Japan by both Japanese and foreign scholars. However, Japanese society is changing and Japanese value attitudes have also been changing, especially in the post-war period. People's collective orientation has been decreasing; many begin to have an individual orientation and a few begin to have a universal orientation.

The universal orientation means a relative priority that a person gives to general human happiness over one's own happiness when a competitive relation takes place between the two. The individual orientation means an opposite priority, namely a priority given to one's own happiness over general human happiness.

People with a strong universal orientation are in a minority in present-day Japanese society. Nevertheless, one should pay attention to this value orientation. In an era of internationalisation, an increase in people with a strong universal orientation will be required to promote human happiness in the entire world.

Value Changes in Japan

A deep change in values from the collective orientation to the individual orientation has occurred in Japan over the post-war period. The Institute of Statistical Mathematics has carried out surveys on the Japanese National Character every five years since 1953. The results of these surveys indicate this change. A very famous question repeated in these surveys examines people's values and many scholars often cite it.

QA. There are all sorts of attitudes toward life. Of those listed here, which one would you say comes closest to your feelings?

(a) Work hard and get rich.

(b) Study earnestly and make a name for yourself.

(c) Don't think about money or fame; just live a life that suits your own tastes.

(d) Live each day as it comes, cheerfully and without worrying.

(e) Resist all evils in the world and live a pure and just life.

(f) Never think of yourself, give everything in service of society.

There are six choices: (a) through to (d) indicate an individual orientation. But (a), (b) and (c), (d) are two different groups. The former group (a, b) indicates an individual orientation which depends on a social system. There must a social system in order for people to get money through hard work or to become famous through earnest study. In this sense, people who select (a) or (b) depend on their social system — obedience to it becomes a means to get money or honour. In behavioural results, obedience to the social system resembles that of persons with a collective orientation. However, the real value orientation underlying the behaviour is individual.

The latter group indicates a different individual orientation. People who select (c) or (d) obey their own thinking or liking. They do not need to obey the social system in order to satisfy their own value orientation. They sometimes look selfish. The centre of their personal value system is the self.

Choices (e) and (f) indicate a strong social orientation, which could come from either a collective orientation or a universal orientation. People who select these choices let social affairs come before their own affairs.

First, the survey results indicate individualisation (The Institute of Statistical Mathematics [ISM] 1982:388). Since the end of World War II in Japan, people who select the social orientation (e, f) have decreased in number and those people who select the individual orientation, especially (c) or (d), have increased. (See Table 1.) Miyajima (1983) described this change as "privatisation," which means a life-style centred on the self.[1] It is certain that people who give precedence to individual-relation things over social-relation things are increasing in number.

The increase in the choices of (c) or (d) shows that there are a lot of persons who do not depend on the social system in recent Japan. However, it is a simple interpretation. The ratio of people who select (a) or (b) has not changed so much. These days, the relations between hard work and wealth, and between hard studying and achieving honour, are not so clear. People who work hard do not always become rich. People who study hard do not always get honour. Therefore, the ratio of choices (a) and (b) is low. In fact, however, there are a great many people who study hard and who work hard in Japan. They realise the possibilities of getting money or honour by working hard or studying earnestly are low. Therefore, to a question like QA, they may answer that they want a life that suits their own tastes or an easy-going life. But it is inferred that they really wish to get money and honour in spite of low possibilities.

After all, people's individual orientation has increased in post-war Japan. People themselves realise this change is occurring and they do not always approve of it. But this change is continuing nonetheless.

Second, the survey results shed light on the individual-collective opposition in Japan. The main objects of the collective orientation are the nation and

TABLE 1   DESIRED WAY OF LIFE BY YEAR AND BY COUNTRY
(PERCENTAGES)

Country/ Year	Wealth	Honour	Tastes	Easy-going	For Justice	For Society	Others
Japan[1]							
1953	15	6	21	11	29	10	8
1958	17	3	27	18	23	6	8
1963	17	4	30	19	18	6	6
1968	17	3	32	20	17	6	5
1973	14	3	39	23	11	5	5
1978	14	2	39	22	11	7	5
1979[2]							
Japan	13	2	40	34	9	2	—
Korea	16	5	41	7	23	8	—
Philippines	34	6	24	16	18	2	—
Singapore	20	3	38	21	12	6	—
India	41	9	15	11	18	6	—
France	5	3	34	14	40	4	—
FRG	12	2	49	12	24	1	—
Italy	9	5	57	17	11	1	—
Britain	8	1	15	43	30	3	—
Canada	9	1	48	29	10	3	—
USA	7	2	43	28	17	3	—
Brazil	13	8	33	16	24	6	—
Australia	7	1	38	38	11	5	—

Sources:
[1] Japanese data (1953–1978): The Institute of Statistical Mathematics, Research Committee on the Study of the Japanese National Character. 1982. *Nipponzin no Kokuminsei* (4) (A study of the Japanese National Character). Tokyo: Idemitsu Shoten. p. 388.
[2] Leisure Development Center (1979). *Thirteen Countries Value Survey*. Tokyo: Leisure Development Center.

occupational groups — companies, government offices, schools, unions, and so on. There are several questions in the survey on the Japanese National Character which examine the relative importance of the individual and the nation, the public (ISM, 1982:325–8). Results are shown in Table 2.

Most people do not assign priority to either the nation and/or individuals. Rather, people thought that improving Japan and making individuals happy are the same thing. People who support the precedence of the nation are decreasing in number. Furthermore, in the recent annual surveys carried out by the Prime Minister's Public Relations Office, more people give priority to the individual than the nation. In the first half of the eighties, the ratios of priority being given to the individual and the nation were almost the same. However, since 1985 the

TABLE 2   QUESTIONS REGARDING THE SELECTION OF
INDIVIDUAL-COLLECTIVE ORIENTATION PERCENTAGES

	1953	1958	1963	1968	1973	1978
QB. Priority given to individual rights or the public interest						
(a) Individual rights	—	—	29	33	32	32
(b) Public interest	—	—	57	57	55	55
QC. What happens more in recent Japan?						
(a) Light treatment of individual rights	—	38	—	—	—	50
(b) Disregard for the public interest	—	29	—	—	—	35
QD. Priority given to individual happiness or improvement *of the nation?*						
(a) Individual happiness	25	—	30	27	30	27
(b) Improvement of the nation	37	—	30	32	26	27
(c) Both the same priority	31	—	34	36	37	41
QE. Types of department chiefs						
(a) Connection only at work	12	14	13	12	13	10
(b) Connection in addition to work	85	77	82	84	81	87

Source: The Institute of Statistical, Mathematics, Research Committee on the Study of the Japanese National Character. 1982. *Nipponzin no Kokuminsei* (4) (A Study of the Japanese National Character). Tokyo: Idemitsu Shoten. pp. 310, 325–8.

individual priority has exceeded the national priority, and in 1988 its ratio is 31 percent compared with 27 percent given to the national priority (Prime Minister's Office 1989b:24–6). It can easily be inferred that such people do not want the pre-war and mid-war system of Japan which forced people to sacrifice their whole lives for the sake of the nation.

The next question, QF, examines the value orientation — individual or collective — to a company (ISM, 1982:310).

Suppose you are working in a firm. There are two types of department chiefs. Which of these two would you prefer to work under?

(a) A man who always sticks to the work rules and never demands any unreasonable work but who, on the other hand, never does anything for you personally in matters not connected with work.

(b) A man who sometimes demands extra work in spite of rules against it but who, on the other hand, looks after you personally in matters not connected with work.

The result is strong agreement with type (b). (See Table 2.) There was no change from 1953 to 1978. Most Japanese support this type of department manager. Other societies display less support for this value. Using this question, a survey was carried out on Hawaiians of Japanese ancestry, Hawaiians of non-Japanese ancestry and Americans (USA proper). The ratios of agreement with type (b) are 63 percent, 57 percent and 50 percent respectively (ISM,1982:89).

These results show the Japanese emphasis on emotional interpersonal relations. Approval of such relations looks like a display of the collective orientation. In fact, they do show traditional Japanese collectivism. But this may not always be the result of a collective orientation. The main reason for such a collective orientation to a company is the Japanese management style. This gives employees many benefits that can only be obtained by belonging to a company. These benefits do not only include fringe benefits, but also social status and power, which are useful inside and outside the company. Belonging to a company or an organisation for work explains who we are and how we behave, which increases our reliability and enables smooth behaviour in Japanese society. Thus, the higher a company's reliability becomes, the higher the reliability of persons belonging to it; the greater the power a company commands, the greater the power of its members. Companies are not only places where we can earn money, but also places for living.

Nevertheless, Sakamoto (1983) pointed out that interpersonal relations in companies are ends in themselves for the middle and older age groups, but become means for the young. In short, for the young, close interpersonal relations in companies are annoying and undesirable, but are means to rise in status and power. Therefore, Sakamoto added that interpersonal relations will change if social sanctions become weak in companies. Although the support for a collective orientation to a company seems not to have changed very much since 1953, the behaviour in displaying a collective orientation has been changing from ends to means. This thinking explains the individualisation that was shown in the results to QA.

The Causes of Individual Orientation

Why did post-war Japan change toward the individual orientation? There are two main causes: one is democracy introduced by the United States of America after World War II; the other is economic growth and the social change that it engenders.

Some critics disparage Japanese democracy because it was put in place by the United States rather than the Japanese people achieving it by themselves. However, regardless of the way the democratic regime was established in Japan, the Japanese were liberated from authoritarian rule by the state because of it. This changed their values. Recently, for instance, moral education textbooks for elementary or junior-high schools have not taught patriotism, loyalty to their masters, obedience and so on. (These were important virtues in pre-war Japanese morals.) On the contrary, they teach pupils the virtues of justice, uniqueness (personal character), freedom and responsibility, and rights and obligations which are very important to maintain a democratic regime.[2] Pupils who have learned such virtues come to have an individual orientation which is different from the value orientations of their parents.

However, the pupils do not come to have a universal orientation. Why? One important reason is that, in the Japanese educational system, the world and the universe, which are the premises of individual existence, are not taught thoroughly. At the same time, sympathy with other human beings, the core of the universal orientation, is also not taught well. As a result, although loyalty to the nation and the race is declining, the concern of the young generation is only with the self.

On the other hand, the rapid growth of the Japanese economy, and the urbanisation and the nuclearisation of the family caused by rapid growth, has brought about a major change in people's consciousness. First of all, the affluent society, which resulted from the rapid growth, enabled people to satisfy their wants.

After the necessary conditions for life are satisfied, people want to satisfy their selective preferences. More and more they want consumer items that match their preferences.

Second, the urbanisation and nuclearisation of the family weakened traditional pre-war social norms and sanctions which were based on territorial (village or neighbourhood) or kinship relationships. At the same time, family and neighbourhood services and amenities became marketable. Nowadays one can live easily by using commercial products without depending on village or kinships relationships. Even living alone has become easy. At department stores and supermarkets one can buy a small portion of food for one person. One can also buy small household appliances, such as a small refrigerator, a small washing machine, and so on. These market changes decrease the practical necessity for a collective orientation in daily life and enhance the possibility of an individual orientation.

As an aspect of consumption it becomes easy to have an individual orientation. As an aspect of production through work, however, the collective orientation is still needed as a means because production is mainly carried out in companies or other social groups and the collective orientation makes for increasing productivity.

In sum, the political, economic and social changes caused an increase in the individual orientation. This change in people's value orientation becomes an explicit problem when some people's individual orientations become competitive relations in the work-place or in other public places.

Although values have changed in post-war Japan, the lack of a universal orientation itself has not become a controversial problem nor raised much interest or concern. However, in these days a lot of problems related to the entire world are successively emerging in Japan, such as trade frictions and global environmental problems. In order to respond to these problems, it is more useful to think about value orientations in the light of the individual-universal dimension than in terms of the individual-collective dimension. The individual-universal dimension is symbolised by the opposition of two attitudes. The first affirms social change toward an advanced industrial society based on a heightened individual orientation. The second rejects that kind of social change and tries to look for a way to strengthen universalistic human co-existence. The latter viewpoint opposes the present social change toward individualisation. At present, those advocating the universal type of thinking are in a minority.

It is hard to tell from survey results how many of the "universalist" type of people are present in Japan. One reason is that, generally speaking, the universal orientation is thought more desirable than the individual orientation. Therefore, when asked whether they have an individual orientation or a universal orientation, people are apt to select the universal orientation. For example, 66 percent of all respondents agree that it is important to "do something for society, because I am a member of the human society" (in the 1973 Japanese National Character survey; ISM 1982:287–8), and 55 percent agreed with the statement, "To do what is of benefit to other people, whether or not it is what I want to do myself" (in the 1978 survey; ISM 1982:288). These are answers that reveal a universal orientation. However, the questions are examining people's behavioural intentions, not their real behaviour. When asked about their evaluation of real social behaviour, different and opposite results appear. To the question, "Do you think that most people try to be as helpful to other people as they can, or do you think that most people think only of themselves?" 74 percent answered "only of themselves" (in 1978; ISM 1982:288). These results indicate one of two things. Either there are many persons in our society who intend to be helpful but do not translate their intentions into actual behaviour, or else bad behaviour stands out and is readily noticed, while good behaviour is not so easily apparent. In either case, it is certain that the majority feels that most people are selfish and lack a sense of responsibility and criticise them for it.

However, in the 1980s the universal orientation began to be paid attention to, not as behaviour based on a special ideology, but as behaviour coming out of daily life. The results of the next question in the Prime Minister's Office survey suggest an increase in the universal orientation. To the question in 1988, "Which is better, the priority of Japan's profits over the entire world's profits or the priority of the entire world's profits over Japan's profits?" the priority of the entire world profits exceeded the priority of Japan's profits (46 percent vs. 38 percent) for the first time, a reversal from 33 percent vs. 40 percent in 1985 (Prime Minister's Office 1989b:37–9). Of course, this universal value orientation does not involve a self-sacrificial devotion to the world or to society to the point of sacrificing one's own personal needs. But, at a certain threshold, it does not mean giving priority to the general human or world happiness over one's own personal happiness when the two are in competition. In fact, since the 1980s, some small social movements, as consumer movements or environmental movements, which embodied universal orientation, came to be observed.

The individual orientation under limited conditions causes problems. It is impossible to satisfy all of people's individual orientations at once. Some people's satisfactions can be obtained only at the expense of other people's satisfactions. In sum, under these conditions to have or not to have the consciousness of co-existence with other peoples distinguishes those with an individual orientation from those with a universal orientation.

In post-war Japan, people's value orientations changed toward the individual orientation from the collective orientation, which was considered to be a characteristic feature of the Japanese. However, since the 1980s a small or medium growth of universal orientation has been observed. The practice of a latent universal orientation has spread. Although people who have a universal orientation and behave accordingly are still in a minority, I predict that the universal orientation will be more popular in future societies. Therefore, it is important to pay attention to this dimension of the individual universal orientation, and to study what causes and affects the formation of these value orientations.

ENDNOTES

[1] In this paper, the private-public dimension is not used. The term "public" is ambiguous at this point in that it does not distinguish between a collective orientation and a universal orientation.

[2] Regarding a content analysis of Japanese moral education textbooks, see Morota (1984). In this thesis, the difference of teaching methods between pre-war Japan and post-war Japan is pointed out. The teaching method during the pre-war period was to make pupils obey their teachers and that in the post-war era is to make pupils think for themselves.

REFERENCES

Braithwaite, V. (1982). "The Structure of Social Values: Validation of Rokeach's Two-Value Model," *British Journal of Social Psychology,* 21:203–11.

Economic Planning Agency (1960). *Annual Report on National Life.* Tokyo: Printing Bureau, Ministry of Finance.

Economic Planning Agency (1965). *Annual Report on National Life.* Tokyo: Printing Bureau, Ministry of Finance.

Economic Planning Agency (1970). *Annual Report on National Life.* Tokyo: Printing Bureau, Ministry of Finance.

Flanagan, S. C. (1982). "Changing Values in Advanced Industrial Societies" *Comparative Political Studies,* 14(4):403–44.

Hidaka, R. (1980). *Sengo no Shisou wo Kangaeru* (Thinking of Post-War Ideology). Tokyo: Iwanami.

Illich, I. (1973). *Tools for Conviviality.* New York: Harper and Row.

Institute of Statistical Mathematics, Research Committee on the Study of the Japanese National Character (1982). *Nipponzin no Kokuminsei* (4) (A Study of the Japanese National Character, Vol. 4). Tokyo: Idemitsu Shoten.

Inglehart, R. (1977). *The Silent Revolution: Changing Values and Political Styles among Western Publics.* Princeton: Princeton University Press.

Maruyama, Y. (1988). "Seikatsu Kurabu Seikyo no Jigyo Soshiki" (The Work Organisation of the Life Club Cooperative), pp. 30–79 in Sato, Y. (ed.), *Joseitachi no Seikatsu Nettowaku* (Life Network for Women). Tokyo: Bunshindo.

Mita, M. (1966). *Kachiishiki no Riron* (Theory of Value Consciousness). Tokyo: Kobundo.

Miyajima, T. (1983). *Gendai Shakaiishiki-ron* (Theory of Contemporary Social Consciousness). Tokyo: Nihonhyoronsha.

Morota, N. (1984). "Senzen, Sengo no Shakaiteki-kachi no Henka" (The Change of Social Values between the Pre-War and Post-War Periods),. *Japanese Review of Social Psychology,* 3:30–40.

Morris, C. (1956). *Varieties of Human Values*. Chicago: The University of Chicago Press.

Prime Minister's Office (1989a). *Monthly Public Opinion Research 4*. Tokyo: Printing Bureau, Ministry of Finance.

Prime Minister's Office (1989b). *Monthly Public Opinion Research 7*. Tokyo: Printing Bureau, Ministry of Finance.

Rokeach, M. (1973). *The Nature of Human Values*. New York: Free Press.

Sakamoto, Y. (1983). "Nihon ni okeru ishiki-doko no aratana danmen" (New Aspects of Changing Consciousness in Japanese Society), *Toukei Suri Kennkyujo Ihou*, 31(2):251–66.

QUESTIONS

DISCUSSION QUESTIONS

1. In countries like Somalia or the former Yugoslavia, many children are socialized by the experience of war. In a sense, they come to think of war as "normal." Is there a realistic hope for peace among people who grow up expecting war?

2. Brainstorm a list of male–female differences. (Follow the most important rule of brainstorming: don't evaluate people's ideas until you run out of suggestions.) Then, try to reach a consensus on the list — which ideas should go and which should stay? Finally, discuss each trait on the list to decide whether it is determined by nature or nurture.

3. Repeat this brainstorming exercise to reach a concensus about Canadian–American differences.

4. When reading over the survey questions Oyama's respondents answered, do you find any questions that seem foreign to Canadian culture? In other words, would you find it difficult to answer any of Oyama's questions? Why?

DATA COLLECTION EXERCISES

1. Find some children's books at a local school or public library and compare their content to Singapore readers described by Quah. Systematically compare North American readers published in the 1960s, 1970s, 1980s and 1990s, using the criteria described in excerpt 2.2.

2. Collect biographical data on at least six international terrorists. Were they, like the Armenian terrorists described in an excerpt above, socialized into the role?

3. Interview a student who has attended school outside Canada. Ask about differences he/she has experienced in classroom demeanour, and about the roles of student and teacher.

4. Are children's cartoons too violent? Watch two hours of television cartoons with a partner and document the types and frequencies of violent action.

1. Go to the library and find out what you can about the "rise and fall" of the Oneida community. Write a brief essay, explaining the community's demise, especially the decline of commitment to the community.

2. In a brief essay, analyze the educational and occupational choices you have made so far in terms of gender socialization. What people and what factors influenced your choices? Did your parents or grandparents have the same range of choices?

3. Do you think it likely that North Americans will embrace universalistic values? Give your answer in a brief essay.

4. Are some people poor and other people rich because of the ways they were socialized? Answer in a brief essay.

SUGGESTED READINGS

1. Elkin, Frederick and Gerald Handel (1989). *The Child and Society: The Process of Socialization,* Fifth Edition. New York: Random House. This is a classic reference work for anyone interested in knowing more about the topic of socialization.

2. Ellis, Dormer and Lyz Sayer (1986). *When I Grow Up: Expectations and Aspirations of Canadian Schoolchildren.* Ottawa: Labour Canada. This study of over 700 Canadian school children examines their opinions (stereotypes) of various occupational choices and their future plans. The authors find that children seem to understand that both boys and girls can work in non-stereotyped fields, but their *own* job choices do not reflect this diversity.

3. Kostash, Myrna (1987). *No Kidding: Inside the World of Teenage Girls.* Toronto: McClelland and Stewart. This Canadian study is a rich analysis of the teen years, based on lengthy interviews with teenage girls who talk candidly about boys, friends, family, and sex.

4. Handel, Gerald (1988). *Childhood Socialization.* New York: Adeline de Gruyter. This is a collection of 19 articles dealing with such topics as the family, schools, peer groups, and television as agents of gender and class socialization. Several of these articles look beyond the North American context.

DEVIANCE AND CONTROL

Introduction

Philosopher Thomas Hobbes believed the State to be the source of social order and the basis for all that is good and stable in human life. But anthropological and sociological evidence gives us good reason to think Hobbes was *wrong*.

For example, in different parts of the world anthropologists have studied small, pre-industrial societies that have very little of what we would call "government" and "laws." Yet these societies seem to work very well indeed. This raises doubt that you need a state, laws, and elaborate means of social control to have social order.

In fact, a great many social ties — among them, a shared culture, kinship, and economic cooperation — all help to maintain order, with or without state intervention.

And, unlike Hobbes, sociology does not hold that social

disorder is particularly abnormal. From our standpoint, rule-breaking is a *normal* part of society and rule-breakers are usually normal members of an alternate, or deviant, social order. By this standard, deviance is *conformity* to a set of values and norms that many (often, middle-class people) don't want to accept as legitimate.

In this context, sociology's job is to study how competing social and moral orders come into existence: how people, in everyday life, create and defend a social order.

Consider these questions:

- How do people walk through crowds without getting knocked down, or knocking anyone else down?
- How do people manage to carry on conversations, a kind of verbal traffic?
- What keeps people orderly when they are standing in line outside a theatre, or waiting to pay at a check-out counter?
- How do people make decisions when they are given confusing or incomplete directions, or complicated evidence?

All of these are familiar problems. What's more, we are all pretty good at solving these problems. We do so without giving them much thought: they are part of a taken-for-granted world of experience. As well, we have learned how to do these things *informally*: no one taught us how to walk in crowds, carry on a conversation, or make practical decisions. In fact, we are all creating and enforcing our "social order" all the time, every day — without state intervention.

As we do so, we are deciding whether, when and how we should make exceptions to the rules we, and other people, have created. By this standard, nothing is absolutely and permanently normal or abnormal, deviant or conforming. The standards are always being negotiated. Our rules of conduct are *all* socially invented.

It follows that nothing is deviant in and of itself. It only *becomes* deviant with reactions from the community that indicate the behaviour is deviant. (So, for example, in excerpt 3.2 below we see a Nigerian sociologist trying to evaluate what "kind" of deviance begging represents.) And in a pluralistic society like ours, different groups of people will have different ideas of what behaviour they consider deviant.

True, there are some forms of deviance, particularly certain crimes, about which there is a lot of agreement. (On this, see excerpt 3.1 below, on the evaluations of a variety of deviant acts in India, Kuwait, and the USA.) Even so, people often disagree on the acceptibility of different types of criminal behaviour and the appropriate punishment. How, then, do we try to control one another, and with what results?

The Role of Social Control

We all exercise *informal social control* over one another through gossip, praise, blame, setting an example, and many other interpersonal means. Since we are social beings who seek the approval of others, informal social control usually works well to keep people conforming to the rules. Sometimes it doesn't work and then we need formal controls: laws and law enforcers.

Usually we think of formal social control — the actions of police, courts, prisons, and the like — as a *response* to crime. But consider the opposite too: social control causes crime. If we had no agencies of social control, we would have no crime and no criminals. All schools of sociology recognize this, but view the relationship between social control and crime in different ways.

The Structural Functionalist View of Deviance and Control

For example, structural functionalists believe that deviance and social control may both have significant social functions. Deviance can be found in every society and every social group. In that sense, deviance — even crime — is a "normal" aspect of social life and may even benefit society.

One refinement of this approach is *anomie theory*, developed by Robert Merton (1957). According to this theory, deviant behaviour is a "normal," functional response to unequal opportunities for success in our society. One kind of deviant response is what Merton calls "innovation": developing non-legitimate, even criminal, means for achieving success (like the "narco-terrorists" in excerpt 3.3).

This adaptation is most likely among poor people who have been socialized to desire success but have little access to legitimate means of gaining success. This is why crime is a North American way of life — a tried and true means of upward mobility in a society where everyone yearns for success.

Here, crime is "functional" because it allows poor people to keep believing in traditional values and institutions when these values and institutions disadvantage huge portions of the population. Yet, there are many senses in which crime is *not* functional to society. To take a simple example, consider the women and children who are victims of violent men, as described in excerpt 3.4 below. How, then, to explain the persistence of crime and social control?

Conflict Theories of Deviance and Control

Deviance only exists when we apply rules to human behaviour. But it matters who makes these rules. According to conflict theorists, knowing who makes the rules, and why, is the key to understanding deviance and control.

Conflict theorists argue that social control extends social inequality into the realm of law. In every society, some people have more power than others. These people use their power to protect their own values, interests, and possessions. That means getting the government to make, and the police to enforce, laws that protect their own interests, not someone else's.

From this standpoint the study of deviance and control is the study of lawmaking: why governments make certain laws, and who these laws favour. By this reasoning, neither deviance nor control is functional to society as a whole. Rather, social control serves one particular group at the expense of everyone else. As we see in excerpt 3.3 below, this is the reason drug traffickers in Latin America are so intent on "capturing" the state. When they *are* the law, they won't be *outside* the law.

But in a great many cases, there is little conflict over whether a norm should, or should not, be enforced. Serious crimes like murder are a prime example of this. And, though conflict theory often depicts poor people as victims of the police and courts, they are more often the victims of criminals. So, it is worthwhile examining what the third major school of sociology, symbolic interactionism, has to say about deviance and control.

The Interactionist Perspective on Deviance and Control

Symbolic interactionists focus on the ways social control affects the individual deviant. Out of this approach have come two distinct but related concerns: the study of labelling and the study of "deviant subcultures."

Labelling theory starts from the assumption that deviance is largely a result of the reactions of others. Labelling theorists do not try to explain why an individual engages in deviant behaviour in the first place: everyone does it sometimes. Instead they study what happens to people after they have been identified or labelled deviant.

This means that labelling theorists begin by looking at the act of labelling itself. They show that the application of a label is stigmatizing. A *stigma* — a mark of shame or social disgrace — discredits an individual or group. What's more, a person seen as deviant by others may come to see him- or herself in the same way. That person will now be more likely to engage in deviant behaviour, because it fits in with his or her new self-image. Repeated deviant behaviour and a deviant self-image is what labelling theorists call *secondary deviation*.

The other side to this interactionist approach focuses on socialization and the fact that some people are more likely than others to learn how and why to be deviant. This line of thinking can be linked to what is called "differential association theory."

This theory assumes that becoming a deviant means conforming to the norms and values of a deviant group or subculture. A *deviant subculture* is made up of people who conform to certain norms and hold certain beliefs which the larger society considers deviant. Members of the subculture may dress, behave, and speak in a way that emphasizes the differences between that group and competing groups (e.g., rival gangs) or "straight" society.

In reading the excerpts that follow, keep in mind that deviance is relative. There are always many disagreements about "right" and "wrong;" social order is fluid and agencies of social control have their own cultural and political agenda.

REFERENCES

Merton, R. K. (1957). "Social structure and anomie," in his *Social Theory and Social Structure, Revised Edition*, pp. 131–160. New York: Free Press.

3.1 Sandra Evans Skovron, Joseph E. Scott and P. Kamalakara Rao

How Offenses are Perceived in the United States, India, and Kuwait

INTRODUCTION

We argued in the Introduction to this section that "deviance" and "conformity" are always being defined and redefined — in short, always being negotiated in groups and societies. Yet the next excerpt shows that there are great similarities in the ways people view different, relatively extreme types of deviance — especially crimes.

A set of surveys carried out in the United States, India, and Kuwait shows student-respondents scoring penalties for deviance very similarly. When these penalty scores are applied to a variety of deviant acts, respondents in these same countries tend to evaluate the seriousness of deviant acts very similarly. There is, however, one very important difference in the rank-orderings: namely, the severity with which (Islamic) Kuwaiti respondents treat offenses against morals.

Kuwaitis consider these offenses against morals, which include such things as adultery, atheism, and homosexuality, to be just as serious offenses as armed robbery and manslaughter, and they propose to penalize them similarly. This tendency reflects the effect of Islamic religious teaching in Kuwait (indeed, in much of the Islamic world), and the reluctance of Muslims to distinguish between sacred and secular, or church and state, concerns. On the other hand, there is some chance this will change with continued exposure to Western ideas; in support of this speculation, see excerpts 6.2 and 12.2 below.

There is little research that addresses the perceived seriousness of crime from a cross cultural perspective. This paper extends the research on cross cultural perceptions of crime seriousness by examining perceptions of a wide range of offenses and sanctions for respondents from three very different cultures: namely, the United States, India, and Kuwait.[1]

Skovron, Sandra Evans, Joseph E. Scott and P. Kamalakara Rao (1987). "Cross Cultural Perceptions of Offense Severity: The United States, India and Kuwait," *International Journal of Comparative and Applied Criminal Justice*, 11(1), Spring, 47–60. Reprinted by permission.

The seriousness of thirty-seven offenses were rated by having respondents assign one of seventeen penalties to each offense. The severity of the seventeen penalty categories were in turn ranked by respondents. As a first step in calculating the perceived seriousness of offenses, the severity ratings of the penalty categories must be analyzed.

There are only slight differences in the penalty rank ordering among the United States, Indian, and Kuwaiti respondents. It may be concluded that the rank order of penalties is essentially similar for the United States, Indian, and Kuwaiti respondents. The perceived seriousness of penalties was essentially similar despite the inclusion of non-traditional and unfamiliar penalties in the penalty list.[2]

The Perceived Seriousness of Offenses

Respondents were asked to rate the seriousness of thirty-seven offense vignettes by assigning one of the seventeen penalty categories to each offense. The mean seriousness scores for the penalty categories were used to calculate the mean seriousness score for each offense. The mean seriousness score for each offense was calculated by summing the seriousness scores of the assigned penalties and then dividing by the number of respondents. This process was repeated for all three samples and yielded seriousness scores for the three groups for the thirty-seven offense items. The offenses were then rank ordered for each group of respondents. The rank ordering of offenses for the United States sample could then be compared to the rank ordering for the Indian and Kuwaiti respondents. The rank ordered offenses for the United States sample, as well as the seriousness scores for all three samples, are presented in Table 1.

Table 1 reveals a number of similarities in the rank ordering of offenses for the United States and Indian samples. However, some differences may be noted. A number of property offenses were perceived much less seriously by the Indian respondents than by the United States respondents. For example, the Indian students ranked items 8 and 11, both property offenses, considerably less seriously than their United States counterparts. There were also differences with regard to white collar offenses. The Indian respondents rated a number of white collar offenses, for example items 14, 15, 16, 24, and 26, more seriously than did the United States respondents.

The rank order of the seriousness ratings of the Kuwaiti respondents differ from those of both the United States and Indian respondents.

To further examine these differences, the offense items were examined by groups or categories of offenses. For purposes of analysis, the offenses were grouped into four categories: violent offenses (items 1, 2, 3, 4, 6, 7, 8, and 10), property offenses (items 11, 12, 13, 20, and 23), white collar offenses (items 14, 15, 16, 17, 24, 25, and 26), and morals offenses (items 9, 18, 19, 21, 27, 28, 29, 30, 31, 32, 33, 34, 35, 36, and 37). Items 22 and 5 were accidental crimes and thus were not placed into any category for this analysis. Mean seriousness scores were then calculated for each category of offense. These scores are presented in Table 2.

Offense	United States N = 535		India N = 300		Kuwait* N = 599	
	Mean Sanction	Rank	Mean Sanction	Rank	Mean Sanction	Rank
A man killed his wife during an argument.	13.163	1	10.883	1	12.353	6
An individual kidnapped a woman to rape her.	12.120	2	10.778	2	12.804	4
A man stabbed his wife with a knife during an argument.	11.974	3	8.921	7	11.557	8
An individual committed a forcible rape.	11.504	4	10.003	5	13.202	2
A man killed a little girl with his car while driving under the influence of alcohol.	11.403	5	9.856	6	11.407	10
An individual intending only to injure someone by throwing a stone accidentally killed him.	10.827	6	8.590	9	8.743	25
An individual forced a woman into prostitution.	10.396	7	10.267	3	13.041	3
An individual robbed a store with a gun.	10.112	8	8.416	12	11.200	12
An individual sold illegal drugs.	9.664	9	7.649	15	11.250	11
An individual threw burning liquid in someone's face which caused scars.	9.576	10	10.042	4	10.141	15
An individual burglarized a neighbor's home.	9.149	11	3.062	36	10.515	14
An individual set fire to a warehouse.	9.041	12	8.295	14	9.738	21
An individual stole things worth about $100.	8.799	13	7.596	16	8.543	28
An individual sold company secrets to another company.	7.931	14	8.558	10	7.880	31
An individual forged an official document.	7.679	15	8.357	13	8.509	29

TABLE 1   Cont'd

Offense	Mean Sanction	Rank	Mean Sanction	Rank	Mean Sanction	Rank
A businessman bribes a government official for a contract.	7.607	16	8.612	8	8.810	23
An individual loaned money at a high interest rate.	7.226	17	6.856	20	8.235	30
An individual used drugs.	6.802	18	6.965	19	9.403	20
An individual committed perjury.	6.734	19	5.643	28	9.457	19
A person forged a check.	6.530	20	8.446	11	8.618	27
An individual operated a public gambling house.	5.805	21	7.170	17	9.977	16
An individual accidentally shot another while hunting.	5.624	22	6.820	21	5.764	35
A young boy stole an automobile.	5.355	23	6.002	26	4.942	37
An employee took a car as a bribe.	5.264	24	7.056	18	7.512	32
An executive falsely advertised the quality of a product.	4.824	25	6.642	25	5.622	36
An individual falsely advertised prices.	4.755	26	6.685	23	6.205	34
A pharmacist sold drugs for an abortion.	4.722	27	5.456	30	8.881	23
A physician performed an illegal abortion.	4.699	28	3.872	34	8.702	26
A woman engaged in prostitution	3.818	29	5.561	29	11.956	7
An individual accused a woman of adultery without adequate proof.	3.179	30	6.664	24	9.808	17
A married man committed adultery.	3.100	31	6.095	27	12.789	5
A married woman committed adultery. .	3.062	32	6.773	22	13.539	1
An individual insulted someone's honor in front of others.	2.823	33	4.646	32	7.258	33
A male engaged in homosexuality.	2.810	34	5.360	31	11.518	9

TABLE 1   Cont'd

75

Offense	Mean Sanction	Rank	Mean Sanction	Rank	Mean Sanction	Rank
A woman had an illegal abortion.	2.731	35	4.339	33	9.355	22
An individual abandons religion and espouses atheism.	1.476	36	3.340	35	10.587	13
A single man committed fornication.	1.295	37	1.000	37	9.532	18

*Permission was obtained from Al-Thakeb, F. and J. E. Scott (1981). *International Journal of Comparative and Applied Criminal Justice,* 5 (Winter): 129–143.

TABLE 2   MEAN SERIOUSNESS OF OFFENSE CATEGORY: UNITED
            STATES, INDIA, AND KUWAIT

Offense Category	United States Mean Seriousness	India Mean Seriousness	Kuwait* Mean Seriousness
Violent	11.209	9.737	11.650
Property	7.775	6.680	8.399
White Collar	6.075	7.538	7.840
Morals	4.100	5.369	10.494

*Permission was obtained from Al-Thakeb, F. and J. E. Scott (1981). *International Journal of Comparative and Applied Criminal Justice,* 5 (Winter): 129–143.

As may be seen in Table 2, the United States respondents perceived violent offenses most seriously, with a mean seriousness score of 11.209, followed by property offenses (7.775), white collar offenses (6.075), and morals offenses (4.100). The rank order of offenses for Indian respondents was somewhat different. The Indian respondents also ranked violent offenses as the most serious offense category, although their mean seriousness score was somewhat less than for the United States respondents (9.737 as compared to 11.209). The second most serious offense category for the Indian respondents was white collar offenses (7.538), followed by property offenses (6.680), with the morals offenses ranked as the least serious (5.369). The Indian respondents perceived white collar offenses somewhat more seriously and property offenses somewhat less seriously than did the United States respondents.

The Kuwaiti respondents differ considerably from the other two samples in their ranking of offense categories. They do rank violent offenses as being most serious (11.650). However, the Kuwaiti respondents ranked morals offenses nearly equal in seriousness to violent offenses (mean seriousness = 10.494). In fact the single most serious offense as ranked by the Kuwaiti respondents was a morals offense. "A married woman committed adultery." The United States and Indian samples both rated morals offenses as the least serious offense category. The Kuwaiti respondents ranked property offenses and white collar offenses as the third and fourth most serious category of offense respectively.

Removal of the morals offenses increased the similarity between the Kuwaiti and Indian and United States samples.

Discussion and Implications

This research has demonstrated remarkable similarity with regard to perceptions of the severity of both sanctions and offenses for comparable samples of United States, Indian, and Kuwaiti respondents. The perceptions of the three sampled groups were essentially comparable with regard to perceptions of the severity of the seventeen sanctions. This finding is particularly remarkable inasmuch as a number of penalties which were unfamiliar to the respondents from some countries were included on the list of penalty categories. For example, such sanctions as "civil death and no job," "banishment," "severing a limb," "whipping," and "stoning to death" are certainly unfamiliar to United States respondents and are not used as sanctions in Western legal systems. Many of these penalties, in particular "severing a limb" and "banishment" are also unfamiliar to most Indian respondents. Despite this, the three groups of respondents were in essential agreement with regard to the perceived seriousness of these penalties.

There was also essential agreement among the United States and Indian respondents with regard to the perceived seriousness of the 37 offense items. Despite a few differences, such as the greater perceived severity of white collar offenses for the Indian students and the greater perceived severity of property offenses for the United States students, marked similarity in perceptions was demonstrated overall.

Consistent with previous research (Scott and Al-Thakeb, 1977; Evans and Scott, 1984) the Kuwaiti sample was the most divergent. However, the differences were largely attributable to the morals offenses. There was a marked degree of similarity to the other samples on the rankings of violent, property, and white collar offenses. Despite the widely divergent cultures, standards, and practices in the United States, India, and Kuwait, this research has, with the exception of morals offenses, demonstrated a high degree of consensus with regard to the perceived seriousness of both sanctions and offenses.

ENDNOTES

[1] University students were used in order to obtain a sample most comparable to the samples from other cultures to be included in this study. It is recognized that student samples are often criticized as being non-generalizable to the wider population. In this research, a student sample was selected because it provides the most control and comparability for the cross cultural comparison. Previous research (Rossi *et al.*, 1974; Evans, 1981; Evans and Scott, 1982a) has indicated that demographic characteristics of respondents such as age, education, and social class have little or no impact on seriousness perceptions. The fact that

students' perceptions of offense severity do not differ markedly from those of the general public is illustrated by the similarities between the United States students' seriousness ratings obtained in this study and those obtained for a community sample in an earlier study (Scott and Al-Thakeb, 1977).

2 The nontraditional penalties are:

Civil Death and No Job
Whipping
Banishment
Sever Limb
Stone to Death

REFERENCES

Al-Thakeb, Fahed and Joseph E. Scott (1981). "The Perceived Seriousness of Crime in the Middle East," *International Journal of Comparative and Applied Criminal Justice,* 5(2): 129–143.

Evans, Sandra S. (1981). *Measuring the Seriousness of Crime: Methodological Issues and a Cross Cultural Comparison.* Unpublished Dissertation, The Ohio State University.

Evans, Sandra S. and Joseph E. Scott (1982a). "Analyzing the Perceived Seriousness of Crime Cross Culturally: The Impact of Respondent Characteristics," presented at the X World Congress of Sociology, August, 15–20, 1982, Mexico City.

Rossi, Peter, Emily Waite, Christine Bose, and Richard Berk (1974). "The Seriousness of Crimes: Normative Structure and Individual Differences, " *American Sociological Review,* 39:224–237.

Scott, Joseph E. and Fahed Al-Thakeb (1977). "The Public's Perception of Crime: Scandinavia, Western Europe, the Middle East and the United States," in C. Ronald Huff (Ed.) *Contemporary Corrections,* Beverly Hills, CA: Sage.

3.2 Patrick Edobor Igbinovia

Begging in Nigeria

INTRODUCTION

In 1861, Henry Mayhew finished cataloguing all the varieties of "street people" to be seen in his native city. The result was a four-volume classic, London Labour and the London Poor. *There, Mayhew devoted space to discussing street pedlars, petty criminals, prostitutes, homeless people, tramps, juvenile delinquents, and beggars. His goal was to distinguish*

Igbinovia, Patrick Edobor (1991). "Begging in Nigeria," *International Journal of Offender Therapy and Comparative Criminology,* 35(1), 21–33. Reprinted by permission.

among the many varieties of poor people: to say which ones can work but won't, which ones work at "reputable" but poor-paying jobs, and which ones do disreputable and even criminal work.

The next excerpt, on begging in Nigeria, is much shorter than Mayhew's opus but has a similar flavour and a similar goal. It aims to explain why there are so many beggars in Nigeria's cities, to distinguish which ones could live by more reputable trades if they chose to, and to advise the government on ways to prevent a "scourge" of begging.

In today's Nigeria, as in 1861 London, the researcher seeks to place blame where it belongs and avoid blaming beggars who, for one reason or another, simply cannot survive without state assistance (unless they beg in the streets). Similar debates are going on in North American cities beset by a "scourge" of angry poor (see, for example, excerpt 4.4 below) and major Third World cities surrounded by shantytowns and filled with "street children." Always, the question is "Who is to blame?" Is it the "deviant" individual, a heartless state, sluggish economy, or some combination of all these elements?

B egging is one of the most serious social problems in Nigeria today. According to the United Nations, there are 450 million beggars and destitutes in the world. Of these, 3 million are in Nigeria ("The Role of Government," 1988). Beggars are a social menace in Nigeria: they roam the streets, harass citizens, disrupt the flow of traffic on the highways, and engage in various forms of crimes. Beggars are also social parasites. Begging has become a social institution — an industry, a commercial enterprise, an occupation for otherwise healthy and able-bodied citizens who have refused to work for a living. Many of the beggars in Nigeria are carriers of terrible and contagious diseases, and they pose serious health consequences for the citizenry (Ndubuisi, 1986). Indeed, beggars not only constitute a scourge to Nigerian society, they also form the dregs of the Nigerian society.

In spite of the prevalence of begging in Nigeria, it has received little scholarly attention. Therefore, the purpose of this essay is to examine the causes and patterns of begging in Nigeria. Several recommendations aimed at preventing and controlling the phenomenon are tendered.

Patterns of Begging

At some time in his career, the Nigerian beggar may work within many classifications. A beggar will generally select a method of operation best suited to his status, his perception of the public, his physical and mental condition, and his financial objectives. A close scrutiny and synthesis of available data marshalled from various reports on begging in Nigeria reveal two broad categories and five types of beggars in Nigeria. The two broad categories of beggars are (a) able-bodied beggars and (b) impotent beggars.

Able-bodied beggars are physically and mentally fit beggars or destitutes who take to begging to make a living. A significant part of beggars in Nigeria are in this group.

On the other hand, the impotent beggars are physically or mentally handicapped or disabled beggars who take to begging because they cannot work to earn a living. The basic difference between the categories of beggars is that the able-bodied beggars are healthy and would work to earn a living — if they chose to, whereas the physical deficiencies of the impotent beggars makes it almost impossible for them to be engaged in gainful employment, unless they were trained to acquire work skills.

The two categories of beggars can be further delineated into five types. These are: (a) Women Beggars, (b) Child Beggars, (c) Immigrant Beggars, (d) Disabled Beggars, and (e) Executive Beggars.

It should be noted that the differences between the various types of beggars can be slight. For example, a beggar could be both an "immigrant" and "disabled" beggar at the same time. With increasing age, an "executive" or "woman" or "child" beggar may become a "disabled" beggar. The "child" beggar may also eventually become an "immigrant" beggar, or in time be elevated to the level of "executive" beggar.

Causes of Begging

What motivates people to become beggars? The causes of begging in Nigeria are multifaceted and range from poverty and custom to disability and religion. Indeed, there is documented evidence to suggest that begging in Nigeria has some cultural and religious foundations. The Yorubas of Nigeria sanction begging for a woman who has given birth to twins. Both Christianity and Islam enjoin their adherents to give alms to the poor as a partial fulfillment of their religious obligations. African traditional religions encourage the giving of alms to the needy and support begging (Ndubuisi, 1987). According to one writer, the majority of beggars in Nigeria today "are able-bodied men and women who (because they are lazy) exploit the sympathetic and religious dispositions of most Nigerians to beg for alms" ("Law against begging," 1987). Consequently, some people take to begging in Nigeria because it is more profitable than gainful employment (Eigbefoh, 1986; Ndubuisi, 1986).

Poor economic conditions and unemployment have also been identified as major causes of begging in Nigeria. Indeed, the increase in the number of beggars in the country can be traced to the Economic Stabilization Act of 1982, which led to the closure of factories and retrenchment of workers. In commenting on this situation, a former worker, turned beggar, said:

> As you see me in this bus, I am a former worker but was retrenched in 1985. Since then I could not find any job. (It is) not that I am lazy, it is just that I cannot find a job. My wife and two children are at home. I don't know when (last) I gave them money. So in the name of God nothing is too small for me. God shall repay you tenfold. (Adebiyi, 1987)

Physical and mental disability has been identified as a possible cause of begging in Nigeria. People who are crippled, blind, paralyzed, deaf and mute, or handicapped in some way and who receive no assistance from their relatives or the government engage in begging as a means to survive. Some people take to begging because their relatives or friends exploit them to make money for themselves. These beggars are often placed at strategic locations to solicit alms. At the end of the day, the bulk of the money collected is taken by their kith and kin, while a token amount is given to the beggars (Oyofo, 1987).

Some psychologists believe that people become beggars because of extreme or excessive economic pressures exerted on them. For example, Omoluabi suggests that certain economic and psychological factors induce people into begging. He explains that individuals who are outgoing or extroverted are more likely to take to begging than those who are introverted (quoted in "Experts' Views on Begging," 1988).

The causes of begging in Nigeria can be summarized as follows: traditional and cultural, customs and religion, poverty and destitution, laziness and indolence, unemployment and the need to make a living or money, deformity and disability, desertion and lack of spouse or family care, inadequate and lack of rehabilitation and vocational centers, old age, influx of illegal and destitute aliens. Indeed, there seems to be considerable agreement among authors that the main causes of begging are deeply rooted in economic conditions. Because economic hardship may induce emotional distress, it can also activate patterns of behaviour associated with begging. In short, economic conditions will precipitate begging, but do not cause it.

Characteristics of Beggars

Information concerning the characteristics of beggars in Nigeria is rather scarce. Beggars usually start their careers at a relatively early age, about two years old, and continue until about the age of 70 years. Yet, a significant number of beggars now begin their career in begging from about the ages of 18 to 45 years old. The work period of beggars often starts as early as 7 a.m. and runs till about 7 p.m. daily. Fridays is the most busy and lucrative day, with Sunday being the least. Begging is at its peak at Christmas periods and during Muslim festivities. On these occasions, religious adherents are expected to generously give alms to the poor and needy.

In general, beggars in Nigeria believe not only that there is nothing socially wrong in begging, but they also believe they were forced into the art by the country's harsh economic conditions ("Menace of Alien Beggars," 1987). Generally, the Nigerian public judge beggars as a nuisance: health risks, molesters, and potential criminals.

Significantly, the modus operandi of most beggars in Nigeria appear to be similar. They all accost the members of the public and greet them in a friendly manner. After the formalities are over, they either ask for help in "the name of God" or tell stories about how unemployment suddenly turned their lives sour. The finale is to ask their victims to help them with whatever amount of money they can afford. Bowls and walking sticks are the preferred instruments used by Nigerian beggars as they solicit for alms. The bowl is used in collecting money. The choice of a walking stick is somewhat guided by the need to use it to feel their way (for those who are blind), and to use it to support or maintain their balance (for those who are physically disabled) as they move around.

Most beggars in Nigeria are males, although a significant number of women and children are now joining their ranks. Similarly, most beggars in Nigeria are nationals of the country, but an increasing number of beggars in the country are from the neighbouring countries. It appears that begging is more prevalent in Northern Nigeria than Southern Nigeria, with a predominance among the Muslim (Islamic) native population of the old Northern Nigeria. When compared with the predominantly Christian South, the practice of begging is heavily concentrated in the Northern States of Nigeria. In sum, the Muslim religion appears to be a stronger factor in sustaining begging in Nigeria than the Christian religion.

Control of Begging

The Nigerian government has made some attempts to control the problem of begging in Nigeria. For example, during the Second All African Games in 1973, the government forcefully removed beggars from the streets and sent them to rehabilitation centers. At the end of the games, the beggars were allowed to return to the streets. A similar action was taken during the World Black Arts Festivals held in Lagos in 1977 — with the same result. Government officials also got rid of beggars in Ilorin in 1987 to "ensure that the President of Nigeria was welcome to an environmentally decent town" ("Sick Beggars," 1988). When the President left the town, the beggars returned to the streets.

There is no doubt that the social utility and effectiveness of most of the rehabilitation programs and institutions in Nigeria, instead of providing the protective cover for destitute people, have, with their bureaucratic ineptitude, regimentation, neglect, underfunding, lack of zeal, and planning turned out to be more like prison yards than rehabilitation centers.

It is essential that the Nigeria government acts to contain the spread of begging before it becomes a veritable scourge. It would appear that there is a strong case for the development of special establishments for beggars and destitutes, and for making them as effective as circumstances allow in terms of equipment, personnel, training facilities, education, funding and care. It should be noted that many of these people are sent to these institutions only because they are physically and mentally handicapped; many are at the institutions because there is nowhere else they can go.

It is imperative that the government begin implementing suggestions and recommendations which have been made for many years. Of primary importance are the following recommendations:

1. There is no national policy on the care, control, and rehabilitation of beggars and destitutes in Nigeria. It is necessary for the government to formulate a policy.

2. The government must build more rehabilitation centers for beggars and destitutes. These centers must be properly equipped and staffed. Clinics and counseling centers for beggars should be established. Those who are placed in charge of the inmates should receive the necessary training to equip them for this role.

3. Adequate funds should be made available by the Federal and State governments to run the rehabilitation centers. In addition, the government must evolve a social security scheme for beggars and destitutes. Under such a scheme, inmates in rehabilitation centers could be paid disability and unemployment stipends or allowances.

4. At the end of inmate training periods, government and charity organizations must take the lead in providing relevant employment opportunities for beggars and destitutes who have acquired sufficient skills. Those beggars and destitutes who wish to be self-employed should be given financial assistance to set up shop. In this regard, government must collaborate with interested private individuals and humanitarian organizations to create job opportunities, to provide financial assistance (to make the centers more financially solvent), and to succour beggars and destitutes.

5. Government must involve the mass media in educating beggars and destitutes on the benefits of rehabilitation and the acquisition of work skills.

6. Beggars should be provided with the opportunity to participate actively and constructively in programs designed to provide them with the skills and experience that will bring value and self-esteem to their lives.

7. Government must involve the families of the beggars and destitutes in the care and rehabilitation of their relatives.

8. Government must educate beggars on the need to help themselves and have family planning. Contraceptives must be provided to beggars and destitutes to help curtail the number of children.

9. Government must prevent and discourage the influx of illegal aliens into the country. It is imperative that our porous borders be properly policed to check illegal immigration.

10. More research should be conducted with a view to gaining further insight into the causes of begging and eventually to enable more meaningful and more beneficial interventions.

To this end, the Nigerian government must ensure that her citizens are elevated from subhuman levels of existence. No effort should be spared to make life more meaningful for the beggars and destitutes in particular, and also for the citizenry in general. This is the true test of civilization.

REFERENCES

Adebiyi, A. (1987). "The new beggars in our society," *Daily Times,* 7 December, p. 26.

Agbese, D. (1988). "Stuck in the groove," *Newswatch,* 11 April, p. 13.

Aimienmwona, J. (1987). "The art of begging," *The Guardian,* 10 June, p. 9.

Eigbefoh, O. (1986). "A nation of beggars," *Daily Times,* 21 July, p. 5.

Ekpei, P. (1988). "Begging for Survival," *The Guardian,* 20 March, p. 13.

"Experts' views on begging" (1988), *Sunday Times,* 17 April, p. 10.

"Executive beggars now in vogue" (1986), *Sunday Times,* 7 September, pp. 1-2.

Federal Republic of Nigeria (1975). *Third national development plan, 1975–1980.* Lagos: Federal Ministry of Economic Development, p. 285.

"Law against begging" (1987), *Daily Times,* 1 January, p. 6.

"Life on the street is better than in the camp" (1988), *Sunday Times,* 17 April, pp. 7,10.

"Menace of alien beggars" (1987), *Sunday Times,* 1 March, p. 9.

Ndubuisi, F. (1986). "Begging, a way of life," *The Punch,* 18 March, p. 5.

Ndubuisi, F. (1987). "Nigeria and her beggars," *The Guardian,* 20 December, p. 9.

Olayiwola, R. (1987). "Resurgence of alien beggars worries Ondo State residents," *Daily Times,* 29 December, p. 3.

Oyofo, S. (1987). "Begging — A new dimension in vogue," *Daily Times,* 27 June, p. 7.

"Sick beggars pose health hazards" (1988), *Sunday Times,* 17 April, p. 8.

Ubaka, G. (1988). "The changing art of begging," *Sunday Times,* 17 April, p. 7.

3.3 Peter A. Lupsha

Narco-Terrorism in Colombia

INTRODUCTION

Everywhere the scale of economic activity has grown larger and, even, globalized. Just as there is a global economy today, so there is a global crime problem. With the growth and spread of criminal activity, the boundaries have blurred between crime and legitimate business, crime and government, and crime and political protest. And just as there is evidence that criminal groups have used legitimate governments and businesses to achieve their goals, so

Lupsha, Peter A. (1989). "Toward an Etiology of Drug Trafficking and Insurgent Relations: The Phenomenon of Narco-Terrorism," *International Journal of Comparative and Applied Criminal Justice,* 13(2), Fall, 61–75. Reprinted by permission.

there is evidence legitimate governments and businesses have used criminal groups, including drug traffickers, to achieve their goals.

The next excerpt tries to untangle some of this web of relationships by looking more closely at one particular example: narco-terrorism in Latin America. The author notes that, often, drug traffickers cooperate with political insurgents (who oppose the government by armed force) because it is convenient for both to form this alliance. (For more on political insurgents, see excerpt 11.4 on social movements in Latin America.) But that doesn't make narco-terrorism a form of political protest. Above all, drug trafficking is devoted to making (and keeping) huge profits. Kingpins of the drug world have no ideological interest in Marxism or any other ideology.

In its truest form, narco-terrorism is aimed at guaranteeing that the state will never interfere with the profit-making of drug traffickers. This is accomplished through a wide range of criminal acts that range from bribery to threat to assassination.

Terrorism, according to the official U.S. definition from the Report of the Vice President's Task Force on Combatting Terrorism (1986), consists of "the unlawful use or threat of violence against persons or property to further political or social objectives. It is usually intended to intimidate or coerce a government, individuals or groups to modify their behavior or policies."[1]

In order to avoid the motivational issue in acts of political terrorism in which, "one person's terrorist is another person's freedom fighter," the United States chose to stress the criminality of the terrorist act itself. Thus criminals such as drug traffickers who engage in the unlawful use of violence to intimidate the states, its agents and authority figures, would be committing terrorist acts. Indeed, this and only this activity, comprises what can be called "narco-terrorism."

In this hemisphere it is more common to find a variety of alliances, or for lack of a better term, "marriages of convenience" between insurgents and drug trafficking organizations. Such relationships tend to be rather short-term and unstable sets of interactions. Typically, they involve the insurgents providing security services for coca leaf plantations and refining laboratories located in their operating areas in turn for direct payment or logistical support activities (arms, equipment, transport, etc.). This type of activity I shall label "*Symbiotic.*"

From such interactions one finds a number of documented instances when the contacts have resulted in arrangements of convenience between drug traffickers and the insurgents' "sponsor-states" or allies.[2] Colombian drug traffickers have, for example, transported arms to both FARC and the "Movimiento 19 de Abril" (M–19) in return for safe transit of their drugs, with payment of transit fees through the insurgents' sponsor states territory. The government of Cuba with its commitment to revolutionary insurgencies in the hemisphere has, for example, served in this role.[3] The critical question is, should such interactions be labeled "narco-terrorism?" I think not. Rather, they are simply example of "covert action operations" or "special measures and activities," which work to further Cuban destabilization objectives in Colombia in a rather cheap, risk-free, and deniable manner. They should thus be classed as such, and not narco-terrorism, for this only weakens the concept's usefulness.[4]

It is also important to realize that the major drug traffickers are not Marxist-Leninists, and they are not aligned with the Cubans. Carlos Lehder Rivas in an interview with the Colombian news magazine *Semana* said that "he had no contact with Cuba," although he had discussed with Robert Vesco the possibility of developing a chain of resort hotels there after Castro had promulgated a law permitting foreign investment.[5] Similarly, Barry Adler Seal reported that when he asked the drug traffickers about the Ochoas' dealing with communists he was told, "No, no, no. We are not communist. We don't particularly enjoy the same philosophy politically that they do, but they serve our means and we serve theirs."[6] The major Colombian traffickers see themselves as businessmen. They are nationalists and capitalists, not Marxists. In a 1988 interview, Pablo Escobar put it this way, "The people accused of drug trafficking are the only ones investing in our country." "The other economic sectors send their money to foreign bank accounts."[7] The traffickers are self-made men, new billionaires, materialists who are bound to have uneasy associations with ideologues and revolutionary insurgents.[8]

A second aspect of drug trafficker, insurgent and insurgent Sponsor-state activity that is frequently confused is the situation of "safe haven." In the Golden Triangle, Lebanon, the Afghanistan-Pakistan-India-Iran borders, and even in our hemisphere, ongoing situations of insurgency and low-intensity conflict work to create "denied areas," that is to say, areas where the United States has little or no access, influence, or control either directly or through its surrogates and allies. The existence of such denied areas creates opportunities for drug traffickers in search of safe havens of operation.

True narco-terrorism includes those activities initiated by drug traffickers who use violence or the threat of violence against persons or property to further their objectives and to intimidate or coerce a government, individuals, or groups to modify their behavior or policies. While the actors may be criminals, not ideologues, their objective is the intimidation of the states. Narco-terrorism is political in this sense. It is directed at the political community and its institutions. Its end is not simply individual intimidation for some immediate and individualistic criminal gain, as is criminal extortion or kidnapping for ransom. Today's narco-terroristic actions go beyond this. At a minimum they are acts of criminal terror for a political goal. It is the action of a purposive interest group seeking to defend its liberty and power. And I think this is a difference of conceptual importance.

This was made clear in a letter sent by the Cartel to the newspaper *El Colombiano* in 1987 at a time when Jorge Ochoa was threatened with possible extradition. "We will declare total and absolute war against the country's political leaders. We will execute principal political party chieftains out of hand."[9] Several weeks later Ochoa was released.

To fully understand true narco-terrorism it is useful to show how it and Colombian drug trafficking developed over time. Cocaine came to Colombia in the early 1970s. A review of U.S. Custom's data indicates that a total of 760 kilos were seized from all of South America between 1970 and 1973. Towards the end of this period occasional larger quantities, such as 30 kilos concealed in fishing poles, were seized. But most of the traffic seized consisted of less than 3 to 5 kilos concealed on or in some human "mule."[10] In 1974, Colombian Griselda Blanco de Trujillo was indicted in Brooklyn, New York for smuggling 150 kilos of cocaine into the U.S., a major arrest for the time. A year later 600 kilos of cocaine, the largest single seizure to that date, was made in Cali, Colombia, and it is said that some forty murders occurred in Medellin as a result.[11] In 1976, Pablo Escobar, a future leader of the Medellin Cartel, was arrested with 39 kilos of cocaine, the largest seizure in Medellin that year. It is said that Guillermo Cano, the editor of *El Espectador*, was killed in 1986 by Escobar's "sicarios" (professional assassins), after making this arrest public in his newspaper.[12]

My purpose in this brief chronology is to illustrate first how short the time span of the cocaine boom has been. In less than fourteen years Pablo Escobar moved from being a small time "mule" to being listed in *Fortune* and *Forbes* as one of the world's leading billionaires.[13]

The reason Escobar's 1976 arrest went unnoticed is that he himself was a young "sicario," assassin, and had the police involved in this incident murdered. This act of assassination, however, was simply criminal terrorism: revenge, security and the elimination of witnesses to a crime. Intimidation may have played a role, but if so, it was likely to have been a minor one. In the assassination of Guillermo Cano a decade later, such private direct material motives were replaced by broader purposive and symbolic ones: not just the elimination of a man, but the intimidation of the media of Colombia. In brief, between 1976 and 1986 criminal terror in Colombia evolved into narco-terrorism.

This path of narco-terrorism in Colombia has, like all paths governed by necessity and driven by exogenous events, been a twisted one. But if there is a single point to mark its beginning, it can be placed as December 1, 1981, when some 223 drug traffickers gathered at the Ochoa clan's restaurant, Las Margaritas, and formed "Muerte a Secuestradores," or MAS (Death to Kidnappers), in response to the kidnapping of Marta Nieves Ochoa by M–19.[14] Rather than paying off, the Ochoas and their friends and allies choose to unite and act. They placed advertisements in newspapers and showered leaflets from small aircrafts down on the crowds at the big Cali-Medellin professional soccer game to record MAS's birth and to offer rewards for information about kidnappers.

With these acts the drug traffickers had taken two important political steps. First, they had united and formed a purposive interest group. Second, they had publicly appointed themselves as administrators of vigilante justice above the law and the state's exclusive monopoly over the legitimate use of force.[15]

The formation of paramilitary groups and death squads like MAS has a long history in Colombia, as private oligarchs, "caudillos," the army, and the state, have used informal means of maintaining power. The formation of MAS, however, was more than just the founding of another death squad. It really heralded the emergence of a new interest group in Colombia politics, a drug "gremio." ("Gremios" are powerful interest group associations which traditionally have played major roles in Colombian politics.) MAS was merely an arm of this drug "gremio."[16]

While the data are fragmentary, it appears that the creation of MAS also helped promote closer ties between right-wing elements in the army and the drug traffickers. Amnesty International reported in 1983 that MAS killings were occurring in army counter-guerilla zones, particularly the Middle Magdalena region. The Amnesty report states "the army's attribution of illegal actions to MAS appeared intended to conceal unlawful actions directed by sectors of the army itself."[17] One has to be careful in interpreting these data, however, because the army, the guerrillas, and the drug traffickers' paramilitary, narco-militias were all co-located in these zones of operation. Indeed, the Middle Magdalena region was where many of the leaders of the Medellin Cartel were establishing large ranches at this time.[18]

Since then, evidence that the drug traffickers have forged ties to key members of the army has emerged. In spring 1989, it was reported that both the former intelligence chief of the Army's Fourth Brigade, Plinio Correa, and the former head of Colombia's special forces, the Red Berets, Eber Villegas, are employees of the Medellin Cartel.[19] But such ties develop slowly and have many motives, so let me return to the chronology of the evolution of narco-terrorism.

In 1981–2 the drug traffickers began to work together, and use narco-terrorism as a means to stop the insurgent criminal terror (kidnapping) they faced from the left. By 1984, the drug traffickers did not appear to need MAS, for the kidnappings of traffickers and their families appeared to have dropped dramatically.[20] Instead, the drug traffickers were developing private armies of security guards, narco-militias, and squads of professional assassins. In the eastern "Llanos" and other insurgent controlled areas, the traffickers were also forming narco-militias and their symbiotic ties with insurgent groups like FARC appeared strained and increasingly conflictual.[21]

By 1984–5 these differences with FARC had become armed conflicts with the traffickers using their narco-militias and sicarios have been used to eradicate the guerrilla presence.[22]

The path of narco-terror took another turn in 1986 when the government, attempting to bring peace to the country, arranged an amnesty with FARC which permitted it to form an overt political arm, the Patriotic Union and to stand in elections. In October of that year Pardo Leal, the presidential candidate of the Patriotic Union, was murdered by "sicarios" employed by Gonzalo Rodriquez Gacha.[23] Throughout 1986 and into 1987 more than forty Patriotic Union candidates and hundred of their supporters were murdered by the traffickers' "sicarios" and narco-militias, as part of the ongoing turf war between them and FARC for dominance over the growing areas of the Llanos. Now both the cities and the countryside had become daily scenes of narco-terrorism.

Back in 1984 when the traffickers were both threatened with extradition and hurt and angered by the Tranquilandia raid, they ordered the assassination of Justice Minister Rodrigo Lara Bonilla. It was an act of narco-terrorism, carried out by a sixteen-year-old "sicario," that shocked the nation.[24] Before then, there had been a time, in the early 1970s, when judges and magistrates in Colombia fought to get drug cases because of the amounts of corruption money that could be made. But by 1980, when two judges were assassinated in Medellin, some eighty judges and forty magistrates chose to resign. Now, after the murder of Minister of Justice Lara Bonilla, new judges and ministers were becoming hard to find.

Supported by an angry President and aroused nation, Laras' replacement, Enrique Parejo Gonzales, carried out the extradition orders that he had set in motion. The first major traffickers to be extradited was Hernan Botero Moreno, a Medellin millionaire and owner of one of Colombia's most important professional soccer teams, the "Atetico Nacional."[25] The rest of the Lara initiated extraditions quickly followed, and after such dangerous service Parejo was appointed Ambassador to Hungary in hopes the "Iron Curtain" would save him from the vengeance of the traffickers. On January 13th 1987, however, narco-terrorism came to Eastern Europe and Ambassador Parejo was shot five times in the head by a team of Colombian assassins who were identified as members of the "Hernan Botero Moreno Brigade."[26]

On February 19th, 1986, narco-terror had come to the United States when DEA informant Barry Adler Seal, who had managed to penetrate the upper echelons of the Medellin Cartel, was murdered by Colombian assassins in Baton Rouge, Louisiana.[27] It came again in 1988 when a Colombian hit team was sent to execute the New York head of DEA, Robert Stutman, and New York's Governor, Mario Cuomo. These assassins were intercepted by the FBI and deported.[28]

In Colombia, Col. Jaime Ramirez Gomez, who had led the raid on Tranquilandia was gunned down by the traffickers' "sicarios" outside Bogota on November 17, 1986.[29] On January 18, 1988, the Colombian Attorney General Carlos Mauro Hoyos Jimenez was attacked in a drug cartel kidnapping attempt. He was wounded in the ensuing firefight and later died.[30] But a taped recording of Pablo Escobar's car phone made shortly after these events pinpointed the Cartel's complicity. Escobar is heard talking to his key "sicario," John Jairo "Popeye" Velasquez, who is complaining that he can't stop the bleeding from Hoyos' wound. Escobar's response, "Get rid of the son of a bitch."[31] Later that day a group calling themselves "the Extraditables" phoned the police with information on where to find the Attorney General of Colombia's body, saying, "Listen carefully: the war will go on...."[32]

It is now thought that the drug traffickers had hoped to use the Attorney General and Andres Pastrana Gomez, the Conservative Party candidate for mayor of Medellin, whom they had kidnapped a week earlier, to negotiate an amnesty with the government for the cartel.[33]

What is important in this bloody litany is that it illustrates the way in which narco-terrorism threatening institutions through the assassination of authority figures, it was seeking to destroy those very institutions themselves. In November of 1985 the drug traffickers paid five million dollars and arms to M–19 for an attack on the Palace of Justice, Colombia's Supreme Court. This violence resulted in eleven justices killed and the extradition files burned.[34] Here we have an instance of narco-terrorism with insurgents acting as the traffickers' surrogates.

It is said that violence begets violence, and this is certainly the case with narco-terrorism. Today the paramilitary militias and sicarios that the drug traffickers created are increasingly turning on the traffickers themselves.[35] In turn, the drug traffickers are hiring retired British, Israeli, and German ex-special forces and special operations skilled military and intelligence mercenaries, along with retired Colombian special forces officers, to professionalize their paramilitary armies.[36] Meanwhile, paramilitary violence in Colombia has grown to epidemic proportions, with more than 3,000 deaths in 1988.[37] In response, the government of Colombia has recently created a 1,000 man special police force to try to deal with it.[38] Narco-terrorism has helped to spawn anarchy in Colombia as the traffickers have sought to assert their control over drug markets and gain their political goals. Cartel leader Pablo Escobar put it this way. "A lot of bloodshed could have been avoided if the government had entered into a dialogue."[39]

In this article I have attempted to examine and clarify the concept of narco-terrorism from the related phenomena that are often confused with it. I have defined narco-terrorism and specified several subtypes of true narco-terrorism. Then by focusing on Colombia, I [have] tried to chart the steps and stages in the evolution of narco-terror, and to point out some of its key developmental turning points and linkages.

ENDNOTES

[1] See Report of the Vice President's Task Force on Combatting Terrorism (GPO: Washington, D.C., February 1986).

[2] See Rachel Ehrenfeld, "Narco-Terrorism and the Cuban Connection," *Strategic Review*, vol. XVI:3, Summer 1988, pp. 3–9 for some examples.

[3] Since the Jaime Guillot-Lara case in 1982, there have been numerous drug traffickers and Cuban defector reports of Cuba's role as a facilitator in drug and insurgent arms traffic. For some examples, see *Miami Herald*, November 20, 1983; February 20, 1983; *Washington Times*, November 19, 1987, March 10, 1988, March 23, 1988.

[4] See David Brock, "The World of Narcoterrorism," *The American Spectator*, June 1989, pp. 24–25 and Rachel Ehrenfeld, "Narco-Terrorism and the Cuban Connection," op. cit.

[5] *Semana*, (Bogota), "Lehder en Los Llanos," No. 89, January 17/23, 1984, p. 31.

[6] DEA reports, cited by Guy Gugliotta and Jeff Lean, *Kings of Cocaine*, (New York: Simon & Schuster: 1989), p. 152.

[7] Cited by Howard Kohn (1989). "Company Town," *The Rolling Stone*, 6 April, p. 90.

[8] See Mario Arango Jaramillo (1988), *Implacto del Narcotrafico en Antioguia* (Medellin, Colombia: Dario Martinez) for a sympathetic and favorable view of the Cartel as beneficial capitalists.

[9] Cited by H. Kohn (1989). "Company Town," *The Rolling Stone*, 6 April, p. 88.

[10] Hearings, House Select Committee on Narcotics Abuse and Control, Testimony of Vernon Acree, Commissioner of Customs, September 28, 1976, p. 430.

[11] Guy Guliotta and Jeff Lean, *Kings of Cocaine,* p. 23.

[12] Howard Kohn, "Company Town," p. 90.

[13] *Fortune,* (Cover: Special Report) June 20, 1988, pp. 27–41.

[14] Fabio Castillo, *Los Jinetes de la Cocaina,* pp. 111–114.

[15] Max Weber (1947). *The Theory of Social and Economic Organization,* translated by A. Henderson and T. Parsons (Glencoe, Il. The Free Press), pp. 155–7.

[16] "Gremios" are powerful interest group associations in Colombia such as the national association of coffee growers (FEDECAFE) who with the army and church have a powerful role in Colombian politics. In 1981 the drug traffickers were forming such a "gremios." See Harvey Kline, *Colombia: Portrait of Unity and Diversity* (Boulder, Col.: Westview Press, 1983) pp. 123–125.

[17] Source not included in the original.

[18] *Semana,* "Garrote a la Mafia," No. 106, May 15/21, 1984, pp. 26–7.

[19] Howard Kohn, "Company Town," p. 72.

[20] See *Semana,* "Paramilitares: ejercito en has sombras," No, 77, August 31–September 6, 1982,. pp. 36–9.

[21] *Semana,* (Bogota) April, 3/9, 1984, pp. 26–8.

[22] *Semana,* (Bogota), January 24, 1989, pp. 22–28.

[23] *El Tiempo,* (Bogota) May 13, 1987, p. 1.

[24] *Semana,* (Bogota), "Muerte Anunciada," No. 105, FMay 8/14, 1984, pp. 22–31.

[25] *Semana,* (Bogota), "Tarjeta roja a Botero," No. 109, June 11, 1984, pp. 24–26.

[26] Fabio Castillo, *Los Jinetes de la Cocaina,* pp. 221–2.

[27] Guy Gugliotta and Jeff Lean, *King of Cocaine,* pp. 234–5.

[28] The deportation was to preserve the anonymity of a key informant whose name might have been revealed at the matter come to trial.

[29] For the best primary source interview materials of the contract to kill Col. Ramirez see Guy Gugliotta and Jeff Lean, *The Kings of Cocaine,* Chapter 27, "The Ramirez Contract," pp. 261–272.

[30] *The New York Times,* January 26, 1988, p. 1.

[31] Reported by Howard Kohn, "Company Town," p. 90.

[32] *Semana.* (Bogota), February 2, 1988, pp. 25–39.

[33] Ibid., p. 25.

[34] Fabio Castillo, *Los Jinetes de la Cocaina,* pp. 188–9.

[35] *El Espectador,* (Bogota) February 19, 1989, p. 2A.

[36] *Semana,* (Bogota), January 2, 1989; *El Espectador,* February 19, 1989; H. Kohn, *Op. Cit.* p. 73.

[37] Allen Riding, *The New York Times,* "Massacres are Jolting Colombia," December 15, 1988, p. 6.

[38] *The Times of the Americas,* Vol. 33:9, May 3, 1989, p. 14.

[39] Cited by H. Kohn, "Company Town," p. 90.

3.4 Rosemary Gartner

Patterns of Victimization Around the World

INTRODUCTION

A growing number of researchers in the field of crime and deviance have recently turned their attention to the study of victims: who gets hurt, why are some kinds of people more likely to get hurt than others, and what can be done about it?

The next excerpt, by Rosemary Gartner, looks at violence against women and children — acts which are usually, though not always, committed within the home, or between intimates. (On this, see also excerpt 7.3 below.) Here, there is little ambiguity about the victims, or the perpetrators of harm: the question is "Why did they do it?" Or, asked in a sociological rather than psychological way, "What are the social conditions under which people are more likely to do that kind of thing?"

What Gartner finds is that, across a wide range of societies, we can see social patterns that predict higher and lower risks of violence. Among other things, these "risk factors" have to do with women's education and participation in the paid work force — in short, women's independence from, and equality with, men. Violence against women tends to increase during the middle of women's transition to independence. Then it declines.

This argument shows that violence against women and children is "normal," in the sense of being predictable, even though (in many countries) it breaks the law. Second, violence against women and children is a universal phenomenon, even though it happens one case at a time, under unique conditions each time.

The mass slaying of 14 women at the University of Montreal in December 1989 shocked all Canadians deeply, but had especially profound effects on women. After the tragedy, many expressed concern about whether it signaled a trend in violence against females — a sort of "backlash" in response to the movement of women into arenas traditionally dominated by males. Those reacting against this fear have noted the Montreal killings were unprecedented and atypical. But, while the likelihood of more massacres of women is extremely remote, is it not possible that such backlash violence could be increasingly directed against individual women in less spectacular, but no less deadly incidents?

Gartner, Rosemary (1992). "Patterns of Victimization," in L. Tepperman and J. Curtis (eds.), *Everyday Life.* Toronto: McGraw-Hill Ryerson. Reprinted by permission.

This question prompted me to look at the relationship between changing gender roles and women's vulnerability to violence (Gartner, 1990b). While females are the victims of homicide less often than males, the size of this female protective advantage varies considerably. For example, in Italy and the United States since 1950, males have faced risks of homicide three times greater than females' risks. In other societies, this female advantage has been negligible: in the 1980s in Denmark and England, for instance, women were killed almost as often as were men. There is much less variation across societies in who kills women. Males are the perpetrators in over 80 percent of the killings of females, and in about 90 percent of the killings of adult females.

Female Homicides and Gender Inequality

Anthropological and historical evidence shows that the killing of women is relatively infrequent, and the gender gap in homicide is relatively large, in many societies that are sharply gender-stratified (Curtis, 1974). In these societies, family arrangements are especially patriarchal, women are not allowed to participate in economically productive activities (or their economic activities are devalued), and females are socialized to be extremely passive and subservient. Yet despite these disadvantages, women appear to be at much less risk of homicide than are men. On the other hand, in many societies where gender inequality is less pronounced, women's risks of being killed are closer to men's risks. This suggests women in contemporary western societies might come to face risks of being killed similar to men's as various forms of gender inequality and discrimination diminish.

To explore this issue, I collected homicide victimization rates of females and males in 18 developed nations for the years 1950 to 1980. I also gathered information on the roles and status of women, and on gender inequality in each nation. This included women's participation in the labour force and in higher education, gender segregation in occupations, and the rate at which women had children outside of marriage, got divorced, and delayed marriage past their early twenties.

Two perspectives on the relationship between greater gender equality and female homicide can be distinguished. One, the "criminal opportunity" approach, deals largely with homicides in the public domain. According to this approach, criminal victimization, such as murder, occurs when a motivated offender encounters a suitable target (victim) in the absence of capable guardians (Hindelang *et al.*, 1978; Cohen and Felson, 1979). How people move through the routine daily activities of life — where they spend time, how many and what types of people they spend time with — all influence their opportunities for being homicide victims. It follows that where women's and men's activities are more alike, their chances of being killed ought to be more alike.

A second perspective on the gender gap in homicide is suggested by feminist discussions of changing gender relations. According to this view, with reductions in gender inequality, women should be freer to avoid or to challenge

TABLE 1   MEAN SEX- AND AGE-SPECIFIC HOMICIDE VICTIMIZATION
RATES[a] FOR 18 NATIONS, 1965–1984

Country	Males over age 14	Females over age 14	Children aged 5–14	Children 1–4	Infants under 1 year
United States	14.92	4.18	.99	2.11	5.40
Finland	4.89	1.51	.55	.89	6.92
Canada	3.28	1.55	.58	1.04	3.17
Italy	2.45	.69	.24	.22	.80
Australia	2.30	1.41	.51	1.06	3.00
Austria	1.67	1.20	.48	.89	6.81
Belgium	1.53	1.13	.33	.73	.98
West Germany	1.48	1.03	.56	1.03	5.59
New Zealand	1.46	.83	.38	1.71	4.49
Sweden	1.41	.83	.44	.84	1.36
France	1.39	.79	.26	.48	1.92
Japan	1.34	.74	.80	2.26	7.64
Norway	1.20	.59	.23	.35	1.80
Ireland	1.09	.43	.10	.18	2.05
Switzerland	1.04	.81	.51	.75	4.57
Netherlands	1.00	.51	.21	.43	1.63
England & Wales	.88	.71	.28	.99	4.30
Denmark	.75	.78	.65	.83	2.21
Mean, all 18 nations	2.45	1.10	.45	.93	3.65

[a]All rates are calculated per 100,000 persons in the appropriate sex or age group, except rates for infants, which are calculated per 100,000 live births.

Source: *World Health Statistics Annual,* World Health Organization, Switzerland.

male domination in a number of spheres of social life. Thus, where women have more alternatives to violent relationships with men, or more resources to protect themselves from victimization, their risks of being killed should be lower than where their choices and opportunities are more limited, if this view is correct.

This approach is more general than the criminal opportunity perspective, in that it can be applied to homicides in both the public and private domains. Women with more resources can leave abusive relationships more easily. They can also protect themselves more adequately in their public lives, for example, by choosing to live in safer neighbourhoods or taking taxis rather than walking late at night. Moreover, women with more resources can direct them toward collective advantages. For instance, they can lobby for more public protection of women, through changes in the substance and enforcement of laws against violence toward women.

The criminal opportunity perspective and the feminist approach seem to pre-dict different outcomes for changes in gender stratification. The former suggests that gender equality *increases* the likelihood of women being killed, whereas the latter predicts that gender equality *reduces* the likelihood of women being killed.

Both may be right, however. Gender stratification is a complex phenomenon. It is composed of both differences in the *roles and activities* women and men per-form, as well as differences in the *status and power* women and men hold. With greater gender equality in *roles*, women's daily activities could expose them to more dangerous situations.

This could increase the opportunities for female victimization. However, with greater gender equality in *status*, women could individually and collectively claim more control over their lives and their environments. This could decrease the op-portunities for female victimization.

In other words, changes in gender stratification could operate to increase or de-crease homicides of females, depending on which process had the strongest effects.

These processes may operate within different time frames and unfold at differ-ent speeds. Over the last few decades, the greatest changes in women's lives have been in their day-to-day activities, as they have moved into the labour force in un-precedented numbers, taken on a wider array of non-domestic responsibilities, and moved away from lives circumscribed largely by family ties. So gender inequality in roles has declined at a fairly steady pace.

Gender inequality in status, however, has been more obdurate. More women are working outside the home and heading households. But gains in status have not kept pace with changes in women's roles. For example, women's economic status has improved little in the last few decades, either in an absolute sense or relative to males. There are many disturbing examples of this, from the contin-ued gender gap in wages to the growing proportion of poor households headed by females.

These differences suggest that recent changes in women's roles and changes in women's status may have had countervailing effects on women's risks of being killed. Moreover, improvements in women's status, however gradual, may have slowed any increase in women's risks of victimization by counteracting the risk-en-hancing effects of women's less traditional roles.

To explore these issues, I combined and analyzed the time-series data on women's roles, status, and homicide for all 18 nations. The patterns I found, then, are general, applicable across these nations. I discovered:

- where women are less embedded in *traditional family and reproductive roles* — that is, where they had children out of wedlock more often, divorced more often, and delayed marriage longer — their risks of being killed were higher, and the gender gap in homicide was less pronounced.

- where women competed with men for *economically productive roles* — that is, where women made up a larger proportion of the paid labour force, and where occupations were less gender-stratified — their risks of being killed were also higher, and the gender gap in homicide was less pronounced.

- however, where women had *greater access to higher education* (and, I would argue, to the status, resources, and power that higher education confers) their risks of being killed eventually declined, and the gender gap in homicide did not narrow.

So, changes in women's roles and changes in women's status appeared to have counterbalancing effects on their risks of being killed. However, as anticipated, gains in women's status seemed to take time to translate into protection against violence. In the short run, as women assumed a greater range of roles and responsibilities, they also became more vulnerable to violence.

I decided to explore a bit further. Did women's less traditional roles always lead to greater risks, or did this depend on how much status women had? Perhaps where gender differences in status were less pronounced, women did not face increased risks of homicide when they moved into non-traditional roles; whereas where gender differences in status remained large, women were vulnerable when they took on more non-traditional roles.

I divided the 18 nations into two groups, depending on the level of female status in the nations (measured by female college enrollments). Some nations in the "high status" group were Canada, Sweden, Finland, and the United States; "low status" nations included Ireland, Japan, Italy, and the Netherlands. I found it was only in the low status group that women's less traditional roles substantially raised their risks of being killed. In the high status group of nations, the rate at which women were killed did not rise as gender differences in roles diminished.

It appears, then, that in societies that allowed fuller participation of women in higher education — a major avenue to higher status — women were not as likely to lose their protective advantage as they competed with men in the labour force or as they moved out of traditional domestic arrangements. Thus, the context within which women participate seems to determine their vulnerability to violence.

What do these findings have to tell us about Marc Lepine's murder of 14 women at the University of Montreal? At first glance, the Montreal killings do not seem to fit the general pattern I found. They occurred in Canada, a nation with relatively high female status. The setting was a university, a source of advances in women's status. On the other hand, most of the women killed were engineering students; they had entered a traditionally male-dominated field. And the verbal and written comments Lepine left behind indicated he was resentful and infuriated by "feminists" and other women who sought opportunities in less traditionally female ways. For him, such women had prevented his success professionally and personally.

Thus, I think the Montreal massacre can be seen both as part of a more general phenomenon of male backlash violence against women, and as a particularly aberrant expression of that pattern. In other words, Lepine's hostility toward successful women cannot be dismissed as merely the attitude of one isolated and psychotic individual. At the same time, it would be a mistake to conclude that seeking gender equality through higher education or professional advancement is a risky strategy for Canadian women.

Child Homicides, Family Structure, and Welfare Spending

The analysis of homicides of females was based on the knowledge that their killers are usually men. That is why it was important to focus on gender relations in explaining changes in women's risks of victimization. Similarly, studying the homicides of children requires some knowledge of who presents the greatest risks to children's lives, and under what circumstances.

Children, like women, face the greatest risks from people they are related to or living with. For infants, the most likely killer is a parent; as children grow older, the risks from their parents decrease, while the risks from other family members or other persons who know them well grow.

Certain types of family structures are known to increase children's vulnerability to violent victimization, including homicide. For example, children with young parents, single parents, step or foster-parents, or many young siblings face elevated risks of being physically abused or killed (Daly and Wilson, 1988). Where such families are also exposed to economic stresses, children's risks are especially high.

These well-known patterns have been explained in different ways. The "systems" or ecological approach proposes that a group's balance of resources for coping with stressors determines the level of violence in the group. From this approach, the family is a microsystem that is sometimes structured to limit the extent to which resources can be marshaled to cope with stressors (Garbarino, 1981). Where parents have fewer personal and social resources to draw on, where they are isolated from support systems, and where family size exceeds resource capacity, child abuse and homicide should be greater.

According to a systems approach, this relationship between family risk factors and violence against children operates at two levels. Not only will individual families that are isolated and resource-poor be particularly prone to child abuse. In addition, large numbers of such families in a social system (for example, a neighbourhood, city, or nation) can raise the risks of violence for all families in the system. This occurs because networks of informal control and support become weakened in the system as a whole.

A second explanation of the higher risks of homicide for children in certain family settings is provided by evolutionary psychology (Daly and Wilson, 1988). According to this perspective, through natural selection, individual decision making is oriented toward promoting one's genetic posterity or reproductive fitness. Consequently, the likelihood of infanticide is greater where a child is

> of dubious quality, ... where there is some doubt that the offspring in question is indeed the putative parent's own [and where there are] extrinsic circumstances that might bode ill for a particular childrearing effort: food scarcities, a lack of social support, overburdening from the demands of older offspring, and so forth. (Daly and Wilson, 1988:44)

According to an evolutionary perspective, certain family structures or parental characteristics may increase the likelihood of child homicide, even when they are not accompanied by resource constraints. For example, teenage mothers should be more likely than older mothers to kill their children, in part because the potential future reproduction of teenage mothers is greater. Children raised by step-parents and unrelated caregivers should be at greater risk of violence, in part because these children do not enhance the reproductive fitness of their caregivers. Furthermore, maternal characteristics that are associated with premature, under-weight, and less healthy babies should also be associated with elevated risks of child homicide.

The systems approach and the evolutionary perspective identify similar types of risk factors for children. According to both, where there are more single and very young mothers, non-intact families, and families with many young children, child homicide rates should be higher. Furthermore, where systems of social and economic support for families are less developed and less generous, child homicide rates should also be higher. I examined these predictions using child homicide data from the same set of nations described earlier for the years 1965 to 1984 (Gartner, 1991). I also collected data on family structures and welfare spending in these nations, including information on births to teenage and single mothers, di-vorce rates, and the ratio of young children to adult women in the population. A number of these high-risk characteristics of families increased between the late 1960s and the late 1970s in these nations. For example, divorce rates more than doubled, and rates of births to teenage and single mothers also grew. I asked if these changes in family structure were associated with changes in the homicide rates of infants and young children and found:

- infants under the age of one were more likely to be killed where rates of births to teenage mothers were higher, and where government spending on welfare programs was more limited;

- children aged one to four were more likely to be killed where rates of births to teenage mothers and to single mothers were higher, where divorce rates were higher, and where government spending on welfare programs was more limited.

Both the systems and the evolutionary approaches suggest that the risks asso-ciated with certain family structures can be lessened by providing families with re-sources to deal with the stresses they face. One way to do this is through government programs designed to alleviate economic deprivation.

To look at this issue, I divided the nations into two groups: one had higher than average government spending on welfare programs, while the other had lower than average spending. I then analyzed family structures and child homicide in these two groups. This analysis revealed that

- in nations where welfare programs were less generous, the risks associated with certain family structures were much greater than in nations where welfare pro-grams were more generous.

In other words, higher government spending on social welfare was associated with lower risks of violence against children that resulted from the prevalence of particular family structures.

Conclusion

There are two important implications of these studies of female and child homicides. First, they show that social processes and structures can raise the risks of being killed for all members in society, regardless of gender or age. Second, they show that some social processes and structures pose particular risks for females and children. Therefore, theories of homicide based solely on studies of males are likely to be inadequate or even misleading when applied to females and children.

REFERENCES

Cohen, Lawrence E. and Marcus Felson (1979). "Social change and crime rate trends: A routine activity approach," *American Sociological Review*, 44:588–607.

Curtis, Lynn (1974). *Criminal Violence: National Patterns and Behavior.* Lexington, MA: D.C. Heath.

Daly, Martin and Margo Wilson (1988). *Homicide.* New York: Aldine de Gruyter.

Garbarino, James (1981). "An ecological approach to child maltreatment," pp. 228–267 in L. H. Pelton (ed.), *The Social Context of Child Abuse and Neglect.* New York: Human Sciences Press.

Gartner, Rosemary (1990b). "Gender stratification and the gender gap in homicide victimization," *Social Problems,* 37:593–612.

—— (1991). "Family structure, welfare spending, and child homicide in developed democracies," *Journal of Marriage and the Family,* 53.

Hindelang, Michael J., Michael R. Gottfredson, and James Garofalo (1978). *Victims of Personal Crime: An Empirical Foundation for a Theory of Personal Victimization.* Cambridge, MA: Ballinger.

QUESTIONS

DISCUSSION QUESTIONS

1. What penalties do you think most Canadians would want to apply to professional beggars — people who *could* work at a conventional job but prefer to beg for a living instead?

2. What kinds of laws would suggest that people in power consider women to be a type of property?

3. Would it be fair to say that begging is a harmless form of deviance that victimizes no one? If so, why are beggars treated with such contempt?

4. What factors are likely to increase the level of violence in conflicts between drug traffickers and governments? Does increasing violence mean that the government is winning the war?

DATA COLLECTION EXERCISES

1. Collect some data from published sources on the causes of begging in North America. What (estimated) proportion is due to drug or alcohol addiction?

2. How might different societies vary in the degree of seriousness they attach to the crimes Gartner discusses in her excerpt? See if you can find a society in which violence against women and children is considered unimportant, or undeserving of harsh penalties.

3. Find published data on attitudes toward drug traffickers in Latin American countries where drugs are grown on a large scale. Are popular attitudes there any more sympathetic to the drug trade than they are here?

4. Using published materials, collect information about abused women and children. How likely are they to end up "on the street" — homeless, as beggars or engaged in prostitution?

WRITING EXERCISES

1. You are a consultant to the ruler of Nigeria. Write a brief evaluation of Igbinovia's plans for dealing with the beggar problem.

2. "The worst consequence of drug trafficking is *not* narco-terrorism, it is the corruption of entire governments and countries." Do you agree? Answer in a brief essay.

3. "There are two ways to deal with an unfair world: retreat or attack. Beggars retreat, drug traffickers attack." Do you agree? Answer in a brief essay.

4. "The ways people in a given society respond to offenses against women and children tells us a great deal about ideas of equality in that society." Do you agree? Answer in a brief essay.

SUGGESTED READINGS

1. Gullestad, Marianne (1984). *Kitchen-Table Society*, especially pages 220–257, 346. Oslo: Universitetsforlaget. This book on domestic life in Norway illustrates the fact that all social arrangements, from the smallest (two-person couples) up to the largest (total societies), are systems of rules and expectations that are constantly being negotiated, revised, enforced, destroyed, and remade.

2. Levinson, David (1989). *Family Violence in Cross-Cultural Perspective*, pp. 9–38. *Frontiers of Anthropology*, 1. Newbury Park: Sage Publications. This essay uses the Human Relations Area Files to find out typical characteristics of societies in which family violence is common, and why domestic violence is justified in different ways in different societies.

3. Bell, Daniel (1958). *The End of Ideology*. New York: Free Press. In this book Bell makes his famous argument that crime is American as apple pie — a "queer ladder of success" in a society driven by the desire for success. What, then, would he have to say about the evidence of (comparable) rates of crime in Moscow, Calcutta, and Paris?

4. Williams, Holly Ann (1990). "Families in refugee camps," *Human Organization*, 49(2):100–109. As civil wars rage around the world, families are forced from their home communities into refugee camps and other temporary shelters. This article explores what happens to family members when they become refugees. In short, there is a breakdown of traditional social controls and an increase in deviance, even violence.

CLASS, INEQUALITY, AND STRATIFICATION

Introduction

Ever since the origin of the discipline in nineteenth century European social thought, sociology has been concerned with the sources and consequences of inequality. The problem of social inequality has been so central to sociology that Robert Brym (1988:4) argues we must see it as one of the field's three "classic questions." Some sociologists go even further, seeing class inequality as "*the* problem in sociology" (Giddens, 1980:19).

Hunter (1986:2) claims that the strong interest in social inequality "lies in the fact that it seeps into and shapes so many aspects of our experience, even if we are not always (or even often) aware of its presence and effects. It is not something which affects only some people or touches only some isolated corner of our lives." In fact, it touches all parts of all of our lives.

Social Inequality and Social Stratification

Social Inequality

Every society that sociologists have studied has proven to have social inequality. By *social inequality* we mean differences in access to scarce and valued resources of ownership, income, occupational prestige, and so on. All societies have at least some inequality, particularly in access to the scarce resource of power and leadership positions. For example, some people get to fill leadership positions and others do not. Typically, men have more power than women. And most societies have much more social inequality than just differences in power.

Many societies contain marked differences in ownership, wealth, income, and prestige. And, time and again, we find that these resources are more easily obtained by men than women, by majority racial and ethnic groups than by minority groups, and by people of higher (rather than lower) social class backgrounds. In short, societies "use" gender, race, and class to distribute scarce resources.

Social Stratification

Another way of saying the same thing is that all societies have "policies" concerning the distribution of scarce resources. These policies are specified both in laws (e.g., laws concerning private property in Canada) and in various norms (e.g., rules on advancement in a bureaucratic workplaces.) Taken together, these laws and norms form the basis of a *stratification system*.

In any "stratification system," the same types of inequalities occur with each new generation. Inequalities between people persist because the same "rules of the game" persist.

Researchers working from two different sociological theories have identified two distinct types of social inequality. One theory comes out of the work of Karl Marx and emphasizes economic ownership. The other comes out of the work of Max Weber and emphasizes more varied forms of inequality — income and wealth, occupational prestige, and power, among others.

Social Class

According to the Marxian approach, *social classes* are defined by ownership of the means of production and labour power, and they exist in all capitalist societies. The "means of production" may include the machines, buildings, land and materials used in the production of goods and services. The owners of the means of production, or their agents, buy "labour power" — people's physical and mental capacity to work for wages (or salary).

With this relationship in mind, Marxists identify three main classes. One class, the *petite bourgeoisie*, own their means of production, work for themselves, and do not employ others. A second class, the *proletariat* or working class, do *not* own the means of production and sell their labour power for wages. A third class, the *bourgeoisie* or capitalist class, own the means of production, purchase labour power, and accumulate wealth from surplus value created by workers' labour.

Marxists believe that a conflict of interests is *inherent* in the organization of capitalism. On the one side, capitalists try to keep wages low and productivity high to maximize their wealth; on the other, workers try to increase their share of the wealth by winning higher wages and improving their working conditions.

Socio-Economic Status

This is an important part of the story, but not the only story. For example, non-Marxists claim that social classes can also be defined through inequalities in income, occupational prestige, and power. Often, they study *these* forms of social inequality to the neglect of "social class" in the Marxian sense. In practice, people ranked separately on income, prestige, and power may fall into different ranks on these different dimensions. For example, people in the middle-income category may receive quite different degrees of prestige for their different jobs, depending on whether they earn their income in white-collar or blue-collar work. Likewise, people with the same amount of income may enjoy very different amounts of control, or authority, in the workplace.

Poverty

So far the topic of inequality sounds very abstract and dry. It becomes much less so when we look at cases of social inequality in other countries, as we do in the following excerpts. And it becomes positively dramatic when we confront some very sobering facts about poverty.

When sociologists distinguish between relative and absolute poverty, they are distinguishing between very different kinds of poor people. Under conditions of "absolute poverty," people do not even have enough of the basic necessities — food, shelter and medicine, for example — for physical survival.

By contrast, "relative poverty" must be judged in terms of the general living standards of a given society or social group. What people consider "poor" varies from one society to another and, within a given society, from one group to another. In North America, we would consider people with much less than the average income to be "poor," even though most of them have enough money to survive physically.

Governments usually measure poverty in relation to "low income cut-off points" which vary with family size and the size of community in which the family lives. Large families who live in large communities generally need more money to live at a given level than smaller families in smaller communities.

Lest we think that poverty is largely a problem of other countries, and not one of Canada's problems, let us consider some aspects of poverty in this country.

The incidence of poverty in Canada is highest in families with three or more children and in those headed by mothers (mostly single parents). Nearly half of all one-parent families headed by women are poor, and this percentage has increased since 1981. Indeed, families headed by lone female parents make up about one-third of all low-income families (Methot, 1987). This process is what some have called the "feminization of poverty."

Among unattached individuals, the incidence of poverty is highest among the young (under age 25), the old (65 and over), and women, largely because these groups are least likely to be in the paid labour force or hold a well-paying job (Methot, 1987). Low incomes are common in families whose members have completed little formal education or are often out of work (that is, were not in the labour force at all, did not work full time all year long, or experienced some unemployment during the year).

Low incomes are especially frequent in the Canadian regions where unemployment and low education are common: for example, in Canada's more rural and remote communities. Here residents tend to be unemployed frequently and for longer-than-average periods of time.

Welfare legislation suggests that the amount of government assistance provided to poor people depends on the perceived causes of their poverty. For example, old people and the physically disabled typically receive the most help. Apparently we consider them the blameless or "deserving poor." Single mothers and chronically unemployed people receive less generous and secure assistance, since many consider them the "undeserving poor." Welfare payments to this latter group fail to meet actual living expenses — especially for people living in large cities where rents are high. Many believe that if welfare payments were higher than the minimum wage, unemployed people would be reluctant to get off welfare and take a job.

Yet many unemployed people cannot find a job. In some regions and for some groups the unemployment rate has been very high, especially during the recession of the last twelve years. Certain groups such as female lone parents of small children cannot afford to pay the daycare costs that would allow them to take a job. Others, such as the physically disabled, cannot find a job suitable to their ability.

By 1990, over one child in six in this country was living in a low-income family. That percentage had increased since the early 1980s, as the proportion of elderly with low incomes was decreasing. Of all age groups, children are the most numerous and blameless victims of poverty. Their poverty demonstrates the error in thinking that a poor person has only him- or herself to blame. It is clear the poverty of children is due to forces beyond their control: especially, the inability of parents to find work and the inadequacy of social supports (like free daycare) that would permit them to do the job.

The poverty problem in Canada is not going to get better without decisive actions that will include (1) the creation of new jobs for people to fill, (2) job retraining for people whose job skills are inappropriate, and (3) social supports, such as free, good-quality daycare, for women who need to go out and earn an income.

As we shall see in the following excerpts on poverty in the villages in Bangladesh and among the urban black "underclass" of America, there is much in common across societies in the causes of poverty, and the necessary solutions to it.

REFERENCES

Brym, Robert J. (1988). "Foundations of Sociological Theory," in Lorne Tepperman and James Curtis, eds., *Readings in Sociology: An Introduction*. Toronto: McGraw-Hill Ryerson.

Giddens, Anthony (1980). *The Class Structure of Advanced Societies,* Second edition. London: Hutchinson.

Health and Welfare Canada (1989). *Health and Welfare in Canada*. Ottawa: Supply and Services.

Hunter, Alfred A. (1986). *Class Tells: On Social Inequality in Canada*, Second edition. Toronto: Butterworths.

Methot, S. (1987). "Low income in Canada." *Canadian Social Trends*, Spring, pp. 2–7.

4.1   Don Black and John Myles

Industrialization and the Class Structure in Canada, the United States, and Sweden

INTRODUCTION

Inequalities of social class occur in most countries, but there are theoretically interesting differences across countries. The first excerpt in this section, by Black and Myles, puts the class structure of Canada in comparative perspective. This allows the authors to compare Canada with the United States and Sweden. Black and Myles use a modified version of the Marxian class categories described above, making further distinctions between large and small employers and between workers and managers and supervisors.

The authors expect that major differences among the three countries will be found in the ways management and economic ownership are organized, and this turns out to be the case. Canada is shown to have relatively more managers and supervisors than Sweden and fewer than the United States. Also, the bourgeoisie is relatively smaller in Canada than in the United States or Sweden.

Black and Myles attribute these differences, in part, to the high level of foreign ownership in the Canadian economy. In effect, Canadians manage what Americans own. Even Sweden, a small late-developing country like Canada, has a larger share of home-grown capitalists. To find out the reasons why, you may want to read a book by Gordon Laxer. (See Suggested Readings below.) You should also read excerpt 10.3 by Peter Townsend, which explains how (and why) foreign ownership of the economy may produce poverty, not wealth, for a large number of citizens.

This paper will address a comparative analysis of the class structures of Canada, the United States, and Sweden. Our general conclusion will be that the Canadian class structure continues to bear the imprint of "uneven development" that is reflected in the size and composition of both the petite bourgeoisie and the working class. We also conclude that dependent industrialization

Black, Don and John Myles (1986). "Dependent Industrialization and the Canadian Class structure: A Comparative Analysis of Canada, the United States, and Sweden," *Canadian Review of Sociology and Anthropology*, 23(2), May, 157–181. Reprinted by permission.

has resulted in the "Americanization" of the Canadian class structure. Within those sectors of the economy traditionally dominated by U.S. capital (and U.S. labour unions), Canada has developed a class structure that is distinctively American. The result is a much greater dispersion of capitalist functions within the labour force.

These conclusions are based on the analysis of identical national surveys conducted in the United States, Sweden, and Canada between 1980 and 1983. In the following sections we briefly outline the conceptualization of classes and the data that provide the bases for these conclusions.

Conceptualizing the Structure of Class Relations

Class location is defined as a position in a structure of power within which producing occurs. Hence, the term class structure refers to the distribution of effective powers over the forces of production including money capital, the means of production, and labour. The schema guiding the analysis is derived from the work of Erik Wright (1978).

The Bourgeoisie, the Petite Bourgeoisie, and Small Employers

The traditional bourgeoisie is defined simultaneously by legal ownership of the means of production and the purchase of the labour power of others. The latter distinguishes such positions from petits bourgeois positions where no labour power other than that of the owner is employed in production. Operationally, these two types of positions are easily distinguished by differentiating between the self-employed who do and do not have employees. What critically distinguishes between these two classes is whether the surplus value produced originates from the owner's own labour power or the labour power of others. Between these two conditions, however, is the situation of many small employers who continue to produce much of the surplus product themselves but also exploit the labour of others. For present purposes, small employers are arbitrarily distinguished from the bourgeoisie by their employment of more or less than ten persons. Given the nature of national random samples, most members of the bourgeoisie captured by this method are at best small capitalists and for most purposes we shall simply collapse "small" and "large" employers into a single category.

Managers and Supervisors

Managers and supervisors are distinguished by the fact that while they lack legal ownership of the means of production, they participate directly in the functions of capital, that is in control over capital, labour, and the means of production. Managers are identified by responses to a complex set of questions concerning participation in policy-making decisions with respect to the allocation of capital, labour, and the means of production within the enterprise. A separate category of "advisor-managers" is also used to identify those who provide advice in the decision-making process but do not directly make decisions. In most of our analyses we do not distinguish between advisor-managers and other managers because of the small size of the advisor category.

Supervisors include those employees who do not participate in making policy decisions but who do exercise authority over others. In constructing this category two forms of authority were identified: 1) sanctioning authority — an employee who is able to impose positive or negative sanctions on others; and 2) task authority — responsibility for coordinating the labour of others. Those with task authority are included in the supervisory category only if they are also part of the formal hierarchy. Nominal supervisors — persons in the formal hierarchy but with neither sanctioning nor task authority — are not included.

Workers and Semiautonomous Employees

The working class in Wright's formulation is a residual category, defined by the absence of direct or indirect powers over the disposition of capital, labour, or the means of production. But were we to define the working class simply as all those who do not participate in the managerial-supervisory chain of command, numerous occupational groups with at least an ambiguous relation to the working class would be relegated to the working class. These include university professors, social workers, engineers, and various other professional and semi-professional groups neither participating in the decision-making process nor controlling the labour of others. Wright deals with this problem by constructing a category of "semiautonomous" employees defined as wage-earners for whom the process of proletarianization is relatively incomplete (i.e. those employees who retain control over how they do their work and have at least some control over what they produce). Operationally, they are identified by a coding procedure based on responses to an open-ended question in which respondents provide examples of how they are able to design and otherwise control important aspects of their work (see Wright, Costello, Hachen, and Sprague, 1982).

The Class Structures of Canada, the United States, and Sweden

Despite obvious (and expected) similarities in the class structure of the three countries, there are notable differences.

First, Canada has a much larger petit bourgeoisie and, correspondingly, a smaller bourgeoisie than either Sweden or the United States.

Second, Canada has a smaller managerial and supervisory apparatus than the United States but a larger one than Sweden. The key to this difference lies at the supervisory rather than the managerial level. This becomes more apparent from the distributions in panel B where the self-employed are excluded and "managers" are broken down into decision-making managers and managers who only advise in the decision-making process.

TABLE 1 THE CLASS STRUCTURES OF CANADA, THE UNITED STATES, AND SWEDEN (%)

A) Total Labour Force

	Canada	U.S.	Sweden
Large employers	0.9	1.8	0.7
Small employers	2.8	6.0	4.7
Petit bourgeoisie	12.3	6.8	5.3
Managers	14.6	17.1	14.7
Supervisors	10.0	12.7	7.0
Semiautonomous employees	16.0	9.4	16.8
Workers	43.4	46.0	50.9
Total	100 (1756)	100 (1415)	100 (1133)

B) Wage Earners

	Canada	U.S.	Sweden
Decision-making managers	14.1	14.8	12.7
Advisor-managers	3.3	5.2	3.8
Supervisors	11.9	14.9	7.8
Semiautonomous employees	19.1	11.0	18.8
Workers	51.6	54.0	57.0
Total	100 (1474)	100 (1207)	100 (1012)

NOTE: N is in parentheses

Third, in contrast to the preceding pattern, Canada and Sweden are remarkably similar with respect to the relative number of semiautonomous employees and, here, it is the United States that proves to be the exception where only 11 percent of all wage-earners fall into this category compared to 19 percent of all wage-earners in Canada and Sweden.

Fourth, the result of a much larger petit bourgeoisie than either the United States or Sweden, a high proportion of semiautonomous workers relative to the United States, and a large supervisory apparatus relative to Sweden, is that Canada has the smallest "working class" of the three countries though the difference between Canada and the United States is not large.

These differences underline the two distinct problems that must be addressed in comparing the class structure of Canada with those of the United States and Sweden. On the one hand, Canada has a larger proportion of petit bourgeois locations and, on the other hand, it has a different distribution of autonomy and authority within the wage-earning population of the class structure. While the relative size of the wage-earning population is certainly related to the size of the petit bourgeoisie, its composition is not.

Some Further Considerations

Relative to the class structures of Sweden and the United States, there is evidence of the "distortions" in Canada's class structure. There are two notable features. First, Canada does have a distinctive occupational and industrial composition, and the size of the working class in Canada reflects these differences. Although Canada's industrial structure per se is of only minor importance in accounting for differences in the size of the working class, the occupational composition of the employed work force is significant. Smaller blue-collar work force is the major component accounting for Canada's smaller working class. What is striking about this is, of course, that there are no comparable effects of occupational or industrial composition in explaining U.S.–Swedish differences in class structure.

A second feature of the Canadian class structure is Canada's larger petite bourgeoisie and, correspondingly, fewer small and large employers. Although Canada's large petite bourgeoisie is mostly a product of the persistence of petit bourgeois production in agriculture, it is also the case that petty commodity production has been more persistent within the Canadian transformative sector than in the U.S. or Sweden. In addition, the typical Canadian employee works for a smaller firm than Swedish or American employees. Both patterns would appear to reflect the truncated character of capitalist development in Canada.

But by far the most striking feature is the extent of incorporation of American practices for organizing class relations in the Canadian workplace. This is reflected in the apparent "overmanagement" of the Canadian working class and the tendency to incorporate employees into the administrative apparatus while simultaneously limiting the autonomy of those excluded from it, particularly in those sectors where the American branch plant has been dominant. It is the degree to which the Canadian class structure is Americanized that constitutes its most distinctive feature, and, to the extent that the American class structure itself is a curiosity among the advanced capitalist countries, this is also its most distinctive "distortion."

REFERENCES

Wright, Erik Olin (1978). *Class, Crisis and the State:* London: NLB.

Wright, Erik Olin, Cynthia Costello, David Hachen, and Joey Sprague (1982). "The American class structure." *American Sociological Review* 47: 709–26

4.2 Abram de Swaan

Jealousy as a Class Phenomenon: the Petite Bourgeoisie and Social Security

INTRODUCTION

The next excerpt discusses the world's first social insurance programs, introduced by governments in Europe and North America between 1880 and 1930. These programs were aimed at reducing economic inequality by protecting the working classes from possible income loss due to illness or unemployment.

Members of the petite bourgeoisie, or small business class, strongly opposed these programs. This is understandable in those cases where programs required employers to contribute to insurance funds for the benefit of their employees. However, the same group also opposed plans where small businesses did not have to contribute. How do we explain this resistance?

According to the author the resistance was an example of "downward jealousy" in class relations. The petite bourgeoisie saw any gain by the working class as a loss for them. According to the author, the petite bourgeoisie opposed the programs because they could not stand to see the working class handed the same degree of security they had struggled so hard to achieve.

This kind of jealousy may be an inevitable part of all economic group relations. People often resent the gains of others when it lessens inequality, the gap between groups. (Perhaps the same motives account for the continued efforts Brahmins make in India to avoid "untouchables;" see excerpt 5.3 on this.) But if the downward jealousy described in this excerpt is inevitable, it does not lend hope for greater equality in the world.

When jealousy emerges as a group feeling, relations between groups tend to acquire a conflict-ridden quality. The advantages, which one side believes to accrue to the other, it perceives as losses to itself, regardless of whether it had to give up or forego anything as a result. Bitterness at the sight of other people's good fortune appears. Such jealous group relations may occur in both directions, upward among the less well off who envy their luckier counterparts, and downward among the better off who cannot bear others to increase their well-being even if it is at no cost to themselves.

Swaan, Abram de (1989). "Jealousy as a Class Phenomenon: The Petite Bourgeoisie and Social Security," *International Sociology*, 4(3), 259–271. Reprinted by permission.

A social psychological interpretation of group relations purely in terms of "jealous relations" risks reduce a real conflict of interests to a mere psychological misperception. Such psychologisation is dangerous since it reduces real interest and justifiable claims to infantile emotions. But this caveat does not rule out an analysis of the role of jealousy in group relations.

Envy and jealousy in game theoretical terms transform "variable-sum" situations into "zero-sum" games. In other words, these emotions increase the conflict potential of the situation because the partners concerned perceive their interests as completely opposed, when an outsider might see mutually satisfying solutions if only jealousy had not changed the parties' evaluations.

These negative comparisons are of the essence when social differentials themselves are at stake. The satisfaction of money need not be in having more of it than others, it may reside in having enough of it for oneself. But the satisfacton that goes with social prestige is by its very nature bound up with being higher than others are, since it involves comparisons. Prestige distributions are always competitive and conflict-ridden.

Relations Between the Petite Bourgeoisie and the Working Class

At this point the argument may be applied to the analysis of a historical episode: the emergence of compulsory social insurance for wage workers and the petit bourgeois opposition against such schemes.

Between 1880 and 1930, compulsory and collective nationwide insurance against income loss from the vicissitudes of industrial working life was introduced in Europe and North America. Elsewhere I have argued that these arrangements were brought about by an activist political regime in coalition with large employers or organised workers, or both (cf. de Swaan 1988, especially Ch. 6).

In general, the opposition against these innovations came most of all from the petite bourgeoisie: from those people who saw themselves positioned "between capital and labour," and who indeed both employed their capital and applied their own labour as independent entrepreneurs.[1] Of course, they often also employed foreign capital and many among them did hire workers, but they themselves worked along with their employees and privately owned the means of production. This definition covers groups as diverse as small and medium farmers, shopkeepers, artisans, traders, manufacturers, and independently established professionals such as lawyers and doctors. These categories shade into other social strata, when the enterprise grows so large that the owner no longer works alongside his employees, or when it becomes so small that it hardly involves any capital at all and comes to resemble casual or "hired-out" labour.

Because the *petite bourgeoisie* was such a motley category and rarely united behind exclusive political organisations of its own, party positions on issues of social legislation cannot be identified unambiguously with the opinions of small entrepreneurs on the issues. More generally, in the present approach, a class need not be treated as a unitary agent, unanimous in its animosity. But by and large small independent entrepreneurs opposed workers' insurance, and often quite vehemently at that.

Why they did so is by no means obvious. In so far as they were employers, they feared having to pay insurance contributions and some schemes indeed imposed fees, many economically marginal enterprises could hardly afford.[2] But some plans excluded enterprises with a small number of employees and all excluded those in which only family members worked. Such proposals were opposed nevertheless.[3] If the insurances were financed from the general tax fund, small entrepreneurs might still resist it for increasing the overall tax burden and their share in it. But those plans that entailed no contribution from general taxes still met with objections from small entrepreneurs. Moreover, had they perceived the issue strictly in terms of financial costs and benefits, the small employers might have appreciated the savings on the disbursements they made privately or through commercial insurance to their incapacitated and aged workers. Support of needy or elderly employees was not usually a legal obligation, but a moral one of widely varying stringency. Yet, by and large, employers did object to the replacement of moral commitment by legal compulsion. It is difficult to understand what privilege was lost thereby, other than the freedom not to fulfil one's moral obligations. Voluntariness allows benefactors and employers to adjust their handouts to the changing proceeds of risky enterprise.

Employers did resent bureaucratic interference with their entrepreneurial autonomy. Especially the small masters, unaccustomed to any administration, hated the "*paperasserie*." The small, independent middle class sensed that social insurance was another major addition to big government, which it feared and hated as much as it did big business, department and chain stores, or consumer cooperatives.

The autonomy of the small entrepreneur was an essential myth. Wage earners were dependent on the whim of their employers, tenants on the caprice of their landlords, but the *petits bourgeois* were boss in their own shop and their own house. That made them superior to working people, both in their own eyes and in those of the workers. In so far as they were indeed independent, their autonomy rested solely on the ownership of the means of production they worked with (and on the ownership of the major durable means of consumption, such as their own house, partly workshop, partly family dwelling).

The basis of relative autonomy was private property. Property served the twofold function of working capital and insurance against adversity. This property was accumulated by individual saving. Social insurance represented an alternative to private property in its providential functions. It entailed the collective and compulsory accumulation of transfer capital to be disbursed in times of need. It thus relieved wage workers from the continuous compulsion to save for the future which was so essential and oppressive a feature of middle-class life. With social insurance, workers, too, would be sure in times of disease and disablement, during old age and often even during periods of unemployment. This caused jealousy among the petite bourgeoisie and made them oppose the insurance plans.

In the second half of the nineteenth century, the small independent entrepreneurs increasingly lost the field to large enterprise. At the same time, workers gained more income and security, while their social prestige also rose. A salaried position increasingly became an alternative for members of the petite bourgeoisie. In other words, workers and *petits bourgeois* increasingly became involved in a competition for status, which was intensified because they often lived close together in the same *quartiers*, shared a common urban neighbourhood culture and met as shopkeepers and customers, or worked together as craftsmen on the shop-floor. Workers who had succeeded in putting away some savings often established themselves in independent business, and businessmen frequently had to hire themselves out as employees or saw their children accept salaried employment.

As class boundaries were vague, changing and precarious, it seemed all the more pressing to maintain the small differences in status between the independent entrepreneur and the wage-dependent worker: "It is likely that fears of proletarianisation led many craftsmen and shopkeepers to exaggerate the remaining "small differences" — home-owning, the absence of unemployment (although not under-employment), or outward badges of respectability" (Blackbourn, 1984:48). The regularly employed workers were equally eager to distance themselves from casual workers, vagrants and paupers whom they considered their social inferiors (cf. de Regt, 1984). The *embourgeoisement*, which characterises so much of working-class culture in the unions, housing societies and friendly societies since the late nineteenth century, served to demarcate a boundary between these decent and steadily employed workers and the others, the dregs of society. The same emulation of middle-class forms of life acted as pressure upon the independent middle class, which in turn sought to maintain its lower boundary by adhering even more strictly to the ways of the propertied classes (cf. Elias, 1982).

During the first half of the nineteenth century, factory labour was generally considered an anomaly which would disappear as increasing numbers of workers would succeed in putting aside a small working capital to establish themselves in independent business. And many workers shared those illusions. They had been craftsmen or peasants before, in rural areas they often still kept a few animals and worked a small plot of land on the side. In the cities, factory work alternated with casual jobs and "cottage industry" at home, while wives or children often also worked in the factory or operated a tiny shop of their own. The ideal for working people was to own a small business or a piece of land, and a house of one's own to live in: private property remained the ideal, to be realised through individual savings. Property was considered as venture capital in the first place, for the owner to work by him or herself; even a privately owned house was first of all a shop or a farm to work in and next, a dwelling space for the family. The second function of private property was to provide financial security. This may seem less obvious now, after traumatic episodes of hyper-inflation, and when small enterprise is associated with risk-taking. But at the time, wage dependency was considered even riskier.

A fundamental equation of nineteenth century society runs: individual savings = private property = economic independence = financial security. In this light the question was why workers did not save to acquire the blessings of propertied existence. The simplest answer is also the best: they did not earn enough to save. But even when they could afford to put aside a small sum, they often spent it anyway. In a social environment of dire poverty, whoever has unused resources at his or her disposal is under constant and intense pressures from less fortunate kin, neighbours and fellow workers to lend or give them money. Refusing such requests means either refusing help to those who once did help one, or destroying long-standing solidarities which might be a vital necessity on some future day and thus a source of security in themselves. In other words, poor people do not save because their peers demand they spend their surplus on them and there is more security in heeding that request than in keeping one's surplus to oneself (and this — with the fear of the taxman — also explains the traditional secretiveness of hoarding peasants in rural societies) (cf. Popkin 1979).

In other words, the formula — savings = property = independence = security — did not apply to the working class. For the small middle class, however, it became a moral precept. Private accumulation was also considered proof of moral and social rectitude and earned one the esteem of one's fellow citizens. On the other hand, the poor who did not save were thought of as improvident spendthrifts who had gambled away their claims to sympathy. This comfortable view of social inequality was not just hypocrisy. Small middle-class families must have made great sacrifices and foregone many pleasures for the sake of private accumulation. And, as the century proceeded, in many cases this self-denial produced ever more niggardly results. Economic independence often did not lead to a secure existence, but on the contrary to ever increasing dependency on banks, large suppliers and big industrial customers. Craftsmen found themselves driven out of business by factory production and shopkeepers by department stores and cooperatives. Small enterprises often proved the most vulnerable to the risks of economic conjuncture, while inflation ate away fastest at small savings which could not easily be invested elsewhere.

The middle-class ideal was still to leave one's sons a "nice business" and marry one's daughters to a propertied suitor. As these goals proved increasingly difficult to realise, small entrepreneurs began to invest in education for their children, ensuring them of a position in the cadre of a corporation or government bureaucracy (cf. Crossick, 1984:21). "In this manner the second generation did not so much climb or step down on the social ladder, it rather made a step aside, crab-wise," into the hierarchy of the new salariat (Blackbourn, 1984:44).

In the last quarter of the nineteenth century, the conditions of the industrial proletariat began to improve. Urban sanitation spread. A beginning was made with working-class housing. The worst abuses of industrial labour were contained by factory legislation. And industrial workers increasingly were being considered as the backbone of the nation, factory production as the true source of national wealth. New ways were being sought to make the existence of wage workers more secure. And if individual workers did not manage to save enough to provide against adversity, then they might succeed collectively in accumulating funds: the recipe of the friendly savings associations. These mutual funds were an important transitional institution on the road to compulsory collective insurance on a national scale.

Wage earners, protected by social legislation and national insurance, were no longer a prey to emiseration at the first stroke of adversity. And this eliminated an important difference between the petite bourgeoisie and the working class, one which was at the core of the status distinction. And so it was experienced by small entrepreneurs, for example by Frank Bulen, as his *Confessions of a Tradesman* of 1908 testify (quoted by Crossick, 1984:263):

> *The doctrines I heard preached by the socialists in the open air simply filled me with dismay. For it was nothing else but the unfit and incurably idle, the morally degenerate, at the expense of the fit, the hard-working, and the striving classes.*

And:

> *It makes me positively ill to hear the blatant cant that is talked about the working man, meaning journeymen and labourers only. The small London shopkeeper toils far harder than any of them, is preyed upon by them to an extent which must be incredible to those who don't know.*

Behind middle-class protests there may have been "a vigilance in maintaining and guarding something": jealousy of a working class that stood to gain the security which once had been the sole privilege of the propertied classes. It is not easy to document this group feeling adequately. It was often hidden behind more elaborate ideological stances, if it was expressed at all. And it may only be uncovered by studying private sources, such as personal correspondence, diaries, and letters to the local press.

The assumption may also serve in interpreting more recent group feelings. For example, in countries such as the Netherlands, where minimum wage incomes are not much above maximum benefits, a downward jealousy can be sensed: what workers earn by hard work, others receive without effort or merit (cf. Verhey and van Westerloo, 1984). Here too, the small financial difference masks a crucial status distinction. And again, these jealous relations are ambivalent, since employed workers are aware they may be next to go on the dole.

ENDNOTES

1 Cf. Crossick (1984:9): "We find the unique feature of the petite bourgeoisie in the fact that its livelihood is derived both from its capital and its own labour.... It is the former that sets it apart from the proletariat, the latter from the bourgeoisie.... Any labour it hires is on a very limited scale."

2 Payroll taxes were sometimes paid by workers, sometimes by employers, most often by both; sometimes the state added its part. In practice, the formal division of shares between employers and workers did not make much difference, since each party would try to make the other pay for it by adjusting wages, and since the parties together would try to compensate for insurance fees by increasing prices.

[3] For example, the English unemployment insurance of 1911 initially covered only heavy industry and the building trades; the French *"insurance sociale"* of 1930 excluded agrarian workers; the Dutch Workmen's Compensation Act of 1901 excluded agrarian workers (cf. de Swaan, 1988: Ch. 6).

REFERENCES

Blackbourn, D. (1984). "Between Resignation and Volatility: The German Petite Bourgeoisie in the Nineteenth Century," in Crossick, G. and Haupt, H.-G. (eds.), *Shopkeepers and Master Artisans in Nineteenth-Century Europe.* London: Methuen.

Crossick, G. and H.-G. Haupt (1984). *Shopkeepers and Master Artisans in Nineteenth-Century Europe.* London: Methuen.

De Regt, A. (1984). *Arbeidersgezinnen en Beschavingsarbeid.* Amsterdam: Arbeiderspers.

De Swaan, A. (1988). *In Care of the State: State Formation and Collectivization of Health Care, Education and Welfare in Europe and America in the Modern Era.* New York/Cambridge: Oxford University Press/Polity Press.

Elias N. (1982). *The Civilizing Process: Power and Civility,* Vol. 2. Oxford/New York: Blackwell/Pantheon.

Popkin, S. H. (1979). *The Rational Peasant: The Political Economy of Rural Society in Vietnam.* Berkeley: University of California Press.

Verhey, E. and G. Van Westerloo (1984). "De Pont van Kwart over Zeven," in *Ons Soort Mensen.* Amsterdam: Raamgracht.

4.3 Mohammed Sadeque

Survival Characteristics of the Poor in a Bangladesh Village

INTRODUCTION

Oppressively poor living conditions are the lot of many people throughout the world. We see a graphic example of this condition in the next excerpt on village life in Bangladesh. (You can read more about Bangladesh in excerpts 7.2 and 8.1.)

There, the working lives of poor people are filled with uncertainty. Some spend every day looking for whatever work they can find, without great likelihood of finding work at all. Even

Sadeque, Mohammed (1986). "The Survival Characteristics of the Poor: A Case Study of a Village in Bangladesh," *Social Development Issues,* 10(1), Spring, 11–27. Reprinted by permission.

employed workers have little economic security. There is a constant threat of employers hiring outside workers for cheaper wages.

At the best of times, a family's income is scarcely enough to meet its basic needs. Food is the number one priority of families and many spend their entire income on food. The residents of Meherchandi live in dilapidated, unsafe huts, in filthy surroundings — many in poor health.

Poverty has also had a disastrous effect on family life. In these families, tension is high, a divorce and desertion common. Education of children is unimportant to these villagers because they see no hope of their children's lives being any better than their own. As a result, few children complete even a minimal education and there is a high dropout rate among those who begin school. People here will never have stable employment and a stable income until they improve their education. Unfortunately, they cannot improve their education until they have stable employment and a stable income.

*I*n Bangladesh, poverty has been one of the major concerns in social studies in recent years. The present study adopted a multidimensional stance to analyze the interrelationship between economic and non-economic features of deprivation and their impact on the survival of the poor. The study is expected to help develop appropriate social policies for Bangladesh where methods for mobilizing the poor do not exist.

Village Meherchandi

The study village was located on the northern border of the University of Rajshahi. Two criteria — land ownership and income — were adopted to single out the poor households which constituted about 86 percent of the 632 households in the study village. *The Second Five Year Plan of Bangladesh* estimates the number of poor and extremely poor at 83 percent and 53 percent, respectively (Bangladesh Planning Commission, 1980).

TABLE 1   LAND OWNERSHIP IN MEHERCHANDI

Land Holding	Percentage of Total Households	Percentage of Total Land
Landless	39.24	—
Less than 1 acre	21.84	6.28
1.00-2.50 acres	23.58	26.93
2.50-5.00 acres	8.70	21.08
5.00-7.50 acres	3.80	16.68
7.50-12.50 acres	1.58	11.33
Over 12.50 acres	1.26	17.70
Total	100.00	100.00

Location, cost consideration, and familiarity with the community prompted the selection of the study village. Data were collected in three stages: preliminary survey of all households in the village, an intensive interview of selected households, and 12 case studies.

Presentation of the Findings

Income-Earning Activities

The daily wage earners had to undertake whatever work they could manage on a day-to-day basis for eking out a bare subsistence. The day laborers were faced with uncertain employment opportunities due to the seasonal nature of agricultural and non-agricultural income-earning activities, unfavorable natural conditions, and the pressure of outside laborers. Others who had relatively stable sources of income could not count on any single activity throughout the year, and had to engage in additional activities to supplement their income.

On the basis of the major income-earning activities, we broadly categorized the households into eight specific groups: day laborers, small farmers, petty service holders, rickshaw pullers, petty traders, artisans, and beggars. The day laborers were the largest group. They constituted 40 percent of the households at the preliminary survey stage.

The monthly average household income of the classified categories based on data collected at the interview phase indicates very low income levels. The average monthly income of all the categories was about Tk.377, or roughly U.S.$13 (1 taka = $0.035). An average household size of 5.48 persons put the per capita monthly income at slightly more than two dollars, which is about one-fourth of the presumed national per capita income in Bangladesh.

The findings in regard to income were supported by case studies. The abysmally low income of the day laborers, service holders, and beggars was confirmed by the case studies.

Meeting Basic Needs

The poor spent all or most of their income for consumption purposes only. Analysis of a month's expenditures shows that more than 90 percent of the total expenses were for daily food requirements (Table 2).

The various household categories show a similar expenditure pattern. Four households (Cases II, III, XI, and XII) spent their entire yearly income on food. Four others (Cases I, IV, VI, and VIII) allocated nearly 90 percent for food. The remaining four cases had to divert part of their incomes for meeting extraordinary expenses such as payment of marriage gift, purchase of medicine, etc. In other words, they decreased food intake to meet other unavoidable expenses.

The poor adopted varied means to survive a decrease in income: credit-buying from village grocers, informal loans, institutional credit, disinvestment of assets (if any) or, in extreme circumstances, starvation.

TABLE 2   EXPENDITURE PATTERN OF POOR HOUSEHOLDS IN A
PARTICULAR MONTH

Expenditure Item	Percentage of Total Expenses
Rice	47.11
Wheat	15.73
Pulses	3.16
Vegetables	5.06
Other Foodstuffs	20.08
Cloth	6.15
Medicine and Medical Expenses	1.53
Recreation	0.82
Social Responsibility	0.36
Total	100.00

Since they purchased foodstuffs daily, they were subject to recurring price fluctuations. Certain essential items of daily living for the years 1981–1983 demonstrated wide variations in local prices.

Because their earnings were uncertain and irregular, so was their food-intake pattern. It was clearly linked to income and the manner in which it was earned. Thus, they had little control over what and when they ate. Food-intake information for a particular 24-hour day and for a particular month strongly suggests the poor recorded a much lower intake of carbohydrates (their dominant form of food) than the desirable minimum of 450 grams of rice/wheat per capita per day.

Food-intake information from the twelve case studies collected for two consecutive months on a weekly basis shows an equally depressing picture. None of these households could afford a minimum carbohydrate diet.

The vast majority of households cooked rice and/or wheat only once in the evening and ate the evening's leftover, if available, the next morning. The curry consisted of leafy vegetables or *marichbata,* a peculiar combination of onions, chilies, and mustard oil. None of the households purchased any fish or meat from the market.

This near-starvation diet had a deleterious impact on health. About one-fourth of all members in the households studied and one-half of the labor force reportedly were suffering from diseases. The incidence of chronic and severe gastrointestinal diseases on a wide scale was clearly indicated. Deficiency diseases related to malnourishment seemed to be highly concentrated among the poorest households.

Health problems were exacerbated by at least two conditions: first, their huts (78 percent had a one-room dwelling of about 127 sq. ft.) were made of rustic material, were substandard, delapidated, and unsafe, and they lacked the minimum facilities of rest, sleeping, and healthful living; second, their living environment was filthy, as only 15 percent used service latrines, whereas the vast majority evacuated their bowels in the fields and banks of tanks, polluting soil and water. Moreover, 50–80 percent of the households utilized home remedies, faith healing, and herbal medicines, and went to locally available quack alopaths and homeopaths when disease conditions deteriorated. Most people had no awareness of prevention.

Education of children was not conceived of as relevant to the realities of living. They could not imagine that the lifestyle of their children could differ from theirs. Only about 25 percent of the children were attending primary schools. The dropout phenomenon was also colossal. Most school-aged boys and girls had to help their parents with household tasks, collect firewood, or earn an income.

In summary, food was the overriding need. Families were so engrossed in meeting this requirement that the rest of their basic needs were grossly neglected — consciously or unconsciously.

Impact on Family and Kinship Relationships

Economic insecurity and hardship and the consequent interpersonal complications appeared to pave the way for the division of joint families into nuclear ones. About 85 percent of the poor households could be classified as nuclear. This division took place upon any pretext. At times, far-sighted parents took the initiative in setting up separate households for married sons in the interest of amity or to make them independent. All the cases except one were nuclear in the present study.

Many of the nuclear families were wracked by internal conflicts and mutual distrust. Familial peace and harmony seemed to be disturbed constantly by two particular conditions: first, grown girls were a perpetual source of anxiety for parents because the burden of a dowry or marriage gift was beyond their means. Second, the poor households recorded about a 25 percent rate of divorce/desertions. Unfortunately, neither the traditional local leadership was of any help in checking indiscriminate divorce/desertions, nor was there any effective legislation passed to protect the victimized married women.

Interestingly, most of the divorced/deserted women earned their own food. We also found instances where rich and powerful employers were having illicit sexual relationships with such working women.

Sons-in-law, on the other hand, enjoyed a somewhat privileged position. Sometimes their fathers-in-law lent or gave them money to do petty business. They also were presented with gifts from their fathers-in-law on special occasions. The primary concern of the girls' parents was to ensure that the marriages of their daughters survived. The weaker social position of women was clearly indicated. It is likely that the daily preoccupation with ceaseless efforts to find work and food changed the traditional mode of kinship relationships. Such relationships (both patrilineal and matrilineal) were limited to the exchange of visits at the most, and proximity was an important determinant. Relatives living in distant villages did not maintain connections with one another.

Status in the Community

Relationships with neighbors could be termed diffused. The pressure of outside laborers and the preference of some local employers to engage outside laborers at cheaper rates might have led to the ejection of a few of the working poor from the local employment market. But the majority were dependent on co-workers and poor neighbors for mutual support during emergencies or on rich and powerful neighbors for employment and other exigencies. There was a patron-client relationship between the rich and the poor, and the poor neighbors reciprocated by offering free services or supporting patrons in local elections (Khan, 1978). This dependence might have lowered their social position.

Their political awareness and participation seemed to be at the lowest ebb. Most adults voted in a ritualistic manner. The desire to achieve economic gains (e.g., relief goods) and the opinion and influence of the patrons acted as motivating factors. Local politics virtually became the monopoly of the local power elites.

Alternative opportunities for participation could be provided by voluntary social agencies and other programs that sprang up in the study community in recent years. Two voluntary organizations established to cater to the recreational needs of the local people had a very brief existence. At the time of research, two other organizations were working as cooperative saving societies.

Attitude

Almost everybody felt God had ordained their sufferings. The old, physically weak, and chronically sick were the most frustrated. Their sense of insecurity was obvious. Their ability to work and earn was their most valued possession and when that was threatened, their physical survival was endangered. Households with very young dependents or grown-up/divorced/deserted young girls were found to sulk in their pent-up frustrations.

Despite the fact that most of the poor were fatalistic, the majority were not content with their living conditions. They were unhappy because they failed to meet even the minimum food needs, let alone other basic necessities. The majority, however, did not give up and continued working hard for their basic survival. We agree with Gans (1970) in asserting that their reaction to present living conditions might be called fatalistic, "not because they were unable to conceive of alternative conditions but because they have been frustrated in the realization of alternatives."

Our observations did not support the prevalence of a so-called culture of poverty among our respondents.

Implications for Social Policy

The study found survival by all the categories of the rural poor to be precarious. The problems of unemployment and lack of purchasing power appeared to have spread widely. The main problem is employment. It is, therefore, urgent that the nation adopt appropriate strategies of planned mobilization of our vast landless manpower through agro-based employment schemes, promotion of rural non-farm activities, and labor-intensive rural industrialization schemes. The traditional rural artisans should be incorporated into these schemes.

The productivity of small, marginal farmers should receive equal attention. Previous studies indicate that they were more productive than larger farms, provided they are given access to a regular flow of necessary credit, extension facilities, and inputs at the proper time (Hossain, 1974). The existing Integrated Rural Development Programme (IRDP) has failed to meet their needs because the cooperatives are dominated by the rural rich (Jones, 1979).

The deteriorating socioeconomic status of disadvantaged women is largely linked to the failure to make them economically independent. Those without any productive role in their families must be provided with one to supplement family income. Others should be taught alternative ways of performing household chores; the time saved may be used in undertaking additional income-producing activities. Moreover, the legislation enacted to protect their rights needs to be enforced.

To enable rootless people to derive the full worth of their work, their asset base has to be steadily created by suitable land and other asset reforms and by funnelling a substantial portion of the annual development funds to them. We found an unprecedented increase in the vulnerability of the old, infirm, and the young dependents who were previously supported by the joint family system. Society must introduce social security measures for them.

Health services were in disarray. The existing *union* level health care centers can be revitalized with essential medicines and equipment, and locally recruited paramedics may be trained to provide elementary health information as well as curative and preventive services. These centers could also serve as a nucleus for providing additional family welfare services.

In conclusion, we may emphasize two things. First, mass illiteracy reinforces the unemployment problem. The nation has to mobilize resources to introduce compulsory education in order to arrest illiteracy and raise the skill level of children and young adults. Second, organizations for the poor need to be turned into viable action groups by a gradual process of education and consciousness-raising. Existing poverty-focused programs and voluntary social agencies may be utilized as institutional bases for reaching and organizing them.

REFERENCES

Bangladesh Planning Commission (1980). *The second five year plan 1980–85.* Dacca: Bangladesh Government Press.

Gans, H. J. (1970). "Poverty and culture — Some basic questions about methods of studying life style of the poor," in P. Townsend (ed.), *The concept of poverty* (pp. 146–164). London: Heinemann.

Gil, D. G. (1973). *Unravelling social policy theory, analysis and political action towards social equality.* Massa: Schenkman.

Hossain, M. (1974). "Farm size and productivity in Bangladesh agriculture: A case study of

Phulpur farms." *The Bangladesh Economic Review,* 2(1), 469–500.

Jones, S. (1979). "An evaluation of rural development programme in Bangladesh." *The Journal of Social Studies, 6,* 51–92.

Khan, F. R. (1978). "Problems and model of the study of elites in a district town in Bangladesh." *The Journal of the Institute of Bangladesh Studies, 3,* 149–172.

4.4 William Julius Wilson

The Black Underclass in America

INTRODUCTION

The next selection by Wilson further explores the sources of poverty: this time, the persistence of poverty among the urban "underclass" in the United States.

The author finds that affirmative action has done little to help poor blacks because affirmative action is aimed at reducing discrimination. Though a problem, this is not what prevents most urban blacks from improving their economic situation. Wilson believes that many of the same factors promote poverty for white and African Americans alike. For example, in any population a high concentration of youth predicts low incomes and high rates of unemployment and crime.

However, race plays a part too. Urban blacks have been particularly hard hit by the shift in the economy to services from manufacturing, the traditional sector of black employment. The problem for poor people is a drop in employment opportunities, just as it is in Britain; see excerpt 10.3 by Peter Townsend. Limited opportunities make it especially hard for black men to support their families and, in this way, erodes their self esteem and sense of family responsibility.

Wilson notes that much of the research on black poverty has focused on the family for explanations. But recent research suggests that, even under slavery, black families were actually quite strong and stable. The high percentage of single-parent families we see today first appeared in the middle of the twentieth century, not during times of slavery.

It is no secret that the social problems of urban life in the United States are, in great measure, associated with race.

While rising rates of crime, drug addiction, out-of-wedlock births, female-headed families, and welfare dependency have afflicted American society generally in recent years, the increases have been most dramatic among what has become a large and seemingly permanent black underclass inhabiting the cores of the nation's major cities.

And yet, liberal journalists, social scientists, policy-makers, and civil-rights leaders have for almost two decades been reluctant to face this fact. Often, analysts of such issues as violent crime or teenage pregnancy deliberately make no reference to race at all, unless perhaps to emphasize the deleterious consequences of racial discrimination or the institutionalized inequality of American society.

Some scholars, in an effort to avoid the appearance of "blaming the victim," or to protect their work from charges of racism, simply ignore patterns of behavior that might be construed as stigmatizing to particular racial minorities.

Such neglect is a relatively recent phenomenon. During the mid-1960s, social scientists such as Kenneth B. Clark (*Dark Ghetto*, 1965), Daniel Patrick Moynihan (*The Negro Family*, 1965), and Lee Rainwater (*Behind Ghetto Walls*, 1970) forthrightly examined the cumulative effects on inner-city blacks of racial isolation and class subordination. All of these studies attempted to show the connection between the economic and social environment into which many blacks are born and the creation of patterns of behavior that, in Clark's words, frequently amounted to a "self-perpetuating pathology."

Why have scholars lately shied away from this line of research? One reason has to do with the vitriolic attacks by many black leaders against Moynihan upon publication of his report in 1965 — denunciations that generally focused on the author's unflattering depiction of the black family in the urban ghetto. The harsh reception accorded to *The Negro Family* undoubtedly dissuaded many social scientists from following in Moynihan's footsteps.

The "black solidarity" movement was also emerging during the mid-1960s. A new emphasis by young black scholars and intellectuals on the positive aspects of the black experience tended to crowd out older concerns. Indeed, certain forms of ghetto behavior labeled pathological in the studies of Clark et al. were redefined by some during the early 1970s as "functional" because, it was argued, blacks were displaying the ability to survive and in some cases flourish in an economically depressed environment.

In the end, the promising efforts of the early 1960s — to distinguish the socioeconomic characteristics of different groups within the black community, and to identify the structural problems of the U.S. economy that affected minorities — were cut short by calls for "reparations" or for "black control of institutions serving the black community." In his 1977 book, *Ethnic Chauvinism*, sociologist Orlando Patterson lamented that black ethnicity had become "a form of mystification, diverting attention from the correct kinds of solutions to the terrible economic condition of the group."

Meanwhile, throughout the 1970s, ghetto life across the nation continued to deteriorate. The situation is best seen against the backdrop of the family.

In 1965, when Moynihan pointed with alarm to the relative instability of the black family, one-quarter of all such families were headed by women; 15 years later, the figure was a staggering 42 percent. (By contrast, only 12 percent of white families and 22 percent of Hispanic families in 1980 were maintained by women.) Not surprisingly, the proportion of black children living with both their father and their mother declined from nearly two-thirds in 1970 to fewer than half in 1978.

In the inner city, the trend is more pronounced. For example, of the 27,178 families with children living in Chicago Housing Authority projects in 1980, only 2,982, or 11 percent, were husband-and-wife families.

Teenage Mothers

These figures are important because even if a woman is employed full-time, she almost always is paid less than a man. If she is not employed, or employed only part-time, and has children to support, the household's situation may be desperate. In 1980, the median income of families headed by black women ($7,425) was only 40 percent of that of black families with both parents present ($18,593). Today, roughly five out of 10 black children under the age of 18 live below the poverty level; the vast majority of these kids have only a mother to come home to.

The rise in the number of female-headed black families reflects, among other things, the increasing incidence of illegitimate births. Only 15 percent of all births to black women in 1959 were out of wedlock; the proportion today is well over one-half. In the cities, the figure is invariably higher: 67 percent in Chicago in 1978, for example. Black women today bear children out of wedlock at a rate nine times that for whites. Almost half of all illegitimate children born to blacks today will have a teenager for a mother.

The effect on the welfare rolls is not hard to imagine. A 1976 study by Kristin Moore and Steven B. Cardwell of Washington's Urban Institute estimated that, nationwide, about 60 percent of the children who are born outside of marriage and are not adopted receive welfare; furthermore, "more than half of all AFDC [Aid to Families with Dependent Children] assistance in 1975 was paid to women who were or had been teenage mothers." A 1979 study by the Department of City Planning in New York found that 75 percent of all children born out of wedlock in that city during the previous 18 years were recipients of AFDC.

Why No Progress?

I have concentrated on young, female-headed families and out-of-wedlock births among blacks because these indices have become inextricably connected with poverty and welfare dependency, as well as with other forms of social dislocation (including joblessness and crime).

As James Q. Wilson observed in *Thinking About Crime* (1975), these problems are also associated with a "critical mass" of young people, often poorly supervised. When that mass is reached, or is increased suddenly and substantially, "a self-sustaining chain reaction is set off that creates an explosive increase in the amount of crime, addiction, and welfare dependency." The effect is magnified in densely populated ghetto neighborhoods, and further magnified in the massive public housing projects.

Consider Robert Taylor Homes, the largest such project in Chicago. In 1980, almost 20,000 people, all black, were officially registered there, but according to one report "there are an additional 5,000 to 7,000 who are not registered with the Housing Authority." Minors made up 72 percent of the population and the mother alone was present in 90 percent of the families with children. The unemployment rate was estimated at 47 percent in 1980, and some 70 percent of the project's 4,200 official households received AFDC. Although less than one-half of one percent of Chicago's population lived in Robert Taylor Homes, 11 percent of all the city's murders, nine percent of its rapes, and 10 percent of its aggravated assaults were committed in the project in 1980. Why have the social conditions of the black underclass deteriorated so rapidly?

Racial discrimination is the most frequently invoked explanation, and it is undeniable that discrimination continues to aggravate the social and economic problems of poor blacks. But is discrimination really greater today than it was in 1948, when black unemployment was less than half of what it is now, and when the gap between black and white jobless rates was narrower?

As for the black family, it apparently began to fall apart not before but after the mid-20th century. Until publication in 1976 of Herbert Gutman's *The Black Family in Slavery and Freedom*, most scholars had believed otherwise. "Stimulated by the bitter public and academic controversy over the Moynihan report," Gutman produced data demonstrating that the black family was not significantly disrupted during slavery or even during the early years of the first migration to the urban North, beginning after the turn of the century. The problems of the modern black family, he implied, were a product of modern forces.

Those who cite racial discrimination as the root cause of poverty often fail to make a distinction between the effects of *historic* discrimination (that is, discrimination prior to the mid-20th century) and the effects of *contemporary* discrimination. That is why they find it so hard to explain why the economic position of the black underclass started to worsen soon after Congress enacted, and the White House began to enforce, the most sweeping civil-rights legislation since Reconstruction.

Making Comparisons

My own view is that historic discrimination is far more important than contemporary discrimination in understanding the plight of the urban underclass; that, in any event, there is more to the story than discrimination (of whichever kind).

Historic discrimination certainly helped to create an impoverished urban black community in the first place. In *A Piece of the Pie: Black and White Immigrants since 1880* (1980), Stanley Lieberson shows how, in many areas of life, including the labor market, black newcomers from the rural South were far more severely discriminated against in Northern cities than were the new white immigrants from southern, central, and eastern Europe. Skin color was part of the problem, but it was not all of it.

The disadvantage of skin color — the fact that the dominant whites preferred whites over nonwhites — is one that blacks shared with Japanese, Chinese, and others. Yet the experience of the Asians, whose treatment by whites "was of the same violent and savage character in areas where they were concentrated," but who went on to prosper in their adopted land, suggests that skin color per se was not an "insurmountable obstacle." Indeed, Lieberson argues that the greater success enjoyed by Asians may well be explained largely by the different context of their contact with whites. Because changes in immigration policy cut off Asian migration to America in the late 19th century, the Japanese and Chinese populations did not reach large numbers and therefore did not pose as great a threat as did blacks.

Furthermore, the discontinuation of large-scale immigration from Japan and China enabled Chinese and Japanese to solidify networks of ethnic contacts and to occupy particular occupational niches in small, relatively stable communities. For blacks, the situation was different. The 1970 census recorded 22,580,000 blacks in the United States but only 435,000 Chinese and 591,000 Japanese. "Imagine," Lieberson exclaims, "22 million Japanese Americans trying to carve out initial niches through truck farming."

The Youth Explosion

Different population sizes also helped determine the dissimilar rates of progress of urban blacks and the new *European* arrivals. European immigration was curtailed during the 1920s, but black migration to the urban North continued through the 1960s. With each passing decade, Lieberson writes, there were many more blacks who were recent migrants to the North, whereas the immigrant component of the new Europeans dropped off over time. Eventually, other whites muffled their dislike of the Poles and Italians and Jews and saved their antagonism for blacks. As Lieberson notes, "The presence of blacks made it harder to discriminate against the new Europeans because the alternative was viewed less favorably."

The black migration to Northern cities — the continual replenishment of black populations there by poor newcomers — predictably skewed the age profile of the urban black community and kept it relatively young. The number of central-city black youths aged 16–19 increased by almost 75 percent from 1960 to 1969. Young black adults (ages 20–24) increased in number by two-thirds during the same period, three times the increase for young white adults. In the nation's inner cities in 1977, the median age for whites was 30.3, for blacks 23.9. The importance of this jump in the number of young minorities in the ghetto, many of them lacking one or more parent, cannot be overemphasized.

Age correlates with many things. For example, the higher the median age of a group, the higher its income; the lower the median age, the higher the unemployment rate and the higher the crime rate. (More than half of those arrested in 1980 for violent and property crimes in American cities were under 21.) The younger a woman is, the more likely she is to bear a child out of wedlock, head up a new household, and depend on welfare. In short, much of what has gone awry in the ghetto is due in part to the sheer increase in the number of black youths. As James Q. Wilson has argued, an abrupt rise in the proportion of young people in *any* community will have an "exponential effect on the rate of certain social problems."

The population explosion among minority youths occurred at a time when changes in the economy were beginning to pose serious problems for unskilled workers. Urban minorities have been particularly vulnerable to the structural economic changes of the past two decades: the shift from goods-producing to service-providing industries, the increasing polarization of the labor market into low-wage and high-wage sectors, technological innovations, and the relocation of manufacturing industries out of the central cities.

Beyond Race

Roughly 60 percent of the unemployed blacks in the United States reside within the central cities. Their situation continues to worsen. Not only are there more blacks without jobs every year; many, especially young males, are dropping out of the labor force entirely. The percentage of blacks who were in the labor force fell from 45.6 in 1960 to 30.8 in 1977 for those aged 16–17 and from 90.4 to 78.2 for those aged 20–24. (During the same period, the proportion of white teenagers in the labor force actually *increased*.)

More and more black youths, including many who are no longer in school, are obtaining no job experience at all. The proportion of black teenage males who have *never* held a job increased from 32.7 to 52.8 percent between 1966 and 1977; for black males under 24, the percentage grew from 9.9 to 23.3. Research shows, not surprisingly, that joblessness during youth has a harmful impact on one's future success in the job market.

There have been recent signs, though not many, that some of the inner city's ills may have begun to abate. For one, black migration to urban areas has been minimal in recent years; many cities have experienced net migration of blacks *to* the suburbs. For the first time in the 20th century, a heavy influx from the countryside no longer swells the ranks of blacks in the cities. Increases in the urban black population during the 1970s, as demographer Philip Hauser has pointed out, were mainly due to births. This means that one of the major obstacles to black advancement in the cities has been removed. Just as the Asian and European immigrants benefited from a cessation of migration, so too should urban blacks.

Even more significant is the slowing growth in the number of *young* blacks inhabiting the central cities. In metropolitan areas generally, there were six percent fewer blacks aged 13 or under in 1977 than there were in 1970; in the inner city, the figure was 13 percent. As the average age of the urban black community begins to rise, lawlessness, illegitimacy, and unemployment should begin to decline.

Even so, the problems of the urban black underclass will remain crippling for years to come. And I suspect that any significant reduction of joblessness, crime, welfare dependency, single-parent homes, and out-of-wedlock pregnancies would require far more comprehensive social and economic change than Americans have generally deemed appropriate or desirable.

The existence of a black underclass, as I have suggested, is due far more to historic discrimination and to broad demographic and economic trends than it is to racial discrimination in the present day. For that reason, the underclass has not benefited significantly from "race specific" antidiscrimination policies, such as affirmative action, that have aided so many trained and educated blacks. If inner-city blacks are to be helped, they will be helped not by policies addressed primarily to inner-city minorities but by policies designed to benefit all of the nation's poor.

I am reminded in this connection of Bayard Rustin's plea during the early 1960s that blacks recognize the importance of *fundamental* economic reform (including a system of national economic planning along with new education, manpower, and public works programs to help achieve full employment) and the need for a broad-based coalition to achieve it. Politicians and civil-rights leaders should, of course, continue to fight for an end to racial discrimination. But they must also recognize that poor minorities are profoundly affected by problems that affect other people in America as well, and that go beyond racial considerations. Unless those problems are addressed, the underclass will remain a reality of urban life.

QUESTIONS

DISCUSSION QUESTIONS

1. Would you expect to find that social inequality, in some form, is "universal," or found in all societies? Why or why not? Discuss.

2. Compare and contrast the concepts of "social class" and "socio-economic status" and give examples drawn from the four excerpts in this Section.

3. Compare Sadeque's and Wilson's views on the causes of poverty in the cases they discuss.

4. Define and discuss the concept of "underclass," as Wilson uses it. Is there an "underclass" in your home community?

DATA COLLECTION EXERCISES

1. Recall the set of class categories used in the Black and Myles study. In what ways might they need to be changed to be useful in analysing the class structures of a wider spectrum of contemporary societies — for example, Russia, Mexico, or

South Africa? Try out your own class categories on a society of your choice, comparing it with a conventional set of categories.

2. Study Canadian newspaper reports to find evidence of "downward jealousy" of the kind discussed by de Swaan. How do you intend to measure it and what do you expect to find after making these measurements?

3. Suggest ways of measuring "relative" and "absolute" poverty in your community. How would they have to differ to be appropriate for the communities studied by Sadeque and Wilson?

4. Gather library data on the extent of social inequality of Canada's native peoples. Are they an "underclass" as Wilson uses this concept?

WRITING EXERCISES

1. Write a brief essay in which you speculate on the ways Black and Myles' results might have turned out if they had done their comparative study of Canada and the United States a hundred years ago.

2. Write a brief essay showing how contemporary discussions of "exploding" health care and old-age pension costs reveal underlying class conflicts.

3. Both Sadeque and Wilson see improved educational opportunities as a partial solution for the inequalities they studied. Write a critical assessment of this view.

4. Write a brief letter to the Prime Minister listing ways in which social class and socio-economic status inequalities may be lessened in Canada (or, if you prefer, in another society of your choice).

SUGGESTED READINGS

1. Howard, Robert (1985). *Brave New Workplace.* New York: Viking. In many countries, there has been a growing trend toward more employee participation in workplace decision-making. This volume critically analyzes that development. The author concludes that most cases of this approach are really managers manipulating their employees. Workers may *believe* they have some control and autonomy, but the most important result is more managerial control over workers.

2. Rossi, Peter H. (1989). *Down and Out in America: The Origins of Homelessness.* Chicago: University of Chicago Press. A penetrating analysis of why, in North America, homelessness and extreme economic hardship increased markedly in the last decade. The author puts forward policy suggestions based on the analysis.

3. Sennett, Richard and Jonathan Cobb (1973). *The Hidden Injuries of Class.* New York: Vintage. An interview study, with provocative interpretations, on how people come to grips with the fact that they are toward the bottom of the community's class structure.

4. Wolf, Eric (1982). *Europe and the People Without History.* Berkeley: University of California Press. A sweeping world-wide perspective on the ways expanding European capitalism and colonialism affected pre-capitalist societies — including their structures of class and stratification.

RACE AND ETHNIC RELATIONS

Introduction

In his classic work *The Vertical Mosaic* (1965), John Porter argued that Canadian society is stratified along ethnic lines. *Ethnic stratification* means that ethnic groups are ranked and treated unequally. This rank-ordering of ethnic groups is dominated by people with the power to define what physical or cultural characteristics are most socially desirable — usually, their own. They rank other groups on the basis of similarity to themselves.

Ethnic Stratification

In a society that is ethnically stratified, each ethnic group occupies a well-defined position in the social structure. Ethnic stratification is only possible when people attach cultural meanings to various physical and cultural traits. For example, as we saw in excerpt 1.4, people may value lighter skin over darker skin. Accordingly, they treat light-skinned people better than dark-skinned ones. Or they may believe that Protestantism is a more "civilized" religion than Catholicism, or vice versa, or that Francophone culture, or aboriginal culture, or British culture, is "better" than some other culture.

All of these beliefs have social consequences. In fact, Porter argued that, in Canada, the relationship between ethnicity and class is so strong that you can predict a person's education, income, and job prestige by knowing his or her ethnic origin.

According to Porter, this correlation between ethnicity and class or socioeconomic status arose from Canada's history of immigration. Certain groups had come to do certain kinds of work in Canada: the earliest Chinese to build the railways, the Ukrainians to farm the prairies, the Italians to build the cities, and so on. Over time, they and their descendants remained at the same socioeconomic level — sometimes, even in the same industry. This happened because of discrimination and a lack of educational opportunity.

Later work shows Porter feared that ethnic minority groups were assimilating far too slowly for their own good, and for Canada's good. He felt higher levels of assimilation would demand more educational opportunity for the members of minority groups. Ethnic inequality would only start to break down when ethnic minorities enjoyed more opportunity for higher education and took advantage of this opportunity.

This is why Porter opposed the perpetuation of a "vertical mosaic," even under the name of "multiculturalism." First, he believed it was unfair: ethnic stratification kept the Charter Groups *in* power and everyone else *out*. Second, ethnic stratification discouraged bright children of ethnic minority backgrounds from pursuing higher education. This reduced the development of talent in society. Third, ethnic stratification often translated into voluntary segregation and this slowed down assimilation. In this way it limited people's usefulness as Canadian citizens.

That was Porter's picture of Canada nearly 30 years ago. But the evidence suggests that Porter's image of Canadian society is less valid today than it once was. The "vertical mosaic" image may have captured what was happening in Canada in the first half of the century and before, but there have been some important changes since then.

Since Porter published his findings in 1965, sociologists have researched every corner of this question. They have used better data and more powerful techniques of analysis than Porter had available. As well, Canada has changed in the last few decades. For all of these reasons, recent researchers have drawn different conclusions from Porter's. In short, today Canada remains a vertical mosaic along racial lines, but not along ethnic lines.

Leaving aside *this* change, Porter may have been wrong to assume that all ethnic groups assimilate in the same ways: namely, through higher education and the adoption of mainstream Canadian values.

Ethnic Identity

A recent study, *Ethnic Identity and Equality: Varieties of Experience in a Canadian City*, by Breton et al. (1990), shows this error very clearly. First, it argues that Porter is wrong to conclude that all ethnic minorities, or non-Charter Group members, remain outside the mainstream of society. When immigrants fail to participate fully in Canadian political life, it is *not* because they are too wrapped up in their own ethnic group. Like other people, ethnic minorities begin to participate more as they get more education.

Second, involvement in the larger society does *not* keep people from holding on to an ethnic identity or ethnic goals. Third, and conversely, holding on to an ethnic identity or ethnic goals does not necessarily keep people from participating in the mainstream society. It may even make it easier! For example, if the ethnic group makes a wide variety of resources and contacts available to its members, this may help people to enter the wider society more successfully.

Excerpt 5.1 below, on local politics in Kenya, makes these same points in a different social context. It shows that ethnic membership is extremely important in a multicultural developing society.

Fourth, different groups display different patterns of ethnic identification and assimilation. In many groups, ethnic language use is a key to cultural identity and ethnic solidarity. In other groups, residential segregation or occupational segregation may be most important. Excerpt 5.2 below, on ethnic conflict in the former Soviet Union, shows religion can play a very important part in signifying group membership and mobilizing resistance against the dominant group.

Finally, ethnic identity is something that continues to change over time. "And because of different internal and external circumstances, the process of evolution is different from one group to another. It may be that the past has a different relevance for some groups than for others" (op. cit.:264).

Like all culture, ethnic culture is a record of the group's history. On the one hand, it preserves a pattern of relationships that may have made sense 1000 years ago; an example of this is the caste system described in excerpt 5.3 below. That pattern may not remain obviously useful, necessary, or just today. On the other hand, it preserves a set of ancient grudges that help to keep the group together.

So, for example, Canadian Jews are slow to forget the treatment of European Jews by Germans and East Europeans 50 years ago. Likewise, Sikhs remember and resent their treatment by Hindus; Palestinians their treatment by Israelis; Koreans their treatment by the Japanese; Croats their treatment by Serbians (and vice versa); Africans their treatment by whites; Ukrainians their treatment by Russians, and so on. As we saw in excerpt 2.3, many Armenians have never forgiven the Turks for their treatment 90 years ago (though all of the Turks involved are surely dead by now).

In short, interethnic fears and hatreds die slowly, and they hold an ethnic group together. They are reawakened by events in other parts of the world: in Europe, Israel, the Ukraine, Africa, and South America. Faraway events all influence the ways we perceive our lives in Canada, as members of local ethnic groups. Concerns with faraway events may lead people to build barriers against other ethnic groups, even when such barriers are not really needed in Canada.

Breton and his colleagues show that ethnicity links people to their historical past and to other parts of the world. In that respect at least, there is a great deal to be said in favour of ethnicity: it ties members of an ethnic group together, wherever they may live in the world. However, there is less to be said in favour of racism, and Canada is becoming stratified by race as it was once stratified by ethnic ancestry.

Now a Racial Mosaic?

The recent study (Breton et al.) reports that some groups face serious obstacles to their full economic and social acceptance. They include the Chinese and West Indians, but also the Jews, who suffer barriers to social acceptance despite their economic success in Canadian society. "Thus being non-white, a new immigrant, or Jewish continues to involve disadvantages for full and equal participation in Canadian society."

Paradoxically, even some people "who want to blend into Canadian society experienc[e] problems of incorporation" (*ibid*). They are stuck inside their own communities, whether they like it or not."

An immigrant community with few resources and little political clout — like the West Indians, Portugese, or even Chinese — can give its members little help in overcoming such rejection. For example, a West Indian living in Toronto will gain much less from involvement in his/her community than an Italian will, since the West Indian community can do little to help its members prosper in the larger society.

In the last excerpt of this section (5.4), the author points out that Canada faces a very high risk of serious racial conflict in years to come. Avoiding this means taking actions to correct the problem of racial prejudice and discrimination. Otherwise we will go the way of Britain and the United States.

REFERENCES

Breton, R., W. Isajiw, W. Kalbach, and J. Reitz (1990). *Ethnic Identity and Equality: Varieties of Experience in a Canadian City.* Toronto: University of Toronto Press.

5.1 Barbara P. Thomas-Slayter

Ethnic and Class Mobilization in Kenya

INTRODUCTION

We have seen, in various excerpts in this book, that societies are often divided in terms of ethnic, regional, and class loyalties. The following excerpt begins by showing that contemporary Kenya is no exception to this pattern. The author also indicates that, as with many other societies, ethnic and regional loyalties are stronger than class loyalties.

The author then shows that ethnic and regional divisions are both useful for, and an obstacle to, the operation of the power elite of Kenya. They are useful because the masses cannot readily come together to oppose the powerful. They are an obstacle, however, for any attempts by the elite to mobilize the masses to do as they wish.

One way that some mobilization has taken place is around local self-help activities called "Harambee." In a modest way, these activities, which are often locally-initiated, empower ethnic and regional groups and the poor. These activities are also being promoted wherever possible by the elite, when they serve their interests.

The author suggests that more widespread mobilization of people around common class interests which cut across ethnic groups and regions will be difficult to achieve because of the stronger ethnic and regional loyalties.

The Kenyan state is trapped by near overwhelming economic pressures arising from its position within the global economy. Moreover, its political situation is tenuous vis-a-vis a growing public dissatisfaction that some Kenyans have been in a position to take advantage of largesse arising through global economic linkages, and vis-a-vis its international allies who, in the declining days of the Cold War, may not be predisposed to meet the costs of maintaining strong friendships with Third World countries. On one hand, the Kenyan state desperately needs to mobilize both the political support and the economic resources of its rural people. On the other hand, it is prevented from fully utilizing these forces by its own fragility and its fears of losing control. Ethnicity remains the most compelling basis for community mobilization, as well as the energizing force which the state fears the most, given its own dependence on problematic, multi-ethnic coalitions while trying to build a strong, multi-ethnic nation.

Thomas-Slayter, Barbara P. (1991). "Class, Ethnicity, and the Kenyan State: Community Mobilization in the Context of Global Politics," *International Journal of Politics, Culture and Society*, 4(3), 301–321.

Ethnicity Versus Class in Kenya

Ethnicity as a Catalyst for Community Mobilization

Throughout Africa, ethnicity is an important phenomenon and remains, today, the single most important variable around which individuals, households, and communities aggregate for common action. Ethnicity can be defined as a perception of common origins, as well as shared history, norms, language, dreams and other ties and attributes which link a person to a given set of people. An ethnic group may be spatially defined as well. The consciousness of special identity permits and encourages people to organize to advance their common interests.

Ethnicity is often a political as well as a cultural phenomenon. Analysts of contemporary Africa emphasize that ethnic awareness, vis-a-vis other groups, is a consequence of the colonial period in which governance was often achieved through promotion of ethnic rivalries. In the post-independence period, ethnic groups, like other groups, place claims upon the state. They compete among themselves and with other groups for state controlled resources. In the political systems operative in many African nations today, ethnic loyalties and organizations play a significant role in advancing the material and other interests of their members. They usually do so through patron-client relationships which are a common phenomenon in the politics of many African states.

Ethnically-based communal solidarity, as found at varying levels of political and social organization, is a potent and often feared force in Kenyan institutional and organizational development. In a formal way, the Government of Kenya avoids overt policies or actions which encourage ethnic rivalries. In this regard, the most widely debated policy of the country has been its refusal to consider a multi-party system. Both former President Kenyatta and President Moi have viewed multiple parties as ethnically divisive and politically destructive, leading to competition based on ethnic loyalties. At top national levels, the Kenyan leadership makes considerable effort to incorporate a broad cross-section of ethnic representation in ministerial positions.

National policy de-emphasizes ethnic loyalties. Political ethnic associations are forbidden, and ethnic loyalties in other organizations are discouraged. Public documents refer to provinces or regions rather than to ethnic groups although they may be virtually synonymous. Despite governmental policy, ethnic loyalties are strong, no doubt in part because of the regional or geographic identification which most ethnic groups retain.

An important undercurrent in Kenyan politics today is a shift in the ethnic basis of political power in the inner circle surrounding the Kenyan president. Under Kenyatta, the Kikuyus were highly influential. President Moi comes from a small tribe within the Kalenjen grouping. Those influential in the president's office reflect a shift away from perceived Kikuyu hegemony to Kenyans of a different ethnic origin.

The convergence of ethnic, regional, and/or district lines has important implications for politics and for community mobilization. For example, the ability of

Kikuyus located throughout the country to mobilize on behalf of local development (Harambee) projects within their home communities in Central Province is a reminder of the power of these ethnic ties. The Government, with its District Focus program of small grants to individual projects through District Development Committees, does not provide a counter-weight to the informal and largely ethnic channels such as the Murang'a Harambee Development Fund, a fund organized by and for Kikuyus from Murang'a District. Given that approximately four-fifths of Kenya's population is rural, that rural communities have distinct ethnic identities, and that ethnic ties are among the most effective means to raise development funds, the question of ethnicity in politics and community mobilization promises to be paramount for some time to come.

Class as a Catalyst for Community Mobilization

While ethnicity continues as a dominant influence, a new and potentially profound force — social class — is a growing factor in the Kenyan political economy. Perhaps the class in Kenya most easily identified is that of affluent, urban elites. Based in Nairobi and often solidly tied to strong positions in the government bureaucracy, these individuals continue to have deep roots in a village community where they are widely regarded as benefactors and "local success stories."

Of great importance is the connection between Kenya's class structure and land ownership. The well-entrenched elite families control not only much agricultural land but also the bureaucracy which shapes the policies affecting it. Large farms are likely to be in the hands of Members of Parliament, senior government administrators and other civil servants, senior police chiefs, KANU officials, current and former chiefs, members of the diplomatic corps, and executives of parastatals (Hunt, 1984:288). The Kenyan elite is specifically and directly tied to large scale and export agriculture, "maintaining relatively high export crop prices through their direct and indirect affiliation with the government" (Bradshaw, 1990:17). Their ways of assuring benefits are numerous, and they link the traditional source of wealth, land, with new forms of wealth based upon ties to foreign capital and emerging commerce and industry. A Member of Parliament may own a large coffee plantation in his rural constituency, have access to bank loans at favorable rates, and serve on government regulatory boards. He is also likely to have multiple investments in private businesses such as textiles, auto assembly, or pharmaceuticals, based on indigenous or foreign capital. He is not required to make public disclosures of his finances. This illustration suggests an intricate network of class-based elites with both rural and urban interests, drawing on domestic and foreign capital, and utilizing both the government's bureaucracy and patron-client linkages.

Along with these privileged economic and political positions go certain assumptions in terms of educational opportunity. There is an extremely narrow educational structure in Kenya with access to university education only for a small percentage of those who qualify. While the system is based on examinations impartially administered, the capacity to compete is developed from the early years of primary school. Access to excellent education — a prerogative of affluence — is an important aspect of class structure in Kenya today.

In spite of the increasing evidence of privilege and wealth, a basic question remains. Can subordinate, impoverished rural people mobilize around issues which would be defined as class issues? By far the majority of the poor, not only in Kenya but in all of Africa, are rural folk who tend to be unorganized and, at best, tied into political organization and mobilization through patron-client networks. Poor rural Kenyans activate whatever purchase they are able to gain on the more influential and prosperous members of their own community. Mobilization that has occurred so far, through the Harambee mechanism, has focused primarily on development needs and questions of access and social mobility, not on redressing injustices or seeking equity. The objective for most has been to gain a toehold in the system. The approach rural Kenyans perceive as most likely to be effective is improved education. Most rural communities have focused their efforts on increasing educational opportunity, primarily through building secondary schools. Thus, transforming the system has not been an objective; rather, most have cherished a hope of gaining access to the system. Since independence, educational opportunity, as a way to gain access, has been the single most important issue around which rural Kenyans have readily mobilized for change.

Class and Ethnicity: Conflict and Convergence

The elite Kenyan in recent years has embodied the convergence of class and ethnicity. Dominant in both spheres, he or she can work through both sets of linkages to maintain a position of strength within Kenyan society. For example, Members of Parliament are usually key patrons as well as members of the dominant ethnic group in the communities they represent. They are also likely to be well connected in the urban setting of Nairobi where they spend most of their time. Connections there may be both within and outside their own ethnic group.

The well-placed, affluent urban "patron" uses his social position well and provides a ladder to members of his own ethnic community, aiding them in a variety of ways from new jobs to permits, to contacts, while also maintaining strong ties with many of those in his own class who may or may not be of his ethnic group. There is, however, intra-ethnic rivalry as well as inter-ethnic rivalry. Clans, factions, schisms within ethnic groups do occur constantly. The levels of cohesion and fluidity vary according to the personalities, the issue and the situation.

The Kikuyus are Kenya's most numerous and most dominant ethnic group. Predominant during the Kenyatta years at high levels of government and economy, they were in a position to take advantage of government policies which strengthened the center. As the ethnic group best organized and most able to take advantage of the informal opportunities for development through Harambee, they have benefitted considerably. Kenyatta's death in 1978 led to a fundamental change in the regional, ethnic and economic basis of the Kenyan power structure. President Moi, whose support comes from a number of smaller ethnic groups to the West of the Rift Valley, has pursued a conscious policy of ethnic diversification. He has reduced Kikuyu influence in the high ranks of government, while at the same time solidifying his own sources of political support. Kikuyus continue to play a significant role in Kenya's economic and political structures, yet simultaneously, they feel they are being cut off from the critical sources of power, namely those surrounding the President.

Central Province, home to the Kikuyu, is the most affluent in Kenya, and, as a group, the Kikuyus are the most prosperous. Harambee contributions provide an indicator. Central Province raised its share of Harambee contributions from 30 percent of the total value contributed throughout Kenya in the mid-1970s to nearly half the value in the early 1980s (Thomas, 1985:207). Central Province's small farmers are major producers of two of Kenya's primary earners of foreign exchange, tea and coffee, and have been more fully integrated into the cash economy, reaping some of the benefits when prices are high. Thus, there is a basis for the fears some have expressed concerning the potential for Kikuyu hegemony. These fears exist despite the fact that within Central Province there are many smallholders and increasing numbers of people dependent upon wage labor.

Moreover, the Kikuyus have forged ahead with secondary education and have the highest rates of Form IV completion for both males and females in the country. There is a dearth of employment opportunities appealing to those who have completed this level of education. Frustrations are quickly generated when the hopes of parents are dashed and the efforts of young adults to enter the system prove futile. In such situations, alienation and disaffection can readily arise.

Overall, evidence suggests that there is a sharply increasing awareness of class differences in Kenya. In the context of a rapidly growing population and galloping unemployment, economic and social inequities may become Kenya's paramount issue. It is likely, however, that these perceptions would be accompanied by a complex overlay of ethnic loyalties. As noted, there is a close fit between region, administrative unit, and ethnic dominance. Large numbers of rural poor depend to some extent on the largesse of their wealthier kinsmen. Most probably, class issues, based on the need for opportunity, justice and equity for Kenya's poor, would be played out within a power structure shaped significantly by ethnicity.

Harambee: Community Mobilization, Urban Elites, and the Global Economy

Harabee is the Swahili term for "Let's pull together." Harambee self-help started as a means for community members to work collectively on small-scale projects such as schools, clinics, or cattle dips. Groups contributed cash, labor and materials, as well as management skills, to building and operating such facilities.

An outgrowth of traditional family and clan responsibilities, Harambee encourages a transfer of individual resources from the prosperous to the poor and from urbanites to rural residents. It provides a mechanism whereby some highly visible private wealth is put to public use in ways which are considered socially and ethically appropriate. Wealthy persons are supposed to distribute largesse, and Harambee provides a way to allow more than a few to benefit from the contributor's bounty while at the same time bringing a variety of returns to the donor. This obligation is intensified by ethnic and regional competition and loyalties, for one who prospers is expected to render some assistance, not only to family members, but to those of his own background who are less fortunate.

After independence, Harambee rapidly became an integral part of Kenya's electoral processes. Political candidates vied to assist with these projects; candidates based their campaigns on pledges to support Harambee schools and other facilities; and communities quickly learned how to manipulate this competition to their own advantage. Since 1978, when Daniel Arap Moi became President of Kenya, the term "Harambee" has been used more broadly to identify not only small-scale, local or district-level projects, but also efforts orchestrated by the center to support nation-wide development objectives, such as a national scholarship fund or a technical university.

Thus, as a form of community mobilization, Harambee has roots not only in family and clan responsibilities, but also in the independence struggle occurring in Kenya from the 1920s onward. Yet, it has evolved in a new wave over the past thirty years, reflecting the political system in which it is situated, the urban and elite sources of support on which it is partially dependent, and the characteristics of the international economy in which it is embedded. For political, economic, and social reasons, Harambee has been an important part of Kenya's development strategy. It is predicated on a philosophy of incremental change initiated by and shaped for grassroots communities. It is also based on principles of wealth-sharing and redistribution.

In recent years, the Government has moved to capture control over Harambee. This is no small task for there are vested interests in the Harambee system. In one way or another Harambee serves the interests of Government, local elites, national elites and poor rural households. The Government has sought control in several ways. First, through the decentralization of the planning and implementation process, the "District Focus," the Government has attempted to incorporate Harambee resource mobilization into the planning process. Its chief purpose has been to regulate the mix of capital costs and recurrent expenditures to control the sources of funds for each of these categories and to specify the relative contribution of state and local community. In part, this effort has been a response to Kenya's fiscal crisis and to policies of the IMF and World Bank which have put new pressures on the Government to regulate Harambee and to limit recurrent costs related to social services.

As a form of community mobilization and as a political phenomenon, Harambee has been characterized by the dispersal of power. Overall, it has constituted a minimal threat to those at the center of governance. In this context, self-help in Kenya must be viewed as politicized but powerless. At the local level it can provide effective grassroots development; at the national level, it does not jeopardize the status quo. However, even its local role may be diminishing as comparisons of Kenya's two most recent Development Plans suggest.

The Plan for 1984–88 specifies that cooperative effort through self-help will be encouraged and should be expanded during the Plan period (Government of Kenya, 1984:45). In a speech in 1985 President Moi stated, "Harambee is a basic Kenyan institution...and the cornerstone for local resources mobilization..." (Moi, 1985:1). This theme was echoed by the Minister for Finance and Planning who, in his Budget message, emphasized the theme of "mobilization of domestic resources for renewed growth" (*Weekly Review*, June 21, 1985:2).

The theme for the 1989–93 Plan is "Participation for Progress." The Plan mentions that the Harambee self-help movement is noted for its contribution to capital formation in the rural areas and notes that Harambee is "one of the concrete ways in which the theme of this Plan 'Participation for Progress' will be translated to positive action" (Government of Kenya, 1989:32). Harambee is lauded in terms of past accomplishments and in terms of its ideological significance. However, the Plan attaches no specifics to the Harambee contribution. One may infer that, at the present time, Harambee's development role is outweighed by its political significance. Harambee has always been important politically, but in the context of a more authoritarian state and increasing state-society tensions, the politics of Harambee take on new meaning.

Clientelist politics, imperfect and inequitable though the system may be, offer some checks and balances and some flexibility for processes of access to and distribution of resources. With the increasing power of KANU this flexibility has diminished; politics is a "top down" process with the players kept in line by the authority emanating from the high levels of the party. Clientelist politics, accompanied by the Harambee approach to development, distract the attention of rural citizens from fundamental changes which would benefit Kenyans more broadly — changes in tax laws, land ownership policies, pricing on agricultural commodities, or regulation of behavior of members of statutory boards.

Harambee broadens political participation and some forms of community mobilization, but it does so primarily within the context of inequitable relationships, reciprocity between unequals, and benefits and services to be rendered to individuals or to specific communities. Rural communities have welcomed the opportunity to "tap" the resources of the center in ways provided by Harambee efforts, and in many cases they have learned to do so with skill and acumen. Nevertheless, this system of mutuality between national leaders and local communities, while enhancing some forms of participation and aiding some communities does not alter fundamental power relationships within the political and economic systems.

Concluding Observations

To date in Kenya, locally-generated self-help through a clientelist political framework has been the primary method communities have employed to try to alter the distribution of goods, services, and opportunities and to try to diminish the inequities which characterize the nation. As an instrument for promoting development, Harambee has fostered an ad hoc approach directed toward "the squeakiest wheel." That is, those self-help groups and those communities which collect the most money and have the most articulate and well-connected leadership can command the most attention from outside donors, including the Central Government. Those who are best able to organize themselves can draw on the loyalties of their members who have prospered beyond the immediate locale.

Among other consequences, this process has sharpened the inter-elite conflicts and intra-elite linkages, as politicians and other leaders at all levels strive to shape coalitions which will benefit themselves and their communities. These elite linkages usually take the form of patron-client relationships with ethnic and regional foundations. In the rural areas ethnicity and geography overlap significantly. Reliance on community or ethnic connections for local development tends to strengthen these loyalties, building vertical connections and obscuring identification with others in a similar socio-economic stratum. This approach also tends to exacerbate differences between rich and poor localities, regions, and ethnic groups.

If economic conditions continue to deteriorate, as appears to be the case for many nations in Africa in mid-1990, and if hopes for increased prosperity dwindle, the paradigm for community mobilization is likely to change. Incremental change through Harambee is unlikely to appeal to growing numbers of frustrated rural and urban Form IV leavers who perceive little opportunity for themselves and observe great wealth at the top of a narrow pyramid within their social structure.

In the context of a deteriorating economy, the Government will probably foster Harambee self-help as a politically defusing mechanism, hoping to avoid political confrontations between dissatisfied rural communities and the Government. However, the options here seem to be declining. Elites, who have been contributing large sums to Harambee, face diminishing sources of largesse. For the urban middle class, employment pressures, inflation, shortage of goods and services, and the impact of various structural adjustment policies are certain to diminish their willingness to contribute to local development projects and to clarify their sense of grave injustice in a system in which a few are acquiring great wealth. Already pinched by numerous demands for their limited salaries, this group of middle management bureaucrats, secretaries, drivers, and office messengers is likely to find self-help contributions a heavy and unwelcome burden.

Most important, however, voices of courage, as well as anger and despair, descry the widening gap between rich and poor. As the Government closes off avenues for encompassing diversity, for constructive participation in the polity, and for assuring its own accountability, frustration is likely to grow and give voice to this despair. In this regard, linkages with the global political economy are complex. On the one hand, those linkages are oppressive in a variety of ways as noted above. On the other hand, through the international media, through the church with its international structure, and through organizations such as Amnesty International, they support the "staying power" of those who are trying to lead the

way toward a more democratic, just, and egalitarian Kenya. In fact, we may be seeing in Kenya the emergence of a clearly articulated ideological stance which will
mobilize Kenyans across most social categories. The visibility and support given to
this effort from beyond Kenya's boundaries is not unimportant.

REFERENCES

Bradshaw, York W. (1990). "Perpetuating Underdevelopment in Kenya: The Link between
Agriculture, Class and State," *African Studies Review*, 33, 1, April, 1–28.

Government of Kenya (1989). Development Plan 1989–1993. Nairobi: Government Printer.

Government of Kenya (1984). Development Plan 1984–1988. Nairobi: Government Printer.

Hunt, Diana (1984). *The Impending Crisis in Kenya*. Brookfield, Vermont: Gauer.

Thomas, Barbara P. (1985). *Politics, Participation, and Poverty, Development Through Self-Help
in Kenya*. Boulder, Colorado: Westview Press.

Weekly Review, The (1990). Issues between January, 1990 and July, 1990. Nairobi: The Weekly
Review, Ltd.

5.2 James W. Warhola

Religion and Ethnic Conflict in the Former Soviet Union

INTRODUCTION

*Like language, religion can be a major focus of group identity. (If you doubt it, read excerpt
10.4 on the new political leaders of Iran.). So controlling religious observance can have the
same effect as forcing everyone to speak the same language: it produces resentment and conflict among minority peoples.*

*In the former Soviet Union, several factors conspired to eliminate religious observance.
One was Marx's opposition to formal religion as an "opiate of the masses." Another was the
Soviet Union's desire, from the rule of Lenin onward, to find ways of unifying a large number
of socially, culturally, and economically diverse peoples in one nation. Related to this was the
belief, not unlike John Porter's (discussed earlier), that ethnic boundaries maintain inequality
and conflict, and reduce a nation's economic competitiveness.*

Warhola, James W. (1991). "The Religious Dimension of Ethnic Conflict in the Soviet Union," *International
Journal of Politics, Culture and Society*, 5(2), 249–270. Reprinted by permission of Human Sciences Press, Inc.

However, the members of Russia's religious groups saw the matter differently. Religion was central to their way of life. It was also a symbol of their personal autonomy: a right they were unwilling to have the state take away. They viewed the denial of religious liberty as an attempt to impose elite, atheistic views. As such, it was a symbol of political domination.

This concern with religious autonomy may not have caused the breakup of the USSR. Yet religious concerns rallied many people who were opposed to the Soviet agenda, whatever their reasons.

*E*thnologists and political scientists have long examined the connection between religious consciousness and ethnic/national consciousness. In the Soviet case the connection is particularly intriguing, given the regime's commitment until 1989 to the deepening secularization of society, and the related attempt to formulate a new, essentially "supranational" *Soviet* culture and national identity. By the time of the 24th Party Congress in 1971 the latter was ostensibly achieved in the form of a "new historical community [*obshchnost*]: the soviet people [*narod*]." By the time of the outbreaks of ethnic violence in 1986 and the Millennium celebrations of 1988 it was painfully clear that neither objective had been reached. If anything it appeared that the several generations of Soviet rule had only spawned an environment more hospitable to the spread of inter-ethnic conflict. The question is how did traditional religious attachments contribute to the perpetuation of ethnonationalist consciousness at the foundation of that conflict?

By the time of the outbreak of Soviet ethnonationalist violence under Gorbachev, virtually every form of nationalist assertiveness had some religious angle related directly or indirectly to it. This is not to say that religion was the primary motive force behind that assertiveness; in fact in virtually no case is there much evidence that it was. But the essentially corroborative tie must not be overlooked because of its somewhat disguised nature.

Religion has generally operated on at least two levels in helping give rise to ethnonationalist political demands. First, on a more superficial level, political issues dealing with religious topics began to surface during the Brezhnev years, but assumed much greater force with the onset of glasnost. These demands ranged from mere calls for relief from administrative and ideological harassment to calls for a qualitatively different relationship between religious bodies and state power. Significantly, by the end of 1989, nearly all of these demands were either met or forthcoming. This created a much different configuration of political power in Soviet society with respect to religion than had been the case since Lenin's decree on the separation of church and state in January 1918.

Yet there is a second, deeper level on which religious attachments shaped the character of politicized ethnonationalism. This is of greater long-term political significance, for it deals with more profound political and anthropological questions of communal identity and behavior. Religious attachments historically have often had the effect of helping to sustain national consciousness by providing a sense of *Gemeinschaft*, or community, that appears to touch human need at a deeper level than mere civil connections possibly could. Significantly, these preservative tendencies in religiosity appear to be especially strong under conditions of perceived mortal threat to the community in question.[1]

Under such conditions, demands emerging from the group against the (perceived) exterminators are not likely to be easily neutralized or even moderated. When national identity is tightly bound with religious attachment, perceived threats to the nation (e.g., per Russifying policies) have given rise, among other things, to a retreat into intensified religious identification. Although virtually impossible to prove conclusively, the perceived threat of extinction may be a critical dimension of heightened ethnonationalism in the USSR, in which the de facto Russifying pressures continued albeit under the ironic, disingenuous rubric of "internationalism."[2]

Curiously enough, however, a similar sense of threat arose among many ethnic Russians. Perceptions of being reduced to second-rate status appear to have fostered in part a resurgence of interest and adherence to Russian Orthodoxy. The core political problem is that these demands and counterdemands were ideologically quite illegitimate until Gorbachev's revision of how national relations were to be properly managed.

Underlying the entire political strategy was the insistence on "internationalist unity" among Soviet nationalities. Yet this may be exactly the point at which the religious element is most likely to come to the fore in ethnonational demands. That is, the point at which a nation's insistence — on the basis of essentially *religious* self-understandings — of its own identity is simply incompatible with official Soviet requirements.

The Shift in Soviet Attitudes Towards Religion

The open vitality of religion in the USSR even after 70 years of episodic suppression suggests that the very efforts to eliminate religion from Soviet society have unwittingly played a part in creating the conditions for the magnitude of ethnonationalism confronting the Gorbachev regime.[3] What evidence supports this?

Several points are worth noting. First, the suppression of religion in the USSR dates from Lenin's Decree on Separation of Church from the State and Schools (January 1918), almost immediately after the Bolshevik seizure of power. In this respect the unprecedented length of the suppression appears endemic to Soviet rule, not a mere Stalinist perversion of socialism. It is instructive that Khrushchev's virulent anti-religion campaign of 1959–64 was not infrequently justified as a return to Leninism. The point was surely not lost on those more recently expressing interest in Orthodoxy as a palliative for the failed ideology.

Second, the recent relief from political suppression appears to have come in two general stages: (1) Gorbachev's calls for cessation of administrative harassment of religion by late 1987, reversing his earlier position, and (2) a virtual sea change in political posture regarding religion nearly across-the-board (that is, both territorially and confessionally) by late 1988.

In fact a fundamental shift occurred in the Kremlin's official orientation toward religion leading up to and subsequent to the Millennium celebrations of summer 1988.

The historical magnitude of the shift is underscored by viewing the Soviet dilemma from the perspective of Robertson's scheme reflecting the large-scale range of possible orientations of government toward religion in the modern era (e.g., after the French Revolution):

(a) conventional religion redundant, new secular religion necessary

(b) conventional religion disruptive, secular rationality necessary

(c) conventional religion redundant, but elemental aspects necessary

(d) conventional religion partially constructive in the making of the modern world, consciousness of appropriate forms of religion necessary.[4]

Within this framework, the official Soviet orientation was option (a) or perhaps (b) depending on one's precise definition of "secular religion." But then the official Soviet position definitely shifted toward the other end of the spectrum, and perhaps into (d). From the perspective of religious liberties this shift may be a welcome change. Yet the *political* fallout from the shift may represent the very core of the ethnic challenge in the USSR.

"Nation-Building" and Religious Consciousness

The modern state itself has sometimes been directly responsible for the formation or sustenance of national identity. Since the early modern era (roughly traceable to the European Renaissance and Protestant Reformation), two broad historical patterns may be noted. First, the state itself acts rather self-consciously as an instrument of forming or buttressing national consciousness, for its own purposes. The modern Leviathan, not accidentally, is called the *nation-state*, purportedly reflecting a congruence of the cultural and political realms.[5] Although the global system of nation-states came to represent the basic framework in world politics by the postcolonial, post WWII era, the fact is that few if any *states* presided over one *nation* in any significant ethnographic sense.

As the 21st century approaches, this ethno-political incongruity shows no signs of diminishing in presence or abating in significance. The evidence points rather to the perdurability of ethnic identity, and to the continuing, if not deepening, relevance of religion in the political realm. With respect to ethnic consciousness, this may be viewed as a personal, existential response to the incongruity of culture and politics, in Gellner's sense of culture. One result of this incongruity appears to be a modern crisis of identity both at the level of Durkheim's "collective consciousness" — modernization qua secularization — and at the level of Jung's "collective unconscious" — the modern nation-state as a destroyer of communal identity in the name of "nation-building" and an ethnically artificial nationalism.[6]

Second, and at least equally problematic, the modern Leviathan essentially presents itself as having a legitimate claim on virtually all public activity within its realm, including religion. The problem is that religion very often is found at or near the very core of national and particularly ethnic identity.

In terms of ethnic identity and religious consciousness, political modernization laid the foundation for a rather artificial divorce between religious consciousness and ethno-civic attachments. The nature of this divorce is becoming more evident as ethnic assertiveness *against central states* perceived as politically illegitimate often finds itself linked with religious sentiment to some degree. It is thus hardly surprising that the current so-called "Islamic revival" appears more a reaction against Western conceptions of the state and the legitimate scope of formal state authority as it is against modernization of society in an economic or technological sense.

With the modern state's arrogation of authority over all dimensions of life, including religion, it is not surprising that *popular expectations* of the state have risen correspondingly. In the late modern era, states' failure to live up to popular expectations often engenders a renewal of nationalism or ethnic sentiment, depending on the group in question. In this sense it is not surprising that such throwbacks to ethnonational roots often involve either a return to religious roots or to a buttressing of the religion-ethnicity nexus.

The etymological roots of the English word "religion" hint at its significance in this regard: "re-ligia," or the "thing that binds a community together." The psychological significance of this is enormous, in light of recent research into the frequent failings of the modern state to live up to implicit or explicit popular expectations placed upon it. Although this pattern is more closely associated with political life in the Third World, the approach is particularly useful for understanding the religion-ethnicity nexus in the USSR. Specifically, Migdal's concept of the "duality" of many states in the third world applies precisely to this aspect of Soviet political life: "unmistakable strengths in penetrating societies and their surprising weakness in effecting goal-oriented social changes."[7] Clearly the strength of the Soviet state in maintaining itself in power exceeded the longstanding aspiration of fostering a religion-free society. Yet the reasons for that inability to ferret out religion go much deeper than a "weak state," and touch on the roots of the human impulse toward religiosity.

Conclusions

In the Soviet case, we see two broad patterns historically having operated at cross purposes with each other: the attempt at forced secularization of Soviet society, and a variety of measures taken to sustain national identity. Ironically, the measures to sustain national identity were to operate within the context of a long-range "internationalist" historical goal of fostering a supra-national "Soviet" identity. By the late 1980s both goals — secularization and internationalism — simply shipwrecked. The forced secularization had a variety of effects, including a reactive religiosity among broad sectors of the population; a particular strength of this reaction where Moscow would have *least* liked to have seen it (among Russian nationalists and in traditionally Moslem areas); and a powerful contribution to the popular indifference to the formerly official ideology.

And what of Soviet "internationalism?" The concept of "internal colonization" used to explain nationalist sentiment elsewhere appears particularly applicable to the USSR. Soviet rule over minority areas, as the Czarist precursor, can hardly be called anything less. At least one observer has noted "growing sentiment in Central Asia that they have been so colonized."[8] The pattern of traditional Soviet (pre-Gorbachev) measures designed to sustain national identity, albeit within the contexts of "the new historical community," "Soviet patriotism," and perhaps worst of all — "proletarian internationalism" — have in fact worked in tandem with the religion-via-forced secularization phenomenon to produce the depth of ethnonationalist sentiment and conflict confronting Moscow.

ENDNOTES

[1] Anthony Smith's, *The Ethnic Origins of Nations,* and particularly chapter 5, deals extensively with this question.

[2] van Dzuba, *Internationalism or Russification?* London: Weidenfeld and Nicolson, 1968.

[3] James W. Warhola, "Religion and Modernization in Gorbachev's USSR," in *Religious Challenge to the State,* Matthew C. Moen and Lowell Gustafson, eds., Temple University Press, forthcoming. Volume 11, no. 1, Winter 1990/91: 40–1.

[4] Roland Robertson, "Classical Sociological Perspectives on Religion and Revolution," in *Religion, Rebellion, Revolution,* Bruce Lincoln, editor; NY: St. Martin's Press, 1985:240–1.

[5] Ernest Gellner, *Nations and Nationalism.* Ithaca: Cornell University Press, 1983.

[6] Susan Greenwood's concept of "transpersonal religion" may be particularly helpful in clarifying the issue of how religion as a "collective consciousness" may politically augment a "collective unconscious" in the form of energized ethnic identity. See "Emile Durkheim and C. G. Jung: Structuring a Transpersonal Sociology of Religion," *Journal for the Scientific Study of Religion,* Volume 29, no. 4, Winter 1990: 482–95.

[7] Joel Migdal, *Strong Societies and Weak States: State-Society Relations in the Third World.* Princeton University Press, 1988, p. 9.

[8] Yaacov Ro'i, "The Islamic Influence on Nationalism in Soviet Central Asia," *Problems of Communism,* July-August 1990, xxxix:4, p. 57.

5.3 S. S. Sharma

The Interaction Between Castes in an Indian Village

INTRODUCTION

In India, different caste groups lead different lives. The status differences between these groups are age-old and protected by religion. (On a similar theme, see excerpt 11.2 on delegitimizing ideologies and ethnocentrism.)

The most extreme form of difference, "untouchability," prohibits contact with the caste-less harijan for fear of pollution and loss of karma. India's "untouchable" harijan perform the lowliest, most menial work. They are India's street sweepers and toilet cleaners, and although India depends on their labour, untouchables are people without any standing in Indian society. They do not even have proper names.

Since the coming of Independence, Indian governments have tried to eliminate this kind of extreme, historic inequality. Yet the next excerpt, by Sharma, shows that today the practice of untouchability persists even though it is illegal. Higher-caste Hindus have largely accepted contact with the harijan in public places. Public interaction in the markets and temples, where untouchables roam freely, allows them to claim to have stopped practising untouchability. Yet the higher-caste Hindus continue to practice untouchability in their private lives.

In many parts of India, untouchability is a sensitive topic that is even hard to study. What is certain is that the harijan want more interaction with, and less social distance from, high-caste Brahmins. So far, this sentiment is not reciprocated.

An attempt is made in this paper to identify the pattern of interaction between the upper caste and the "untouchables" or the scheduled castes. The present study proposes to use an interactional approach for exploring the existing relations. The assumption is that so long as the upper castes feel polluted by a bodily contact of the scheduled caste, the scheduled castes are in effect "untouchables."

Since it is an exploratory study, 30 heads of households of each of the castes, Brahmin and scheduled castes, were interviewed. The respondents were selected on the basis of their preparedness to grant interviews. This became necessary, because it is too sensitive an area of enquiry in the village. Of the respondents,

Sharma, S. S. (1986). "Untouchability, a Myth or a Reality: A Study of Interaction Between Scheduled Castes and Brahmins in a Western U.P. Village," *Sociological Bulletin*, 35(1), March, 68–79.

however, 4 scheduled castes and 3 Brahmins refused to answer one question; 2 scheduled castes declined at another stage and three Brahmins and two scheduled castes dropped out at the last stage of the survey. The Brahmin caste was selected on the basis of the researcher's own experience as a rural Brahmin. A schedule of 10 questions was prepared. The questions were explained to the respondents so that reliable information might be obtained. The systematic information was supplemented by asking the respondents to narrate the most remarkable events of untouchability which they experienced in their life. The field work done during June, July and August 1984 was conducted in Machhra Village.

The Village

Machhra is about 20 km from Meerut on the Meerut-Lucknow Road. It is a multi-caste village with a population of about 2587 voters. The Tyagi caste is numerically at the top, being 22.24 percent The others are Brahmins 20.1 percent, the scheduled castes 19.13 percent, Muslims 9.8 percent, Balmiki 4.1 percent, Nai 3.1 percent, Gujars 2.94 percent, Saini 2.82 percent, Potter 2.5 percent, Badhai 2.4 percent, Khatik 2 percent, Sikkigar 1.58 percent, Bania 1.28 percent, Jogi 1.2 percent, Sunar 0.92 percent, Dhinwar 0.93 percent, Chhipi 0.66 percent. The Tyagis, the Brahmins and the Gujars are land-owners and cultivators. This village has provided an M.L.A. from among the Brahmins to the preceding U.P. Legislative Assembly. The village is irrigated and electrified.

The Economy

The whole life of the village depends on land. The main feature of landed property in the rural setting is that it is unequally distributed. Landownership has been the privilege of higher castes, barring a few exceptions of Harijans. This village is not typical in this sense. The survey of 30 families of Brahmin caste revealed that on average a Brahmin household holds 30 bighas of land and its range varies from 10–80 bighas. On the other hand, scheduled caste households own eight bighas of land on average and the range varies between five and 14 bighas. Every one of the scheduled castes is either an agricultural labourer or an unskilled mason, or a rope-maker or a cot-weaver. His earnings are insufficient by any criterion. He lives in unhygienic conditions with inadequate accommodation.

This village has educational facilities from elementary to graduate level. Among the schedule caste respondents, about half (13) are illiterate, almost the same (12) have primary education and only one-tenth have gone up to Junior High School. Of the 28 Brahmin respondents about one-fifth (6) are illiterate, 12 are primary, five are Junior High School, three are High School, one is B.A. and one is M.A.

The Brahmins and scheduled castes differ in respect of employment of educated boys, also. The former have 21 such cases. It is significant that one-third could get jobs after completing High School, nine after Intermediate, two after B.Sc. and three after Post-Graduation. In case of the latter, the situation is by and large the same. In all, 5 could get a job and among them 3 after Intermediate, one after Graduation and one after Post-Graduation. In the families under study, 17 educated Brahmin boys have settled in agriculture. Such families have sufficient land to absorb the younger generation in agriculture. Only three have been reported as educated unemployed. One has qualified for the Intermediate, another has failed at the Graduate level and the third possesses a professional degree in teaching. The situation is worse in the case of the educated scheduled caste boys. There are 12 cases who have left education. They are selling their physical labour in the village and report themselves as unemployed. In general, scheduled caste boys finish their education at High School level or below and only a few continue beyond.

Untouchability

Information was obtained from the respondents along two lines: First, by studying a few cases according to case study method; second, by posing specific questions related to the context in which the respondents feel untouchability is observed viz. social, political, and economic.

Case I:

A scheduled caste Sub-Inspector of Police while on duty had to stay for a night with the Pradhan in a village in U.P. The Pradhan sent one of his sons to the local scheduled caste family to bring utensils to be used at dinner for the Sub-Inspector, who somehow, came to know of it and instantly refused to take dinner at the Pradhan's house and insisted on having it at the scheduled castes's house from which the utensils were brought.

Comments: Vertical occupational mobility is not a ladder for vertical social mobility.

Case II:

The same scheduled caste Sub-Inspector of Police happened to be deputed as Security Officer in an Industrial Organization in Rajasthan. He along with his colleagues was served tea by a tea-stall boy. When one of them came to know that the tea-stall boy was a scheduled caste, all of them were annoyed and asked the owner of the shop not to keep the boy at his shop. The Sub-Inspector introduced himself as Chaudhry and thus could get acceptance in the High Caste group.

Comments: The urban setting is not quite different from the rural one with respect to observing untouchability.

Case III:

The same scheduled caste Sub-Inspector of Police got admitted to a Sanitorium at Bhowali in District Nainital. One of the Muslim employees there somehow, came to know his caste. The Muslim employee advised him to conceal the caste otherwise he would be deprived of facilities and services of the staff. He pretended to be a Jat and thus could adjust to the situation.

Comments: It is not true that untouchability has been removed from public places.

Case IV:

At the instance of one Tyagi leader from among the most respected and influential traditional elite caste, a scheduled caste in the village happened to invite a few Brahmins and Tyagis to a feast. The Tyagi who was an enthusiastic social reformer advised the scheduled caste host to serve dishes to the Brahmin and Tyagi guests. The Brahmins as well as the Tyagis, but for the Tyagi social reformer, left the feast untouched.

Comments: Untouchability is a reality. Food is considered to become polluted the moment it is touched by the hand of a scheduled caste.

Case V:

In October, a cultural activity called "Rama Lila" is celebrated in the form of a drama depicting the fight between Rama the symbol of God and Ravana the Demon King. It is strictly prohibited on the grounds of purity to allocate the role of Rama to a scheduled caste boy. However, one educated scheduled caste boy was accepted as a member of the Organizing committee of the Drama Club.

Comments: God is considered to become polluted even when he is impersonated by the scheduled caste.

Deprivations

An attempt was made to identify the nature of deprivation felt by the scheduled castes in this village. To make the observations precise and specific, a few items indicating social, economic and political deprivations were projected in the interview.

With regard to public places, it was reported by the scheduled castes that they do not dare enter the temple. It was observed that the Brahmins too are not regular in visiting the temple, nor do they perform many rituals. Many do not even wear the sacred thread. The scheduled castes feel their entry into the temple is not by itself a sufficient indicator of their being accepted by the Brahmins.

With regard to private places, the general impression of the Brahmins of this village is that their women folk are more conservative than the men. The women work as a constraining counter force on males in bringing about any social change with regard to untouchability in private life and after much conflict and altercation between the men folk and the women folk, the women prevail.

With regard to political affairs which fall under public dealings, neither caste observed any untouchability. Politics, it was reported, encouraged a closer contact between the two castes and members of both castes were satisfied with this state of affairs.

To explore the intensity of social interaction on the part each caste, a question was raised: "Are you interested in having social interaction with each other?" The four alternative responses were mentioned as "most," "more," "less," "least." The responses "most" and "more" have been taken as an indicator of "active" and "less" and "least" of passive extent. The results are shown in Table 1.

The difference between the responses of scheduled castes and Brahmins is so great that the hypotheses of equal intensity of interaction are rejected. Scheduled castes are actively interested in interaction with Brahmins, whereas Brahmins are passive in this regard.

There is sufficient qualitative evidence to indicate there is acceptance of scheduled castes more in public than in private places. Brahmins and scheduled castes were asked: "In which situation do the scheduled castes and Brahmins insist on acceptance?" The former in our study is denoted by refusal to scheduled castes to enter into temples and the latter is denoted by denying scheduled castes permission to enter the inner part of the house and to take meals on a common table. The responses are given in Table 2.

The difference between the responses of scheduled castes and Brahmins is very high. Brahmins insist on accepting scheduled castes in public places whereas the scheduled castes insist on being accepted in private places.

A closed question was put to identify the reasons for non-acceptance of the scheduled castes as viewed by the Brahmins and scheduled castes themselves. The earlier studies have suggested ideological and material reasons. The indicators of ideological reasons were, for the purpose of this study, the theory of Karma and nature of food, and of material reasons were poverty and lack of possessions. A choice between ideological and material and undecided reasons was given in the responses. The responses are presented in Table 3.

TABLE 1   DESIRED INTENSITY OF INTERACTION AMONG BRAHMINS AND SCHEDULED CASTES

Caste	Desired Intensity of Interaction		
	Active	Passive	Total
Scheduled Castes	15	11	26
Brahmins	10	17	27

TABLE 2   ACCEPTANCE OF SCHEDULED CASTES IN PUBLIC AND PRIVATE PLACES

Caste	Acceptance of Scheduled Castes			
	Public	Accepted in Private	Both	Total
Brahmins	22	1	7	30
Scheduled Castes	7	16	5	28
Total	29	17	12	58

TABLE 3   REASON FOR NON-ACCEPTANCE OF SCHEDULED CASTES

	Reason For Non-Acceptance			
	Ideological	Material	Undecided	Total
Brahmins	19	5	3	27
Scheduled Castes	9	18	1	28
Total	28	23	4	55

The discrepancy between the responses is highly significant. Brahmins consider ideological reasons for non-acceptance of scheduled castes, whereas the scheduled castes consider material conditions responsible for non-acceptance of themselves by the Brahmins.

Conclusions

In this study, an attempt was made to enquire into the pattern of interaction between scheduled castes and Brahmins in Machhra village. The study confirmed that untouchability is observed by Brahmins in social life, whereas it is not in political aspects. Perhaps the social is the core and the political is the periphery for both castes. Contrary to the widely held belief that occupational mobility may lead to upward social mobility, the study indicates that an educated scheduled caste with an achieved status of police official was not considered as touchable by the higher castes even in a public place like a hospital. Ascription takes precedence over achievement. The scheduled castes insist on being socially accepted in private places. The Brahmins prohibit them from doing so but concede their free entry into public places. The reasons are obvious in that the Brahmins do not make their daily prayers in the temple of the village and those who do so have started to have mini temples in their residences. Thus it should not be interpreted as a substantial change. Lastly, the Brahmins and scheduled castes are diametrically opposed to each other with respect to reasons for untouchability. Ideology is the basis of untouchability according to Brahmins and material conditions are vital according to the scheduled castes.

5.4 Jeffrey G. Reitz

Racial Discrimination in Canada and Britain

INTRODUCTION

Canadians pride themselves on having avoided large-scale race riots of the kind that have oc-curred in the United States, Britain, and other countries This success, along with the coun-try's formal commitment to multiculturalism, has led many Canadians to assume there is no "race problem" in Canada.

But the next excerpt, by Jeffrey Reitz, draws a different conclusion. It argues that, in fact, there is a race problem in Canada that is no different, and no less, than what exists in Britain. This is proven by identical results obtained in job discrimination research done in the two countries; the data argue that there is no less discrimination against black people in Canada than there is in the United Kingdom.

Reitz says that we may be sitting on a racial time-bomb. He cites four particular factors which are controlling the outbreak of racial conflict today, but may disappear in the future, leaving Canada to play out Britain's earlier racial conflicts. We may be facing the creation of a black underclass of the kind described in excerpt 4.4 by Wilson.

What should we do if Reitz is right? At the very least, we should stop being smug and com-placent. We also need to take steps to overcome racial discrimination in the workplace and else-where; this may avert the disaster Reitz is projecting. And even if Reitz is wrong, the country has lost nothing by opposing racism: it has simply made good on the promise of multiculturalism.

Credible comparative evidence on racial discrimination in Canada compared to Britain or the United States is sparse, but the evidence that exists runs counter to the usual assumption of less discrimination in Canada. Our interest here is specifically in discriminatory behaviour, that is to say, the denial of access to jobs and other significant resources in society, solely on the basis of race.

Comparative Evidence on Racial Discrimination: Britain vs. Canada

Generally, in Britain, racial minorities are less well off than they are in Canada. West Indian men in Britain are substantially less well-educated than whites, have lower occupational status, earn less when employed full time, and have almost

Reitz, Jeffrey G. (1988). "Less Racial Discrimination in Canada, or Simply Less Racial Conflict? Implications of Comparisons with Britain," *Canadian Public Policy/Analyse de Politiques*, XIV(4), 424–441. Reprinted by permission.

double the white unemployment rates. In Canada, West Indian men have comparatively high levels of education in relation to other groups. While their incomes are lower than the incomes of whites, their unemployment rates are only marginally higher than white unemployment rates. Thus West Indian men in Canada experience less economic disadvantage compared to West Indian men in Britain. In Britain, Asians, mainly Indians and Pakistanis, are relatively better situated than are West Indians, but so are Asians in Canada, including many Chinese and Indo-Chinese as well as Indo-Pakistanis.

The higher status for Canadian racial minorities does not necessarily reflect less discrimination. Higher status is expected because occupationally-selective Canadian immigration policies have brought more highly educated and employable immigrants to Canada, and because the buoyant Canadian economy provides opportunities for minorities, insulating them from the "last hired, first fired" syndrome.

Actual racial discrimination in employment in Britain and Canada can be compared in data gathered from experimental field trials. In Toronto, such discrimination field trials were conducted by the Social Planning Council (SPC) of Metropolitan Toronto. Because these studies were modelled closely on similar British studies in London and Birmingham (McIntosh and Smith, 1974), results can be directly compared.

The field trials, including telephone applications by actors with varying accents, and walk-in applications by black and white actors presenting comparable qualifications, produced remarkably similar results in the two countries. (See Table 1.) In both studies, whites more often received positive responses to telephone applications than did non-whites. (See panel A.) In Toronto, whites received positive responses in 86.9 percent of applications, whereas non-whites received positive responses in only 60.1 percent of applications, a difference of 26.8 percent.[1] In London and Birmingham, the corresponding percentages were 89.3 percent for whites and 73.9 percent for non-whites, a difference of 15.4 percent. These data do not support the hypothesis of less discrimination in Canada. In actual in-person job offers, whites in both countries had about a three-to-one advantage over non-whites.[2]

In other words, the data show the measured extent of direct racial discrimination in employment in Toronto is not less than its extent in London and Birmingham.

A follow-up SPC employer survey showed how little Toronto employers are aware of discrimination or other race-related problems within their organizations (Billingsley and Muszynski, 1985). Employers oppose government intervention in hiring decisions. These results, too, correspond closely to British findings (Carby and Thakur, 1977), and suggest that in both countries, major voluntary changes in employer behaviour will not occur soon.

Some comparative evidence relevant to racial discrimination in housing is also available. According to demographic analyses, residential concentration of racial minorities in Britain in the first years following their settlement was not

TABLE 1 COMPARISON OF EMPLOYMENT DISCRIMINATION FIELD
TESTS: BRITAIN, 1974; CANADA, 1985

	Canada[1] (Toronto)			Britain[2] (London, Birmingham)		
A. Telephone application results						
	Percent positive	Percent negative	(N)	Percent positive	Percent negative	(N)
White	86.9	13.1	(237)	89.3	10.7	(84)
Non-white	60.1	39.9	(474)	73.9	26.1	(69)
B. In-person application results						
	Number	Percent[3]			Number	Percent
White offer	27	75.0			23	71.8
Both offer	10	–			49	–
Non-white offer	9	25.0			9[4]	28.1
No offer	155	–			52	–
Total	201	100.0			133	100.0

[1]Source: Henry and Ginzberg (1985:27); study included newspaper advertised non-skilled jobs both white collar and blue collar; West Indian workers only.
[2]Source: McIntosh and Smith (1974:41-42); study included industrial non-skilled jobs only; West Indian and Asian blue collar workers only.
[3]Percentages are calculated based on cases in which jobs were offered to either a white or a non-white, but not to both.
[4]In the British study, it was noted that several of these jobs offered to non-whites were very low paying; the authors excluded them from some of the results they reported. In the Canadian study, no data on pay were provided.

significantly greater than current patterns in Canadian cities. Studies in Britain by Collison (1967:281) and Peach (1982:36) found that indexes of residential racial dissimilarity (the proportion of racial groups who would have to move to bring about a similar distribution across all groups) were between 0.3 and 0.6 in the 1960s. For Canadian cities, Balakrishnan and Kralt (1987:143–54) found index values between 0.4 and 0.6 in 1981. Residential concentrations evidently were comparable at comparable stages in the development of racial minority communities in the two countries.

Social Factors Moderating Racial Conflict

The extent of overt racial conflict in Canada is quite plainly less than in Britain. In the British inner cities of London, Birmingham, Liverpool, and Bristol, hostility and violence have become the norm in relations between young, unemployed blacks and the police. In Canada, chronic violence is not nearly as visible a part of race relations. Furthermore, in Canada there is far less controversy about the status of minorities.

The favorable tone of racial politics in Canada is expressed in positive ways, too. Canadian policy-makers now repudiate past instances of racial bias, such as the incarceration of Japanese-Canadians during World War II.

There is no contradiction between the observation that racial conflict is less in Canada, and the evidence presented above that racial discrimination is not less. By racial conflict, I refer here primarily to minority group responses to discrimination and inequality: the extent to which discrimination is perceived, the extent to which it is thought to be unjust, and the extent to which it becomes the focus of social and political resistance.

What conditions may be operating to moderate racial conflict in Canada, independent of levels of racial discrimination? The following discussion will identify four specific factors, which seem to account for lack of racial conflict in Canada compared to Britain. These are: 1) the generational composition of racial minorities, 2) the economic status and position of racial minorities in relation to overall economic trends, 3) the structure of immigration institutions, and 4) multi-ethnic political structures and culture.

Generational Composition of Racial Minorities

The emergence of a native-born generation within immigrant groups has been crucial to the development of race politics in Britain. British-born blacks have a distinctive social experience, different from the immigrant experience. They often lack the clear economic niche of the immigrant generation, they have no return-migration option, their expectation for equality is greatly increased, and they have an increased identification with minority communities within the country. Increased racial conflict has resulted. Rex and Tomlinson (1979:212), in their study of racial minorities in Birmingham, were "very struck by the gap between the attitudes expressed by the parents on the one hand (which ... were relatively conservative and complacent), and those expressed by young people ... on the other.... Our data showed increasing militancy amongst this group."

In Canada, most racial minority group members are recent immigrants, and a major generational transition lies in the near future. Whereas in Britain, 43 percent of racial minority group members are British-born, in Canada only 23 percent are Canadian-born.

The British experience suggests that existing inequalities will be less acceptable to the large new Canadian-born generation, and will provoke a significantly stronger political reaction than we have seen from the immigrant generation.

However, the generational transition will not necessarily have the same outcome in Canada as in Britain. Racial tensions in Britain were greater than in Canada even when immigrants predominated in minority communities. There are other factors which may serve to moderate racial conflict in Canada.

Socio-economic Position of Racial Minorities

As was mentioned above, racial minorities in Canada have higher entrance status than racial minorities in Britain. It is likely that the greater economic integration of racial minorities in Canada will produce lower potentials for conflict because higher status increases the sense of having a stake in society.

In the short term, any British-Canadian differences in levels of conflict resulting from higher entrance status in Canada probably will be small. In the first years following immigration, immigrants to both countries have jobs more or less as expected. West Indian, East Indian and Pakistani immigrants to Britain in the 1950s and 1960s settled in traditional industrial areas of London and the Midlands (Peach, 1966; 1967; 1968), so initially, unemployment rates were extremely low. Likewise in Canada, the racial minority population has settled mainly in the affluent cities of Toronto and Vancouver, and to a lesser extent in Montreal, cities of southern Ontario and the West.

Concentration of minorities in affluent regions helps to insulate them from the impact of recessions, despite racial discrimination. As time passes, however, racial minority groups cannot remain immune to impacts of economic trends. In a buoyant economy, expansion creates opportunities for minorities; in an economic downturn, privileged groups close ranks, carefully guarding their own interests against those of newcomers.

In Britain, the industries initially most attractive to immigrants were textiles and heavy manufacturing, and immigration boosted local economies (cf. Cohen and Jenner, 1968). These industries were precisely those most hard hit by the new international competition, and by the economic downturn in that country. The lower educational levels of the earliest immigrants to Britain reduced their capacity to adapt to changing economic circumstances.

For Canada the important economic trends lie in the future. No one knows what impact the current national and international economic restructuring will have on particular industries in which racial minorities are concentrated.

The Immigration and Citizenship Issue[3]

Historical British-Canadian differences in immigration and citizenship policy appear to have affected the levels of racial conflict in the two societies, again for reasons having little to do with predispositions toward racial tolerance. In Britain, controversy over immigration control and the creation of British citizenship clearly aggravated domestic race relations. Canada's immigration and citizenship policies, comparatively speaking, have enjoyed a political consensus.

The British immigration policy in place after World War II was, for Commonwealth members, essentially an open door. The policy, which provided for free movement within the UK, colonies, and independent Commonwealth, was defended as a cornerstone of non-racist international relations.

A changing world economic order in the post-war period resulted in unexpected numbers of black immigrants moving to Britain, and the open-door policy came under severe attack domestically. Because immigrants were being accepted as a Commonwealth obligation, with no controls over numbers or qualifications, they came to be perceived as a welfare problem with an open-ended price tag. The open-door policy was quickly abandoned by both parties. A series of highly controversial immigration and citizenship acts were passed, instituting skill-based selection criteria and a kind of retroactive citizenship status governing residence rights in Britain. Racial motivations behind these policies were clear. These events negatively affected the entire atmosphere of race relations in Britain.

Canada's immigration policy reflects its world-system location, which was different from that of Britain. Canada formulated a nation-building immigration policy directed at national social and economic goals (Hawkins, 1972; Parai, 1975). Toward such ends, Canada admitted immigrants selectively, based on social and economic needs, or "absorptive capacity." In the 1960s, in moves to end racial discrimination in immigration policy, geographic selection criteria were abolished, and economic and occupational selection criteria were formalized in a point system. While skill-graded selection criteria may have reduced the number of racial minority third world immigrants, this was never considered a racially-motivated policy because the legitimacy of selection criteria was well-established (cf. Kalbach and McVey, 1979).

The elimination of geographical selection rules produced, in the late 1960s and early 1970s, a shift in ethnic composition of immigration to those of predominantly non-European origins, and an increase in total immigration. An immigration "Green Paper" (Department of Manpower and Immigraton, 1974) was debated, and a new Immigration Act in 1976 empowered Parliament to set annual immigration targets. Total immigration declined to about 100,000 per year. Hong Kong and other Southeast Asian countries became more significant as source countries. In Canada there is popular confidence that immigration serves economic expansion, and this perception dampens controversy.

Canada's broad but selective program of immigration may have had other effects in reducing racial conflict. For one, Canada's policy has affected the higher socio-economic status of racial minorities in Canada. The potential effects of this in reducing racial conflict were outlined earlier. Canada's broader policy, which encourages immigration from all sources, probably also has increased the diversity of cultural origins among the racial minorities in Canada compared to Britain.[4] Ethnic boundaries among racial minorities impede group formation, including the formation of potential conflict groups. Rather than forming political alliances, diverse immigrant groups tend to remain distant from each other.

This factor could operate to reduce racial conflict in Canada compared to Britain, though its force would attenuate as homeland attachments fade over time and through generations.

Multiculturalism, Bilingualism, and Race

Canada's ethnic and linguistic diversity is the feature most often cited as a source of greater racial tolerance. It may, however, be much more important as a force deflecting minority group responses to inequality, thus moderating racial conflict.

Multicultural advisory structures in government are far more developed in Canada than in Britain, but such structures are concerned with cultural status, and not with economic status. Survey data show equity issues are relatively more important to disadvantaged ethnic groups including racial minorities (cf. Reitz, 1980:381).

Advisory structures specifically devoted to race issues are emerging mostly at the municipal level. These structures appear to have been responsible for more significant accomplishments in Britain than in Canada, at least in terms of promoting employment equity within municipal government itself (cf. Ouseley, 1981; 1984). They have had little independent clout, however, and have been ineffective in producing broader changes. Katznelson (1973) showed that race advisory groups, in Britain and the U.S., co-opt minority leaders, and marginalize racial politics. In the long run, co-optation reduces conflict, not inequality.

In the field of equal rights legislation Canada had a headstart over Britain, because of Canada's longer multicultural history. However, such legislation, while important and necessary, is unlikely to produce fundamental change in either country. The procedures are complaint-driven, individually-initiated, and conciliation-oriented. They cannot be used to initiate investigations of entrenched inequities affecting entire groups. Thus, they may make a greater contribution to the avoidance of racial conflict by providing a political safety valve, than to the reduction of underlying inequality. Smith (1977) showed perceptions of discrimination within minority communities in Britain declined following the passage of the first Race Relations Act, while actual discrimination did not decline.

The bilingual structure of Canadian society impedes the formation of a common political consciousness among racial minorities. Immigrants to Canada include both Anglophones and Francophones. Efforts to mobilize racial groups are impeded by the linguistic boundary. As time passes, the effect of this factor could increase, as each linguistic minority integrates within its respective linguistic majority.

Summary

This discussion has examined evidence that the degree of racial discrimination in Canada compared to Britain is similar, while the degree of racial conflict in Canada has been much less. It is possible for social conditions and processes to moderate social conflict without necessarily ensuring that underlying issues and inequities are addressed. It is suggested that such conditions and processes may apply to race relations in Canada.

Racial conflict is likely to increase in the future with the generational transition. There are many unknowns, however, including economic trends in specific industries affecting the distribution of opportunities for minority group members. This analysis suggests that levels of racial conflict in Canada may remain comparatively low, even if levels of racial discrimination remain as high as in Britain.

ENDNOTES

[1] The procedure called for non-whites to make the approach first, to ensure that negative reactions are not a result of employers regarding the job as already committed to the white applicant.

[2] After the adjustment noted in Table 1, note 4, discrimination appears greater in Britain, but the difference is not significant. (See note 5 to Table 1.) Other differences in Table 1 are contrary to the hypothesis of less discrimination in Canada.

[3] The following section draws from Reitz (1988).

[4] In both Britain and Canada, the proportion of the population which is of West Indian origin is approximately one percent. However, the other non-European origin groups in Canada are distributed differently and are more diverse than those in Britain. There are relatively few persons of Indian and Pakistani origins in Canada compared to Britain, and relatively more persons of various Asian origins in Canada.

REFERENCES

Balakrishnan, T. R. and John Kralt (1987). "Segregation of visible minorities in the Metropolitan areas of Montreal, Toronto and Vancouver." Pp. 138–57 in L. Driedger (ed.), *Ethnic Canada: Identities and Inequalities* (Toronto: Copp Clark Pitman).

Billingsley, B. and L. Muszynski (1985). *No Discrimination Here? Toronto Employers and the Multi-racial Workforce* (Toronto: Social Planning Council of Metropolitan Toronto and The Urban Alliance on Race Relations).

Carby, Keith and Manab Thakur (1977). *No Problems Here? Management and the Multiracial Workforce* (London: Institute of Personnel Management, in co-operation with the Commission on Racial Equality).

Cohen, B. G. and P. J. Jenner (1968). "The employment of immigrants: a case study within the wool industry," *Race,* 10:41–56.

Collison, P. (1967). "Immigrants and residence," *Sociology,* 1:277–92.

Department of Manpower and Immigration (1974). *Immigration Policy Perspectives.* Canadian Immigration and Population Study, volume 1 (Ottawa: Information Canada).

Government of Canada (1984). Response of the Government of Canada to "Equality Now!," the report of the Special Parliamentary Committee on Visible Minorities in Canadian Society (Ottawa: Supply and Services Canada).

Hawkins, Freda (1972). *Canada and Immigration: Public Policy and Public Concern* (Montreal: McGill-Queen's University Press).

Henry, Frances and Effie Ginzberg (1985). *Who Gets the Work? A Test of Racial Discrimination in Employment* (Toronto: The Urban Alliance on Race Relations and the Social Planning Council of Metropolitan Toronto).

Kalbach, Warren E. and Wayne W. McVey (1979). *The Demographic Bases of Canadian Society* (Toronto: McGraw-Hill Ryerson).

Katznelson, Ira (1973). *Black Men, White Cities* (London: Oxford University Press).

McIntosh, Neil and David J. Smith (1974). *The Extent of Racial Discrimination,* Vol. XL Broadsheet No. 547 (London: PEP, The Social Science Institute).

Ouseley, Herman (1981). *The System: a Study of Positive Action in the London Borough of Lambeth* (London: Runnymede Trust and The South London Equal Rights Consultancy).

——— (1984). "Local authority race initiatives." Pp. 133–59 in Martin Boddy and Colin Fudge (eds.), *Local Socialism? Labour Councils and New Left Alternatives* (London: Macmillan).

Parai, Louis (1975). "Canada's immigration policy, 1962–1974," *International Migration Review,* 9:4:449-77.

Peach, Ceri (1966). "Factors affecting the distribution of West Indians in Britain," *Transactions of the Institute of British Geographers,* 38:151–63.

——— (1967). "West Indians as a replacement population in England and Wales," *Social and Economic Studies,* 16:3:289-94.

——— (1968). *West Indian Migration to Britain* (London: Oxford University Press, for the Institute of Law Relations).

——— (1982). "The growth and distribution of the black population in Britain, 1945–1980." Pp. 23–42 in D. A. Coleman (ed.), *Demography of Immigrants and Minority Groups in the United Kingdom* (London: Academic Press).

Reitz, Jeffrey G. (1980). "Immigrants, their Descendants, and the Cohesion of Canada." Pp. 329–417 in Raymond Breton, Jeffrey G. Reitz and Victor Valentine, *Cultural Boundaries and the Cohesion of Canada* (Montreal: Institute for Research on Public Policy).

—— (1988). "The institutional structure of immigration as a determinant of interracial competition: a comparison of Britain and Canada," *International Migration Review,* 22:1:117–46.

Tomlinson, Rex, John, and Sally (1979). *Colonial Immigrants in a British City* (London: Routledge and Kegan Paul).

Smith, David J. (1977). *Racial Disadvantage in Britain: the PEP Report* (Harmondsworth, Middlesex: Penguin Books).

QUESTIONS

DISCUSSION QUESTIONS

1. Language and religion are two important aspects of ethnic identity. What are some other aspects, and are they equally likely to support a drive for national autonomy? Why or why not?

2. Religion can often be the basis for stratification and conflict. Do religions always have this effect, or are they equally likely to bring people together in large, peaceful groupings? What determines the social effect of a religion?

3. "The Indian caste system raises doubts that racism is only, and always, caused by colonialism and its aftermath." Discuss.

4. Which is the best way of mobilizing people in Canada — by ethnicity or class? Why is that?

DATA COLLECTION EXERCISES

1. Collect information on one or more groups in the world — whether linguistic, religious, or racial — which favour ethnic or racial purity. What factors gave rise to this desire? What means does the group use to achieve its goal?

2. Has the creation of non-white empires (e.g., by the Mongols, Chinese, Japanese, Persians, Turks or others) historically had the same result as the creation of white empires: namely, a colour hierarchy within (and later, outside) the empire? Collect historical data on one empire to answer this question.

3. To what degree is the drive for national sovereignty based on ethnic differences, and to what degree is it based on differences in wealth and power between minority and majority groups? Collect some data from either Spain or the former USSR to answer this question.

4. Collect information on job discrimination against racial minorities in a developing society (e.g., India, Brazil, or Algeria). Would you predict an eventual increase in inter-racial conflict there? If not, what other conditions are necessary for such conflict to occur?

WRITING EXERCISES

1. Write a brief essay analyzing civil war in some part of the world (e.g., Yugoslavia, South Africa, northern Ireland or elsewhere) in terms of one of the excerpts presented in this section.

2. "Nothing is more important than learning, practising, and teaching our children our ethnic heritage." Write a fiery manifesto defending this point of view.

3. "In theory, you can get different kinds of people working with one another to form a nation. In practice, they'll never really come together." Write a brief essay defending or opposing this point of view.

4. "Religious doctrines are, more often than not, used to justify imperial aspirations — demands for more status, more power and more wealth." Imagine you are an important religious leader (e.g., the Pope, the Archbishop of Canterbury) and write a brief letter replying to this charge.

SUGGESTED READINGS

1. Flere, Sergej (1991). "Explaining ethnic antagonism in Yugoslavia," *European Sociological Review,* 7(3), December, 183–193. This excerpt is about a conflict between ethnic groups that results from regional disparities in the former Yugoslavia. The precipitating factor is the breakdown of legitimation around the state's way of regulating conflict between contending ethnic groups.

2. Hraba, Joseph (1989). "The ethnic hierarchy in The Netherlands: Social distance and social representation," *British Journal of Social Psychology,* 28, 57–69. This article shows Dutch respondents putting Europeans at the top of a social distance scale and former colonials next down the list, with Turkish immigrants at the bottom. The hierarchy does not run from darkest-to-lightest-skinned people, as Washington (Section 1) would have expected. The author explains why.

3. Telles, Edward E. (1992). "Residential segregation by skin color in Brazil," *American Sociological Review,* 57, April, 186–197. Brazil has high levels of racial interaction, at least among the poor (who intermarry and form friendships across colour lines). And the "official" ideology of Barzil's government says that there is little or no racism. Yet residential segregation does exist in Brazil and whites are more segregated from blacks than from mulattoes.

4. Breton, Raymond et al. (1990). *National Survival in Dependent Societies: Social Change in Canada and Poland.* Ottawa: Carleton University Press. This volume focuses on policy directions around ethnicity and "multiculturalism" in the two countries. Canada has become more multicultural, while Poland changed in the opposite direction.

GENDER RELATIONS

Introduction

In Section Two, we described the learning of gender as a key aspect of socialization. "Learning gender" means internalizing rules of behaviour and learning to act in culturally approved ways *as males* or *as females*. Our experiences, the ways we learn to interact with other people, and the words we use to categorize reality all combine to reinforce these gender differences. But the process is so smooth and the outcome so successful that we grow up thinking of gender differences as natural. How does this happen?

The Reproduction of Gender

Children are born into a social environment that emphasizes gender difference. From the beginning, most of their social encounters reinforce a particular set of understandings about gender and the gendered division of labour.

The mass media reinforce gender stereotypes particularly effectively. Advertisers, newscasters, entertainers, and writers of television programs present a consistent and stereotyped message that reinforces the ideal of female economic and social dependence. For example, they idealize romance, marriage, and motherhood. In this way, young women are encouraged to see these events and relationships as natural, desirable, and inevitable. The media also idealize the show of aggression and dominance in men. By doing this they deny men the cultural right to express kindness and gentleness.

Early on, children learn to make distinctions between males and females and categorize the world in these terms. By internalizing the social expectation of a gendered division of labour, children grow up believing that men and women are suited to different adult responsibilities. Their own sense of self and the expectations they have of others reflect and reinforce this early understanding. Later on, they make (largely conventional) education, career, and relationship choices that further reinforce gender distinctions. In the end, they have reproduced gender inequality by continuing to attach social importance to gender differentiation. This cycle is called the "reproduction of gender."

Because gender differentiation is so pervasive, it is hard to break the cycle. No matter how we encourage children to think otherwise, the world they see inevitably reflects gendered stereotypes. The nurturers they encounter at home, on television, at day care and school are women; the decision-makers are men. For children, the exceptions do not disprove the rule.

Ellis and Sayer's (1986:55) study of Canadian school children shows the way children resolve a contradiction between cultural ideals and their experience. Girls in our society know that women *could* work in non-traditional jobs, but this knowledge does not become personally relevant. The researchers report "Many of [the girls] seemed to be saying 'Yes, women can become doctors, but I want to be a nurse,' or 'Bank managers can be women as well as men, but I am going to be a teller.' "

Gender Inequality

In every society, people expect different behaviour from boys and girls, men and women. Women's role in reproduction — their biological hold on motherhood — has led people to make a connection between women and domestic work that is hard to change. The result is a split between the private, domestic world of women and the public world of men.

We find the public-private split reproduced with varying degrees of rigidity throughout the world. In Middle Eastern societies like Saudi Arabia (see excerpt 6.2), men and women live in more or less separate worlds. Women's participation in public life is extremely limited, largely confined to gender-segregated institutions. In excerpt 6.3 you will see that Mexican women are *supposedly* less restricted in their activities. In practice Mexican husbands do not like their wives to take paid employment and try to regulate their other actions too.

By contrast, middle-class Kenyan women have much more freedom. At least on the surface, their lives are similar to the lives of many North American two-earner couples. Excerpt 6.4 discusses the domestic division of labour among middle-class Kenyan couples: what it comprises and how it survives.

The Domestic Division of Labour

Throughout the world, women are saddled with most of the responsibility for housework and childcare. Data for developing regions is sparse, but United Nations analysts (*The World's Women 1970–1990*; *Trends and Statistics* 1990:82) offer two generalizations. "First, women everywhere have nearly total responsibility for housework. Second, men in developing regions generally do even fewer household chores than men in the developed regions."

The next Section shows, in some detail, that the structure and organization of family life has changed dramatically in the second half of the twentieth century. Family changes and changes in the organization of paid work have had more impact on women than men. Women have entered the labour force in large numbers, but men have not made the parallel shift to assuming more responsibility for domestic work.

One consequence is that women have less free time than men and feel overburdened. Descriptions like the "double day" or the "second shift" remind us that women continue to do (or organize) the largest share of housework and childcare. The one area of change in western countries is shopping! Men do nearly 40 percent of family shopping (*ibid*: 82).

Labour Force Participation and Occupational Segregation

World-wide, it is hard to determine precise rates of labour force participation for women. That is because much of women's work is in the informal economy (see excerpt 6.3) and so it is not officially counted. In 1990, the highest rates of economic activity for women were in the USSR (60 percent), eastern Asia (59 percent), and North America (50 percent). Lowest participation rates are found in Latin America and the Caribbean (32 percent), Southern and Western Asia (24 percent and 21 percent), and Northern Africa (16 percent). (See *The World's Women 1970–1990*; *Trends and Statistics* 1990:84.)

Like the domestic division of labour, occupation segregation is universal. In western economies, women typically work in clerical, service, and sales jobs. In Africa and Asia, women work in agriculture. It is no accident that these "women's" jobs all have low status and provide few financial rewards.

The Femininization of Poverty

In the West, the consequences of gender inequality are most dramatic for women caught between domestic and wage-earning responsibilities. For example, the single mothers of young children often cannot earn enough to maintain a decent standard of living *and* cover their child care costs. Welfare payments are below the poverty line and there is a penalty for earning over a minimum amount. Older widowed or divorced women with little or no labour force experience are disadvantaged by old age security schemes that assume homemakers will be supported by a spouse's pension. Not surprisingly, single mothers and older women who live alone face a higher risk of poverty than any other groups, and make up a high percentage of the poor.

The Women's Movement

Throughout the world the Women's Movement has been an important force for change. A first and crucial step was to draw public and academic attention to issues of sexual inequality. Working within formal political organizations and in grass-roots community groups, women have effectively challenged the roots of gendered inequality.

A second wave of feminism, which began in the 1970s, has initiated reforms including new educational and employment opportunities, protections for women's rights to reproductive choice, and demands for freedom from abuse. The goal of equality is elusive and the road is full of obstacles, as the world recession creates a climate of anti-feminist sentiment.

People's attitudes about men and women tend to resist change, despite legislative attempts to limit systemic discrimination. Among Western countries Sweden is perhaps the forerunner in legislative initiatives to ensure that women have reproductive control, equality in the workplace, and the equal participation of spouses in family duties. But even in Sweden, occupational segregation and a gendered division of domestic labour persist. There, most women still work in "women's" jobs, where they receive lower salaries. At home, domestic work and childcare still remain largely women's work.

Conclusion

Two main vehicles for changing structured gender inequality are economic independence and reproductive control for women. In advanced industrial economies, increasing numbers of women work for pay. Increasingly, the educational and occupational histories of young women resemble those of young men. Women and men now have more opportunity to exercise choice concerning their domestic arrangements — to remain single, cohabit, or marry.

It is when women marry (as about 90 percent do) and become parents (as about 90 percent of married women do) that the equality gap begins to widen. The conflicting demands of paid work and caring for young children are difficult to resolve and they become more problematic in hard economic times. North American societies have to do more to address the issues of inflexible work structures and little public involvement in childcare.

REFERENCES

Ellis, Dormer and Lyz Sayer (1986). *When I Grow Up: Expectations and Aspirations of Canadian Schoolchildren.* Ottawa: Labour Canada.

United Nations (1991). *The World's Women 1970–1990; Trends and Statistics.* New York: United Nations Publications.

6.1 Kerstin Nordenstam

Male and Female Conversational Styles

INTRODUCTION

As we saw in the Section on "culture," when we acquire language, we acquire a way of categorizing experience. Sexist language makes women's experiences different (at best) or invisible (at worst). Studies of the implicit meaning of generic terms such as "man" and "he" find that listeners envision a male when they hear these terms. The women's movement has done a great deal over the past two decades to draw attention to the subtleties of language use and suggest alternatives. (For example, substitute the words "police officer" for "policeman.")

Conversational patterns construct, maintain, and reflect status differences between men and women. American studies find that men tend to dominate conversations, speak loudly, and (often) ignore the conversational contributions of women. More women than men use conversational devices that soften the impact of their message or imply hesitancy. But women seem to do more conversational "work" than men: that is, take more responsibility for keeping up the conversation.

The next excerpt is a study of tape-recorded conversations of Swedish men and women. Those selected for study chose their own partners. There were three kinds of groups: men–men groups, women–women groups, and married couples. In this study married women talked more than their husbands and took more responsibility for initiating topics. However when women talk to each other, their conversation is far more animated.

To study language variation in as informal a situation as possible, I used tape recordings made by the participants in their homes. The choice of topics of conversation was entirely free. To make possible gender differences apparent, I compared the language usage of single-gender dyads (conversations between two women or two men) with language usage in two-gender dyads (conversations between a woman and a man).

Material

My material consists of tape recordings of men and women, born in Sweden and living in Gothenburg. These individuals were chosen as a random sample from different age and social groups. A person, around either 25 or 50 years old, selected a

Nordenstam, Kerstin (1992). "Male and Female Conversational Style," *International Journal of Sociology of Language*, 94, 75–98. Reprinted by permission.

conversational partner from among his or her friends or relatives and kept a conversation going for about half an hour. The recordings were made by the participants. The person selected for the task received a state raffle ticket as remuneration. It was made clear they were taking part in a language study. The recordings were made in 1979.

I have chosen three groups of conversations: six dyads where a man talks to another man, called MEN, six dyads where a woman talks to another woman, called WOMEN, and six dyads where a man and a woman talk to each other, called MARRIAGES.

Word Distribution

As is shown in Table 1, the number of words in the corpus is approximately 86,000, distributed over 8,400 utterances. The average number of words per utterance is 10.3. MEN have the longest utterances, with an average of 12.3 words per utterance, and WOMEN the shortest, with an average of 8.2 words per utterance. The figure for the MARRIAGES is 11.3.

However, in the married couple's conversations, the average male utterance consists of 8.7 words, the average female utterance of 13.9 words. This is the reverse of the proportion in the single-gender dyads.

The distribution of words in the dyads varies between an equal distribution of the two parties using 50 percent of the words each, to the most unequal distribution of 72 percent versus 28 percent. The most equal distribution occurs in the WOMEN's dyads. Here none of the talkers utters more than 58 percent of the words. In the MEN's dyads, in four of the six dyads, one person utters more than 60 percent of the words, while in the two-gender dyads the number of words uttered by one party exceeds 69 percent in three of six dyads.

TABLE 1   DIFFERENCES BETWEEN THE THREE MAIN GROUPS

	Men (%)	Women (%)	Marriages (%)	m	f	Total (N)
Number of						
words	20,268	28,048	29,362			86,678
utterances	2,371	3,427	2,602			8,400
turns	2,223	3,089	2,437			7,785
Words/utterance	12.3	8.2	11.3	8.7	13.9	10.3
						($p < 0.001$)
Simultaneous speech/	94	192	119	56	63	405
cooperative overlap	(4.2)	(6.2)	(4.8)			($p < 0.01$)
Interruption of turns	74	73	149	82	67	296
	(3.3)	(2.3)	(6)			($p < 0.001$)
Back-channeling signals	148	338	129	65	64	615
	(6.2)	(9.9)	(4.9)			($p < 0.001$)

Inequality of distribution is greatest in MARRIAGES. The three most talkative married people (with 69 percent, 71 percent, and 72 percent of the words) are also women (500, 507, 618). These three women are the ones selected for the recording and have chosen their husbands as conversational partners. The men who choose their wives to talk to do not act in the same way. Only one (635) talks more than his wife (61 percent).

I interpret these findings as the married women's fulfilling their task particularly thoroughly. There is a general tendency for the people who have been allotted the recording task to talk more than the others.

The three husbands chosen by their wives as conversational partners seem uninterested and uneasy and yawn on several occasions. No woman yawns in my recordings. Could yawning be a characteristic of male conversational style?

Topic and Topical Organization

We know from other studies and our own experiences that men talk to each other about manly things — cars, sports, jobs — and women talk to each other about womanly things — children and personal relations. This is also the case in my study. In my study, however, the women also talk about their jobs and courses. As regards the married couples, the tendency is the same, but here the wife tends to talk about one thing and the husband about another. (See 635, where he talks about tape recorders and other equipment, and she talks about black currants and neighbors.)

I tried to estimate my informants' interest in people by counting the number of people they mentioned by name. WOMEN talking to each other mention almost twice as many names as MEN do talking to each other (48 and 26 respectively). As for the MARRIAGES, the wives mention almost four times as many people as the husbands (30 versus eight).

Furthermore, as in other findings men talk about other men, while women talk about both women and men in my corpus.

Topic Shift

The number of main topics is 236: MEN 77, WOMEN 91, and MARRIAGES 68. Thus WOMEN change topics most frequently, followed by MEN. The person selected for the recording initiates a larger number of topics than his or her counterpart in the single-gender dyads. 59 out of 77 new topics in MEN were initiated by the people selected. The corresponding figure for WOMEN is 56 of 91. For the MARRIAGES, however, there is no difference: 34 of 68 main topics are introduced by the person allotted the recording task. Here, sex seems a stronger variable: 42 out of 68 initiatives are taken by women. Thus, Zimmerman and West's (1975) hypothesis that *men decide the topic of conversation* in mixed groups does not apply to my corpus.

Topic changes can be managed in different ways. The sudden change of topic I call *abrupt*. The person who takes the turn presents a topic not previously discussed. No boundary markers are used. Second, topic change may be *smooth*, characterized by the occurrence of a formal boundary marker (such as "by the way," "this is changing the subject but"), meta comments, fillers, and the like, usually combined with clues as to content like *preclosings* or formal topic endings.

Since Tannen sees abrupt topic shifting as a sign of *high-involvement style* (1984:30), I sorted out the instances of topic shifts that could be considered abrupt.

For WOMEN, around 30 percent of the 91 main topics discussed in this group are introduced abruptly. For MEN, the figure is 23 percent, and for MAR-RIAGES 19 percent. Out of the 13 abrupt topic shifts in the latter group nine are made by women. So there is a tendency for women to begin new topics in a more direct way than men do.

The MEN's dyads, on the other hand, make extensive use of phrases like "this is changing the subject but," "talking about this," "while I remember," etc., which often give a formal impression. WOMEN do not normally use expressions like "by the way" for renewal of a topic though it is common in the other groups.

Abrupt topic shifts may be the consequence of a quick talking pace and a great deal of personal involvement between the conversational partners. The partners in my corpus generally help each other carry on a conversation.

Topic Shift After Pause

Another way of measuring the pace and involvement in a conversation is to check which topic shifts are preceded by an interturn pause.

In MARRIAGES, 37 percent of the topic shifts are preceded by a pause, in MEN 22 percent, and in WOMEN only three percent.

I believe the pause before topic shifts is usually a sign of these talkers' uneasiness. They have difficulties finding a "natural" topic of conversation. Some MEN mention this difficulty directly.

None of the female dyads seem inhibited: they neither turn off the tape recorder, nor talk about difficulties in the situation, nor pause when introducing a new topic. In dyads where men are present, one party is often in focus. [Speaker] A in (620) explicitly expresses the idea that he, not his partner, is the object of study. Men's conversations are often more like interviews than dialogues.

In sum, when women talk to each other and to their husbands, their language usage is characterized by several of the features Tannen (1984) finds typical of *high-involvement style*. Women

* prefer personal topics,
* shift topics abruptly,
* introduce topics without hesitation.

I now want to report on other traits which Tannen (1984:30) includes under pacing: *cooperative overlap* and *participatory listenership*, to see if they too are typical of women's conversational style.

Interruption and Simultaneous Speech

To discuss *cooperative overlap*, we must first sort out the difference between interruption and simultaneous speech.

I define interruption as a turn taking which violates the current speaker's turn. The speaker is not allowed to finish his turn. This could occur with or without simultaneous speech.

I use the term *simultaneous speech* for overlapping speech which does not violate the speaker's turn. This includes three types.

1. *Overlap.* Speaker shift takes place at a transition point, when the first speaker has more or less finished his turn but makes a short addition. It is to be seen as bad timing on the part of the second speaker and is common in rapid spontaneous speech.

2. *Butting-in interruptions.* The listener tries to take over the turn but is not successful.

3. *Cospeech.* The listener is talking at the same time as the speaker in short sequences of parallel speech. He fills in comments and phrases, usually of a supportive nature. I distinguish these from back-channeling signals by virtue of their length and sentence structure. Thus I classify "of course'" as a back-channeling signal, and "yes do that" (555:240) as simultaneous speech.

Cospeech is a sign of the listener's involvement in the speaker's talk. The floor is, as it were, equally shared.

I regard *overlaps*, *butting-in interruptions* and *cospeech* as generally cooperative strategies.

Distribution of Interruptions

MEN have 74, WOMEN 73, and MARRIAGES 149 interruptions. Figured as a percentage of the number of turns in each group, six percent of the turns are interrupted [in MARRRIAGES], compared to the all-MEN's group where 3.3 percent and the WOMEN's group where 2.3 percent of the turns are interrupted. In the single-sex groups, interruptions are also significantly unequally distributed (5 percent level), and men use interruptions more often than women do. Previous researchers have proposed interruption is a male strategy of dominance. My results support this idea.

In MARRIAGES husbands interrupt their wives more than vice versa, but the difference is not significant. The wives keep up with their husbands fairly well. One reason for this could be the speech setting. The home is the women's domain.

My most striking finding, however, is that the marriage situation gives rise to so many more interruptions than talk between friends.

Distribution of Simultaneous Speech

There are 305 cases of simultaneous speech: MEN have 94 cases, WOMEN 192, and MARRIAGES, 119 (significant at the one percent level). There are also more women talking simultaneously with their partners in the mixed groups, 63 against 56, but here the difference is not significant.

Women's talk during the other speaker's turn is a normal part of relaxed informal conversation between equals. Women also address the talker, frequently interpolate remarks, and offer enthusiastic comments during the other speaker's turn. In all-women interaction, such behavior is seen as evidence of active listening. Men's interruptions, on the other hand, seem to have as their goal the seizing of a turn. This is why men's use of interruptions in mixed conversations can result in women's silence (Coates, 1986:153).

This could explain why, in my study, simultaneous talk is not as common in MARRIAGES or in the MEN's dyads as in the WOMEN's dyads. The speech situation is not as relaxed in the first two groups, and the participants are not equals to the same extent as in the same-sex women's dyads. However, interruptions are comparatively common in MARRIAGES, where the "manly" norm prevails.

Thus, WOMEN, when talking to each other, use cooperative overlap to a much greater extent than MEN do. I define cooperative overlap as synonymous with simultaneous speech.

Back-Channeling Signals

Back-channeling signals are uttered during the other speaker's turn, usually at a transition point. Their function is (a) for a listener to show she or he has heard and/or understood and/or agrees with the speaker, and (b) to support the speaker's continuing her/his turn (Linell and Gustavsson, 1986:54). Different types of back-channeling signals are found in my material; "yes" with various elaborations is the most frequently used, while exclamations are few (Nordenstam, 1987:47).

Back-channeling signals are most frequently found in the all-WOMEN's group. Out of 615, 338 are found there. In the all-MEN's group there are 148, and in MARRIAGES, 129 (significance 0.1 level). The hypothesis that *women back each other up more than men do* when in single-sex groups is supported. (See Table 1.)

In MARRIAGES the 129 back-channeling signals are equally distributed between women and men. The comparatively high number among men is probably a consequence of women's talking in the longest turns, which is bound to evoke a certain number of back-channeling signals from their husbands.

All the exclamations or exclamatory questions of surprise, the emotionally loaded exclamations or questions, are uttered by women: "oy," "oh," "ugh yes," "ugh no," "you don't say." Men, on the other hand, only burst out in a balanced way: "eh," "ok," "yes ok," "that's it," "yes right."

The tendency is the same if we look at variants of "yes" (Nordenstam, 1987: 49). WOMEN have the greatest number of types. And in MARRIAGES it is the same impatient husband who utters all four variants (618). Clearly enthusiasm is lowest among the married couples.

Thus, not only the quantity of the back-channeling signals but also the quality of those used by the women reinforces the idea that women are better listeners than men. Their involvement is certainly higher.

MEN dyads

The male dyads often organize themselves hierarchically. They have difficulty finding topics of conversation and are obsessed with the tape recorder. They talk in significantly longer turns than the WOMEN's dyads. They use more formal topic shifters and tend to introduce a new topic after an interturn pause. They interrupt each other significantly more often than WOMEN. Only men yawn.

WOMEN dyads

Female dyads discuss their own personal relations or those of their friends. As mentioned above, MEN talk more about jobs, sports, etc. WOMEN talk about both men and women, whereas MEN mainly mention other men. WOMEN talk about a greater number of topics. New topics are introduced without hesitation. (There are hardly any interturn pauses.) WOMEN use abrupt topic shifts more often than MEN and do not have difficulty finding topics of conversations. They do not seem bothered by the tape recorder. WOMEN support each other while talking: they use significantly more cooperative overlaps when talking simultaneously than men. They also use significantly more back-channeling signals. Thus they are better listeners than MEN. Their back-channeling signals are of a higher intensity and thus qualitatively different from MEN's. WOMEN in single-gender dyads use a high-involvement style.

MARRIAGE dyads

In the conversation of the married couples, some of the characteristics of the single-sex dyads remain, others are lost. Thus with respect to topic choice there are certain similarities: women show a greater interest in human relations and talk about both sexes, while men mainly mention other men. Husbands more often introduce new topics after interturn pauses that signify hesitation than wives do, but the difference is smaller here than in the single-gender dyads. Wives use more abrupt topic shifts (but the figures are too small to be significant), and they initiate more topics. They also talk in longer turns than their husbands do.

My study supports Fishman's (1978) proposal that *interaction is the work women do*. This work seems to be particularly well handled by the wives in my study in that they also do their recording task so conscientiously. I interpret their greater talkativeness and their initiative with respect to finding conversational topics as greater eagerness to be useful in contributing to the study.

The married couples' conversation shows signs of competitiveness. There are comparatively many interruptions and few instances of cooperative overlap and back-channeling signals, compared with the conditions of the WOMEN's group in particular. The enthusiasm is low in the married couples' conversations. It seems the high-involvement style women use when talking to each other is not used when they talk to their spouses. The husbands seem indifferent to the idea of recording half an hour's marital conversation in their homes.

Is it, then, presumptuous to conclude by suggesting we might twist another of Tannen's concepts (1984:58 and 66) and regard men as *enthusiasm constraints* on women in casual conversation?

REFERENCES

Coates, J. (1986). *Women, Men and Language.* London and New York: Longman.

Fishman, P. (1978). "Interaction: the work women do." *Social Problems* 25, 397–406.

Linell, P. and L. Gustavsson (1987). *Initiativ och respons. Om dialogens dynamik, dominans och koherens.* SIC 15. University of Linköping, Department of Communication Studies.

Nordenstam, K. (1987). *Kvinnlig och manlig samtalsstil.* Göteborg: Institutionen för nordiska språk.

Tannen, D. (1984). *Conversational Style: Analyzing Talk Among Friends.* Norwood, NJ: Ablex.

6.2 Yakin Erturk

Differences in the Status of Moslem Women in Turkey and Saudi Arabia

INTRODUCTION

In many Middle Eastern countries gender inequality is maintained by a rigid system of gender segregation. For example, when leaving their homes, Middle Eastern women have traditionally worn the abaya, a heavy floor-length cloak that covers them completely. The supposed reason for the abaya is to protect women's sexual purity. This custom owes more to entrenched cultural traditions than to Islamic religious principles.

The next excerpt compares the status of Moslem women in Turkey and Saudi Arabia. Both are predominantly Moslem societies, but Turkey has been far more liberal regarding women's rights. The 1926 Civil Code outlawed polygamy and gave women the right to divorce and child custody. Turkish women have had the vote since 1930 and actively participate in the public realm.

Erturk, Yakin (1991). "Convergence and Divergence in the Status of Moslem Women: The Cases of Turkey and Saudi Arabia," *International Sociology*, 6(3), September, 307–320. Reprinted by permission.

Saudi Arabia, by contrast, is a far more traditional society. Like Bangladesh (described in excerpt 8.1) it is also a rigidly segregated society. Women have recently gained access to education and employment opportunities, but these are within strictly segregated institutions. Saudi women do not drive cars, although they have gained a measure of independence with the allocation of special women's sections on public buses. The author predicts that reducing the proportion of foreign workers will, in turn, create pressure to use the labour of skilled Saudi women, which will in turn create pressure for further emancipation.

This paper will explore points of divergence and convergence in two Muslim societies representing different models of national transformation and compare the impact of these experiences on the status of women. While the cultural and structural variability is illustrated by focusing on such seemingly contradictory examples it will also be argued that it is not Islam per se (i.e. the implementation of the *Sharia*) that accounts for the subordination of women but rather that it is the religious, political and social tradition which is so profoundly embedded in the intimate levels of consciousness and identity of gender roles. Therefore, it is necessary to approach the problem at two levels:

1. The *structural* level, where Islam as a way of life is interpreted and institutionalised within a concrete socio-political entity within which the status of women is determined. Analysis at the structural level will require us to examine the formal aspects of gender relations and ask, "Is the public domain accessible to women?" The emphasis will necessarily be the quantitative representation of women in the public sphere of life and the socio-political orientation of the state which organises this realm.

2. The *conscious* level, where Islam as an ideology is internalised into identities and personal structures of both men and women. As a result, gender inequalities become perceived as natural rather than social. At this level of analysis the concern is on the qualitative aspects of identity and gender relations. Therefore, here the question shifts to whether sex-role stereotyping is eliminated at all levels of social relations and consciousness, while at the same time creating alternative gender roles.

The Cases of Turkey and Saudi Arabia

A. *Turkey*. Turkey represents a secular approach in terms of the relationship between state and religion. Turkish secularism implies the subordination of the latter to the former rather than a complete divorce between the two. In the process of national transformation, modernising elites of Turkey chose to separate the two institutions and introduce reforms aimed at emancipating women from centuries of seclusion. It must be emphasised, however, that the actual seclusion of women under Ottoman rule was more of an urban upper-class phenomenon, just as the main impact of the secular emancipatory reforms that followed was on that group of women. The Civil Code of 1926 outlawed polygamy and gave women the right to divorce and child custody. Civil marriages replaced religious marriages. In 1930 women were granted their right to vote and to be elected to office. While the Turkish modernisers took measures to integrate women into the public domain, crucial aspects of gender relations (sexuality, domestic division of labour, and so on) and the sex bias of the public/private domains remained untouched.

After the 62 years since the reforms were initiated, in practice the situation is far from what might be expected. Women in the rural areas have faced more of a paradox than emancipation in the face of some of these changes.[1] The laws granting them rights are quite irrelevant to the objective conditions of their daily lives. Many especially in the Eastern provinces are still married by religious ceremony and some are still subject to polygamy. In both cases under the new secular/modern system, the conventional legitimacy of their marital status and the protective mechanisms it provided for women no longer hold. As a result these women are confronted with real hardship in cases where the husband abandons them or dies. Furthermore, they are unable to make any legal claim over their children or inheritance from their husbands. Since they lack the know-how and means by which to function within the modern external institutions (such as courts), they are left to the mercy of their men and the effectiveness of the traditional mechanisms by which rights and obligations were customarily arranged.

As for urban women, the situation varies significantly by social class. For the majority of lower- and middle-class women, the burden of having to contribute to the family budget has been added to the existing burden of domestic responsibilities. At the same time, the working woman had to assume a somewhat "Victorian modesty" to prove her worthiness of being admitted to the "club." They "voluntarily" accepted the ideology of the public domain for the sake of not only being accepted by it, but also for the greater cause of the new role granted to them in the modern nation-state. The first generation of Republican women in particular promoted emancipation as part and parcel of nationalism and the road to modernity. One positive outcome of the state-initiated reformist approach was that the indiscriminate recruitment of women during nation-building into many jobs avoided the emergence of sex stereotyping, especially in the professions.

In the light of recent developments, however, it is questionable whether this trend still holds. As the social transformation becomes more settled and the need for mobilising female labour becomes less urgent, women are being discretely discouraged from the more prestigious positions within the occupational hierarchy. The most obvious areas for such closure are the high administrative positions in state and private enterprises (Gülmez, 1972) and in the medical profession, where women are particularly discouraged from becoming surgeons. Often the ideological justification offered is that some positions are neither compatible with female psychology and a woman's innate qualities nor with their primary duties as mothers and wives. Despite these drawbacks, perhaps the most significant and irreversible outcome of women's entry into the occupational structure is the fact it provided new role models for the younger generations (Öncü, 1981). At the same time, however, the growing fundamentalist movement cannot be overlooked as a competing trend. There appears to be an increasing appeal of the Islamic ideology to young university students even in major urban centres. This has undermined the significance of the urban/rural-modern/traditional dichotomy which was believed to have characterised the women of the Republic of Turkey. Instead, a secular/Islamist differentiation among the educated urban women is gaining precedence.

Kemalist reforms paved the way for the emancipation of women, while at the same time undermining their motivation to struggle for change. In other words, the reforms had a co-opting effect. The average middle-class woman saw little need to struggle for her liberation since she faced no obvious formal barrier. However, this co-optation has not been free of contradictions for urban middle-class women. Pressures arising from the conflict within and between the traditional demands of the private domain and the public domain are forcing women to search for alternative ways of organising their lives and exerting their power to produce new gender roles at home and at work. In addition, the intensity of labour migration within the past two decades had an impact on traditional relations as this process left women with the responsibility of managing their household affairs. In some cases, women joined the labour force as the primary providers for their families. This change, in turn, has required new legislation to accommodate the emerging needs. For example, since 1981 women are allowed to pass citizenship rights to their offspring (a right previously obtained only through the father). Parallel to these changes is the emergence of a more radical women's "consciousness" along feminist and Islamist lines. The latter sees the ultimate liberation of women in a total submission to the will of Allah; the former regards all forms of submission as an obstacle to women's liberation.

B. *Saudi Arabia.* Saudi Arabia came into being as a result of the hegemony of one tribe over others. The power of the Al-Saud hegemony relied on: 1) the Wahhabi[2] connection, which provided the ideological legitimacy of the Saudi regime; and 2) strategic marriages, which allowed them to form alliances with other powerful tribes (Salameh, 1980). This process was supported by oil wealth which reinforced the political-religious alliances of the Al-Saud and Al-Shaikh families.[3] Thus, the material and ideological preconditions for the preservation of traditional institutions were secured. It became feasible for Saudi Arabia to "modernise" without having to restructure their society. Women could participate in the public domain only within private/segregated female institutions. Especially after 1960, the Saudi government extensively supported the education of women and created new employment opportunities in health, commerce and social services among others.[4] The import of sophisticated technology along with foreign domestic labour has freed women from household chores. Private drivers and special women's sections in public buses have given women some physical mobility and independence. These practices allow women to acquire a more diversified image of themselves and their abilities.

How much opportunity will be made available to Saudi women, however, is a contested issue. The contradictions confronting the regime manifest themselves in the constant loosening and tightening of "Islamic principles." It is therefore not possible that under the existing political order the public integration of Saudi women will improve.

Saudi society is literally divided into black and white, private and public, with little chance to deviate from the norm except in secrecy. This sex-divided society is most readily observable in the dress code, i.e. black *abaya* for women and white *deshdasha* (robe) for men. It is also reflected in the organisation of the urban physical environment. Even modest houses or apartments are designed with internal divisions to allow for the observance of the public/private domains.

Overemphasis on morality and strict control of public behaviour has created widespread hypocrisy in Saudi society. Taboos are broken behind the walls. The private domain, which is reserved for the observance of honour, purity and morality, in some cases serves also for "immorality." The by-products of the oil boom — supermarkets, videos, cars, telephones, foreign domestic help, and so on — have, on the one hand, increased the concern for morality, and, on the other, undermined control over individual behaviour. And the veil, in fact, provides a disguise for those women who indulge in the "forbidden."

While the contradictions produced by the concern to preserve segregation, on the one hand, and the need to educate Saudi women, on the other, is mounting, the system is responding with new ideologies of consumerism and "Saudi superiority." The former acts to keep women preoccupied with the consumer market; the latter emphasises the need to distinguish oneself as a Saudi in the face of an influx of expatriates. The veil and the *abaya* symbolically serve such distinctness. Even the more critical Saudi women carefully arrange their veil in the "proper" style so as not to be mistaken for a foreigner. The ideology of "Saudi superiority" works in two ways to preserve the status quo: 1) it assures the conformity of Saudi men and women, and 2) it makes self-appointed managers out of them as they keep an eye on the expatriates they work with. In other words, the Saudis in both state and private institutions act as *managers of the managers*. The native/foreign distinction is also supported by a higher pay scale for Saudis.

Beneath the black and white outer appearance, there is a quiet but persistent revolution. The risk involved in being rebellious bears a heavy price. Even those who are less challenging must put in much effort to gain very little. For example, in 1980 a group of Saudi women from King Saud University decided to attend a conference at the male campus. They observed the veil carefully so that their intentions would not be misinterpreted. The authorities were taken by surprise. They did not lose much time, however, in controlling the situation by confining the women to a separate room where they were allowed to listen to the speaker and submit their questions in writing. Subsequently the issue was never again brought up — as if it never happened.

In November 1990 about 50 women, completely veiled, were reported to have driven their cars in the streets of Riyadh to protest against the Saudi tradition which prevents women from driving. The protestors used the Gulf Crisis as a pretext. They claimed that in the event of war men would be away fighting and they would be left immobilised. This time, however, the response of the authorities was direct. Six protesters who were professors at King Saud University were suspended from their jobs. The reaction of other women in Saudi Arabia has been mixed. The fundamentalists charged the protesters with being infidels. Others from the professional community expressed concern that the act would have adverse consequences for women in the long run. Aside from such incidents there are a number of women writers who write regularly in local magazines and newspapers on women and oppression. Life for these women is not easy. They are constantly harassed by the authorities, their right to publish is periodically or permanently withdrawn, and pressure is brought to bear on their male guardians who are ultimately responsible for their conduct. Most of these women do not attribute the restrictions imposed on them to Islam, rather they see Islam as a political weapon used by the regime. The following quotation from a Saudi woman in the *Wall Street Journal* reflects a commonly held viewpoint. "The royal family is using religion like a lash on our backs to stay in power. They know it's all hypocrisy. The Koran doesn't require veils. We should be a model Islamic society and not accept the word of fanatics" (House, 1981).

Declining oil prices and a multitude of problems arising from the presence of a large foreign workforce is increasing the pressure on Saudi rulers to replace the expatriates with an indigenous workforce. This is a potential challenge to the existing balance which is allowing them to maintain the sex-segregated institutions of education, law, banking, and so on. The Saudisation of the labour force, which must rely on every skilled and experienced Saudi, will require the recruitment of those women who have already acquired these skills in the all-women institutions.[5] A drastic restructuring of society will follow. Within this process, Saudi women, as double victims of oppression, are strategically placed to become a potential force in giving direction to change, more so than their male counterparts.

Concluding Remarks

In both societies the patriarchal-Islamic culture continues to impose standards by which the moral and structural positions of women are defined. Women's natural drives, individuality and independent participation in the public realm are seen as destructive of the institution of the family, and hence society. Therefore, the protection of the family and social order justifies the subordination of women to patriarchal institutions. These linkages are, no doubt, manifest in the Saudi society where male and female distinctiveness is emphasised in segregated but sometimes parallel spheres of activity. The situation is somewhat discrete in Turkey. The Saudi case further illustrates that women are the central targets of regimes which appeal to political-religious alliances for their legitimacy. Similar trends are making their way into the Turkish political life.

The Turkish experience shows that the problem of women in Moslem societies is not merely one of gaining entry rights to the public domain. As important as this is, it can only lead to piecemeal reforms and a few token women in high positions. This is only a precondition. Beyond this it requires alternative models of gender roles at all levels of social relations. This can only be achieved by a conscious effort for change — individually and collectively. In this respect, women in Moslem societies are in a more advantageous position vis-à-vis men. They have access, even under the veil, to the male world. They can observe and become acquainted with male gender roles. In contrast, men's familiarity with women is, in most cases, limited to the more subordinate and traditional female roles. As a result they are not equipped when confronted with women in an unfamiliar context. At the societal level this gap provides women with the opportunity to challenge conventional expectations and to impose an alternative image and self. Of course, the hard reality of political regimes, rising Islamic fundamentalism, and the brutal force men exercise over their wives and daughters cannot be dismissed. Hence, efforts for change must be directed towards both the external and internal obstacles embedded in identity as well as institutional structures.

ENDNOTES

[1] While legal changes concerning the status of women and the family were being introduced, Turkey was also experiencing processes such as national integration, rural transformation and the internal contradictions created by Turkey's position within the world system. These latter processes have probably had a more profound impact on the role and status of rural women. Most studies reveal the changes have preserved traditional formations while modifying their form.

[2] Wahhabism, a movement started in the eighteenth century by Abdul Wahhab, called for a return to the fundamentals of Islam as preached by the Prophet Mohammed. The association of Abdul Wahhab and the Al-Saud family formed the basis of Al-Saud's victory over other tribes and the unification of Arabia.

[3] The members of the Al-Shaik family who hold religious power today are descendants of Abdul Wahhab.

[4] Teaching, social work, and medicine were the first areas to open up for Saudi women. Positions in the service sector followed. With the exception of medicine, all jobs are carried out in segregated institutions. In the past ten years women have also been appearing on television as news readers or programme directors.

[5] According to the Central Department of Statistics, the employment status of the Saudi population over 12 years of age shows that, while 59.3 percent of the men are in the labour force, this is true for only 4.8 percent of the women. Over 90 percent of the Saudi women in the workforce are secondary school and university graduates. It would not be wrong to assume that women in the labour force are employed in professional and administrative positions. These figures do not include the traditional informal sector. (Although the above data were published in 1977, women's participation in the labour force could not have increased significantly.)

REFERENCES

Gülmez, M. (1972). "Kamu Yönetiminde Feminizasyon Olayi" (Feminisation in Public Administration). *TODAIE Dergisi* 5(3):51–71.

House, K. E. (1981). "Modern Arabia: Saudi Women Get More Education, but Few Get Jobs,"
The Wall Street Journal, 4 June.

Kingdom of Saudi Arabia, Ministry of Finance and National Economy, Central Department of
Statistics. *Labour Force in Saudi Arabia, 1397 A.H.–1977 A.D.* Riyadh: Central Department
of Statistics.

Öncu, A. (1981). "Turkish Women in the Professions: Why so Many?" in Abadan-Unat, N. (ed.),
Women in Turkish Society. Leiden: E.J. Brill. pp. 81–193.

Salameh, G. (1980). "Political Power and the Saudi State." *Merip Reports,* October: 5–22.

6.3 Sylvia Chant

Female Labour in Querétaro, Mexico

INTRODUCTION

*In Latin America, women's labour force participation rates are very low compared to other
world regions. One of the reasons for such low involvement is the strong resistance of men.*

*The next excerpt is based on a study of households in three very poor areas of the
Mexican city of Querétaro. Querétaro is rapidly industrializing and the best job opportunities
are in the industrial sector, but most women work in the informal (non-industrial) economy.
The informal economy is unregulated, labour-intensive, unskilled, and low paying. A
woman's most common job is making tortillas.*

*Expectations about the household division of labour and male authority are very rigid in
this society. Women are expected to do all of the domestic work; men are expected to be economic providers. Even male children do not help their mothers with domestic jobs.
Furthermore, Mexican husbands strongly oppose wives' employment. They are concerned
that wives might earn more money than they, that other people might think they (husbands)
were unable to support their wives; as well, they fear that paid employment gives wives an opportunity to be unfaithful. (For more on the topic of "sexual property," see excerpt 7.1.)*

Chant, Sylvia (1987). "Family Structure and Female Labour in Querétaro, Mexico," in Janet H. Momsen and
Janet Townsend (eds.), *Geography of Gender in the Third World.* Albany: State University of New York Press,
pp. 277–293. Reprinted by permission.

This study concludes that female heads of families are financially better off than married women. Female heads are able to work, having no husband to prevent them. So in Mexico, marriage gives women economic security (through their husbands) but denies them economic independence.

This chapter seeks to show the effects on female employment of household-related factors in three shanty towns in Querétaro, an industrializing city in Mexico. The data are derived from a 1983 survey of 244 low-income households selected randomly from lists of owner-occupiers. It is suggested in the present study that a non-nuclear family structure maximizes a woman's opportunities to participate in economic activities outside the home.

The Labour Market in Querétaro

Rapid industrialization, much of it due to the investment of foreign capital, has fundamentally altered Querétaro and in 1983 its population was about 350,000.

Querétaro has become a key centre for industrial location under a nationwide programme of economic decentralization. Industry employed 38 percent of the workforce in 1980 and an estimated one-quarter of the industrial labour force were women (Meza, 1982). However, women tend to figure more prominently in "informal" occupations than in industrial employment. "Informal" employment is a term used to describe economic activities which are small scale, which operate outside the law, which are labour intensive, which use rudimentary technology and which are characterized by low and irregular earnings (Bromley, 1982; Gugler, 1981; Lailson, 1980; LACWC, 1980; Moser, 1978, 1981). The "formal" sector is the converse of this, being distinguished by large-scale enterprises, foreign capital inputs, mechanized production and social and labour legislation. The informal sector itself is highly differentiated, and the term often acts as a catch-all for a variety of non-institutionalized employment; but it has often been seen as inferior to "formal" sector work.

Employment Patterns in the Study Settlements

In the sample, if we discount the 169 (69 percent) who are full-time housewives, only six percent of the female household heads and spouses at work were in manufacturing, 32 percent are domestic servants and the overwhelming majority (55 percent) are in commerce or in the hotel and restaurant trade. Traditionally these occupations have been associated with informal employment. In Querétaro, two-thirds of the working male heads of household in the study settlements were in "protected" employment, but only one-quarter of female workers. Although factory work was considered desirable by both men and women in the interviews, it was not the main occupation of working-class females. While 27 percent of all employed male household heads in the study settlements worked in formal manufacturing enterprises, only two percent of employed female household heads and spouses do so. Additionally, men in factory employment earned an average of 3586 *pesos* a week as manual workers, whereas women earned half this amount.

In the study settlements, informal employment is most common in commerce and private services, in which women outnumbered men. The most common form of female commercial enterprise is the making and selling of *tortillas*, the Mexican staple foodstuff. In about one-third of these cases the wife makes them and the man sells them, otherwise women produce and sell direct to a specific clientele they have built up. Women also produce other types of cooked food, or engage in small-scale manufacture of plant pots, dolls and soft toys. Net income in informal commerce for men amounted to an average of 3232 *pesos* a week, whereas their wives and female heads of household make an average of 1741 *pesos*. This is probably because women spend more time producing items than trading and thus earn less. Furthermore, women are more restricted in their choice of market locations. Women, therefore, are not only heavily involved in unprotected, non-unionized employment; they also rank low in the hierarchy of informal sector jobs, being in the worst paid activities with least status. Why do fewer women work than men, and why are they concentrated in different forms of economic activity?

Undoubtedly, this derives in part from the demand side. Querétaro industry is heavy, it produces many high-technology goods and parts for export, it is subject to state legislation, and it does not commonly employ home-based piece-workers. Thus there is little opportunity for women to work in manufacturing, so they take up informal employment. On the supply side, low levels of education, high fertility and a cultural formation emphasizing domesticity also decrease women's chances of getting out of the home.

Household Constraints on Female Labour

Age

In the study settlements, the correlations between age and female employment accord with the results of previous studies — among women of working age and under 25 a total of 49 percent are in paid work or self-employed; this is a much higher proportion than in any other age group. However, when these figures are controlled for marital status different results emerge: 66 percent of unmarried daughters of all ages are in paid work, but only 10 percent of married mothers. Among married mothers the highest rate of participation in the labour force is in the age group 40–44; about half the married women of that age work. The highest rate of employment for female heads of households is between the ages of 30 and 34, when children are probably too young to work and the mothers have no other option. So, age is interlinked with marital status: where there is a high frequency of marriage break-up, for example, women are far more likely to enter the labour force.

Family Size

It is generally thought that women with smaller families are less bound to the home and more likely to engage in paid work. However, in the Third World, the prevalence of part-time, informal, home-based jobs for women means frequently there is little connection between the two variables. In the study settlements in Querétaro, women working outside the home in paid employment had the largest average number of children (5.4), compared with full-time housewives (4.1), and female workers in small family businesses (3.4). Logically this would also be affected by the age of the children, but no significant differences between age groups were found.

Education

In Mexico, in 1980, only 16.7 percent of all men were recorded as illiterate compared with 21.3 percent of all women. In the study settlements in Querétaro the discrepancy seems even more marked. One-quarter of the 211 male household heads had no education whatsoever, and the proportion rose to more than half for the 33 female heads. Only three female heads had completed more than four years of primary education.

Educational requirements even for manual work in the formal sector, for example, exclude half the workforce from protected employment. In the study settlements, male and female factory workers had an average of six years' education (i.e., they had completed primary school). The men with the least education worked in construction and agriculture (average of two to three years' schooling), the women with least education in commerce and private services. Most domestic servants had no education whatsoever.

Culture and the Sexual Division of Labour

Fieldwork in Querétaro indicated men had three main reasons for not wishing their wives to work. First, the wife might earn more than her husband and "get ahead," though this is unlikely in practice. Second, it might suggest to other families that the husband is unable to fulfil his role as breadwinner and to other men that he is failing to exercise authority over his wife: in other words, that he is weak. And third, the greater freedom of movement accruing to working wives is viewed suspiciously by their husbands, who fear it may result in their spouses being unfaithful (Chant, 1984a). This last explanation means women are less likely to be allowed to apply for jobs where they will work alongside men, and it may account for the concentration of women in occupations noted for their isolation, such as domestic service.

The Effect of Family Structure on Female Employment

Nuclear families represented 68 percent (167) of the sample households. Single-parent families (headed by women) represented nine percent (22) of the total. Extended families (families residing with kin) constituted 23 percent (55). Four-fifths (44) of this group were headed by males and one-fifth (11) by females. One interesting feature emerging from the Querétaro data is that the prevalence of the nuclear family may be related to male authority. In-depth interviews with a sub-sample of 47 families revealed many women would welcome the opportunity of introducing a relative into the house, but there was much male resistance to this. As many as four-fifths of the male heads of nuclear families were unwilling to share their homes with a relative, for fear of losing exclusive ownership of the family's property, or because they feared lack of privacy, or were jealous that another man, even a brother-in-law, would share the same house.

The structure of the nuclear family lends itself most easily to a strict sexual division of labour, the male partner earning a wage and the woman in the home doing the housework and looking after the children. That women bear children, and that men earn more in the Mexican labour market combine to favour the man's position as breadwinner, apart from cultural influences. This rigid division of male and female labour often results in a marked imbalance of power, with female subjugation to male authority reinforced by economic dependence. In as many as half the nuclear families in the Querétaro study, men regularly withheld half their wage packets from their wives and children. The amount and regularity of family privation varied according to the strength of the husband-father's commitment to his dependants.

The husband's economic support was often negligible, yet if his was the only wage in the family and he was opposed to his wife working, she was on weak ground if she wanted to earn a wage of her own and thus raise the level of household well-being. In single-parent families and in extended families where there may be several adults under one roof, the cultural norms may be sufficiently diluted to allow greater equality within the household and thus improve the women's status. The exigencies of life in low-income communities have been seen in the past as forcing certain families to seek alternative roles to survive (Nalven,1978; Lomnitz, 1977): this appears in Querétaro to apply most to non-nuclear families. In "unconventional" family structures, albeit often through economic necessity, women have more freedom both to enter the labour force and to choose the kinds of jobs they do.

Only one-third of the female spouses in nuclear families have paid work, compared with nearly half of the women in male-headed extended families and four-fifths of female heads. What explains this variation? Several authors assert the rise of the nuclear family in industrializing economies is accompanied by an improvement in the status of women. This is not borne out by the data from Querétaro. There it appears to be the women from non-nuclear households who gain access to work in urban areas, and not those nuclear families.

The organization of housework is one factor explaining why women in some families are more likely than others to take paid employment. Domestic work is often seen as women's main obstacle to entering the labour force. Nowhere is this truer than in the study settlements, which lack many basic urban services such as piped water, sewerage, rubbish collection and paved roads, and where housing is of poor quality. Deficient housing and servicing make the domestic workload much greater for women in shanty towns than for their counterparts in more consolidated neighborhoods, and it is therefore probably far more difficult for them to take up paid work in addition to their domestic chores.

Family structure may reduce some of these problems by allowing housework to be shared. In nuclear families the frequency and amount of help is considerably lower than in non-nuclear households, and often housework is done by the female spouse alone. The reasons are as follows. First, because the woman has no other role except her domestic one, it is assumed she can manage that labour in its entirety. Second, even where her husband encourages the children to help, they may be too young to do so. Third, there may only be male children, and in a culture which discourages male participation in "female spheres," boys should not be seen to help their mothers. In non-nuclear families the help of both sons and daughters in single-parent households (movitated by the fact their mothers have full-time jobs), and of female relations in extended families, means there are often two, if not three, people to shoulder the burden of housework.

Another factor influencing female work-roles is the relative need for women to work. In many single-parent families, women have to take up paid work, especially if their children are young. In extended households, because the housework is shared and because there are more people to support, there is less pressure on women to be in the home on a full-time basis and a greater need for them to earn money. In nuclear households women not only find it far more difficult to balance the two work-roles, especially if they have no daughters to whom they can delegate some of the domestic tasks and if they are rearing young children, but also, if the husband is earning, there is less apparent need for them to enter the labour force. They conform to a cultural pattern whereby the man alone provides for his wife and dependants.

In single-parent households, sons and daughters help financially because women's earnings need to be supplemented. In extended families, the greater number of adults allows more people to enter the labour market. A notable finding of the Querétaro study was that in families where wage-earning was divided between two or more people there was a greater tendency to pool all earnings in a collective family budget and to allocate finance more equitably among the dependants (Chant, 1984a). The built-in checks to egoism caused by sharing earnings could mean the family (and its male head where relevant) has a vested interest in sending as many members as possible out to work and maximizing potential income. In one in two of the nuclear households the husband-father does not share his earnings, and he feels he has nothing to gain if his wife goes out to work.

Male authority is modified in non-nuclear structures. In single-parent households the absence of the male leaves the woman the freedom to decide whether to take up paid work (though she often has to). In extended households, the presence of several earners means no man has the position of sole provider and arbiter of expenditure. Women who are not dependent on one wager-earner alone are in a stronger position to press for the right to employment outside the home.

Furthermore, the sharing of workroles, both paid and unpaid, appears to spread an ethic of equal participation in the strategies and benefits of family life: it makes it less easy to justify the division of labour on the basis of sex. For example, if one adult woman in the family has paid employment, it is difficult to substantiate an argument that another woman may not.

A final influence on the entry of women into the labour force is the support gained through having other women resident in their homes. For example, there is often more than one adult woman in the home in male-headed extended families; this contributes to female solidarity and strength and helps women challenge male authority.

Conclusion

We have discussed the way household type and composition influence women's involvement in the labour force in Querétaro, Mexico. These "supply" constraints include cultural norms, age and fertility, and the predominance of the nuclear family, in which few women are allowed by their husbands to enter the labour market. The nuclear family is conducive to a strict segregation between male and female roles, whereas other family patterns not only make it functionally more feasible for women to work, but also allow a degree of deviation from the standard ideology that a woman's place is in the home.

Female heads have the freedom to determine how they will organize the family's earning strategies. Female spouses in male-headed extended families enjoy a reduction in their housework burdens if these are shared by other family members, they have greater support for their claim to work from other female members, and the sharing of decision-making and finance among several adults means the male head has less of a prerogative in dictating what his wife will do and more of a vested interest in maximizing the earning potential of the household.

REFERENCES

Bromley, R. (1982). "Working in the streets: survival strategy, necessity or unavoidable evil?" in Gilbert, A. in association with Hardoy, J. E. and Ramirez, R. (eds.), *Urbanisation in contemporary Latin America: critical approaches to the analysis of urban issues.* Chichester: John Wiley, 59–77.

Chant, S. (1984a). *Las Olvidadas: a study of women, housing and family structure in Querétaro, Mexico,* unpublished Ph.D. dissertation, University College, London.

Gugler, J. (1981). "The rural-urban interface and migration," in Gilbert, A. and Gugler, J., *Cities, poverty and development: urbanization in the Third World.* Oxford: Oxford University Press.

Lailson, S. (1980). "Expansion limitada y proliferacion horizontal. La industria de la ropa y el tejido de punto," *Relaciones del Colegio de Michoacán,* 1(3), 48–102.

Latin American and Caribbean Women's Collective (1980). *Slaves of slaves: the challenge of Latin American women.* London: Zed Press.

Lomnitz, L. A. de (1977). *Networks and marginality — life in a Mexican shanty town.* New York: Academic Press.

Moser, C. (1978). "Informal sector or petty commodity production: dualism or dependence in urban development?" *World Development*, 6(9–10), 1041–64.

———— (1981). "Surviving in the surburbios," *Bulletin of the Institute of Development Studies*, 12(3), 19–29.

Nalven, J. (1978). *The politics of urban growth: a case study of community formation in Cali, Colombia,* Ph.D. dissertation, University of California at San Diego, reprinted by Ann Arbor: Michigan.

Meza Vargas, M. A. (1982). *"Desarrollo industrial en el estado,"* in PRI, *Consulta popular en las reuniones nacionales:* Querétaro, 22–24, Mexico City, PRI.

6.4   Sharon Stichter

Changing Gender Relations in Middle-Class Kenyan Families

INTRODUCTION

Research on changing families finds that, universally, an increasing number of marriages are monogamous, neolocal (i.e. the couple lives separately, not in an extended family household), love-based (rather than arranged), and (relatively) egalitarian. Not surprisingly, middle-class Kenyan families are increasingly reflecting this change of direction.

Among urban middle-class Kenyans, polygamy is increasingly rare, particularly where women's education is high. Family wealth is increasingly derived from waged work, and women are active in the labour force. In this setting, children are an economic cost, not the asset they are in rural communities, so couples cannot afford to have large families. Educated Kenyan women want more egalitarian relationships than were the norm in the past.

The next excerpt asks whether these changes have affected the balance of power within households. This is a question echoed by sociologists in many countries, including Canada. The author concludes that women have gained little in decision-making power, despite their economic contributions. Indeed this is the conclusion sociologists reach in most studies of decision-making among western couples. (See, for example, excerpt 8.4 on women's "double burden" in Japan and Great Britain.)

Stichter, Sharon (1985). "The Middle-Class Family in Kenya: Changes in Gender Relations," *African Urban Studies*, 21 (Spring) 39–52. Reprinted by permission of the author.

Unfortunately, this kind of research is new in the developing world, so we have no way of telling how much better off these women are than their mothers or grandmothers.

This paper addresses the changes in women's position in the family resulting from creation of an urban middle class in Kenya. It focuses on male-female relations in terms of (1) material appropriation and exchange within the conjugal unit, (2) conjugal power and decision making, and (3) domestic labor. The underlying question is whether more egalitarian, "joint" relations are coming into being in the domestic domain, such as are said to exist in contemporary European and U.S. middle class families.

Middle-Class Families in Nairobi

A survey of 317 families living in two housing estates on the edge of Nairobi, Buru Buru and Umoja, was carried out in July and August 1979. Systematic random samples of 10 percent and five percent of households were chosen in Buru Buru and Umoja, respectively, and both the wife (or wives) and the husband were interviewed. The two phases of Buru Buru together had about 1,897 units, and Umoja had 2,903 units at the time of interviewing. The cost of the housing varies, Umoja being much less expensive.

The sample is representative of Nairobi's small but growing African middle class. White-collar workers predominate in the sample. Nearly 70 percent of the women interviewed were active in the labor force.

Aspects of Household Structure

The fact that any African marriage is at least potentially polygynous dilutes the wife's claims on her husband's income in comparison to those she might make under monogamy. The rate of reported polygyny in this sample was only four percent, much below the levels found by Parkin (1978, p. 45) in 1968 in the low income estate of Kaloleni. In the three estates examined here, being the only wife was significantly and positively correlated with the educational level of the wife and with being Kikuyu. It was negatively correlated with large age and education differences between husband and wife, with the age of the husband, and with being a Luo. Having only one wife was noticeably not correlated with either the education of the husband or with household income; in fact, the polygyny rate was highest in Buru Buru 2. This suggests that increasing male incomes and education levels may not lead to a decline in polygyny, but that, as Parkin argued for the Luo, increasing female education levels may.

It is impossible to assess the rate of "disguised polygyny," the practice whereby a man keeps a mistress or "outside wife" in separate accommodation. Rumor had it that some of the single women in Umoja were in fact "outside wives."

The majority of marriages, even among the urban middle class, are contracted according to custom, even if there is also a church ceremony. The latter effectively assures the first wife of at least a superior status in relation to any succeeding co-wives and is also a sign of economic status, since the celebrations are expensive. Whatever the marriage type, a wife has little protection against her main risks: lack of support for herself and her children and physical abuse. A marriage reform bill, which would have unified marriage types, made polygyny contingent on the agreement of the first wife, and outlawed the custom of wife-beating, has twice been voted down in parliament. A bill which would have enforced child support also failed to pass.

In customary marriages (nearly all), the bridewealth payments continue to define the position of the wife as subordinate; 90 percent of the marriages in this sample involved bridewealth. The persistence of polygyny, bridewealth, large household size, frequent and extended visits from relatives, and control of older generations over land inheritance all suggest the "nuclear family" and the "conjugal estate" are at best only weakly emergent among the Kenyan middle class. Yet, the forces of change are great. Wealth increasingly depends on salaries, and families are increasingly able to guarantee status and property (such as educational advantages) to only a small, rather than a large, family. Strong cultural forces for change operate through the mass media and the education system. The education of women may be particularly important. Educated Kenyan women express a desire for a more emotionally close and egalitarian relationship with their husbands, for monogamy, and for the husband's involvement in childrearing (Whiting, 1977; Parkin, 1978, p. 261; Kayongo-Male and Onyango, 1984, pp. 65–67).

Access To Conjugal Resources

How are income resources dispersed and controlled in the domestic unit? Informal conversation suggested wives are likely to put a greater proportion of their resources into a household pool than do husbands. One indication of the husband's willingness to pool his resources with his wife is the presence of a joint bank account. Only 22 percent of the men in the sample reported they maintained such accounts, 29 percent in Buru Buru 2 and 13 percent in Buru Buru 1 and Umoja. Some of these men could also have had individual accounts. Wives were asked whether they kept their earnings separate or put them into a common household fund; 44 percent said they put most of their earnings into the common fund. Even if resources are pooled, there is not necessarily equality of control. Women were asked: "Who decides what is done with the money you contribute?" Twenty-two percent reported that they did, 66 percent said the spouses decided together, and 12 percent said the husband decided.

The wives were asked: "Between you and your husband, who usually pays for the following items?" (See Table 1.) These items are assumed to be a reasonable list of the major budgetary outlays of urban African households. Any sharing of costs can be interpreted as a decline of male financial dominance and an increase

TABLE 1   DIVISION OF FINANCIAL RESPONSIBILITY (IN PERCENT)

| | Husband | | | Wife | | |
	Only	Mostly	Equal	Mostly	Only	Total
Rent/mortgage	52	29	14	2	3	100
Furniture	41	27	25	3	4	100
School fees	42	23	25	4	6	100
Food	26	15	35	4	20	100
Clothing						
Husband	43	35	19	1	2	100
Children	25	13	46	4	12	100
Wife	27	16	28	8	21	100
Wages, housegirl	19	16	23	10	32	100
Average	34	22	27	4	13	100

in the wife's financial responsibilities. On average, husbands continue to be responsible for the major household costs. Strong wifely financial autonomy and equality in financial contributions are rare.

Wives tend to be responsible for the housegirl's wages and their own clothing, while husbands tend to be responsible for the rent or mortgage, the children's school fees, large furniture items, their own clothing, and the car if there is one. Food and clothing for the children tend to be shared.

To explore the correlates of wifely financial responsibility, a scale was created from the accumulated, equally weighted scores on budgetary items. It ranges from one to five; the higher the score, the greater the wifely responsibility. The responsibility scale is most highly correlated with whether the wife is employed. Lower but significant relationships (positive or negative) were found with the wife's education level and age, difference in the spouses' ages, husband's education, household income, ethnicity (for Luo), whether the husband helps with the housework, and the presence of a housegirl. Multiple regression analysis indicated the wife's employment explains 41 percent of the total variance, the other factors each contributing only very small increases in explanatory power.

Jointness, or the "husband and wife equally" response, is more frequent as the wife's employment, education, and income rise. Responses vary markedly according to estate. Umoja, with the lowest level of female employment, also has the lowest level of "jointness" and the highest evidence of male dominance (Stichter, 1987). This finding is consistent with studies in Lusaka and Lagos, where it also was found that pooling is more common among middle-class than among lower class couples and increases as income and education increase (Munachonga n.d.; Karanja-Diejomaoh, 1978; Mack, 1978).

Domestic budgeting is acknowledged by observers and popular commentators to be a problem in Kenya and women are demanding more influence on decisions.

For example, women protest the widespread assumption that the wife's salary is meant to be spent on the household while the husband's may be spent on entertaining friends or on rural business enterprises (Kayongo-Male and Onyango, 1984, pp. 29–30). They also complain about the lack of financial trust and openness in marriage as well as their lack of control over their own earnings.

Conjugal Decision Making

Oppong (1974) argued that the greater a woman's financial contribution to a marriage, the greater will be her decision-making power within it. This study only provides qualified support for this view. The questions were framed in hypothetical terms, asking whether the husband or wife, or both together, would decide on buying a car, buying land or investing in business, where to send the children to school, and hiring a housegirl. These are major decisions for Kenyan middle class families. Equal weight was allotted to each decision, but the decision scale understates women's contribution because everyday decisions such as what to have for supper are not included. Scores ranged from one to three; the higher the score, the greater is the wife's decision making power. Many of the same factors correlate with decision-making as with financial responsibility. Husbands have more power over decisions in Umoja and least in Buru Buru 2. Their separate role in major decisions probably declines as income and wife's employment increase; her greater power over decisions, however, is almost solely in the area of hiring housegirls. Similarly, the "decide together" response increases as one moves from the lower to the higher income estate only if the housegirl question is omitted from the analysis (Stichter, 1987).

Hiring the housegirl is usually the wife's prerogative, and paying her is frequently also her province. (See Table 1.) This reflects the fact that domestic work is considered the woman's responsibility, although she is allowed to hire a substitute. As her income increases, she is likely to do just that. The presence of a housegirl is significantly correlated with women's employment and with household income. None of the factors examined, including wife's financial contribution to the household, appear to account in a major way for the variance in the

TABLE 2   SPHERES OF FAMILY DECISION MAKING (IN PERCENT)

Decision	Husband	Together	Wife	Total
Car purchase	30	69	1	100
Land/business	23	75	2	100
Schooling	13	79	8	100
Housegirl	4	40	56	100
Average	18	65	17	100

wife's decision making power. The most likely hypothesis is that it is mainly in domestic areas such as household help and children's schooling that the wife's decision making increases as her financial contributions do. In large-scale but relatively rare decisions, such as a car, or land, or businesses, her contribution is less often seen as relevant. There is no strong trend toward separate, autonomic decision making. The most frequent response shown in Table 2 is "decide together." Kenyan middle class wives appear to have difficulty translating earnings into truly joint decision making.

Domestic Work

It is still the wife who performs most household tasks, with help from a maid or housegirl. The wife usually purchases food, prepares and serves meals, does the washing, and takes care of the children in the evenings. The housegirl helps with all of these tasks, except shopping, at which the husband helps. The housegirl's range of tasks and total work contribution are surprisingly limited. The husband's contribution is in purchasing children's clothing and furniture, making small repairs, and in some cases taking children to and from school.

The wife and housegirl perform the most time-consuming and house-bound tasks. The husband's domestic contribution does not vary much across the estates and is not highly correlated with any of the major social background variables, such as age, education, income, or ethnicity. Segregation of tasks between husband and wife is notable.

The incidence of housegirls was virtually identical in Buru Buru 2 and Buru Buru 1 — 79 percent and 78 percent, respectively; only 43 percent of the Umoja sample had them. Typically, they are poor, uneducated, village girls. Surprisingly, only about one-quarter of them were close relatives of their employers, which was even less likely in higher income families.

The housegirl system poses a number of labor management problems for the wife. The first is finding and retaining a housegirl in a situation of fairly high turnover. This is normally the wife's responsibility, and it may involve a trip to the rural area. If a housegirl leaves, the wife may lose a week or two of work finding another one, with the result that her employer will be annoyed and inconvenienced. The second problem is in the quality of work. This is not only a question of theft or carelessness with household valuables; many women worry about the quality of childcare.

Many wives worry about their inability to influence their children or to provide adequately for them.

Conclusion

Middle income urban married couples in Nairobi usually pool at least part of their income yet adhere to much separation in decision making and household tasks. The husband's dominance in major financial decision making persists. Wives often do not have much autonomy within marriage. Housework is still largely the responsibility of wives, although most working wives are able to hire housegirls to help.

Lewis (1977) has observed that for Ivorian women of all classes, marriage remains as desirable an asset as it was traditionally. Their control over their own financial resources makes it possible for them to maintain leverage and autonomy within marriage. Smock (1977) describes Ghanaian middle class women as having moved from traditional autonomy to modern subordination. The Kenyan situation differs from these West African cases in that traditional spousal decision-making arrangements do not seem to have accorded the wife as much independence as was the case in some West African societies. This research suggests that the problem in Kenya is that traditional subordination in marriage persists, despite contemporary economic change.

REFERENCES

Karanja-Diejomaoh, W. (1978). "Disposition of Incomes by Husbands and Wives: An Exploratory Study of Families in Lagos." In C. Oppong, ed., *Marriage, Fertility and Parenthood in West Africa*. Canberra: Department of Demography, Australian National University.

Kayongo-Male, D. and P. Onyango (1984). *The Sociology of the African Family*. London: Longman Group Limited.

Lewis, B. C. (1977). "Economic Activity and Marriage among Ivorian Urban Women." In A. Schlegel, ed., *Sexual Stratification: A Cross-Cultural View*. New York: Columbia University Press. Pp. 161–91.

Mack, D. E. (1978). "Husbands and Wives in Lagos: The Effects of Socioeconomic Status on the Pattern of Family Living." *Journal of Marriage and the Family* 40:807–16.

Munachonga, M. n.d. "The Conjugal Power Relationship: An Urban Case Study in Zambia." Falmer, U.K.: Sussex University. Xerox.

Oppong, C. (1974). *Marriage among a Matrilineal Elite: A Family Study of Ghanaian Senior Civil Servants*. London: Cambridge University Press.

Parkin, D. (1978). *The Cultural Definition of Political Response: Lineal Destiny among the Luo*. New York: Academic Press.

Schuster, I. M. G. (1979). *New Women of Lusaka*. Palo Alto, Calif.: Mayfield Publishing.

Smock, A. (1977). "Ghana: From Autonomy to Subordination." In J. Giele and A. Smock, eds., *Women: Roles and Status in Eight Countries*. New York: John Wiley.

Stichter, S. (1987). "Women and the Family: The Impact of Capitalist Development in Kenya." In M. Schatzberg, ed., *The Political Economy of Kenya*. New York: Praeger. Pp. 137–60.

Whiting, B. (1977). "Changing Life Styles in Kenya." *Daedalus* (Spring): 211–25.

QUESTIONS

DISCUSSION QUESTIONS

1. Ask men and women in the class to consider their occupational choice in light of gender socialization. What (or who) has influenced their choice?

2. What brought about changes in the attitude of North American men to paid work for women? Do you predict similar attitude changes in Latin America?

3. Has Stichter overstated the case about Kenyan women's lack of decision-making power? Do you think the results would be much different for a study conducted in Canada? Would it matter *where* in Canada the study were done?

4. Is feminism passé in North America? Why or why not?

DATA COLLECTION EXERCISES

1. Replicate Nordenstam's study of male–female differences in conversational style. Do you notice similar differences in your North American sample?

2. Using the United Nations sourcebook *The World's Women* (see suggested readings below), create a table to compare political participation, labour force participation, fertility, and divorce rates for women for countries by region. What does this show you?

3. Select representative questions from the Canadian Gallup Poll (look in the reference section of a university library) to evaluate changing attitudes to maternal employment over the last two or three decades.

4. Ask 20 men and women at your college or university what job they expect to be doing in ten years. Then, using current labour force data, calculate the extent to which identified jobs are sex-typed. Also, try to find current income data for the jobs.

WRITING EXERCISES

1. Is gender inequality inevitable? Answer in a brief essay.

2. Can women have it all: career, relationship, and children? Create a brief dialogue between two women who take opposing sides in this question.

3. Write a brief essay analyzing gender inequality in two developing countries. Be sure to compare rates of labour force participation, occupational segregation, and participation in political life, among other things.

4. Write a brief essay about the anti-feminist backlash in North America. What is the basis of its appeal? Do you think it will it gain or lose strength in the 1990s?

SUGGESTED READINGS

1. Statistics Canada (1990). *Women in Canada: a Statistical Profile*, second edition, Ottawa: Minister of Supply and Services. This book is an excellent reference for information concerning a number of aspects of Canadian women's lives including family, education, health, labour force activity, income, and so on.

2. Steinem, Gloria (1992). *Revolution from Within: A Book of Self Esteem*. Toronto: Little Brown and Company (Canada). This personal exploration by the editor of *Ms.*

Questions

magazine is at once readable, affirming and insightful: a good read for men and women alike. As Steinem demonstrates, "It's never too late for a happy childhood."

3. Tavris, Carol (1992). *The Mismeasure of Women.* New York: Simon and Shuster. This book looks at the large number of studies comparing men and women and the biases that underlie them.

4. United Nations (1991). *The World's Women 1970–1990; Trends and Statistics.* New York: United Nations Publications. Like the Canadian reference, this book is an invaluable source for understanding and comparing changes in women's lives.

FAMILY

Introduction

North American family life has changed a great deal in the last half of the twentieth century. Compared to families in the 1950s, families today are smaller and much less stable. Divorce is more common and far more people live alone. The birth rate has dropped to below replacement level. Attitudes have also changed. For example, we have much more tolerance for "nontraditional" relationships, including homosexual couples and couples who live together without marrying.

Indeed, these changes have been so dramatic, and have occurred so quickly, that they have caused alarm in some quarters. Anti-feminist groups like R.E.A.L. Women in Canada decry the state of family life and the implications of women's labour force participation and divorce on children. They would like to see a return to the "Father

Knows Best" world of the past. But as comfortable as that image may be to some people, it is impossible to recreate now. New family patterns are too well established to reverse.

Not only North American or Western families are changing. Cross-cultural studies show that families *everywhere* are changing and becoming more similar in structure. In societies where extended family living has been the pattern, an increasing number of couples are living away from their parents, because of work or education. Young people expect and exercise more choice in marriage partners. And, although this is not universal, there is a trend toward more equality between spouses than in the past.

Fertility Changes

In the industrial world, including Canada, fertility is below replacement. Indeed, low levels of childbearing in the developed world have been consistent enough to have been given the label "the second demographic transition" by van de Kaa. (See excerpt 12.4 below.) Without immigration, the populations of most Western countries would shrink. Low fertility also ages the population: the smaller the proportion of young people, the greater the proportion of elderly.

Canada's declining birth rate reflects a smaller average family size and the postponement of childbearing, but also an increased number of childless families. However, about 90 percent of women in industrial countries have at least one child, and Canadian women conform to this trend.

One of the most significant recent changes in women's lives is increased control over reproduction. For the first time in history, women have safe and reliable contraception available to them. In Canada and the United States there is strong resistance to the use of abortion as a means of birth control. This is not so in China, where the dramatic success of the 1979 one-child policy depended on a wide net of medical services including contraception and abortion. In India, sex ratios that strongly favour males suggest that, as economic pressure increases, some families resort to female infanticide or selective abortion (to eliminate female fetuses).

The general availability of contraception has *not* reduced teenage pregnancy, particularly in the United States where rates are the highest in the developed world. Countries with liberal attitudes to contraception and sex education have much lower rates of teenaged pregnancy. In Sweden for example, there are very few unwanted births to women of any age or marital status.

Divorce Trends

In the industrial west, *both* marriage and divorce are more popular than ever. Divorce rates have increased throughout the world, particularly over the last two decades. The United States has one of the highest rates anywhere. While Canadian divorce rates are not as high as those in Sweden or the United States, they too have jumped since the 1968 Divorce Act changed the grounds for divorce. The crude divorce rate (the number of divorces per 100 000 married people in the population) was 54.8 in 1968. It rose to 124.2 in 1969 and 621.0 in 1970. Between 1970 and 1987 the divorce rate tripled.

In Canada and a number of other countries, divorce rates declined slightly in the mid-1980s, suggesting that divorce had "peaked." However, by 1986 in Canada rates again began to rise, so it is difficult to predict an upper limit.

One of the most important consequences of increased divorce is the larger number of women and children who suffer financially as a result. The phrase "feminization of poverty" was first used to describe the large number of divorced or widowed women who, because of little or intermittent work experience and the responsibility to care for young children, cannot support themselves or their children adequately. So, for example, research in the United States (Arendell, 1987) finds that at divorce, women's standard of living decreases by about 50 percent while men's standard of living actually increases.

Why did divorce rates increase so dramatically and why have they remained so high? There are no simple answers. In some research, high divorce rates are associated with increases in longevity, standards of living, women's labour force participation, and cohabitation. In other research, divorce has been linked to poverty and economic downturns. In any case, it would be simple-minded to conclude that changing these correlates would strengthen marital *commitment*. We seem to have developed extremely high expectations of marriage, and these expectations are not tied to a relationship with a particular spouse. As a result, a large fraction of adults divorce, but the majority of divorced people remarry.

Nontraditional Unions

Marriage is not universal in Canada, but most people (about 90 percent) marry. At any point in time there are far fewer married people in the population than that. An increasing number of people choose to live singly or in nonmarital unions. The change reflects changing attitudes and increased affluence. Now, a great many adults can earn enough to live comfortably singly. They may live alone because they have made a long-term commitment to single living, or because they have not yet married or remarried.

In Canada and the United States, (unmarried) cohabitation has become an increasingly accepted prelude to marriage. Yet "living together" is far less common here than in Scandinavia, where it is rare for a couple to marry *without* living together first. In many parts of the world, particularly Latin America, long-term cohabitation is a common alternative to marriage.

It is difficult to measure trends in cohabitation in Canada because no one counted cohabiting relationships officially before 1981. Then, six percent of all heterosexual couples were unmarried. By 1986, the number had reached eight percent. About half of these couples will eventually marry, and many will then divorce; in fact, the odds of divorce are higher for couples who previously cohabited than for couples who did not.

Women's Labour Force Participation

One of the most significant recent changes in family living has been the increased labour force participation of married women. In 1941, only four and a half percent of married Canadian women were in the labour force. By 1951, the proportion had risen to 11.2 percent and by 1961, to 20.8 percent. In 1991, 68 percent of women with children at home were working or looking for work, an increase of over half a million women since 1981 (1991 figures reported in the *Toronto Star*, March 3, 1993). The increase can be attributed primarily to economic need.

Some people are tempted to draw a causal connection between increased rates of divorce and the increased labour force participation of married women. Indeed, the "new right" do just this. But as Kingsley Davis (1984) argues, this is not a simple one-way relationship. Once divorce rates reach a certain point, married women will enter the labour force as insurance. This is the only rational thing to do.

So, the vast majority of women readers of this book can expect to juggle family responsibilities and paid employment for some part, or all, of their lives. Within their families, they will try to negotiate greater involvement by other family members. As a consequence they will feel over-worked and, if Arlie Hochschild's (1989) American research is generalizable to Canadian families, underappreciated.

Because of entrenched beliefs about the gendered division of labour, the vast majority of men continue to avoid "sharing" the responsibility for domestic work and child-care. On the other hand, there is increased evidence that many fathers regret the lack of time they have to parent. It seems likely that conventional work structures will have to be changed to meet the needs of employed parents; but so far, this idea has not met with much enthusiasm in North America.

Family Futures

In the past, family sociologists could speak confidently of predictable stages of a "Family Life Cycle." The usual stages were courtship, marriage, parenthood, post-parenthood, and grandparenthood. But today it is increasingly difficult to refer to predictable and patterned stages. Our families no longer look like the 1950s model of the nuclear family, and for most families, the changes have been positive. Most have centred around women's shifting family and economic responsibilities.

Now, Canadian women play a much larger part in making family decisions than their mothers or grandmothers did. That freedom has two sources: women's increased economic independence and their greater ability to control reproduction. Consequently, women today can live singly or as part of a couple, marry or not, parent or not.

Yet despite the available choices, most Canadians continue to value and choose marriage and children. For most of us, families remain a central prop throughout life.

REFERENCES

Arendell, T. J. (1987). "Women and the economics of divorce in the contemporary United States," *Signs*, 13(1), 121–135.

Davis, Kingsley (1984). "Wives and Work: The Sex Role Revolution and Its Consequences," *Population and Development Review*, 10, 397–417.

Hochschild, Arlie (1989). *The Second Shift: Working Parents and the Revolution at Home*. New York: Viking.

van de Kaa, Dirk (1987). "Europe's second demographic transition," *Population Bulletin*, 42(1), March, 1–57.

7.1 Alice Schlegel

Marriage Practices and the Value of Virginity

INTRODUCTION

Arranged marriages have occurred in every culture around the world. Until recently, most Eastern marriages (in Africa, Asia, and the Middle East) were arranged by parents of the couple. (On this, see the next excerpt by Ahmed.) Typically, the couple would live with the groom's family in a large extended family household. Brides were usually quite young, sometimes prepubescent. Part of the negotiation in arranged marriages focused on determining the value of the dowry (household goods and/or money given by the bride's family to the groom's family) or brideprice (gifts or money given by the groom and his family to the bride's family). Cross-culturally, brideprice is a more common practice than the giving of a dowry.

The next excerpt looks at the relationship between gift giving and pre-marital sexual permissiveness. It seems that virginity among brides is valued in societies where dowry or inheritance by women is common. As the excerpt explains, in these societies the emphasis on virginity is designed to make it hard for "inappropriate" young men to seduce (and possibly impregnate) women from higher status families. When no property accompanies the marriage, virginity is of little interest. "Thus there is an association between the giving of property and control of the girl's sexuality." It seems that ideas about virginity are rooted in practical concerns about maintaining family status.

There may be some connection between marriage transactions and the value on virginity, but it is not readily apparent what that connection is.

To illuminate this question, it is necessary to understand the varying effects marriage transactions — the movement of goods (most usually) or services at the time of a marriage — have on the transmission or retention of property and on the social debts incurred thereby. This question was addressed in Schlegel and Eloul (1987, 1988) and will be summarized here. Following that, marriage transactions and attitudes toward virginity will be analyzed. It will be argued that the virginity of daughters protects the interests of brides' families when they use marital alliances to maintain or enhance their social status.

Schlegel, Alice (1991). "Status, Property, and the Value of Virginity." Reproduced by permisssion of the American Enthropological Association from *American Ethnologist,* 18(4), November, 719–734. Not for further reproduction.

The form of marriage transaction that has received the most attention in the literature is bridewealth, goods given by the groom, usually with the assistance of his kin, to the family of the bride. Bridewealth generally does not remain with the family that receives it: it is used to obtain wives for brothers of the bride or an additional wife for her father. Thus, goods and women circulate and counter-circulate.

Women exchange is also a form of replacement, the exchange being direct rather than mediated by a transfer of property. Women exchange and bridewealth are most frequently found where women have economic value through their large contribution to subsistence (cf. Schlegel and Barry, 1986). In each case the result is a kind of social homeostasis.

Brideservice is often considered analogous to bridewealth, with payment in labor rather than goods. They differ in that the benefit of brideservice goes directly to the bride's household and is not circulated as are bridewealth goods. Thus, families with many daughters receive much free labor, while families with few get little.

While gift exchange, in which relatively equal amounts are exchanged between the families of the bride and groom, can occur at all levels of social complexity, it is often found in societies with important status differences in rank or wealth. Since residence is predominantly patrilocal in gift-exchanging societies, the bride-receiving household is socially in debt to the bride-giving one. The exchange of equivalent goods is a way of ensuring intermarrying families are of the same social status, as indicated by the wealth they own or can call up from among their kin and dependents.

Status is a major consideration in dowry-giving societies. The bride's dowry is sometimes matched against the groom's settlement, thus ensuring equivalence, a usual practice among European land-owning peasants or elites. Dowry can also be used to "buy" a high-status son-in-law, a common practice in South Asia and one also known in Europe.

The final form of marriage transaction examined here is indirect dowry, which contains some features of both bridewealth, in that goods are given by the groom's family, and dowry, in that the goods end up with the new conjugal couple. Sometimes the groom's kin give goods directly to the bride, but more often they give goods to her father, who then gives goods to the new couple. Indirect dowry appears to be a way of establishing the property rights of the conjugal couples that make up larger households, in anticipation of eventual fission. In addition, it allows for status negotiation without either family being put in the other's debt (cf. Schlegel and Eloul, 1988).

There are variations within these major types, and additional features that are secondary and limited in distribution. In complex societies, the form of transaction may vary according to region or class. When the forms differ by status, the preferred form, practiced by the elite, is the one considered here.[1]

Marriage Transactions and the Value on Virginity

Information on the value placed on virginity comes from two sources. The primary one is the code, "Attitude Toward Premarital Sex (Female)" in Broude and Greene (1980). Using the Standard Sample of 186 preindustrial societies, Broude and Greene found information on this subject for 141 societies. Their code is divided into six levels of value: (1) premarital sex expected; (2) premarital sex tolerated; (3) premarital sex mildly disapproved of but not punished; (4) premarital sex moderately disapproved of and slightly punished; (5) premarital sex disallowed except with bridegroom; and (6) premarital sex strongly disapproved of. For the present study, the first three categories were collapsed into "virginity not valued" and the second three into "virginity valued." I have made four alterations to the code based on my reading of the ethnographic literature.

The second source is data collected by Herbert Barry and me on adolescent socialization in Standard Sample societies not coded by Broude and Greene. The data were collected on adolescent behavior, not cultural attitude; coders were asked to assess whether premarital sex was tolerated. Because the code is less detailed than Broude and Greene's and because it measures behavior rather than attitude, I offer information only on societies in which premarital sex is not tolerated and thus, by definition, virginity is valued. The value on virginity is not randomly distributed among societies with all types of marriage transaction. Table 1 shows the distribution, which is statistically significant: $p < .0001$. Even when those societies without marriage transactions are eliminated, the distribution is still statistically significant: $p < .001$.

Others have also found associations between premarital sexual permissiveness and structural or cultural features. (See Broude's [1981] summary.) Sexual permissiveness is associated with the simpler subsistence technologies, absence of stratification, smaller communities, matrilineal descent, matrilocal residence, absence of belief in high gods, absence of bridewealth (but bear in mind that in earlier studies,

TABLE 1   A TEST OF THE VALUE ON VIRGINITY ACCORDING TO THE TYPE OF MARRIAGE TRANSACTION

| Virginity valued | Marriage transaction[a] | | | | | |
	None	Bride-wealth[b]	Bride-service	Gift exchange	Dowry and indirect dowry	Total
Yes	3	16	6	9	18	52
No	26	27	10	3	7	73

$N = 125$; Chi-square = 27.13; $p < .0001$.

[a]Women exchange is omitted because of the small number of cases.
[b]Includes token bridewealth.

bridewealth has been conflated with indirect dowry), high female economic contribution, little or no property exchange at marriage, and ascribed rather than achieved status. These features are all highly intercorrelated, and some correlate with types of marriage transactions (Schlegel and Eloul, 1988).

Goody (1973, 1976) has shown virginity is prescribed in societies in which dowry or inheritance by women is customary, and this article pursues that line of thinking. The advantage of an explanation grounded in type of marriage transaction is that it does not simply assign premarital permissiveness to the less complex societies and restrictiveness to the more complex; it suggests motives for parental control of adolescent girls' sexuality.

Why Value Virginity?

I argue virginity is valued in societies in which young men may seek to better their chances in life by allying themselves through marriage to a wealthy or powerful family. In preserving a daughter's virginity, a family is protecting her from seduction, impregnation, and paternity claims on her child. This is most critical when certain kinds of property transactions are involved. In societies in which dowry is given (or daughters inherit), it would be attractive to seduce a dowered daughter (or heiress), demanding her as wife along with her property. Her parents would be reluctant to refuse, since the well-being of their grandchildren would depend upon their inheritance from both of their parents, and another man would be unlikely to marry the mother if it meant he had not only to support her children but to make them his heirs.

To illustrate that upward mobility through marriage with a dowered daughter or heiress is not foreign to dowry-giving societies, consider a common theme of European fairy tales. A poor but honest young man goes through trials to win the hand of the princess, who inherits her father's kingdom. Or, he wins her heart, and through the good offices of a fairy godmother or other spirit helper, they evade her wrathful father and are eventually reconciled with him. This more or less legitimate means to upward mobility is not so different from the illegitimate one, by which he wins the girl through seduction.

This line of reasoning was familiar to the 17th- and 18th-century English. As Trumbach tells it:

> Stealing a son ... was not the great crime. It was, rather, the theft of a daughter that was the real nightmare. For a woman's property became her husband's and she took his social standing.... To steal an heiress was therefore the quickest way to make a man's fortune — this was the common doctrine of the stage before 1710 — and it had a special appeal to younger sons. [1978:101–102]

All of the dowry-giving societies in the sample value virginity except the Haitians. Nevertheless, as Herskovits, writing about Haiti, points out: "Even though pre-marital relations are commonplace, ... the pregnancy of an unmarried girl is regarded as both reprehensible and unfortunate, and she is severely beaten for it by her family" (1971:111).

The majority of societies that exchange gifts and give indirect dowry also expect brides to be virgins. This is particularly true in the case of gift exchange, in which a bride's family gives property along with her, receiving a more or less equivalent amount from the family of the groom. As noted earlier, gift exchange is a way of ensuring the two families are of equal wealth or of equal social power. Impregnating a girl would give a boy and his family a claim on that girl and an alliance with her family, even though they would have to come up with something themselves for the exchange. As in dowry-giving societies, an emphasis on virginity discourages a man who is tempted to jump the status barrier by claiming fatherhood of a woman's child. The sample does, however, include three exceptions to the general requirement of virginity in gift-exchanging societies, and it is instructive to examine these deviant cases.

Malinowski (1932) has discussed the sexual freedom of Trobriand Island girls at length. However, Trobriand Islanders do not, at least ideologically, associate sexual intercourse with pregnancy. Weiner (1976:122) relates two cases in which pregnancy was attributed to magic, and her informants maintained women could conceive without male assistance. No boy, then, can make a claim on a girl simply because he has been sleeping with her and she has become pregnant.

Among the Omaha, virginity was not considered important for most girls (as coded in Broude and Greene [1980]), but according to Fletcher and La Flesche (1911), virgins were held in greater esteem than those who had lost their virginity. It was a privilege to marry a girl who had been tattooed with the "mark of honor," which was given to a virgin of a prominent family. Only the marriages in prominent families involved significant gift exchange. In ordinary marriages, the young husband was expected to work a year or two for his father-in-law, making brideservice more common than gift exchange. Thus, it was in the important marriages, accompanied by the exchange of goods of much value, that the bride was expected to be a virgin. Omaha elite families faced the danger that a daughter might be seduced by a youth who would persuade her to elope. As long as his family recognized the marriage and brought some gifts to the bride's father, the marriage was legitimate in the eyes of the community. Maintaining the virginity of high-status girls protected their families from unwanted alliances.

In Samoa, similarly, girls from untitled families had sexual freedom (as coded in Broude and Greene [1980]) but the daughters of titled chiefs did not. Children could be affiliated to the mother's group rather than the father's, Samoa having an ambilateral descent system. If the mother's rank was higher than the father's, the children's status would be elevated above their father's. High-status families would wish to guard their daughters against potential social climbers, who might be tempted to improve their children's position in life by seducing and marrying socially superior girls. It appears that only the arranged marriages, generally of high-status people, involved much gift exchange. Most marriages were of the "elopement" type and were much less expensive than the arranged ones (Shore, 1981).

When no property accompanies the marriage, virginity is of little interest. If the groom gives goods or labor, the picture is mixed, but fewer societies are restrictive than permissive. In societies in which the bride's side gives considerable property, as with gift exchange, dowry, and, in many cases, indirect dowry, virginity is most likely to be valued. Thus, there is an association between the giving of property, particularly from the bride's side, and control of the girl's sexuality. I have interpreted this as a means by which the families of girls prevent their being seduced by ineligible boys, resulting in alliances that could be an embarrassment.

Discussion

The question of the value on virginity revolves around whether premarital sexual intercourse leads to pregnancy, and whether biological fatherhood alone gives a man a claim on a child and its mother.

Virginity is not such an issue if abortion is freely available, as in Southeast Asia. Even there, however, the idealization of virginity is most common in Eurasia, and it is found in some other areas, such as Polynesia or native North America, where certain categories of girls are expected to be virginal. It is noteworthy that belief in the purity or spiritual power of virginity, chastity, and celibacy developed in those regions where dowry or gift-exchange was the established form or the form practiced by the elite and aspired to by those who would imitate them. Ideology does not arise *de novo* but is grounded in existential concerns and issues. I suggest the ideology of virginity has its source in pragmatic concerns about status maintenance and improvement.

The elite have secluded their daughters, possibly in imitation of the Hindu, Buddhist, or Moslem aristocrats whom they have emulated in other ways (cf. Reid, 1988:163).

Although abortive techniques are widely known and practiced, even where proscribed (Devereux, 1976), abortion is a last-ditch measure for preventing unwanted births and must take a distant second place to the maintenance of virginity.

Impregnating a girl does not automatically give a boy or man a claim to her child or to her. In the Trobriand Islands, as we have seen, biological fatherhood alone is simply not recognized. In other places, it may be recognized without giving the impregnator a paternity claim. Such a claim may have to be paid for through bridewealth and marriage to the mother; if it is not, the child is absorbed into the mother's kin group. This practice appears to be more common in Africa than in other regions. I suggest the acceptance of illegitimate children is greater when children are a distinct economic asset.

If children are not an unqualified asset to the mother's family, the rules of social life are likely to include the prescription that fathers take responsibility for their children, thus bringing biological and social fatherhood closer together. The responsibility for one's child can be restated as the right to that child, and biological fatherhood becomes a claim on social fatherhood. When the status of the mother is equal to or lower than that of the impregnator, it is to her advantage to press for marriage or at least support, so long as the impregnator is willing (or is unable to escape). When the mother is of greater wealth or higher status, particularly when her status or property will be inherited by her child, it is to the advantage of the impregnator to press *his* claim on the child and its mother. It is in such situations, I propose, that virginity is valued, as it is the surest way of preventing such claims.

ENDNOTES

[1] Coding on marriage transactions can be found in Schlegel and Eloul (1987). The Pawnee form has been recoded from absence to gift exchange, based on Grinnell (1891). The Somali, Teda, and Toda forms have been recoded from bridewealth to indirect dowry, based on Lewis (1961), Chapelle (1957), and Walker (1986), respectively.

REFERENCES

Barry, Herbert, III, and Alice Schlegel (1986). "Cultural Customs That Influence Sexual Freedom in Adolescence." *Ethnology* 25:151–162.

Broude, Gwen J. (1981). "The Cultural Management of Sexuality," in *Handbook of Cross-Cultural Human Development*. Ruth H. Munroe, Robert L. Munroe, and Beatrice B. Whiting, eds. pp. 633–673. New York: Garland.

Broude, Gwen J. and Sarah J. Greene (1980). "Cross-Cultural Codes on Twenty Sexual Attitudes and Practices," in *Cross-Cultural Samples and Codes*. Herbert Barry III and Alice Schlegel, eds. pp. 313–334. Pittsburgh: University of Pittsburgh Press.

Devereux, George (1976). *A Study of Abortion in Primitive Societies*. Rev. ed. New York: International Universities Press.

Fletcher, Alice and Francis LaFlesche (1911). *The Omaha Tribe*. Annual Reports of the Bureau of American Ethnology 27:17–672.

Goody, Jack (1973). "Bridewealth and Dowry in Africa and Eurasia," in *Bridewealth and Dowry*. Jack Goody and S. J. Tambiah, eds. pp. 1–58. Cambridge Papers in Social Anthropology no. 7. Cambridge: Cambridge University Press.

——— (1976). *Production and Reproduction*. Cambridge: Cambridge University Press.

Grinnell, George B. (1891). "Marriage among the Pawnee." *American Anthropologist* 4:275–281.

Herskovits, Melville J. (1971[1937]). *Life in a Haitian Valley*. Garden City, NY: Doubleday and Company.

Lewis, I. M. (1961). *A Pastoral Democracy: A Study of Pastoralism and Politics among the Northern Somali of the Horn of Africa*. London: Oxford University Press.

Malinowski, Bronislaw (1932). *The Sexual Life of Savages in Northwestern Melanesia*. London: Routledge and Kegan Paul.

Reid, Anthony (1988). *The Lands Below the Winds. Southeast Asia in the Age of Commerce 1450-1680*, Vol. 1. New Haven, CT: Yale University Press.

Schlegel, Alice and Herbert Barry III (1986) "The Cultural Consequences of Female Contribution to Subsistence." *American Anthropologist* 88:142-150.

——— (1991). *Adolescence: An Anthropological Inquiry*. New York: Free Press.

Schlegel, Alice and Rohn Eloul (1987). "Marriage Transactions: A Cross-Cultural Code." *Behavior Science Research* 21:118–140.

—— (1988). "Marriage Transactions: Labor, Property, and Status." *American Anthropologist* 90:291–309.

Shore, Bradd (1981). "Sexuality and Gender in Samoa: Conceptions and Missed Conceptions," in *Sexual Meanings*. Sherry B. Ortner and Harriet Whitehead, eds. pp. 192–215. Cambridge: Cambridge University Press.

Trumbach, Randolph (1978). *The Rise of the Egalitarian Family*. New York: Academic Press.

Walker, Anthony R. (1986). *The Todas of South India: A New Look*. Delhi: Hindustan Publishing.

Weiner, Annette B. (1976). *Women of Value, Men of Renown*. Austin: University of Texas Press.

7.2 Ashraf Uddin Ahmed

The Transition from Arranged Marriage in Bangladesh

INTRODUCTION

Sociologists have often found it useful to distinguish between Eastern and Western models of the family. Western families have typically been monogamous and love-based, households are small and nuclear, and couples live "neolocally," away from both sets of parents. By contrast, Eastern families have been based on arranged marriage, often contracted when brides are very young. Couples live with or very near extended family members; typically, they bear many children, and sons are valued more highly than daughters. The wealthiest men in society often practise polygamy.

Over the last few decades, Eastern marriage patterns have started to change in several ways. Now, couples marry later, exercise more choice in marriage partners, and more couples live in separate households. (See, for example, excerpt 12.2 below.)

The reasons for this change vary slightly from society to society. For example, in China, highly effective family planning policies were initiated in the 1970s, legislating a minimum age of marriage and limiting family size to one child. In the Middle East, change was accelerated by a dramatic rise in the standard of living and a subsequent increase in women's education. In Bangladesh, as the next excerpt shows, change was precipitated by socioeconomic deterioration.

Ahmed, Ashraf Uddin (1986). "Marriage and its Transition in Bangladesh," *International Journal of Sociology of the Family*, 16(1), Spring, 49–59. Reprinted by permission.

*I*n South Asian countries, irrespective of cultural conditions, a transition is visible in the pattern of family formation, the mating process, divorce and remarriage. In the last few decades, Bangladesh has also experienced transition in these aspects. The deterioration of socio-economic conditions has resulted in changes in the marriage pattern. For example, a dowry system is supplanting the older bride price system, and family background is no longer given its former importance in marriage negotiations. This paper attempts to evaluate these changing patterns and their linkages with socio-economic factors in Bangladesh society.

Marriage

Arranged marriage is dominant in most African and Asian countries. The proportion of marriages which are arranged nevertheless varies across nations. South Asian countries, except Sri Lanka, will probably be the highest in terms of the percentage of arranged marriages.

The arranged marriage performs the following functions: (1) it helps to maintain social stratification in general, (2) it affirms and strengthens parental power over the children, (3) it helps keep the family traditions and value systems intact, (4) it helps consolidate and extend family property, (5) it enhances the value of the kinship group, (6) it helps keep the tradition of endogamy if one desires (Goode, 1963; Chekki, 1968), and (7) it helps young people from getting into the uncertainty of searching for a mate.

Muslim Marriage

In Islam, marriage is a civil contract as opposed to a sacrament (Korsen, 1979). The Qu'ran encourages marriage. For those who do not have enough money to set up a separate house or to provide the basic necessities, however, it encourages abstinence until their condition improves. Besides this economic restriction, Islam has put restrictions on the eligibility of marriage partners such as uncle-niece, or aunt-nephew. Cross-cousin rather than parallel-cousin marriage is more common in Muslim societies, more so than any in other societies. For men to marry non-muslims is permissible, but for women it is not.

Hindu Marriage

From ancient times, marriage among Hindus has been considered as a ritual and a sacramental union. Marriage is an indispensable event of Hindu life, and the unmarried person is considered unholy. From the religious point of view, the unmarried person remains incomplete and is not eligible for participation in some social and religious activities. Except in a very few cases, the importance of marriage transcends not only the entire family but also the past ancestral line as well as future generations.

The Hindu religion has given great importance to progeny whereby fathers and their ancestors are assured a peaceful and happy afterlife. The customs and the rites of Hindu religion demand male children from each married couple. Parents want to make sure their sons marry and continue to have male children. Pointing to the tradition and custom of the Hindu religion, Basham said, "a father who did not give his daughter in marriage before the first menstruation incurred the guilt of procuring abortion (a very sin, worse than many kinds of murder) for every menstrual period in which she remained unmarried" (1963:167). These factors partly explain why marriage is universal and why child-marriage has been well accepted in the Indian sub-continent.

Child Marriage

The child-marriage system was started by the Hindus, and later adopted by the Muslims. In the mid-nineteenth century, this practice became more common among Muslims and lower-caste Hindus. The proportions used to vary by regions. In some areas Muslims had a higher child-marriage rate, and in other areas, the Hindus did. After a long struggle, progressive Indian leaders with the help of the British government succeeded in 1929 in making a law on age at marriage, known as the Sarda Act. According to this act, the minimum age at marriage for girls was fifteen years. The law, however, has largely remained unenforced to this day.

Having a female child was considered by Hindus to be a sign of God's unhappiness with a girl's parents. If parents had a girl-baby, they were reluctant to mention it to friends and relatives. Girls are always an economic burden to the parents until their marriage because they cannot contribute to the household income like sons. This has been strengthened by the partial acceptance of the Muslim *purdah* system, which does not allow them to work outside the household. Besides, the society places a high value on the chastity or virginity of the girls before marriage. Girls are also a psychological burden to the parents. If it is known that a girl is no longer a virgin, it will be difficult for her parents to find a husband for her. All these fears and responsibilities induce the parents to marry off their daughters as soon as possible no matter how old they are. The situation is gradually changing, however.

Economically, child-marriage is profitable to the parents. The amount of dowry or bride price is usually significantly smaller when it is a child-marriage than a youth marriage. The overall cost of gifts is usually less. To minimize the ceremonial costs, parents sometimes try to arrange the marriage of two sons or daughters at a time, even if the younger one is not of marriageable age.

Besides the economic factors, child betrothal occurs in order to maintain social ties between families. In some cases, two couples who have been good friends commit to the marriage of their children even when their children are not yet born. For Hindus, this practice may occur among friends within the same caste or subcaste. Among Muslims, it occurs among brothers and sisters, and this extends to friends. As most of the marriages are arranged, parents take it for granted that these marriages will eventually take place without objection from their children.

Mate Selection and Social Mobility

Most marriages in a traditional Muslim society are arranged by parents or guardians. Conventionally, parents of boys take the initiative. Sometimes they talk directly to the parents or propose through a *ghatak* (marriage broker) or through relatives and friends of either family. When parents of both families find the would be in-laws are suitable, the marriage takes place. Where marriage is arranged, the interests of the families get priority over the interests of the couple. Sometimes, the marriage partners do not get to see each other before the marriage. This is primarily a marriage between families and is termed a "blind marriage" by Parish and Whyte (1978).

Classical Islamic law sets two conditions — consent of the parties involved and a contract specifying the bride price (*mehr* [mahr]) to be given by the husband to his wife in the presence of witnesses. The consent sometimes is not free from the influence of parents.

Love marriage is thought to be disruptive to family ties, and is viewed as a children's transference of the loyalty from a family orientation to a single person, ignoring obligations to the family and kin group for personal goals. There is an old saying "love is blind." It overshadows the quality of spouses. It is a weak criterion for selection of a mate. People believe love after marriage is a heavenly or spiritual thing. God helps those who have sincere love for their spouses by giving them a peaceful life.

If parents are looking for a mate for their son, they first inquire about non-economical factors — beauty, age, family status, modesty, religiousness and literacy — and then economic factors — the amount of dowry and gift. Although dowry and gifts are important, there is no standard set for these. For daughters, parents inquire about the occupation, income, education and social status of the family of the would be son-in-law. The economic factors into which they inquire are the extent of land holding by his family if they are in rural areas, otherwise economic solvency or well-being of the family.

In Western societies, personal beauty of a girl is an important quality in the marriage market. A beautiful girl of low social class has a chance to marry a man at a much higher social class. She has a chance to trade her beauty at a higher price in the marriage market. Although this is true to some extent for every society, the chances of her upward mobility are much lower in a traditional society, where most of the marriages are arranged by guardians, so beauty does not get much importance in marriage negotiation.

Among the factors considered as important determinants in mating, education appears to have a stronger influence in the marriage market. Education increases the chances for hypergamy. If a man with a good education reduces his expectation for dowry and increases his willingness to make bridal gifts, he might be able to marry into a higher social class than his own, although this is forbidden in Islam. Education still has a strong influence in the marriage market, but it may not remain the same in the future if the employment situation in the non-agricultural sector does not improve. A business profession with some educa-tion is gradually overriding the value of an educated bridegroom.

Occupation, which has a strong relation with education, is another important factor for men. Employment in urban areas plus education has more demand in the marriage market. Of course, it depends on the type of occupation. Recently, men working in the Middle-East or in any foreign country have been preferred by the bride's parents. Parents think to marry off their daughters to economically sol-vent and socially well-placed mates. Economic solvency often gets the highest pri-ority among the factors. On the other hand, when parents look for a mate for their sons, they place greater importance on the social status of the bride's family in ad-dition to the economic factor. Marriage is therefore emerging as one way social mobility might take place. If the family status of a person is high, but achieved personal quality is low, the person has a chance either to marry in the same social class or one relatively lower than one's own. As a result, downward mobility takes place in one family and upward mobility in the other family. On the other hand, if the family status of a person is low but his achieved personal quality (or human capital) is high, the person has a chance to marry in a social class higher than one's own and thereby upward mobility takes place. Otherwise, most marriages occur within the same social class (homogamy).

Hindus practice endogamy. The first criterion is caste and sub caste identity. Within caste or sub caste, the factors of dowry and selection process are the same as discussed before. Cross-caste marriage does not occur unless it is love marriage. A negligible percentage of marriage can be found around the border line of sub-castes. Love marriage seldom occurs among Hindus. In Bangladesh, marriages be-tween relatives appear to be declining. Three factors seem to have contributed to this fact. The first is the rise of dowry which resulted from the delay of men's mar-riages and a surplus of marriageable women. The second is the rise in men's spatial mobility resulting from increased literacy and non-agricultural occupations. The last factor is the diffusion of the Western belief that these marriages produce sickly children.

Is There a Marriage Squeeze in Bangladesh?

A few decades back, there was a scarcity of potential wives in the area. This short-age of marriageable women may be regarded as one cause of child-marriage. The impact of the demographic transition, high fertility and declining mortality, has resulted in an age-distribution with a broader base. Although the sex-ratio at birth has been about 105 males per 100 females for a long time, this does not imply the number of potential husbands is higher than the number of potential wives. This is because the age of eligibility for marriage is not the same for men and women. Parents of girls, particularly in rural areas, consider their daughters marriageable at menarche. On the other hand, men are not usually considered marriageable until they have stable source of income either from a job or from their parents' property. This contributes to the age difference between spouses.

In urban areas, young men are deferring their marriages. Under present economic conditions, men are finding it difficult to marry because the amount of money they earn cannot buy the basic necessities for even two people, aside from the problem of housing. As a result, men's demand for dowry is becoming a dominating factor in the marriage market, although the government has officially banned the dowry system. If the job market for educated women were better, the situation would be somewhat better; their potential earnings would be a substitute for dowry.

In rural areas, the situation does not differ much. People who own cultivatable land and can earn their own living are more likely to get married earlier. The surplus of labor in rural areas has also affected the marriage pattern there. Besides these economic factors, the age distribution of a growing population demonstrates that the potential wives outnumber the potential husbands, since the population of the preceding age groups are often larger than the following age groups.

Another factor, labor migration to the Middle-East, has affected the marriage market. Most of these migrants appear to be single. This employment opportunity has delayed the marriages of some people. On the other hand, it has helped some people to afford to marry. In general, however, it has contributed to late marriage for most of the people involved.

Lastly, the liberation movement had some effect on the number of potential husbands, as the number of deaths of young men was much higher than other age groups.

These factors are working together for the creation of late marriage and for increasing the number of single people. This marriage squeeze has emerged in all the South Asian countries (Caldwell, Reddy and Caldwell, 1983) and in other parts of Asia.

Discussion

Social development has made changes in Bangladesh. The concept of marriage might have not changed much, but the process of family formation and mating process has.

In mate selection, the persons involved in marriage are having more to say. Economic considerations are coming to have increasing importance, as are the achieved qualities of the marriage partners. In absence of other capital, human capital is becoming the strongest determinant in the selection since 90 percent of the population live below the poverty level in this country. As a result, transfer of assets among them is gradually declining due to their inability to produce a surplus. Human capital thus is becoming a dominant exchange commodity in marriage. The rationality of this consideration lies in the condition of the job market, which is to say on the demand for human capital.

The urbanites are gradually being highly exposed to Western culture. These people like to imitate the imported culture. Consequently, urban culture is not highly traditional. Also, the severity of economic pressures is making people less able to perform according to the demands of the traditional culture. Although this country is one of the least developed countries, nevertheless the society is experiencing a change in the pattern of family formation, family type and marriage decision. These changes are somewhat in the direction of the characteristics of the Western World, as limited by a poor economy.

Both demographic and socio-economic conditions have contributed to the marriage squeeze. The situation might improve if employment opportunities for women and the overall literacy rate increase. The concept of marriage as universal in the society may not remain as strong as it used to be. From the marriage squeeze, a positive effect, a reduction in population growth, is emerging.

REFERENCES

Basham, A. L. (1963). *The Wonder that was India.* New York: Howthorn Books, Inc.

Caldwell, J. C., P. H. Reddy, and Pat Caldwell (1983). "The Causes of Marriage Change in South India." *Population Studies,* 37:343–361.

Chekki, D. A. (1968). "Mate Selection, Age at Marriage and Propinquity Among the Lingayats of India." *Journal of Marriage and the Family,* 30:707–711.

Goode, William J. (1963). *World Revolution and Family Patterns.* London: The Free Press.

Parish, William L. and Mortin L. Whyte (1978). *Village and Family in Contemporary China.* Chicago: The University of Chicago Press.

7.3 Linda MacLeod

Wife Battering in Canada

INTRODUCTION

Linda MacLeod, author of the next excerpt, estimates that each year a million Canadian women are beaten by their husbands. In Canada in 1988, 57.4 percent of all female victims of homicide were killed by someone with whom they shared a domestic relationship. Typically, marital homicide is related to wife battering: wives who kill their husbands do so in self-defense. Other wives are killed by abusive husbands in an escalating cycle of abuse. (You may want to review excerpt 3.4 by Gartner before reading this next piece. It provides the "big picture" on this worldwide problem of violence against women.)

MacLeod, Linda (1987). *Battered but not Beaten: Preventing Wife Battering in Canada.* Reprinted by permission of the Canadian Advisory Council on the Status of Women, Ottawa.

The excerpt begins by describing two explanations of wife battering: power-based theories and learning theories. Power-based theories suggest that wife battering is an extension of socially accepted expressions of male power. Men physically assert themselves to re-establish their power.

By contrast, learning theories focus on the consistent finding that a high proportion of abusers and survivors of abuse were abused as children and in turn abuse their own children. In other words both men and women learn to abuse (or accept abuse) as a response to frustration. Neither abusers nor survivors have learned other more appropriate ways of dealing with failure or frustration.

Many battered women, according to MacLeod, do not identify with either theory. Instead, they feel great ambivalence about their relationship. They do not necessarily see their husbands as more powerful, nor do they want to live with abuse. As MacLeod argues, unless social service workers understand the ambivalence battered women feel they will not be able to provide the kind of help battered wives will find useful.

Battered women and batterers come from all walks of life. They may be working outside the home or in the home. They may be unemployed or have a steady job. They may be rich or poor, well-educated or illiterate, of any nationality or race, young or old, with or without children.

Despite the difficulty of understanding wife battering, two major types of explanation have been widely used to respond to battered women, their children, and the men who batter them.

Power-Based Theories

These theories explain that violence against women is perpetuated by society's power structure which makes men dominant over women through the creation of separate and unequal roles for each gender. This dominance is reinforced through institutional rules and structures based on male supremacy.

As staff members of the Women's Research Centre in Vancouver have stated:

> *Wife assault is a reality in our society because men have the socially ascribed authority to make the rules in marriage, and because violence against their wives is accepted in the eyes of society, as an appropriate instrument of control. The social and economic structure of marriage as an institution in which women are dependent on men, requires this assignment of authority to men.*[1]

Power-based theories of wife battering emphasizing sex-based inequality and the patriarchal structure of society have gained acceptance by policy-makers and service-providers in this field. This explanation for wife battering appears in most writings on the subject and helps guide intervention services for battered women, their partners, and their children.

Research on the power dynamics in battering families also asserts that power is more highly valued in battering families than in non-battering families. On the surface, this power may not always overtly rest with the man. However, research findings suggest that, in families where the woman is dominant in terms of decision-making or earning power, or where the woman is perceived to be superior in some other way, violence is often used by the man to shift the balance of power. Many counsellors reported that many men resort to physical violence when they feel their wives are more articulate than they are. These men frequently complain that they can't win an argument with their wives, so they "shut them up" by the use of force.

In power-based theories, the acceptance and social reinforcement of violence in the family is a means to establish and to maintain the male in a dominant relationship over his wife.

Because male roles are socially created as dominant over female roles,

> *Wife assault arises out of the socio-cultural belief that women are less important and less valuable than men and so are not entitled to equal status and respect. Thus, central to the task of dealing with the problem of wife assault is the need to recognize that wife assault is a social problem experienced by many Canadian women each year rather than an isolated interpersonal problem between two particular spouses.*[2]

Learning Theories

Learning theorists argue that witnessing or suffering violence teaches people to use violence to try to solve problems or deal with stress.[3] This argument is supported by research and by statements from service-providers which reveal that many batterers come from families where their mothers were battered and/or where they themselves were physically, sexually, or psychologically abused as children.[4] These findings are corroborated by the statistics collected for this study. Sixty-one percent of the partners of the women who stayed in transition houses in 1985 had been abused as children. Thirty-nine per cent of the battered women reported being physically abused as children, 24 percent reported being sexually abused, and 48 percent reported being emotionally abused as well. Of the women who said they physically abused their own children, 69 percent said they had themselves been physically abused during their childhood.

Learning theorists also argue that the use of violence as a discipline tool can teach violence. In this vein, researchers report a "strong relationship between parental punishment and aggression" and suggest that

> *increasing evidence indicates that a high price is paid for maintaining order in the family through violence. The norms that legitimate violence assure a family institution and a society characterized by violence for years to come.*[5]

Learning theorists also frequently explain the perpetuation of violence by stating that victims, friends, and society as a whole unintentionally reinforce the violence.

> *The victim after the beating, may indeed do as he insists; others may treat him with more respect and often he feels more in control. Even if he feels remorseful or guilty about her injuries he (and sometimes the victim herself) tends to blame the victim for "causing"*

him to "lose control." He denies responsibility for the negative behaviour. Due to the tacit acceptance of family violence in society and to the lack of clear messages that his violent behaviour must stop, his violence is rarely punished.[6]

Finally, learning theorists suggest that witnessing violence vicariously can teach some men to use violence within or outside the family. This tenet has created concern about pornography as a teaching tool for violence.

These types of explanations, one based on the structure of power in our society, the other on learning theory, have clarified our understanding of wife battering, and have helped to guide intervention efforts. Yet many shelter workers and other service-providers lamented, "These theories that seem so clear to us just don't seem to ring true for too many of the women who come to us."

How do Battered Women Understand the Battering?

Battered women speak of a shifting, ambiguous power. They spoke sometimes of feeling powerless against their partners. They also spoke of their power in the relationship and of the powerlessness of their partners. Many believe women are more powerful than men, as the quote below elucidates:

I can't quite make sense of what the women here [at the shelter] are saying about the patriarchal structure of society and about power and society making men more powerful and all that. When I was growing up, my mother was for sure stronger than my Dad in every way but physically. She was smarter, could do more, and more people respected her. I think it's the same with my husband and me. There's no way he's stronger than me, except physically, and that's why he hits me, because he feels so low.

Other women elaborated this theme in terms of a mother-son model of relationships between themselves and their partners.

My husband and all the men I've ever known are like little boys. We're really like their mothers, underneath. Everyone keeps telling me to leave him; they say he'll destroy me. But they don't know how strong I am and how weak he is underneath.

Others spoke of the power they feel in the relationship.

Sure I feel sorry for him. He says he would have nothing without me and the kids. I know he's pretty rotten sometimes. But he really needs me. I guess that's why I keep going back. He makes me feel important.

Still others spoke of their partners as victims or losers in society.

You can talk about men being powerful in our society if you want, but you're not talking about my husband. My husband's never had any power in his whole life. He's never had a chance. He was born poor. He was born Indian. He's never felt better than anyone. He's never felt better than me. It's because he's so low that he hits me.

Many battered women do not feel like powerless victims, and will not respond positively to services which treat them like victims instead of survivors.

These experiences remind us of the complexity of the realization of power in individual relationships. They also remind us that power in our society is not just gender-based; it is also class-, race-, and age-based.

Many battered women also understand battering as something that "got out of hand," as an extension of a normal part of a normal relationship. Many battered women feel their relationship started out much like any other relationship and, in fact, some emphasize that they feel they had an unusually loving, intense, and close relationship.

Intimate relationships, by definition, generate a wide range of emotions. The image of romantic love idealized in our society is characterized by highs and lows. Being "in love" is living "on the edge," participating in a kind of emotional aerobics. The socially accepted use of drugs, the preoccupation with "having it all," with creative stress, the fitness craze, and even our social addiction to soap operas and violent television shows emphasize high energy and intense emotional highs and lows.

For these reasons, wife battering at the outset is often difficult to prevent, or even to identify, because some violence (rough sexual play and psychological games intended to elicit jealousy) is intertwined with our ideal of "being in love" (isolation and possessiveness). In different socio-economic groups, this violence may be more or less psychological, or more or less physical, but the romantic desire to be alone together in a private world and the desire to have constant physical contact with your loved one are simply the "positive" faces of the jealousy and isolation which become part of most wife-battering experiences.

Battered women often talk of the intensity of their love for the batterer. Throughout this study, many battered women made the following kinds of statements: "I've never had better sex with anyone," "I just can't believe he'd hit me. I know he really loves me as much as I love him," "No one's ever loved me the way he does." Battered women also speak of the highs and lows of the relationship:

> *You know, life was a roller-coaster with Bill. In the end, of course, that became unbearable — all the tension. But in the beginning, it was just so thrilling. I never wanted to come down.*

Many battered women are guilty of no greater "weakness" than being in love with being in love. It's their attempt to stay in love, to retain an idealized vision of their partner, that often prevents many battered women from realizing they are being battered until the battering has become a part of life.

Women who are battered do not generally define themselves as battered the first time they are battered. In fact, because wife battering includes emotional, verbal, and financial battering, as well as physical and sexual battering, it may be difficult to define when the first incident actually occurred. This ambivalence is evident in the words battered women use to describe their early experiences with the batterer. It is not uncommon for battered women to say:

> *I was flattered by his jealousy at first — I thought it meant he loved me. He said he would rather stay home, just with me, than go out with friends. I loved the attention and closeness at first. I thought he was the most romantic man in the world.*

Even the first case of physical abuse is not always clear-cut. In many cases, the woman is "just pushed." While pushing can result in severe injuries, depending on the location of the push — down the stairs, over a chair, into a pot of boiling water on the stove, etc. — the push itself can be easily re-interpreted by the batterer and by the woman who is battered as something minor. The results of the push can be viewed as an accident.

> *I was just baffled the first time he hit me. It wasn't really a hit, you know, not like a punch or even a slap; he just pushed me really hard. I broke an arm, but it was from falling backward over a chair, not from his push.*

Another woman's statement mirrors these sentiments:

> *I couldn't believe my husband had hit me. I just kept asking, is this the same man who loves me so much that he can't stand it if another man talks to me? It was really easy for me to accept his explanation that he'd had a hard day at work and a little too much to drink. I couldn't see anything else without having to ask if he really did love me, and that was just too painful. It wasn't until much later, years of violence later, that I could see that the way he loved me — his jealousy, his possessiveness — were also part of the violence.*

Is this "illogic" really so different from the logic which we call compromising, or "forgiving and forgetting," when it does not involve identifiable violence?

While violence almost always escalates, it may not do so for months or years. The result is that women accept the violence as unpleasant but bearable, given the good things about the relationships (and most battering relationships do still provide sporadic periods of closeness during the honeymoon phases of the violence) until they are so enmeshed in the cycle of violence and so demoralized and trapped by it that they can't "just leave."

Many service-providers, and even women who have been battered, counsel that leaving or calling the police "the first time it happens" is the most effective way to ensure it won't happen again. However, given that it may be hard to define "that first incident," especially since definitions of intolerable violence are culturally relative and since most women have a lot of emotional and practical investment in their relationships, this advice frequently has an unreal, hollow ring to it.

American author Susan Schechter points to the "normalcy" of the early reactions of most battered women, at least in terms of the current "rules" of intimate relationships, in her comment: "Most people feel ambivalent when ending a long-term relationship. Major change is always difficult, often slowly and haltingly undertaken."[7]

There is growing evidence that leaving provides no guarantee the battering will stop and may even escalate the violence. In the present study, 12 percent of the women were separated or divorced. Anecdotal information suggests the majority of these women were battered by their ex-husbands, some by new partners. Michael Smith, in his telephone survey of 315 Toronto women, found that, while the rate of abuse for all women interviewed was 18.1 percent, for women who were separated or divorced, the rate jumped to 42.6 percent.[8]

The reactions of most battered women are often strong and logical and must be treated this way if we are to reach out to battered women and provide services for them which "ring true," will be helpful, and will be used by a greater number of battered women. It is easy to scoff at, or be discouraged by, the astonished response of many women to the suggestion that they leave their violent husbands: "But he's my husband, and the father of my children. I can't just abandon him." It's easy from an outside vantage point which assumes the batterer, the battered wife, their relationship, or all three are defective, to dismiss as misguided sentiment the woman's heroic attempts to keep her marriage together, to keep her children from knowing about the violence, to insist that she loves her husband. The woman's actions and statements are easy to dismiss as long as we assume the battered woman, along with her partner and their relationship, are somehow different from us in terms of the basic personality of the man and woman and in terms of the initial quality of the relationship.

However, as this study has established repeatedly, research shows that battered women do not fit one psychological or socio-economic mould. Few common characteristics which are not the direct result of the battering have been cited. In fact, in the one study known to the author where the personality traits of battered women *before* the violence were discussed, Lenore Walker found women who are battered "perceive themselves as more liberal than most" in their relationships with men[9] — a far cry from the stereotype of the battered woman as a traditional woman totally oppressed by, and dependent on, her partner.

It is *after* prolonged battering, as a result of the battering, that battered women begin to display certain similar psychological traits. After prolonged battering, women suffer from low self-esteem and isolation. They are emotionally dependent on the batterer, are compliant, feel guilty, and blame themselves for the violence, and yet demonstrate great loyalty to the batterer. Not only do they want the relationship to continue, they state they are staying for the sake of the family. They believe the batterers' promises to change and frequently believe the violence would stop if only their partners would get the one lucky break they've always wanted.[10]

To understand the actions and perceptions of battered women, it is important to think of how we all act in relationships, what we want, and the extent to which many of us will go to preserve a relationship. As one shelter worker poignantly said:

> *Relationships are hard to come by. Sure we should help women know that they have worth outside their marriages, but a marriage isn't just status and a piece of paper ... it's warmth, belonging, and a future. Battered women don't always get these good things out of their relationships, but most of them did in the beginning, and they just keep hoping it will come back. People will go to any lengths to feel loved, and love is not just waiting around the next corner for every battered woman who leaves her batterer.*

Even the majority of women who report the violence do so out of hope that she and her partner will be helped to return to their pre-violent state. Of course, she may also hope she will get attention and be listened to because she is frequently lonely and unnurtured as a result of the isolation most batterers impose on their victims. She may also hope he will be punished or "get his just deserts." But behind it all, she often just wants them to be happy again. The importance of these hopes should not be diminished.

Unfortunately many of the services which have been created for battered women and for their partners have been built on the assumption that the relationship is not worth saving and ignore or belittle the woman's hopes to save and rekindle it. The hope of the service-providers is most often to save or protect the woman as an individual or to help or change the batterer as an individual in some way. This well-intentioned, institutional hope often buries the woman's pleas for a different kind of help. This discrepancy between the battered woman's hopes and the hopes of the service-providers renders many of the initiatives taken inappropriate and frustrating for the women who are battered and contributes to the burnout and despair of the people who try to help the women, their children, and their partners.

ENDNOTES

[1] Helga Jacobson, Co-ordinator. A *Study of Protection for Battered Women* (Vancouver: Women's Research Centre, 1982). p. 5.

[2] Marion Boyd, ed. *Handbook for Advocates and Counsellors of Battered Women* (London, Ontario: London Battered Women's Advocacy Clinic Inc., 1985), pp. 12–13.

[3] Anne Ganley, "Causes and Characteristics of Battering Men," in *Wife Assault Information Kit* (Victoria: Ministry of the Attorney General. April 1986), pp. 68–69.

[4] Research supporting this hypothesis is summarized in Straus and Hotaling, *The Social Causes,* pp. 14–15.

[5] Ibid., p. 15.

[6] Ganley, "Causes and Characteristics," p. 70.

[7] Susan Schechter, *Women and Male Violence: The Visions and Struggles of the Battered Women's Movement* (Boston: South End Press, 1982), p. 20.

[8] Michael D. Smith, *Woman Abuse: The Case for Surveys by Telephone.* The LaMarsh Research Programme Reports on Violence and Conflict Resolution. Report #12 (Toronto: York University, November 1985), p. 29.

[9] Walker, "The Battered Woman Syndrome Study," p. 8.

[10] Alberta, Social Services and Community Health, Breaking the Pattern: *How Alberta Communities Can Help Assaulted Women and Their Families* (Edmonton: November 1985), p. 17.

7.4 A. Goldstein and S. Goldstein

The Challenge of an Aging Population in China

INTRODUCTION

Western countries started to experience declining fertility and increased longevity in the early 1800s and the transition has lasted more than a century. As a result, the population has gradually "aged." In other words, the proportion of older people in the population has increased over time.

In Canada, life expectancy has increased by about 25 or 30 years during the twentieth century. In 1900, only five percent of the population was over 65; today it is over 10 percent, and by 2020, the fraction will be closer to 20 percent. As well, the older population itself is aging as more and more Canadians live well into their 80s and 90s (though rarely beyond that, here or elsewhere; see excerpt 9.1 on the topic of longevity).

Compared to Canada, China is demographically quite young. A much smaller fraction of the population is over 65. But, because of the very large population of China, the absolute number of old people in China is very large.

Arranging for the care of so many old people is a challenge for the Chinese. China does not have a system of old-age security like Canada's. Such a provision was unnecessary in the past when life was short, people lived in extended family households, and there was a strong tradition of filial piety. However, the success of the one-child policy, instituted in 1979, means that most children born now are only children. Fewer people will be available to care for the aged in the next century.

China's current population policy envisages an eventual stable population of about 700 million. Before then, if the one-child family policy is fully successful, the population is expected to reach a peak of 1.2 billion by 2010. It is projected to fall below 1.2 billion only by 2040. Until then, the large cohorts already born will move through the age hierarchy to swell the absolute number of aged persons. Because of concurrent reductions in the number of births, the aged proportion of the total will also rise.

Goldstein, A. and S. Goldstein (1986). "The Challenge of an Aging Population: The Case of the People's Republic of China," *Research on Aging*, 8(2), June, 179–199. Reprinted by permission.

The Traditional and Legal Positons of the Aged

The aging of China's population must be considered within the context of the traditional position of the elderly in Chinese society, a position that in many respects remains today. In the traditional Chinese family the aged held particularly high status (Yang, 1965). Such a position is understandable in a primarily illiterate society where experience rather than formal education is the main source of knowledge.

The communist ideology promulgated since 1949 has had considerable influence on these traditional attitudes. Because the young formed a dynamic element in the establishment of the new regime and in spreading its doctrines and policies, young people assumed roles of political importance. Furthermore, a stress on the capacity of all Chinese to be productive implies the young are to be as respected as the old. This attitude was emphasized by the restructuring of the work unit in rural areas under the commune system, which deemphasized the family as the basic unit of production and thereby also weakened the position of its older members. In urban areas, where education and modern technology became widespread, the young also held an advantage. Nonetheless, although they no longer exercise authoritarian power within the family, the elderly continue to command a high degree of respect (Tien, 1977), and the traditional patterns of interdependence between generations have been largely maintained (Davis-Friedmann, 1983).

Legally, the position of the aged is defined by the Constitution of 1982 (Chinese Documents, 1983:27): "Children who have come of age have the duty to support and assist their parents." The Marriage Law of 1980 goes further to stipulate, "When children fail to perform the duty of supporting their parents, parents who have lost the ability to work or have difficulties in providing for themselves have the right to demand that their children pay for their support" (Beijing Review, 1981a). The Marriage Law even carries the burden of support to the next generation; grandchildren are also enjoined to support grandparents if the parents have died. Failure to meet these obligations is punishable under China's Criminal Code (Beijing Review, 1981b:23).

China is clearly attempting to reinforce and take advantage of the traditional obligations of children toward their parents. In the absence of any national social security system, such support is undoubtedly seen as especially essential in rural areas, where 80 percent of China's population lives. The provisions therefore shift the primary burden of support onto the family rather than onto the government, the commune, or the work unit.

Policies Indirectly Affecting the Aged

The One-Child Family Policy

China's one-child family policy not only subverts traditional values favoring large families, but jeopardizes the system of social security that depends on children's support of elderly parents. The problem is exacerbated by the still widespread custom of patrilocal residence after marriage. A couple, especially in rural areas, whose one child is a daughter can likely look forward to an old age without grandchildren or a child close by.

The one-child policy is also eroding one of the traditional roles of the elderly, that of child care. Even if grandparents live in the same place with their offspring, they will have few grandchildren to care for.

Moreover, although children are supposed to care for their parents, it is difficult to assess either how adequate such care is or how much of a strain it places on the younger persons. If one couple must support four elderly people the costs may be excessive (Du, 1984).

Job Assignment Policies

Upon graduation from secondary schools or universities, students are assigned jobs wherever the government believes they are needed. Although a majority may be placed close to their family homes, many are not. The situation may be particularly acute if rural-born youth are given urban job assignments as China's strict policies to control urban growth generally preclude other family members from joining the urban resident. Therefore, even if an aging couple has children, these children may be in distant places and unable to provide the physical or psychological support older persons need.

The New Economic Responsibility System

In rural areas, the individual responsibility system has placed a premium on intensive labor in the fields, so as to produce surplus crops that individual families can sell. Such hard work is likely to bypass the aged who no longer have the stamina to spend long hours in the field. In addition, the proliferation of small-scale light industry, which is also part of the new economic development, is geared to the absorption of the younger segments of the rural population.

A third aspect of the responsibility system does, however, offer opportunities for the elderly. The system encourages the cultivation of private plots and private raising of livestock. Produce from such enterprise can be sold in the free markets. Such enterprise has traditionally occupied elderly peasants and has helped to contribute to household income (Davis-Friedmann, 1983:16–22).

Programs for the Elderly

Retirement Policies

China's retirement policies, although designed to apply to the rural as well as urban population, are adhered to more in urban places. As a result, relatively more individuals fall into the "aged" category in cities and towns than in the countryside. Male factory workers and cadres retire at age 60; female workers and cadres at age 55, unless they are engaged in heavy work, in which case they retire at 50. Intellectuals and cadres may work up to age 65.

Among nonagricultural workers, a child may take over the job of a parent upon the parent's retirement. With about 4 million urban young people entering the labor force ages annually, a labor surplus exists. Most young people can expect to wait a year after graduating before receiving an assigned job. They can avoid such a delay if a parent retires and the child thereby "inherits" the job. Considerable pressure may, as a result, be exerted by the young on parents in their early 50s to retire earlier than necessary under law. The pressure is especially great for mothers to do so.

The Childless Elderly

The childless elderly have been promised "Five Guarantees": food, clothing, medical care, housing, and burial expenses (*Beijing Review*, 1984). Rural brigades that are developing retirement policies may provide extra services to the childless. Such policies are designed not only in recognition of the particular needs of the childless aged, but to prove that having only one child need not lead to misery in old age. The press now often reports how young people organize themselves to help the childless elderly — doing household chores, shopping, running errands, or just visiting (e.g., *Beijing Review*, 1982b; Jian, 1983). In addition, some administrative units (such as municipalities or provinces) now provide old age homes for those without children or close relatives.

Pension Systems

Formal retirement programs or facilities specifically for the rural aged are rare, but a few brigades have rudimentary pension systems.

Moreover, production-team-sponsored retirement plans are likely to undergo change because of the institution of the responsibility system. Under this new system, individual families negotiate directly with the brigade for the amount of cultivation to be undertaken and are responsible directly to the brigade for delivery of their crop quotas. The production team has thereby had its functions and sources of income curtailed, and programs for social welfare are becoming the responsibility of the brigade or commune. (See *Beijing Review*, 1982b.)

For urban residents, a more widespread pension system is in place. According to the Constitution, "The state prescribes by law the system of retirement for workers and staff in enterprises and undertakings and for functionaries of organs of state. The livelihood of retired personnel is ensured by the state and society" (Chinese Documents, 1983:26). This provision translates, in part, into pension systems developed and administered by individual factories or work units.

Other Programs for the Aged

The urban aged who are not eligible for pensions fall primarily into two groups: (1) those who left the labor force before a pension system was instituted by their work units or after having worked for less than 10 years in a unit with a pension system; and (2) those — mainly women — who never were members of the labor force. As indicated above in principle, and as mandated by the Constitution, these aged are to be cared for by their children. Only the childless aged become the state's responsibility. Figures released by the State Labor Bureau (*Beijing Review,* 1981b) suggest only about 45 percent of urbanites above retirement age are covered by pension systems.

The state also recognizes the need to supplement income for persons not eligible for pensions and allows such individuals to engage in small-scale private enterprise. This most often involves setting up a stand for the sale of clothing or small dry goods.

Licenses for such stalls are typically issued by the city's Industrial and Commercial Bureau for a one-time fee of Y5. Only persons without employment in the formal sector, or support from that sector in the form of pensions, can apply.

With the advent of springtime in China, still another segment of the elderly population enters the informal sector, as ice cream (popsicle) vendors appear on almost every street corner. Most commonly older women, the vendors are licensed by the city and buy their products from state shops.

Such economic avenues for older people with no direct, official support have met several important needs. Not only do they provide some income for the elderly, but the variety of merchandise made available thereby to the masses also fills a need for more color and variety in consumer goods.

Several other ways have been found to utilize the elderly population. Older men may direct traffic in congested neighborhoods. Men and women help enforce regulations in free markets. Older persons sit on the Neighborhood Committees, help to ensure neighborhood sanitation, help enforce family planning regulations, and generally see that the neighborhood functions properly. Others may act as mediators in disputes or as after-school counselors (Wu, 1984).

Because highly skilled workers are at a premium in China, the elderly skilled are used to teach others. Thus, a factory may ask a technician to stay on after retirement to help train younger workers. Other retired workers may go "on loan" to factories in other cities or towns, and such a sojourn may last 2–3 years.

Despite all these efforts, however, large numbers of older people are left with essentially nothing to do. As one Chinese social researcher interested in the problems of his nation's aged commented, "Many are just waiting to die."

Challenges for the Future

In many respects, the elderly in China are better off today than in the past. Family solidarity continues to provide a support system for the aged, whereas at the same time government policies are beginning to provide economic security independent of the family's role.

In rural areas, the welfare of the aged is closely tied to the economic well-being of the communes but, increasingly, also to the ability of individual households to realize higher incomes under the responsibility system. As the rural population ages dramatically over the next 50 years, the changing balance between labor force participants in their prime productive ages and the aged may have a serious negative impact on the well-being of the aged. A key determinant of continued agricultural productivity will be the extent to which China will by then have been able to modernize agriculture.

In urban areas, wherever larger proportions of the retired population are covered by pension systems, the oldest segment of the aged are the most disadvantaged as they are in large part not covered by retirement benefits. This disparity should disappear as the aged segment of the urban population comes to be constituted almost entirely by persons who have worked most of their lives in state enterprises.

The welfare of the aged is thus inextricably related to the degree to which China is able to modernize and to continue to increase its output value of agricultural and industrial products. Such development is, in turn, predicated on achieving success in the nation's overall population control programs, including family planning and rural-to-urban migration.

Traditional values about family solidarity are likely to be put under considerable strain as family size and residential patterns change. New ways of expressing and maintaining family ties will have to be found. The programs beginning to be developed for the aged will have to be greatly expanded in the future, and their cost is likely to be high. The very decentralized mechanisms by which they are currently being funded will likely also require alteration. In addition, other social welfare programs will need to be instituted both to meet the social needs of the elderly and to utilize their energies and expertise to the fullest extent possible.

REFERENCES

Beijing Review (1981a). "China's Marriage Law." March 16: 24, 24–27. (1981b). "Growing old in China." October 16: 24, 22–28. (1982a). "Five-guarantees households in the countryside." March 1: 25, 9. (1982b). "Support and respect the elderly." May 3: 25. (1984). "Old people — a new problem for society." January 23: 27, 10.

Chinese Documents (1983). Fifth Session of the Fifth National People's Congress. Beijing: Foreign Language Press.

Davis-Friedmann, D. (1983). *Long Lives: Chinese Elderly and the Communist Revolution.* Cambridge, MA: Harvard Univ. Press.

Du, R. (1984). "Old people in China: hopes and problems." *Beijing Rev.* 27 (April 16): 31–34.

Jian, C. (1983). "Volunteer service shows improving social mores." *Beijing Rev.* 26 (December 12): 24–25.

Tien, H. Y. (1977). "How China treats its old people." *Asian Profile* 5 (February): 1–7.

Wu, Y. (1984). "A new look in gerontology." *Beijing Rev.* 27 (April 16): 34–35.

Yang, C. K. (1965). *Chinese Communist Society: The Family and the Village.* Cambridge: MIT Press.

QUESTIONS

DISCUSSION QUESTIONS

1. In excerpt 7.1, Schlegel draws an analogy between upward mobility through seduction of a dowered daughter, and the European fairy tale theme of the poor peasant wooing the princess. Can we extend this analogy to modern soaps or pulp fiction?

2. Do you predict that people will put a greater emphasis on chastity as a result of the spread of the AIDS virus? Why or why not?

3. How would you explain wife-battering?

4. As a group, describe and compare experiences of child-care (parental care, relatives, private day care, public day care, nannie or housekeeper, and so on). What are the pros and cons of each method? Which method would you recommend?

DATA COLLECTION EXERCISES

1. A Canadian study of university students published in 1993 found that approximately 30 percent of the female college students had been victims of physical abuse while dating. Interview students on *your* campus to determine the extent of the problem there.

2. Using Statistics Canada sources, find out whether assaults against women are increasing or decreasing. What about marital homicide?

3. Given the current sexual permissiveness in our society, it may be hard to believe the strong stigma against "divorcees," "living in sin" or having an "illegitimate" child that prevailed in Canada before the 1960s. Sample magazines or newspapers from the 1950s and 1970s for comparison.

4. Investigate and compare old age security benefits for four countries. How does Canada rank in comparison?

WRITING EXERCISES

1. Write your own *ideal* marriage contract.

2. Write a brief essay describing how far you think the Canadian government should go to assume responsibility for the care of dependent Canadians.

3. Script a brief discussion between two friends, one arguing that family life would be incomplete without children, the other describing the benefits of childlessness.

4. Does pornography contribute to violence against women? In a brief essay, evaluate the arguments on both sides and draw your own conclusion.

SUGGESTED READINGS

1. Arendell, T. J. (1987). "Women and the economics of divorce in the contemporary United States," *Signs*, 13, 1, 121–135. This article documents the different costs of divorce for women and men. Men's economic position typically improves with divorce, while most women are far worse off economically. Arendell discusses the reasons for this inequity and outlines some policies needed to narrow the gap.

2. Baker, Maureen (1990). *Families: Changing Trends in Canada*. Toronto: McGraw-Hill Ryerson. This multi-authored text focuses on changing families in Canada.

Topics covered include the origins of the family, mate selection, economic conditions and family structures, alternatives to traditional marriage, marital dissolution, family law, and patterns of family violence.

3. Burch, T. K. and B. J. Matthews (1987). "Household formation in developed societies," *Population and Development Review*, 13, 3, September, 495–511. The authors of this article discuss trends in family structure and household size over the last quarter century. From their analysis one would be tempted to predict a continued trend to ever smaller households, although cost will be a limiting factor.

4. Trent, Katherine and Scott J. South (1989). "Structural determinants of the divorce rate: a cross-societal analysis," *Journal of Marriage and the Family*, 51, May, 391–404. The authors of this study look for universal predictors of divorce. Using data from 66 countries they find that the best predictors are level of socioeconomic development and women's labour force participation; however, for both variables the relationship with divorce is U-shaped, not linear.

WORK AND ORGANIZATIONS

Introduction

In *Megatrends*, John Naisbitt wrote that the history of work in America could be neatly summarized with these words: "farmer, worker, clerk." These were the most prevalent occupations as America moved from having an agricultural to an industrial to a post-industrial (or service-based) economy. This basic pattern in the evolution of work has also occurred in Canada and in many other wealthy, developed countries.

Such patterns have long fascinated sociologists who believe that a job is more than just a means to a paycheque or a certain social standing. Work, for most people, places great demands on one's time and energy; for those reasons alone it must be considered an important part of life.

Work is also important because it affects people's physical and psychological health. Lots of jobs are stressful and some are downright dangerous. People get injured, killed, and even murdered in workplaces. Less dramatically, the work we do can sometimes cause us to adopt lifestyles that may not be good for us.

Consider, for example, the changes in lifestyle that went along with the shift from being a society of farmers to a society of clerks. Farmers work outside and get plenty of fresh air and on-the-job exercise, while clerks work indoors at relatively sedentary work. Farmers need to be reasonably robust, clerks don't. Isn't it likely, then, that this shift in the kind of work being done helps to explain why people in post-industrial societies have to struggle so hard to achieve fitness and avoid fatness?

Researchers in Britain recently concluded that the sedentary lifestyles of women are also a major cause of osteoporosis (loss of bone calcium) which commonly leads to hip fractures and brittle bones in the elderly. This doesn't mean that working conditions were healthier, on balance, in the past. That is highly unlikely. It just means that the relationship between work and health goes far beyond whether a given working environment is a health or safety risk to its members on any given day.

In its broadest sense, the philosophical question of what constitutes "healthy" work — that is, work fit for human beings to do — has been at the core of sociological enquiry since the founding of the discipline. Marx, Durkheim, and Weber all wrote extensively about the nature of work and the significance of changing patterns of work. All three men were keenly aware of the fact that the nature of work was rapidly and radically changing in Europe during their own lifetimes. All three saw benefits in the newly emerging work structures and none of them romanticized the old structures that were being supplanted. But all three also warned that there were some chillingly inhumane aspects to the new modes of production.

The Insights of Karl Marx

For Marx (1936, 1963, 1985), capitalist industrial production was inhumane because it alienated workers from themselves and others. It did this by thwarting their natural desire to see the creative act of making a product through from beginning to end. Under the new industrial system, workers were not allowed to perform multiple or complex tasks. It was more efficient to have them do only a few simple repetitive actions that required endurance but not skill.

The only "ability" valued in the new mode of production was a capacity to suppress one's own natural and individualistic work rhythms in order to conform to the rhythms set by the machines. Thus, in the new system, the machine of the production process, rather than the workers, set the pace of work. This inverted the traditional relationship between man and machine. Users became used by their tools, turning unskilled production workers into, in Marx's words, mere "appendages of their machines."

The new system, according to Marx, also led to a dehumanizing of social relationships mainly by upsetting the power balance between the social classes. Because the new system was so much more efficient and productive than the old, it vastly increased the wealth and therefore the power of the factory owners, making them into the dominant class in society. At the same time, the new system sent the fortunes of workers in an opposite direction. The system's very efficiency meant that fewer workers were needed; therefore, the ranks of the unemployed would swell.

Furthermore, the low skill requirements of the new system effectively meant there would be more sufficiently qualified potential applicants for every job. As workers lost bargaining power vis-a-vis their employers they would suffer the fate any suddenly weakened competitor suffers in any adversarial system.

Their lives would get bleaker and nastier as more and more interpersonal relationships became poisoned by the new economic order. Employers would begin to see workers not as people but as "production costs" and exploitable resources. Workers would start to view one another not as friends and neighbours but as competitors for scarce jobs. And eventually, Marx believed, the workers would become bloody-minded and start to see the employing class as exploiters and enemies.

The Insights of Emile Durkheim

Durkheim (1951, 1965) also worried about alienation resulting from the modern practice of breaking work up into narrowly specialized tasks. But he framed the issue in slightly different terms. Like Marx, he focused on how people can become alienated from one another. But Durkheim was also interested in "anomie" — the problem of modern people feeling alienated from the traditions and values of their own culture. And for Durkheim, the main problem of alienation was not so much that it fuelled social conflicts but that it left people feeling rootless, disoriented, and disconnected.

Durkheim's argument was based on the premise that a society's work provides the solidarity — or glue — that binds a society together. He believed that small, agricultural, pre-modern societies were held together by "mechanical solidarity." That was his term for the social cohesiveness that results from people working together in close proximity, doing similar jobs that result in a similar standard of living for all of them. Their similar experiences provided a natural basis, Durkheim believed, for a shared culture. In such a society neighbours could still dislike and disagree with one another but they wouldn't be likely to view one another as odd or incomprehensible strangers.

Durkheim contrasted this image with the situation in modern industrial societies, where people do a wide variety of work in a wide variety of workplaces for widely varying rewards. In modern societies people don't usually work with or even near their neighbours. It is common to not even *know* the names of one's neighbours, let alone their occupations. And because of jargon, there is a good chance you still wouldn't know what your neighbour does for a living, even if he told you. "You say you're a Valuation Systems Specialist? Oh."

In short, there is less common ground among people in a modern society because we share fewer life experiences. We have a harder time relating to one another and so misunderstandings, misinterpretations, and mistrust are more frequent. As a result, there is a tendency for society to fragment as individuals stick to their own familiar and comfortable group.

Traditional cultural beliefs and customs that used to provide people with a common cultural identity are replaced by numerous subcultures with their own unique and exclusionary beliefs. In other words, society becomes "unglued," dissolving into a loose conglomeration of individuals and groups who feel disconnected from one another and from the past.

Counteracting this, according to Durkheim, was a new form of social glue called "organic solidarity." It was based on an intellectual recognition that the division of labour makes us all mutually dependent on one another. We may not know, like, or understand our neighbours anymore. But at least we know we need them to keep making their unique contribution to society. And they know they need us to do the same. The question is: is that abstract knowledge strong enough to hold society together? Durkheim had serious doubts on this score.

The Insights of Max Weber

Weber's (1958, 1961, 1964) worries about the human costs of the division of labour grew out of his analysis of bureaucracies. He believed modern bureaucratic organizations are the most rational and efficient forms of organization ever devised. But their rational and efficient structures also caused Weber to write fearfully about the "iron cage of bureaucracy." Like Marx, Weber saw workers in a bureaucracy subordinating their own work rhythms and styles to those of the system.

Reason and efficiency are intolerant masters: in a large organization, there is only one way — the best way — of doing things. And Weber, like Durkheim, knew modern social relationships are more reserved and impersonal than they used to be. But that too could be blamed on the bureaucratic values of rational efficiency. There is no room for sentiment in an objective assessment of facts.

And yet, what Weber also showed is that this anti-sentimental, rigorously rational point of view is built on a particular set of non-rational beliefs. Weber's comparative research on religion showed that all of the basic features of "modern" work — bureaucracy, the capitalist marketplace, legal rationality, the modern city, and fascination with science and technology — emerged in the same time and place: namely, in northwestern Europe after 1400. This coincided with the rise of Protestant — and especially, what Weber called "ascetic" Protestant — religion.

This type of religion, as we noted in the Introduction to Section 1 on culture, was committed to activism in this world. It promoted certain habits of thought and behaviour — prudence, thrift, efficiency, and the so-called "Protestant work ethic" — which are basic to the work lives of people today.

Conclusion

By looking for the costs as well as the benefits associated with a shift in work, Marx, Durkheim, and Weber raised the kinds of questions that people continue to ask today about newly emerging kinds of jobs. Who benefits? Who suffers? Can I do this kind of work? Do I want to? How would a new job fit into the other aspects of my life?

Most likely a change in the nature of work will be seen as neither wholly welcome nor wholly unwelcome. Remember, Marx, Durkheim, and Weber were ambivalent about modern work too. For Marx, it brought more than just alienation and misery for workers. It also brought them class consciousness, made socialism inevitable, and vastly increased the size of the economic pie to be divided up. Similarly, the fragmentation that worried Durkheim is also the basis for the pluralism and tolerance of modern society. And Weber knew that the same lack of sentiment that rationalism creates also excludes any irrational feelings such as bigotry, chauvinism, and favouritism.

The excerpts in this section are all about people coping with rapidly changing work environments. Sultana Alam and Patricia Schulz's excerpt is about female farm workers in Bangladesh who can no longer find enough work to do. Val Moghadam's excerpt is about the first generation of workers in Iran to enter the modern industrial sector. Ester Reiter's excerpt is set in Canada and concerns a rapidly expanding group within the service sector: namely, fast-food workers.

Finally, the excerpt by Sheng Xuewen, Norman Stockman, and Norman Bonney offers a cross-cultural perspective on one of the biggest shifts occurring in the world of work today. It's about the entry of women into the paid work force and the consequence this has for the sharing of housework between spouses.

As you will see from these excerpts, changes to work can create a wide variety of effects and provoke a wide variety of responses.

REFERENCES

Durkheim, E. (1965). *The Division of Labor in Society*. New York: Free Press.

——— (1951). *Suicide: A study of sociology*. J. Spaulding & G. Simpson (trans.). New York: Free Press. (Original work published 1897.)

Marx, K. (1936 [1867]). *Capital*. New York: Modern Library.

——— (1963). In T. B. Bottomore and M. Rubel (eds.), *Selected Writings in Sociology and Social Philosophy*. T. B. Bottomore (trans.). Harmondsworth: Penguin. (Original work published 1844.)

——— (1985). *Early philosophical manuscripts*. Harmondsworth: Penguin. (Original work published 1844.)

Weber, M. (1958a). "Class, status, party," chapter 7 in H. Gerth and C. W. Mills (eds.) *From Max Weber: Essays in Sociology*. New York: Oxford.

——— (1958b). "Bureaucracy," chapter 8 in H. Gerth and C. W. Mills (eds.) *From Max Weber: Essays in Sociology*. New York: Oxford.

——— (1961). *General Economic History*. New York: Collier Books.

——— (1964). "The types of authority and imperative coordination," section 3 in T. Parsons (ed.) *The Theory of Social and Economic Organization*. New York: Free Press.

8.1 Sultana Alam and Patricia Schulz

Women, Work and Poverty in Bangladesh

INTRODUCTION

Canadians are used to hearing media stories from time to time about the decline of the family farm and the loss of a whole way of life that goes along with farming. The pain that farm families feel sometimes causes commentators to talk of the "current crisis" in Canadian agriculture. In fact, the "crisis" is worldwide and has deep historical roots. The mechanization of agriculture and the consolidation of farms into larger and larger units owned by fewer and fewer people starts at the beginning of the modernization process and continues through it.

The next excerpt describes the situation in Bangladesh, a densely-populated country much different from Canada in that it is very poor, mostly rural, and still in the early stages of modernization. Yet, Saskatchewan's struggling farm women would probably find it easy to relate to some aspects of what the women in Bangladesh face. Both groups of women face the problem that farm work is no longer a viable way to make a living and that farm skills are not readily transferred to other jobs.

Locally available farm work is relatively scarce for both groups, in part because there are too many women chasing too few jobs. Both groups have asked their governments for assistance and both rely on family supports to survive. Both groups have also found ways to help their most needy members. In Bangladesh, for example, the women have evolved an informal job sharing system. Finally, history suggests that both groups will keep trying to preserve their way of life but that the crisis will continue.

The present study is a qualitative exploration of the situation of women heads-of-households as reported by rural women in Bangladesh. The study attempts to understand how poor women view the emergence of the woman head-of-household, the causes to which they attribute the new formation, the resources commonly used by women heads-of-households and the adjustments made by the community to accommodate women who find themselves on their own.

The sample is based on landless and poor women living in Shagatha Thana, in Rangpur district in northeastern Bangladesh. The area was chosen because it is economically depressed and contains a large proportion of widowed, divorced, and deserted women.

Alam, Sultana and Patricia Schulz (1985). "Women and Poverty in Bangladesh," *Women's Studies International Forum*, 8(4), 361–371. Oxford, England: Pergamon Press Ltd. Reprinted by permission.

Methodology

The data for this report are based on several sources:

1) A demographic survey of four women's groups with a total membership of 182. The purpose was to provide clues as to the living arrangements of single women, and about the age, number of children, kind of support received by women heads-of-households who are otherwise unable to find reabsorption with relatives.

2) Five group interviews during which 25–40 women participated. The interviews were discussions of the problems of widows, divorced and deserted women.

3) Individual interviews with selected women who are single, heads-of-households, or related to such women.

4) Individual interviews with the organizing staff of the NGO which operates in Shagatha.

The Results of the Survey

Out of 182 women in the survey, 70 (38 percent) are single, and divide into 54 widowed, 12 divorced and four deserted women. A majority of the single women live as heads-of-households. Forty (57 percent) of all single women are the primary adult managing their households. 22 of the 30 single women who live as members of households headed by relatives live with adult sons. Only five women live with parents, and three with brothers.

Women who find relatives willing to provide shelter and social protection are older with grown sons or are able to invoke social shame mechanisms. The latter includes very young women whom society defines as being in need of protection, and women who have been abandoned without a divorce and are legally unmarriagable.

The mean age of women living with sons is 46.1; that of women who live with parents and brothers is 25.7. The mean age of women who head their households is 41.1.

As already indicated, deserted women are the most effective among single women in mobilizing family support for reabsorption. Widows are the next most effective group. Least fortunate are divorced women. Only 25 percent of divorced women are living as members of households headed by relatives. (See Table 1.)

Women and Poverty in Bangladesh

Slightly over a quarter of the women — 49 (27 percent) — have been married more than once. Of these, 40 have been married twice; seven have had three marriages and two, four marriages. The younger age groups are more prone to multiple marriages. The mean number of marriages in the oldest age group (45+) is 1.19 while the mean number for the 25–34 age group is 1.51. Even among the group under 24 years of age, the mean number of marriages is higher than for the higher age ranges.

TABLE 1   LIVING ARRANGEMENT BY MARITAL STATUS

	Head of household	Lives with others	Total
Deserted	0	4 (100%)	4 (100%)
Widowed	31 (57%)	23 (43%)	54 (100%)
Divorced	9 (75%)	3 (25%)	12 (100%)
Total	40	30	70

Although women heads-of-households are not reabsorbed in other households they are still eligible for support, ranging from the gift of a coarse sari (costing Taka 80), help in paying for a doctor, or medicine, to periodic contributions of rice or wheat. The survey sought information about such contributions over the previous year. Only nine (23 percent) of the 40 who head households receive regular support, 22 (55 percent) receive support sporadically, and the remaining nine receive no support at all.

The Interviews and Field Observation

The Living Arrangements of Women Heads-of-Households

Few women heads-of-households own their own homesteads. Most depend on kin to provide them with housing. The women share the courtyard with their relatives but cook and eat separately. A few do not have kin who are able to help and squat on land belonging to others. Uniformly, the households under women are small, and consist mainly of children or adolescents who are not able to bring in full wages. A few examples reported by the women show the variations in arrangements.

Lives with parents but eats separately. Sharifa, 32, was deserted by her husband because her parents could not meet his demand for Taka 1000 with which he wanted to start a grain business. She lives in the homestead of parents, occupying the kichen-cum-bedroom hut but eats separately. The parents are too poor to feed her. Sharifa supports herself by working like her mother: in other homes sweeping and clay-plastering yards and floors, fetching water, grinding spices, and helping with rice husking.

Lives with mother and assumes primary responsibility for household. Alta, a widow of 28, with no children, lives in her mother's homestead. Her mother is old, has no land, but occasionally gets wheat from government relief programs. Alta supports her mother with food and other necessaries. She works in other homes and occasionally takes orders for thin quilts.

Lives next to parents in house provided by other relatives. Mallicka, a widow of 36, lives next door to her elderly parents and two brothers who are between the ages of 18–22. Space for her small hut was provided by an uncle who owns the adjoining homestead. The expenses for building her hut were pooled through the help of her savings, and contributions from her parents and brothers.

Mallicka, like the other women, works in other homes. She owns a cow which her father cares for. She has three sons who have been farmed out to other people because she cannot support them.

Lives with brothers but eats separately. Bele, 38, was divorced by her husband nine years ago after a history of conflict with her mother-in-law. She was married nine years. She lives in a house built by her three brothers. The brothers are all married and have families of their own. They all live in the same courtyard, occupy separate huts and eat separately. Bele's brothers are landless and work as agricultural day laborers. She raises chickens and works in peoples' homes. She also sews quilts on order.

Bele has eight children, all of whom were taken back by their mother-in-law. Her oldest son visits occasionally and gives her Taka 15-20 for personal expenses.

Owns own home. Shopiron, age unknown, mother of three sons, owns her own house and lives with her youngest son who is twelve. Her eldest son is married and lives in another village. Her second son, also married, lives with his wife and daughter in a separate hut in the same courtyard but cannot feed his mother. He has no land and works occasionally as an agricultural wage worker. Shopiron occasionally gets relief, works in other homes. Her youngest son does weeding and grazing.

Women in De-centralized Living Structures

Many women whom the community identifies as living with relatives rather than "living on her own" because they eat jointly, in fact occupy highly decentralized structures in which the women take equal economic responsibilities, and in which the level of poverty is such that all attention is consumed by the need to secure food on a day-to-day basis. Two such examples include:

> Bachani, 28, separated a year ago from her husband who left her to return to his first wife. Bachani has no children and moved back to her parents' homestead. Her parents are deceased and she lives with two minor brothers between the ages of 14 to 16. All three work. Bachani works in the homes of neighbors, her brothers do light work such as weeding and grazing.

> Shona, 38, is widowed. She poaches on someone's land on which she has built a shack and lives there with her eldest son who is crippled, and a younger son around 10. Her daughter is married and lives with her husband. Shona begs for a living as does her eldest son.

The Social Status of Women Heads-of-Households

When women heads-of-households are provided housing, they are given the least desireable, least durable, and least central hut in the courtyard. They take second place in the use of common facilities, waiting for others to finish using the stove, never claiming a fallen branch for fuel but using leaves and stalks, declaring an occasional fruit-tree in the homestead off limits for their own children.

Families, having once invested in the marriage of a daughter or sister, deeply resent the obligation to support her in difficult times. The resentment is most acutely felt by women who are young and considered of "marriageable" age.

There is constant pressure from relatives for their remarriage. If their parents fail to find a match, they are taunted and ridiculed by cousins and aunts. Soon parents join in pushing the women to take whatever work they can find. The women feel that every mouthful of food they consume is begrudged. They survive by "making ourselves small," by attempting to strike an impossible balance between being both non-existent and helpful around the household.

Women heads-of-households, by assuming responsibility for earning their food, avoid the overt expressions of resentment directed at women dependents. But they do not fully escape the fate of the single woman. The presence of these women and their children in the same courtyard provokes guilt over their helplessness and generates anger. Women heads-of-households indirectly affect the quality of life possible to other occupants in the homestead. Sons and brothers are forced to put on a show of greater poverty than they really experience. They are forced to eat less well than they would otherwise do, to conceal the sari they have bought for their wives or daughters. To do otherwise would undermine their plea of inability to support relatives.

Employment and the Woman Head-of-Household

Traditionally the most important form of employment for landless women is the tedious, time consuming process of parboiling, drying, and husking rice. Husking usually requires two to three women.

Because rice is better preserved from mould and insects with the husk on, families prefer to store the rice as is after harvesting, taking out small quantities two or three times a week for husking. This results in a steady flow of work for landless women. However, rice mills have sharply cut into this form of employment. While rice mills have been introduced, no steps have been taken to create alternative employment for women.

Food-for-work programs provide some work for women. These programs centered around the construction of rural roads, embankments, and irrigation canals pay in kind (wheat or rice). They are eagerly sought by women because they pay up to three seers per day as opposed to the local rate of one seer of rice.

In practice, though, food-for-work programs do not provide work regularly even on a seasonal basis. In Shagatha, the women report having worked on only two food-for-work programs in three winters and some found only three days during each project. In addition, the women have had to fight bitterly to receive their full payment.

The women understand that economic hardship is forcing families to withdraw support from widows and divorced or deserted women. In their view, women would receive a warmer welcome were they self-sufficient, but:

"At the same time there is even less work for us. There is a lot we can do to earn money. But where is the opportunity?"

The homes of the well-to-do landowners employ only a handful of women. The mainstay of single women, particularly women who head households are their relatives who form part of that thin stratum of subsistence cultivator families owning 3–6 bishas (1–2 acres) of land. This group provides the little employment that women heads-of-households are able to find in rice husking and heavy housework (clay plastering, fetching water, repairing clay stoves, etc.).

In most cases when relatives do the hiring, the work is "created" for the less fortunate women. The work would normally be undertaken by the householders themselves with the help of neighbors on an exchange basis. In token of the artificial nature of the services received, the women are paid half the normal wages.

Women in the landless groups contribute towards community solution by observing a system of triage among themselves. In an unspoken arrangement, the women who are less in need remain behind so that women who are on their own can have first choice of the available jobs. This ensures that women heads-of-households get four to five days of work a week at half pay, while other single women may average one to three. Among the former, again, those who own goats or a cow or chickens take second place to their counterparts who are solely dependent on wage work.

One response from policy-makers to the plight of women heads-of-household has been to institute relief programs directed at older widows and mothers with young children. These programs suffer from the usual corruption through which a large portion of the supplies are misappropriated by local politicians who administer the programs.

How Women View the Emergence of a New Formation

The women in Shagatha universally view the emergence of the woman head-of-household with alarm and ascribe it to two factors.

1) Women ascribe the loss of support from parents, brothers, and sons to economic pressures. There is no doubt in the women's minds that living conditions have deteriorated significantly in the last 20 years, making it impossible for families to welcome single women when they lose their husbands. A large segment of families that are now landless owned land one or two generations ago. Compounding the problems of rural families cut off from land is the lack of employment. And with the disappearance of work, there is the loss of what the women term their "value" in the eyes of society.

> *"Today there is no food, no clothes. If a daughter is sent back to her family by her husband now, she catches hell. Because of the lack of things women have lost their value. We have no worth left."*

Younger women whose parents are alive see the impossibility of fathers and mothers to feed another mouth. Women who are in their late twenties and whose parents are either deceased or too old, are more sensitive to the in-built conflicts of interest between their brothers and themselves.

> *"Brothers do not want to feed us any more. So long as our mothers are alive, brothers take care of us. After that they want to steal from us. No matter how much fathers leave, daughters get nothing."*

Women who are older and have grown up sons, also perceive growing insecurity:

> *"Now, there is no caring. Now sons say I cannot even take care of my wife. What can I do for my mother?"*

Older women see themselves as vulnerable once their daughters-in-law become assertive. They do not deny that relationships between mothers- and daughters-in-law have always been tense. The difference is that nowadays sons are more apt to welcome a reduction in the number of mouths they must feed.

2) However, when the women talk about husbands, they talk about qualititative changes in the attitudes of men.

In the view of the women, men today have become acquisitive and greedy. They are moved by the new vogue for dowries to marry and leave wives. As a result, the risk that a woman will be sent back to her family has greatly increased. Shagatha, like other rural areas of Bangladesh, is beginning to experience modernization. As a result, the system of dowry has begun to spread. Prior to the 1970s the system that prevailed was the system of "Pon" or a bride-price. In all probability Pon only meant that the women's parents did not have to pay dowry.

All the group interviews rapidly developed into discussions over the new trend for dowries and its negative effects on marital stability.

> *"There was not so much breaking of marriages before. Now greed is pushing a lot of men to leave their wives and make demands from new wives."*

Another woman dwells on the inhuman burden dowries place on families, and the way it leads to the devaluation of daughters:

> *"It is better not to have daughters. Mothers have to work hard and beg to meet demands (for dowries). Men today have gone mad. They want watches, bicycles, Taka 1000, plus clothes. Even then they are not content and think nothing of leaving their wives when they please."*

The women speculate about the sources of the new marital instability and blame the men.

> *"There are so many marriages today (i.e. multiple marriages for one person). And it is not the women who leave. Women look for security, calm. It is the men who leave."*

They find the plea that men leave their wives because of poverty unconvincing and point out that every man who has left a woman in Shagatha has gone on to remarry or to return to a former wife.

According to the women, men have also become more pleasure-seeking, more self-centered, and more oriented towards using women as objects.

> *"Now the eyes of men have become bad (corrupt). They roam from woman to woman. At first they marry within their villages. Then they go away where nobody knows them and do what they please."*

The women feel helpless. They complain about their loss of authority over sons and nephews who do not listen when their elders rebuke them for leaving their wives.

8.2 Val Moghadam

Industrial Development and Working-Class Politics in Iran

INTRODUCTION

The Iranian Revolution of 1979 overthrew the Shah and shocked many Marxist scholars. They were surprised that the revolution established an Islamic Republic rather than a socialist state. In Marxist theory, religion was supposed to be a spent force by the time societies reached Iran's level of industrialization. Also, the Iranian working class's most revolutionary elements came not from the most advanced sectors of the economy but from the more traditional, backward sectors.

Val Moghadam's excerpt below provides some clues as to why the revolution took the course it did. First, since Iran had only recently industrialized, its modern and urban roots were not deep. Many urban workers were newly arrived immigrants from rural areas and they retained traditional views. So in a sense Iran was not quite as modern as it superficially seemed and therefore religion wasn't yet a spent force.

Second, Moghadam's excerpt suggests workers in the large, modern, industrial sector may have been reluctant to play the "revolutionary vanguard" role because their lives were relatively comfortable. As a labour "aristocracy," they enjoyed high wages, high status, and easy,

Moghadam, Val (1987). "Industrial Development, Culture and Working-Class Politics," *International Sociology*, 2(2), 151–175. Reprinted by permission.

secure jobs. They had a lot to lose in a revolution. By contrast, workers in the traditional sectors toiled in exploitative sweatshops. Thus, it was in the sweatshops rather than in huge modern enterprises that workers were more apt to feel they had "nothing to lose but their chains."

In Iran, the industrial strikes of October 1978 to February 1979 and the rise and fall of workers' councils in the modern industrial sector during and immediately after the revolutionary uprising, raised the question of the consciousness and capabilities of Iran's industrial working class. The councils were established in plants where the owners and/or managers had fled or had been expelled during the anti-Shah upheavals and immediately afterwards (Azad, 1980; Bayat, 1983; Goodey, 1980; Moghadam, 1984). The councils assigned for themselves the right to manage wholly or in part the production, distribution and financial operations of the workplace. Problems ensued and the councils were undermined by the new Islamic regime and as a result of contradictions internal to the councils themselves.

This raises three fundamental questions about industrial workers in Iran. First, how to interpret workers' role in the Revolution: Was it reformist, revolutionary, self-interested, progressive? Second, was the Revolution a step forward or a setback for the working class and the labour movement? Third, what are the prospects for a revival of the labour movement?

This paper examines the political activities of workers in one major industrial region of Iran, Tabriz and environs. Tabriz was chosen because during the 1978–79 Revolution and afterwards, Tabriz acquired the distinction of being the site of the most radical of the workers' councils. Tabriz is in East Azarbaijan, and is a major Iranian city.

I interviewed one of the founding members of the Tabriz industrial workers' councils, in 1985 in Paris. Javad, once an activist worker, was now an unemployed member of the Iranian exile community. Javad presented a fascinating picture of work, culture and politics in Tabriz. This paper combines ethnography and structural analysis in seeking to illuminate linkages between industrial development, culture and working-class politics in Iran.

An Industrial Worker Speaks

In 1985, Javad was 28 years old. He had fled Iran two years earlier for political reasons. Javad's social class background was industrial working class. His father and grandfathers had been industrial workers. At age 12 or 13, Javad began employment in workshops, primarily machine shops. He worked variously as an office sweeper and a tea-boy. He remarked, "Because of the sufferings I experienced in the workshops, I was very receptive to Left ideas."

I asked him about his family life and the importance of religion. "My mother and father didn't like clerics; they didn't like beards," he laughed. His parents were, however, believers: "My mother always prayed." His father became religious, he said, only as he grew old, because "he was afraid of what might happen after he died." It also emerged that his parents had urged him to attend school.

After obtaining his high school diploma, Javad attended the Institute of Technology, a vocational/technical school in Tabriz. At the Institute, Javad attended book exhibits, read widely, encountered radical students, participated in mountain-climbing expeditions that were really political discussion sessions, and engaged in fights with religious (anti-Left) students. When the anti-Shah movement began, Javad joined other Left students, putting up leaflets, organising protests and other such activities. Javad became drawn to Peykar, one of several Left-wing political groups that emerged during the anti-Shah movement. After the Shah was deposed, he joined Peykar.

After the Revolution, Javad worked in a motor assembly factory with 100 employees. This plant was among the many medium-sized industrial establishments that sprang up during the 1960s and 1970s. By Iranian standards, this plant is termed "large," as is any industrial firm employing over 10 workers. In this plant, Javad was a skilled worker, and there were 75 production workers; the balance of the workforce was comprised of drivers (transport workers) and white-collar employees (*karmand*). Javad became the workers' "political representative." At the same time, he became active in the councils' movement, then spreading throughout the industrial sector in Iran (Azad, 1980). In this capacity, he had contact with other factories in and around Tabriz.

Industrialisation and the Stratification of the Tabriz Working Class

Beginning in the early 1960s, the Pahlavi state initiated a capitalist development project based upon import-substitution industrialisation (ISI) and agrarian reform. ISI provided state protection for domestic industry and led to the proliferation of manufacturing that produced commodities primarily for the home market.

Parallel to the rise of a modern industrial sector was the persistence and expansion of "traditional" industrial activities (Moghadam, 1985).

In Iran, large numbers of people are engaged in traditional handicraft industries, among them silversmiths, coppersmiths, carpet weavers, leather and wood workers. Such industries are mostly carried out in or around the Bazaar, Iran's traditional urban markets. I call this the workshop sector of Iranian industry.

The workshop sector is at once functional and dysfunctional for the large modern industrial sector. It is functional in as much as it carries out operations — such as repair, maintenance and production of goods and services geared toward a certain market — that are not within the purview of the modern sector. More importantly, it is functional because it absorbs the surplus population at no or extremely low cost to the state and to capital. It is dysfunctional in so far as the proliferation of workshops could compete with the modern sector. The intensification of this competition — preferential treatment of larger firms and the government's attempt to regulate the Bazaar's operations — led to opposition.

In the early 1970s, the ILO mission that visited Iran recognised that, given the high rate of population increase and the inability of the formal sector to absorb the entire labour force, the general pattern would be the continued growth of the labour force in the informal sectors of both the countryside and the city (ILO, 1973). By the end of the 1970s, much of Iran's "dynamic" manufacturing was in the informal sector in rural areas.

A notable feature of Iranian industry is the small size of the majority of the establishments. Data for 1972 show over 97 percent of establishments employed fewer than 10 persons, yet, as there were over 219,000 enterprises in this category, they accounted for nearly 600,000 workers. This constituted two thirds of Iran's total industrial workforce at the time. Thus a typical industrial worker in Iran was either self-employed, engaged in a family business, or employed in a small workshop (Wheeler 1976:14). Table 1 illustrates this pattern.

The differentiation of industry, of the labour force and of labour markets, has social, political and ideological implications. These divisions became critical during the Iranian Revolution. Javad had his own classification of the Tabriz industrial labour force. In his schema, industrial workers in Tabriz could be separated into three spheres: 1) construction, 2) small-scale manufacturing, and 3) modern industrial plants, especially those with over 100 workers. The majority of workers were in construction or in small-scale manufacturing and most were in the latter. Construction workers were often semi-proletarians, still tied to the countryside. As Javad said, "It took these people a long time to sever their connections to the village." Most researchers agree that much of the Tabriz working class is in its second or third generation of industrial work. Javad concurred with this.

We shall apply the term workshop sector to Javad's second category, small-scale manufacturing. The structure and features of production in the workshop sector are very different from those in the large industrial sector. Javad called

TABLE 1   EMPLOYED POPULATION OF EAST AZARBAIJAN, BY EMPLOYMENT STATUS (1972)

Employment Status	Number ('00s)	Percentage
Total	7972	—
Employer	172	2.1
Self-employed	3468	43.5
Government employee (*Karmand*)	236	2.9
Government worker (*Kargar*)	104	1.3
Private sector wage and salary earner	2134	26.7
Unpaid family	1837	23.0
In training	11	0.13
Not adequately described	10	0.12

Source: *Iran Statistical Yearbook, 1976.*

it "anarchy in production." He meant it was not systematic or regularised. He also explained that most workers in Tabriz began employment at age 12 or 13, and many began at age eight or nine. These were not "young adults," as Javad commented. "They were children; they would cry."

The mentality of workers in this category was different from that of workers in the large, modern industrial sector. According to Javad, a construction worker, for example, aspired to become a *bana* (independent self-employed builder), while many of those labouring in the workshop sector longed to have their own shops. In neither the construction nor the workshop sector was the question of workers' control considered. "The objective is petty bourgeois self-employment," Javad said. There is no concern about alienation. There is, instead, social mobility consciousness, as distinct from class consciousness Javad asserted. Referring to workers for whom the 60-hour work-week is the norm, Javad declared: "They are incredibly exploited, but all they want is to be *aadam* (human being), or *ostad* (master), or *karfarma* (employer)."

Workers in the informal sector, for the most part, can identify more easily with traditional religious values than with secular or socialist ideas. Having come from rural areas and facing the complex realities of Iranian urban life, they can expect to be susceptible to recruitment by a religious populist movement. Workers with urban backgrounds are more likely to be interested in secular ideas and modes of life.

It was in the large modern industrial factories that the sporadic strikes, beginning in the early 1970s, took place. In this spate of strikes, many focussing on job classification as well as on wages, Tabriz industrial workers were well represented. It was also in this sector, that the industrial strikes which shook the Pahlavi regime took place, from October 1978 to February 1979. Finally, it was in this sector that the workers' councils emerged during and after the Revolution (Moghadam, 1984).

I asked Javad if he had noted any tendency for workers in Tabriz to leave the large factories and set up their own small enterprises. Javad did not think this was common in Tabriz. Indeed, it would be a rare worker, he said, who would leave a large modern plant to set up his own workshop. On the other hand, there was some labour transfer from the workshop sector to the modern industrial sector.

Javad said when workers became exposed to the very different conditions within the large plants, the personal relations, long hours, hard work, low income and other features of the workshop sector lost all appeal. And what about workers' own "control" over labour power and skill? Javad's reply was that, although in the large plants there was external control, supervision and management, he experienced more "freedom" (*azadi*).

Javad explained that in the industrial sector in Tabriz, many workers are rural-born and have lived in Tabriz for about ten years. Javad asked me to imagine a recent rural migrant coming to a large factory, where he would be given a uniform, shoes, insurance, an 8-hour working day, a 45–46 hour working week. "This is quite different from the countryside," Javad said, "where one could work 45 hours in three days." In the large factories, wages were much better, working conditions easier, and such options as profit-sharing, a luxury.

And what of labour productivity? Javad's response: it was higher in the workshops. The workers in the workshops laboured extraordinarily hard, he emphasised, and real skill was developed in the workshops. By contrast, the famous machine-tool factory in Tabriz was always in the red, he said. The factory and the workers worked at low capacity, Javad said. Javad's point about low productivity in the large modern industrial sector was not the first time I had come across it. Sources on Iranian industry all note the low levels of productivity (relative to workers in the same plants in advanced industrial countries). Other comments about industry at the time concerned the higher production costs in Iran and the higher wages accrued to labour. The Iranian labour force was decidedly *not* the cheap and docile labour force found in many other Third World countries.

Neither was management terribly advanced, it appears, in the large modern sector. Johnson (1980), who studied high-level manpower in Iran, makes the point about the less-than-developed techniques of scientific management in the large firms. This, presumably, gave industrial workers some of the leeway Javad referred to. By contrast, the relations in the workshop between master and apprentice are of a different order: "The owner is constantly there," as Javad pointed out. There are, clearly, very different relations of domination and subordination in the respective sectors.

Javad was aware of the thesis of a labour aristocracy, of a self-conscious and conservative stratum of the working class which recognises its privileged position. Iranian industrial workers had, by the mid-1970s, become conscious of their important role in the economy and society. This was encouraged by the regime, which, while banning independent labour organisation, exalted industrial workers. In addition, during the 1970s, Iran suffered from a shortage of skilled labour. There was an effort to reduce worker turnover by means of material incentives: higher wages, benefits, profit-sharing, etc. All the talk about the skilled labour shortage and material incentives served to produce a positive self-image on the part of Iranian skilled industrial workers. They were cognisant they were being counted on to realise the Shah's dream of transforming Iran into a major industrial power by the end of the century.

Perhaps due to their privileged position and relative "youth," the modern industrial workers of Tabriz (and the oil-workers of the southern refineries) were the last to join the Revolution. By contrast, construction workers, students, clerics and others had demonstrated against the regime earlier. However, once the industrial workers joined the Revolution, the Pahlavi state could no longer stand up, due to the importance of the industrial firms.

Javad emphasised the role of the Left in the Tabriz industrial strikes. The slogans and placards were written by Leftist workers, he said. Left groups, such as Peykar and Fedaii, were very active in Tabriz, recruiting workers, encouraging and organising the strikes, and so on. As a result, once the workers decided to turn against the state, they took on a militant stance. In their joint statement of 13

Aban 1357 (4 November 1978), the Tabriz workers of the tractor-assembly and machine-tool plants raised both political and economic demands. Among other things, they called for the dismantling of existing workers' organisations and yellow unions, the formation of genuine councils and unions "which defend the rights and social prestige of the workers," and no intervention by outside authorities in the factories' internal affairs (Azad, 1980:16).

Industrial Workers and the Councils

Most of the workers in Tabriz who created and were active in the councils were Left-inspired, city-born and bred workers like Javad, and supporters of Peykar, Fedaii, or Mojahedin. A small number were independent radical workers (that is, not affiliated with political groups). According to Javad, the Left groups would vie with each other in attempts to recruit these workers. Though Javad expressed some criticisms of the Left organisations, after the Revolution he joined the ultra-Left group Peykar. Javad was by no means disdainful of the Left for its activities among workers in Tabriz. Nor was he resentful of the non-working class Leftists, whom he referred to as the "intellectual kids," who agitated among the workers. He expressed respect and admiration for those among them who were "martyred."

In Tabriz, for the most part, the councils' membership was comprised of skilled workers. Almost from the beginning, the councils encountered difficulties. Not least of their problems was the social and ideological heterogeneity of the working class. Javad remarked that, before the Revolution, most skilled workers were not religious. Other workers were observant and believers ("like my mother"), or were what he called "open-minded religious persons" as opposed to "reactionary religious persons." After the Revolution, Javad said: "We had all kinds of workers: Left, Right, religious, progressive, reactionary." This was not a homogeneous or united class.

One notable achievement of the industrial workers of East Azarbaijan was the formation, in the winter of 1979–80, of a coordinating council overseeing and uniting eight factory councils. Altogether, the coordinating council represented 5,000 workers (Azad, 1980).

According to Javad, most of the radical workers were city-born and bred (i.e. from Tabriz rather than villages). Women workers, a very small minority of the Tabriz industrial workers, also participated in the councils.

Then the Islamic associations were created by the ruling Islamic Republican Party (IRP). These bodies competed with and eventually supplanted the workers' councils. With the purification (*paksazi*) of 1359 (1980), a large number of workers were affected. Javad emphasised the suppression that took place in the factories at that time. This included the expulsion and disappearance of activist workers followed by a "tightening of control" in the factories. To recapture factory management and administration from the councils, the regime tried to divide workers on the basis of religion. Another, later, tactic was ironically achieved through a measure widely favoured by workers and the Left — the nationalisation of industries. This allowed the government to undermine activist councils by manipulating inputs. Control was often effected through pure intimidation, and it worked.

Working-Class Politics and Working-Class Culture

The difficulties encountered by the councils, by radical workers and by the Left, were significant. The internal differentiation of the Tabriz working class and the segmentation of the industrial labour force, proved an enormous obstacle. Particularly vexing was the Islamic resurgence, the new Islamic populist discourse and many workers' resistance to Left agitation. Javad remarked: "We easily put up posters in universities, but not in the factories. We found that the workers' consciousness was at odds with our received ideology. It did not match the formulae we had learned." Islam is but one factor in the backwardness of workers, Javad believes. It's not determinant. More important, according to Javad, is the backward culture and ideology of workers, their undeveloped working-class consciousness and the absence of a modern, forward-looking and democratic culture.

The Revolution politicised the workers, Javad said, but did not transform them culturally. His experiences in Tabriz, Javad informed me, reveal "we cannot begin with Marxist slogans; we must begin with the actual working class itself." He pressed the point: "We did not realise at the time that there was such a thing as a reactionary worker. In the council, we'd make allowances for and forgive the pro-Khomeini, anti-Left, or anti-socialist worker." Why? Because he was a worker, because of "false consciousness."

The question of the consciousness of workers is complex. When thinking about industrial labour and working-class politics, we face two paradoxes. The first is that at the same time that the factory is regarded as the crucible of class consciousness and collective resistance, it is presented as an arena of potential embourgeoisement and labour aristocracy. The second paradox pertains more to the advanced industrial economies of the West, where the factory is also presented as an arena of undisputed domination, of fragmentation, degradation and mystification (Braverman, 1974).

Javad agreed with my view that Iranian workers today are more advanced than before, because of their experience in the Revolution (in addition to the dynamics of the labour process). However, a deeper and more continuous process of their cultural development and political maturation is needed. For Javad, the struggle around genuine workers' councils and syndicates is imperative, while seminars should also be organised to provide workers with intellectual understanding of their role in production and society.

I have advanced the proposition that the formation of councils and the movement around workers' control, on the one hand, and the popular demand for nationalisation of "the commanding heights of the economy" (industries, banks, insurance companies, foreign trade), on the other, is prefigurative of the democratic-socialist project of autonomy, social ownership and rational planning. For these and other reasons, I regard the Iranian Revolution as essentially progressive, and make a distinction between the Iranian Revolution and the Islamic Republic. Tilly has argued the elements of a repertoire can change with new experiences of collective action — mass demonstrations, strikes, other forms of grievance and protest and revolutions. Inasmuch as the revolutionary experience in Iran added critical elements to the repertoire of the working class, I regard the Revolution as a step forward for the workers' movement. And because industrial development is very much on the agenda of the present Iranian regime, there is no reason to believe the working class has been decentred. When one recalls the major strike in 1985 by steelworkers that derailed the state's plan to break up the huge Isfahan steel complex and render numerous workers redundant, one senses the industrial workers will be heard from again.

REFERENCES

Ashtiani, A. (1986). "Continuity and Discontinuity in the History of the Iranian Working Class." Unpublished manuscript.

Azad, S. [Moghadam, V.] (1980). "Workers' and Peasants' Councils in Iran." *Monthly Review,* October.

Bayat, A. (1983). "Workers' Control after the Revolution." *MERIP Reports,* May.

Braverman, H. (1974). *Labor and Monopoly Capital.* New York: Monthly Review Press.

Goodey, C. (1980). "Factory Councils in Iran." *MERIP Reports,* June.

Graham, R. (1979). *Iran: The Illusion of Power.* New York: St. Martin's Press.

Halliday, F. (1979). *Iran: Dictatorship and Development.* Harmondsworth: Penguin.

International Labour Organization (1973). *Employment and Income Policies for Iran.* Geneva: ILO.

Johnson, G. C. (1980). *High-Level Manpower in Iran.* New York: Praeger.

Moghadam, V. (1984). "Industrialization Strategy and Labor's Response: The Case of the Workers' Councils in Iran." Paper presented at the conference on "Trade Unions and the Changing International Division of Labour," University of Ottawa, Canada, November.

—— (1985). "Accumulation Strategy and Class Formation: The Making of the Industrial Labor Force in Iran, 1962–1977." Unpublished dissertation. Washington, D.C.: The American University.

Wheeler, A. C. R. (1976). *The Development of Industrial Employment in Iran before 1353 (1974–75).* Geneva: Population and Manpower Bureau, UNDP-ILO Planning and Employment Project.

8.3 Ester Reiter

Work in a Fast-Food Factory

INTRODUCTION

Picture yourself working in a "post-industrial information age economy." Chances are you're seeing a futuristic-looking office filled with computers, fax machines, and other high-tech equipment. It's less likely that you've pictured yourself in a high-tech restaurant, wearing a uniform and giving people their burgers, fries, shakes, and change. In fact, though, both kinds of workplace are common in a post-industrial economy.

In this excerpt, Ester Reiter describes this second kind of "post-industrial" workplace by showing us the work that goes on in a Toronto Burger King. Apparently industrial-age assembly line work procedures haven't died out after all.

Fast-food workers, like factory workers, use expensive pieces of machinery to perform simple repetitive tasks under close supervision in an assembly line environment. Like factory workers, they have little scope for individual innovation and find their work pace set by the machines they tend. Any deviation from the routine prescribed by head office is forbidden since it would likely reduce efficiency.

But fast-food workers face an added burden: as service workers who meet the public, they become part of the package being sold. They are on display, so they must submit to having their personal appearance, speech and demeanor monitored, molded and, as much as possible, standardized. An irregular personality, it seems, is every bit as unacceptable to the system as an underdone french fry or burnt burger.

This paper focuses on the technology and the labour process in the fast-food industry. Using Marx's description of the transitions from craft to manufacture to large-scale industry, it considers the changes in the restaurant industry brought about by the development of fast-food chains. The description of life in a fast-food factory is based on my experience working in a Burger King outlet in 1980/1.

Founded in 1954 by James McLamore and David Edgerton, Burger King became a wholly-owned subsidiary of Pillsbury in 1967. The company grew from 257 restaurants at the time of the merger to 3,022 by May 1981. About 130,000 people are employed in Burger Kings all over the world. By November 1982, there were 87 Burger King stores in Canada, 40 of them company owned.[1]

Reiter, Ester (1986). "Life in a Fast-Food Factory," pp. 309–326 in Craig Heron and Robert Storey (eds.), *On the Job: Confronting the Labour Process in Canada*. Kingston and Montreal: McGill-Queen's University Press. Reprinted by permission.

Until approximately 25 years ago, all restaurant work involved an extensive division of labour: a complex hierarchy within the kitchen required workers with varying levels of skill and training. For a restaurant to be successful, all workers' had to co-ordinate their efforts. A supervisor's function was not only to ensure that the work was done, but to see that the various parts of the operation were synchronized.

This production arrangement resembles what Marx called "manufacture." The skill of the worker remains central to the production process. The commodity created (the meal served to the customer) is the social product of many workers' efforts. Human beings, using tools to assist them in their work, remain the organs of the productive mechanism.

In the fast-food industry, the machines, or the instruments of labour, assume a central place. Instead of assisting workers, the machines are dominant. Marx described this as the transition from "manufacture" to "large-scale industry."[2] Since the motion of the factory proceeds from the machinery and not from the worker, working personnel can continually be replaced. Frequent change in workers will not disrupt the labour process — a shift in organization applauded by *Harvard Business Review* contributor, Theodore Levitt.[3] According to Levitt, this new model is intended to replace the "humanistic concept of service" with the kind of technocratic thinking that in other fields has replaced "the high cost and erratic elegance of the artisan with the low-cost munificence of the manufacturer."

The labour process admired by Levitt has been adopted by many of the large fast-food companies including Burger King.

Managing a Store

The brain centre of all Burger King outlets lies in Burger King headquarters in Miami, Florida. There the Burger King bible, the *Manual of Operating Data*, is prepared. The procedures laid down in the manual must be followed to the letter by all Burger King stores. To ensure procedures are followed, each outlet is investigated and graded twice yearly by a team from regional headquarters.

In order to maximize volume and minimize labour costs, there is tremendous emphasis on what Burger King management calls speed of service. Demand is at its peak during the lunch hour, which accounts for about 20 percent of sales for the day; the more people served during the hour twelve to one, the higher the sales volume in the store.

Ideally, service time should never exceed three minutes.[4] Labour costs are also kept down by minimizing the use of full-time workers and by hiring minimum-wage part-time workers. Workers fill out an availability sheet when they are hired, indicating the hours they can work. Particularly when students are involved, management pressures them to make themselves as available as possible, though no guarantees are provided for how many hours a week work they will be given, or on which days they will be asked to work.

Scheduling is done each week for the coming week and workers are expected to check the schedule each week to see when they are supposed to show up. The *Manual of Operating Data* recommends as many short shifts as possible be assigned, so that few breaks will be required.

Food and paper costs make up about 40 percent of the cost of sales in Burger King outlets. These costs are essentially fixed, owing to company requirements that all Burger King outlets buy their stock from approved distributors. In effect, individual stores have control over food costs in only two areas — "waste" of food and meals provided to employees. Both together make up less than four percent of the cost of sales.

Store operations are designed from head office in Miami. By late 1981, it was possible to provide store managers not only with a staffing chart for hourly sales — indicating how many people should be on the floor given the predicted volume of business for that hour — but also where they should be positioned, based on the type of kitchen design. Thus, what discretion managers formerly had in assigning and utilizing workers has been eliminated.

Having determined precisely what workers are supposed to be doing and how quickly they should be doing it, the only remaining issue is getting them to perform to specifications. "Burger King University," located at headquarters in Miami was set up to achieve this goal. Burger King trains its staff to do things "not well, but right," the Burger King way.[5] Tight control over Burger King restaurants throughout the world rests on standardizing operations — doing things the "right" way — so that outcomes are predictable.

Working at Burger King

I did fieldwork at a Burger King outlet in suburban Toronto in 1980/1. The Burger King at which I worked was opened in 1979, and by 1981 was the highest volume store in Canada with annual sales of over one million dollars.

Workers use the back entrance at Burger King when reporting for work. Once inside, they go to a small room (about seven by twelve feet), which is almost completely occupied by an oblong table where crew members have their meals. Built-in benches stretch along both sides of the wall, with hooks above for coats. Homemade signs, put up by management, decorate the walls.

The crew room is usually a lively place. An AM/FM radio is tuned to a rock station while the teenage workers coming off or on shift talk about school and weekend activities or flirt with each other. Children and weddings are favourite topics of conversation for the older workers. Each worker must punch a time card at the start of a shift. A positioning chart, posted near the time clock, lists the crew members who are to work each meal, and indicates where in the kitchen they are to be stationed.

There are no pots and pans in the Burger King kitchen. As almost all foods enter the store ready for the final cooking process, pots and pans are not necessary. The major kitchen equipment consists of the broiler/toaster, the fry vats, the milkshake and coke machines, and the microwave ovens. In the near future, new drink machines will be installed in all Burger King outlets that will automatically portion the drinks. At Burger King, hamburgers are cooked as they pass through the broiler on a conveyor belt at a rate of 835 patties per hour. Furnished with a pair of tongs, the worker picks up the burgers as they drop off the belt, puts each on a toasted bun, and places the hamburgers and buns in a steamer.

The more interesting part of the procedure lies in applying condiments and microwaving the hamburgers. The popularity of this task among employees rests on the fact that it is unmechanized and allows some discretion to the worker. However, management is aware of this area of worker freedom and makes efforts to eliminate it by outlining exactly how this job is to be performed.

Despite such directives, the "Burger and Whopper Board" positions continue to hold their attraction for the workers, for this station requires two people to work side by side, and thus allows the opportunity for conversation. During busy times, as well, employees at this station also derive some work satisfaction from their ability to "keep up." At peak times, the challenge is to not leave the cashiers waiting for their orders.

As with the production of hamburgers, the cooking of french fries involves virtually no worker discretion. The worker, following directions laid out in the *Manual of Operating Data*, empties the frozen, pre-cut, bagged fries into fry baskets about two hours before they will be needed. When cooked fries are needed, the worker takes a fry basket from the rack and places it on a raised arm above the hot oil, and presses the "on" button. The arm holding the fry basket descends into the oil, and emerges two minutes and twenty seconds later; a buzzer goes off and the worker dumps the fries into the fry station tray where they are kept warm by an overhead light. To ensure the proper portions are placed into bags, a specially designed tool is used to scoop the fries up from the warming table.

Even at this station, though, management is concerned about limiting worker discretion. Despite the use of a specially designed scoop to control the portions each customer is given, a sign placed in the crew room for a few weeks admonished crew about being too generous with fry portions.

At the cash register, the "counter hostess" takes the order and rings it up on the computerized register. The "documentor" contains 88 colour coded items, ensuring that all variations of an order are automatically priced. As a menu item is punched in at the counter, it will appear on printers in the appropriate location in the kitchen. In this manner, the worker at sandwiches, for example, can look up at the printer and check what kind of sandwich is required. When the customer hands over the money, the cashier rings in "amount tendered" and the correct amount of change to be returned to the customer is rung up. Thus, cashiers need only remember to smile and ask customers to come again.

The computerized cash register not only simplifies ordering and payment, but is used to monitor sales and thus assist in staffing. If sales are running lower than expected, some workers will be asked to leave early. Output at each station is also monitored through the cash register. Finally, the computer at all company stores is linked through a modem to the head office in Miami. Top management has access to information on the performance of each store on a daily basis, and this information is routed back to the Canadian division headquarters in Mississauga.

Skill levels required in a Burger King have been reduced to a common denominator. The goal is to reduce all skills to a common, easily learned level and to provide for cross-training. At the completion of the ten-hour training program, each worker is able to work at a few stations. Skills for any of the stations can be learned in a matter of hours; the simplest jobs, such as filling cups with drinks, or placing the hamburgers and buns on the conveyor belt, can be learned in minutes. As a result, although labour turnover cuts into the pace of making hamburgers, adequate functioning of the restaurant is never threatened by people leaving. However, if workers are to be as replaceable as possible, they must be taught not only to perform their jobs in the same way, but also to resemble each other in attitudes, disposition, and appearance. Thus, workers are also drilled on personal hygiene, dress (shoes should be brown leather or vinyl, not suede), coiffure (hair tied up for girls and not too long for boys), and personality. Rule 17 of the handout to new employees underlines the importance of smiling: "Smile at all times, your smile is the key to our success."

While management seeks to make workers into interchangeable tools, workers themselves are expected to make a strong commitment to the store. If they wish to keep jobs at Burger King, they must abide by the labour schedule. Workers, especially teenagers, are expected to adjust their activities to the requirements of Burger King.

The Workers

One of the results of the transformation of the labour process from one of "manufacture" to that of "large-scale industry" is the emerging market importance of the young worker. While artisans require long training to achieve their skills, a machine-tender's primary characteristics are swiftness and endurance. Thus, young workers become ideal commodities: they are cheap, energetic, and plentiful. As well, they can be used as a marketing tool for the industry: the mass produced, smiling teenager, serving up the symbols of the good life in North America — hamburgers, cokes and fries.

Making up about 75 percent of the Burger King work force, the youngsters who worked after school, on weekends, and on holidays were called "part-timers." The teenager workers (about half of them boys, half girls) seemed to vary considerably in background. Some were college-bound youngsters who discussed their latest physics exam while piling on the pickles. Others were marking time until they reached age 16 and could leave school.

The daytime workers — the remaining 25 percent of the workforce — were primarily married women of mixed economic backgrounds. Consistent with a recent study of part-time workers in Canada, most of these women contributed their wages to the family budget.[6] Although they were all working primarily because their families needed the money, a few expressed their relief at getting out of the house, even to come to Burger King. One woman said: "At least when I come here, I'm appreciated. If I do a good job, a manager will say something to me. Here, I feel like a person. I'm sociable and I like being amongst people. At home, I'm always cleaning up after everybody and nobody ever notices!"[7]

Common to both the teenagers and the housewives was the view that working at Burger King was peripheral to their major commitments and responsibilities; the part-time nature of the work contributed to this attitude. Workers saw the alternative available to them as putting up with the demands of Burger King or leaving; in fact, leaving seemed to be the dominant form of protest. During my period in the store, on average, eleven people out of ninety-four hourly employees quit at each two-week pay period. While a few workers had stayed at Burger King for a few years, many did not last through the first two weeks. The need for workers is constant.

Burger King's ability to cope with high staff turnover means virtually no concessions are offered to workers to entice them to remain at Burger King. In fact, more attention is paid to the maintenance of the machinery than to "maintaining" the workers; time is regularly scheduled for cleaning and servicing the equipment, but workers may not leave the kitchen to take a drink or use the bathroom during the lunch and dinner rushes.

The dominant form — in the circumstances, the only easily accessible form — of opposition to the Burger King labour process is, then, the act of quitting. Management attempts to head off any other form of protest by insisting on an appropriate "attitude" on the part of the workers. Crew members must constantly demonstrate their satisfaction with working at Burger King by smiling at all times. However, as one worker remarked, "Why should I smile? There's nothing funny around here. I do my job and that should be good enough for them." It was not, however, and this worker soon quit. Another woman who had worked in the store for over a year also left. A crew member informed me that she had been fired for having a "poor attitude."

Management control and lack of worker opposition is further explained by the fact that other jobs open to teenagers are no better, and in some cases are worse, than the jobs at Burger King. The workers all agreed that any job that paid the full rather than the student minimum wage would be preferable to a job at Burger King; but they also recognized that their real alternatives would often be worse. Work at a donut shop, for example, also paid student minimum wage, under conditions of greater social isolation; baby sitting was paid poorly; and the hours for a paper route were terrible. Work at Burger King was a first job for many of the teenagers, and they enjoyed their first experience of earning their own money. And at Burger King, these young men and women were in the position of meeting the public, even if the forms of contact were limited by a vocabulary developed in Burger King headquarters: "Hello. Welcome to Burger King. May I take your order?" Interaction with customers had some intrinsic interest.

In sum, workers at Burger King are confronted with a labour process that puts management in complete control. Furnished with state-of-the-art restaurant technology, Burger King outlets employ vast numbers of teenagers and married women

— a population with few skills and little commitment to working at Burger King. In part, this lack of commitment is understood through reference to a labour process that offers little room for work satisfaction. Most jobs can be learned in a very short time (a matter of minutes for some) and workers are required to learn every job, a fact that underlines the interchangeable nature of the jobs and the workers who do them. The work is most interesting when the store is busy. Paradoxically, work intensity, Burger King's main form of assault on labour costs, remains the only aspect of the job that can provide any challenge for the worker. Workers would remark with pride how they "didn't fall behind at all," despite a busy lunch or dinner hour.

It would be reassuring to dismiss the fast-food industry as an anomaly in the workplace; teenagers will eventually finish school and become "real workers," while housewives with families are actually domestic workers, also not to be compared with adult males in more skilled jobs. Unfortunately, there are indications that the teenagers and women who work in this type of job represent an increasingly typical kind of worker, in the one area of the economy that continues to grow — the service sector. The fast-food industry represents a model for other industries in which the introduction of technology will permit the employment of low-skilled, cheap, and plentiful workers. In this sense, it is easy to be pessimistic and agree with Andre Gorz's depressing formulation of the idea of work:

> The terms "work" and "job" have become interchangeable: work is no longer something that one does but something that one has. Workers no longer "produce" society through the mediation of the relations of production; instead, the machinery of social production as a whole produces "work" and imposes it in a random way upon random, interchangeable individuals.[8]

The Burger King system represents a major triumph for capital. However, the reduction of the worker to a simple component of capital requires more than the introduction of a technology; workers' autonomous culture must be eliminated as well, including the relationships among workers, their skills, and their loyalties to one another. The smiling, willing, homogeneous worker must be produced and placed on the Burger King assembly line.

While working at Burger King, I saw the extent to which Burger King has succeeded in reducing its work force to a set of interchangeable pieces. However, I also saw how insistently the liveliness and decency of the workers emerged in the informal interaction that occurred. Open resistance is made virtually impossible by the difficulty of identifying who is responsible for the rules that govern the workplace: the workers know that managers follow orders from higher up. The very high turnover of employees indicates workers understand that their interests and Burger King's are not the same. As young people and women realize that their jobs in the fast-food industry are not waystations en route to more fulfilling work, they will perhaps blow the whistle on the Burger King "team." The mould for the creation of the homogeneous worker assembling the standardized meal for the homogeneous consumer is not quite perfected.

ENDNOTES

1 Promotional material from Burger King Canada head office in Mississauga, Ontario.

2 Karl Marx, *Capital,* vol. 1 ([1867]; New York 1977), ch. xv.

3 Theodore Levitt, "Production Line Approach to Service," *Harvard Business Review* 50, no. 1 (Sept.-Oct. 1972): 51–2.

4 A "Shape Up" campaign instituted at the beginning of 1982 attempted to set a new goal of a 2 1/2-minute service time.

5 Personal communication, Burger King "professor," 4 January 1982.

6 Labour Canada, *Commission of Inquiry into Part-Time Work* (Ottawa 1983) [Wallace commission].

7 Personal communication, Burger King worker, 8 August 1981.

8 Andre Gorz, *Farewell to the Working Class* (Boston 1982), 71.

8.4 Sheng Xuewen, Norman Stockman, and Norman Bonney

Women's Working Lives in China, Japan and Great Britain

INTRODUCTION

Until recently, women's traditional work, which included childcare and unpaid housework, was not treated as a serious topic of study by the (mostly male) profession of sociology. Because no money changed hands, it was not viewed as "real" work. That attitude began to fade, however, when women began to enter the paid labour force (and academe) in large numbers.

The next excerpt examines the extent to which husbands in China, Japan, and Great Britain start to take on more of the domestic work when their wives get paid jobs outside the home. Since their husbands never relieve them of all their housework, women who take paid employment are always, in effect, taking on a second job. The researchers find, however, that the weight of this "dual burden" varies significantly from country to country.

Xuewen, Sheng, Norman Stockman, and Norman Bonney (1992). "The Dual Burden: East and West (Women's Working Lives in China, Japan and Great Britain)" *International Sociology*, 7(2), 209–223. Reprinted by permission.

Ironically, an important variable in women's dual burden has now become whether her paid work is seen as "serious" and "real." In China, husbands make a greater effort to share the housework equitably, in large part because their wives work full-time and earn almost as much money as they do. By contrast, Japanese and British husbands are less likely to pick up more of the housework when their wives get paying jobs — partly because they see their wives primarily as housewives dabbling in part-time work.

The Chinese women pay a price for being taken seriously, though. Despite getting more help from their husbands, they have the largest dual burden of any group studied.

M odern societies are confronted with structural dilemmas as to how to allocate labour between the conflicting priorities of production in manufacturing and service industries in the public sphere and production and reproduction in the private domestic sphere. Political processes at the level of the state influence the institutional solutions which are evolved to determine the allocation of labour between these spheres. At the micro-level individuals, couples, families, communities and individual enterprises are confronted with similar dilemmas. In particular, and related to the interests of this paper, parents of young children are faced with how to allocate their time and labour between parental, domestic and employment responsibilities.

This paper examines three societies which have adopted different responses to these dilemmas.

Methodology

The findings reported below draw from data collected by sample surveys in China, Japan and Great Britain. The respondents in the three samples were all employed married mothers of pre-school and school-age children. The Chinese and Japanese surveys used a common methodology, involving the administration of a self-completed questionnaire to mothers of children attending workplace nurseries, kindergartens and child-care centres, in Beijing, Shanghai and Xian in China and a sample of urban areas in Japan in 1987. There were 2,072 respondents in China and 1,865 in Japan.

The British data are taken from interviews with 1,000 respondents in each of six medium-sized British urban labour markets in 1986 and 1987. The data reported in this paper derive from a sub-sample of respondents who were female, married, employed and who had children of school or pre-school age. The data derive from 466 such women interviewed in 1986 and the 246 re-interviewed in 1987.

China: the Dual Burden

In urban China, a 48-hour, six-day working week is the norm for both mothers and fathers of young children. Eighty-two percent of the respondents and 83 percent of their husbands have such working hours. Women's working careers exhibit only brief interruptions following childbirth. Eighty-four percent of the sample had held jobs continuously since they left school and almost three-quarters had returned to paid work within six months of the birth of the child. When asked for their reasons for working, Chinese women were most likely to mention financial necessity.

Chinese women's employment patterns are much closer to men's than they are in the other samples. There is, for instance, no gender difference in the time of travel to and from work in China. Almost all of the female Chinese sample has regular worker status rather than being temporary workers or engaged in family enterprise. Their average income is much closer to their spouses than is the case in Britain or Japan. Educational differences are also far less marked.

Chinese women in the urban labour force are not under pressure when married or pregnant to sever their employment. Indeed the situation is the reverse. Enterprises are currently extending the statutory 56-day maternity leave by up to six months, during which time the female worker qualifies for full pay. Further leave can be obtained for up to two years, but with 75 percent of the pay in the first year and 50 percent in the second. Mothers retain their employment position throughout this period, but may lose seniority rights. There are extensive child-care facilities for pre-school children. A further factor minimising the effects of maternity on employment is the one-child policy which has been very effective in urban areas.

Chinese women exhibit slightly more dissatisfaction with their working life than do their Japanese peers, and are much more likely to consider there to be unreasonable differences between women and men in their employment. 50.5 percent of Chinese respondents, compared to 15.7 percent of Japanese respondents indicated affirmative responses to the question: "Are there any unreasonable differences between men and women at your workplace?"

The most frequently cited "unreasonable difference" amongst the Chinese sample was "few opportunities to receive training" (29.7 percent compared to 9.9 percent among the Japanese sample). The Chinese sample was also twice as likely (15.3 percent compared to 8.8 percent) to cite lack of promotion possibilities as a source of dissatisfaction. This greater dissatisfaction among Chinese women with gender inequalities at work may seem paradoxical, given their greater objective equality with men. The paradox may be resolved by emphasising the greater expectations for gender equality aroused among Chinese women by the official ideology. Chinese women expect a dismantling of gender divisions, and are therefore more disillusioned by those remaining gender differences at work.

With respect to domestic labour, the data indicate a greater sharing of tasks between marital partners in China than in either Japan or Great Britain. Table 1 indicates the gendered division of domestic labour in the three samples for a range of tasks. In each society exclusive female responsibility for washing-up, cooking, cleaning the house and washing clothes is considerably more common than is exclusive male responsibility. In China, however, there is a much more marked incidence of partners sharing these tasks.

TABLE 1   THE DIVISION OF DOMESTIC LABOUR TASKS IN CHINA,
JAPAN, AND BRITAIN (PERCENTAGES)

Task	Female, entirely or mainly			Both			Male, entirely or mainly			Other		
	C	J	B	C	J	B	C	J	B	C	J	B
Washing-up	36	91	53	36	3	36	20	1	5	8	5	6
Cleaning the house	47	89	77	39	6	17	10	2	3	4	3	3
Washing clothes	43	92	94	44	4	5	9	2	1	4	2	0
Cooking	35	94	77	37	2	19	13	1	4	15	3	0

The differing domestic divisions of labour in China and Japan was also demonstrated in an item which requested respondents to describe the husband's role in household work. While 75.3 percent in China said the husband did most of it, shared it with his wife or did it together with his wife, only 4.1 percent reported this to be the case in Japan, and whereas — according to the respondents — over half of Japanese men (54.7 percent) do almost no housework, the comparable figure for China was 7.3 percent.

The greater sharing of domestic roles in China can be attributed to the logistics of managing a household when both partners are undertaking demanding extra-familial employment. There is evidence from the Japanese and British data that where the female partner is in full-time paid work, there is a less extreme gendered division of domestic labour compared to cases where the respondent is in paid work for fewer hours. In general, dual full-time labour market partnerships lead towards less inequality in the domestic division of labour. In China the prevalence of dual full-time working partnerships is a factor contributing towards a less extreme domestic gender role segregation. Where both partners face demanding extra-familial employment responsibilities, the male is under pressure to contribute more to household labour. While much needs to be done to achieve full gender equality in China, the evidence presented above is an indication of considerable changes on this front in urban areas since pre-revolutionary times.

Such advances have not, however, been made without a price. Because of their extensive employment and domestic commitments, Chinese women were much more likely than their Japanese counterparts to say they found housework a heavy or very heavy burden (62.5 percent compared to 38.2 percent), that their work was too tiring (31.9 percent compared to 12.7 percent) and that their hours of work were too long (39.7 percent compared to 15.7 percent). They were also more likely to report they did not get enough sleep (35.8 percent compared to 29 percent). Despite these negative aspects of their circumstances, the Chinese women were more likely to express satisfaction with their family life (93.1 percent compared to 82.7 percent), they were far less likely to be dissatisfied with their husbands' contribution to domestic tasks (25.8 percent compared to 48 percent), and they expressed more satisfaction with their relations with their husbands (96.2 percent compared to 81.9 percent) than did the comparative group in Japan.

Japan: Working Housewives

The pattern in Japan contrasts markedly with that of China. Home and paid work are spheres which are much more differentiated by gender in Japan. Typically in Japan, women leave the labour force upon marriage or the birth of a child, and when they return to paid work they return to subordinate and marginal employment (Eccleston, 1989: Ch. 6; Smith, 1987). This is borne out in the data which demonstrate labour market interruptions occasioned by childbirth and child care being much more common in Japan than China. Over half the sample was not in paid employment for two to five years for such reasons. Only 39 percent had worked continuously since leaving school, compared to 84 percent in China. Forty-one percent were employed in temporary work and 22 percent in private or family enterprises. Fifty-eight percent worked less than an 8-hour day compared to 8 percent of their husbands. Their income averaged just under 1 million yen per annum compared to 3.3 million yen for their husbands.

The data are consistent with the view that female self-identity in China is more anchored in working life, while in Japan it is more rooted in the home. Thus, despite their lower involvement in — and rewards from — paid employment, the Japanese respondents were slightly more satisfied with their working life than their Chinese peers. 70.4 percent of the Japanese sample expressed satisfaction with their working life, compared to 66.2 percent of the Chinese respondents. The Japanese women also expressed significantly less dissatisfaction than the Chinese on such aspects of work as the work being too tiring, the hours being too long, the work not being suitable, and a lack of promotion possibilities. The major exception concerned income. About a quarter of respondents in both China and Japan mentioned dissatisfaction over income. For the Japanese, this represented by far the most frequently mentioned source of dissatisfaction, whereas for the Chinese it was only the third most frequently mentioned item.

Japanese respondents were considerably more likely to agree that the husband should go out to work and the wife should be a housewife. 38.1 percent of the Japanese respondents and 19.2 percent of the Chinese expressed degrees of agreement with this view. Japanese respondents and their husbands, according to the wives' reports, were much more likely to endorse the view that housework and child-care were the responsibility of the wife even if she was in paid work, than were their Chinese equivalents. Twenty-nine percent of respondents and husbands endorsed this view in Japan, and 1.8 percent and 9.8 percent respectively of these categories supported it in China. The Japanese respondents were also more likely to say that a married woman in paid work would neglect housework (23.7 percent compared to 0.3 percent) and that the increase in married women working might result in family problems (40.1 percent compared to 13.8 percent).

Japanese respondents also displayed less enthusiasm for married women engaging in paid work, in that only 63.7 percent of them endorsed the view that "the increase in married women working will promote social equality and progress," compared to 83.5 percent of the Chinese sample.

Because of their lesser involvement in paid work, the Japanese respondents were less likely than the Chinese to report experiencing too heavy a burden of housework and child-care deriving from their work commitments (31.4 percent compared to 37.5 percent). Only 38.2 percent of the Japanese respondents, compared to 62.5 percent of the Chinese felt housework was a heavy or very heavy burden. Amongst the Japanese there was, however, a difference in this respect between those in part-time and those in full-time paid employment. The latter found housework more burdensome than did the former (44.6 percent compared to 29.7 percent respectively). In both countries, then, being in full-time paid work contributed to a feeling that housework was burdensome.

Seventy-eight percent of the Japanese respondents, compared to 51 percent of the Chinese, believe men are advantaged over women in family life, politics, law, and social ideas and customs. Few of them, unlike their Chinese counterparts, believe paid work can produce equality between husband and wife (2.3 percent compared to 19.8 percent in a fixed choice item which allowed other responses on the virtues of married women working). Reflecting their relative social isolation in the household, Japanese respondents were also more likely to recognise the value of paid work in providing a link with society than were the Chinese (16.7 percent cf. 3.4 percent). Thus, while the housewife role finds considerable endorsement among Japanese mothers, it is not without a recognition of the penalties that it results in for them.

Great Britain: Part-Time Workers

Data for the British sample are closer to that of the Japanese than the Chinese model, although gender role segregation in domestic labour tasks does not appear to be as extreme. The British respondents worked fewer hours than the Japanese. Seventy-six percent of the Britons worked part-time — fewer than 30 hours per week, compared to 45 percent of the Japanese. The median number of hours of paid work per week was 18 in Great Britain compared to 37 in Japan and 48 in China. The net wages of respondents in Britain were 35 percent of their husbands' net average wage. In Japan, the comparable figure was 41 percent and in China it was close to 100 percent. Part-time work in Great Britain is generally of low status and poorly rewarded. Seventy-five percent of female employment is in routine non-manual sales and service occupations and semi- and unskilled manual work. Such occupations are often resorted to by mothers of young children since they provide part-time work at hours consistent with their domestic child-care responsibilities. As in Japan, maternity results in women, if they return to paid work, occupying low-status and marginal types of employment.

In China, both wife and husband average 43 minutes daily travel times to and from work. In both Britain (data relate to Aberdeen only) and in Japan, the median travel time for women is 20 minutes, while the median times for their husbands are 44 minutes in Britain and 33 minutes in Japan. These differences could be due to a number of factors. In China, work allocation procedures give workers much less choice as to where they work and women may not have the opportunity to choose to work closer to home. In Britain and Japan, in contrast, women are more able to choose work which fits in with their domestic responsibilities, and their shorter travel to work times may reflect their greater symbolic attachment to the home compared with their husbands. In Britain, an additional factor is that female respondents were much more likely than their partners to travel to work by bus or on foot. Male partners were more likely to travel in their car.

Working Japanese and Chinese parents are much more able to take advantage of kindergartens and child-care centres than are their British equivalents. The latter depend upon relatives, friends and neighbours for such assistance. The marital partners are the major providers of care in this respect, juggling their work schedules to take turns looking after the children. The male partner's role is particularly important when children are below school age. In 21 out of 33 such cases in Aberdeen, male partners were the source of child care. Only two were cared for in day nurseries. When children are of school age, mothers fit their working hours around the school-day. The constraints of providing care for children in the absence of formal institutional provision is one reason British women's hours in paid work are relatively low.

Only 9.5 percent of the British respondents are dissatisfied with their hours of work, compared to 39.7 percent of the Chinese and 15.7 percent of the Japanese. Twenty-two percent of the Britons are dissatisfied with their level of pay, compared to slightly higher proportions of the other two samples who indicate that their income is too low or unstable. Twenty percent of the Britons were dissatisfied with their promotion prospects, compared to 15.3 percent of the Chinese and 8.8 percent of the Japanese. Twenty-two percent of the British sample expressed overall dissatisfaction with their job, compared to 34 percent of the Chinese and 30 percent of the Japanese.

The British were also most likely to express satisfaction with their leisure. The figures were 49 percent for Britain, 42 percent for China and 41 percent for Japan. For British women, part-time work resolves the competing pressures of domestic obligations and paid employment and generates higher levels of satisfaction with employment and leisure.

Like the Japanese respondents, traditional gender role attitudes were espoused by substantial proportions of the British sample. Fifty-two percent expressed degrees of agreement with the statement, "I'm not against women working, but men should still be the main breadwinner in the family," and 18 percent agreed, "In times of high unemployment married women should stay at home." Evidence of a commitment to the domestic sphere was also expressed by the minority of respondents who had never engaged in paid work while their last child was of pre-school age. Only 19 percent reported they would have preferred to work. Of those who had worked while their child was small, 40 percent reported they would have preferred to stay at home.

Fifty-nine percent stated the female partner *should* be ultimately responsible for ensuring the housework is properly done; 43 percent believed the male partner *should* be ultimately responsible for ensuring the family gets an adequate income and 26 percent believed the female partner *should* be ultimately responsible for looking after the children. An item similar to these attitudes, i.e., "the husband should go out to work, the wife should look after the home" was endorsed by 38 percent of the Japanese but only 19 percent of the Chinese. Similarly, 29 percent of Japanese respondents, but only 1.8 percent of the Chinese, supported the view (in a forced choice item with three other possible responses) that "even if the wife is working, housework and child-care should mainly be done by the wife."

Overall, the Chinese respondents were least committed attitudinally to gender role differentiation. Surprisingly, given the emphasis of the literature on the strength of the "housewife" role in Japan, it is difficult with the data available to detect any difference between Japan and Great Britain in the prevalence of attitudes supportive of this role set.

Conclusion

Each of the societies examined has found distinctive institutional solutions to the problems of allocating the labour and time of parents of young children between the competing demands of employment and family life. Certain common features can be discerned, particularly the greater dual burden falling upon employed mothers in each society. In each society they combine primary responsibility for domestic work with their paid employment. There are, however, important variations in this pattern, with women in urban China having a greater total load of obligations, a relatively advantaged position in the sphere of employment and greater help in the home from their husbands. In Britain and Japan the pressures generated by the dual burden are resolved more by mothers of young children lowering their activity and status in paid employment. This process is most marked in Great Britain.

REFERENCES

Eccleston, B. (1989). *State and Society in Post-War Japan*. Cambridge: Polity Press.

Ministry of Internal Affairs, Statistics Bureau (1985). *Labour Market Statistics*. Tokyo.

Smith, R. J. (1987). "Gender Inequality in Contemporary Japan." *Journal of Japanese Studies* 13 (1): 1–25.

QUESTIONS

DISCUSSION QUESTIONS

1. What does a person's job say about him or her as a person? Are we defined by the work we do? Are we *accurately* defined?

2. "De-industrialization" was a term formerly used to describe what happens when an economy loses a big share of its manufacturing jobs. The term had a negative connotation because it was associated with economic recessions and depressions and with rising unemployment. Today, the term "post-industrial" is used to describe an economy that has seen its manufacturing sector shrink. Is the difference between these two terms semantic or real and substantial?

3. Durkheim didn't think modern societies would have just one unified culture because people's life experiences would be too varied and dissimilar. Yet Ester Reiter's excerpt shows a modern corporation doing its utmost to ensure one experience — eating a Big Whopper — will be the same no matter where it happens. Can the standardized products and practies of corporate consumer capitalism provide the basis for a common culture?

4. One way to create jobs would be to reduce the hours people work and to reduce their pay accordingly. This would free up some work for the unemployed. Discuss why you think a substantial fraction of working people would (or wouldn't) be willing to trade more leisure for less pay.

DATA COLLECTION EXERCISES

1. Compile a list of Canada's ten most dangerous occupations by gathering statistics about on-the-job injuries and on-the-job fatalities. Are there any surprises on your list?

2. One of the rewards of hard work is supposed to be economic success. And one of the rewards of economic success is that you no longer have to work so hard. Gather data on the length of the work week in nine countries. Randomly pick three poor countries, three affluent ones, and three that are rapidly becoming affluent. Do nations work less as their wealth increases?

3. Find 20 students who say they have made a definite decision to pursue a specific career. Ask them how they came to pick the career they did. After comparing their answers, try to generate a hypothesis about which factors are most important in the career-selection process.

4. Agricultural workers make up less than four percent of Canada's labour force. With that in mind, find out how many people have agricultural jobs in China, India, and Indonesia. What percentage of their labour force works in agriculture? Now, calculate how many people in those countries would have to give up farm work if agriculture were as small a part of the job market as it is in Canada. Where would such large numbers of people seek work if they were no longer needed as farmers?

WRITING EXERCISES

1. Choose one occupation in which either women or men are severely under-represented. Write a brief essay accounting for this under-representation.

2. Studies show the average person will change jobs several times during his or her working life. In light of this fact, write a brief essay describing some ways to maximize one's chances of remaining happily employed at all times.

3. Under free trade, some Canadian jobs will be relocated in other countries. Write a brief essay describing the kinds of jobs that are most likely to stay in Canada. Explain why Canada is a particularly suitable location for those types of jobs.

4. Write a brief essay about a place you have worked. Describe how the workplace culture (or working atmosphere) was influenced by the kind of work done there.

SUGGESTED READINGS

1. Armstrong, Pat and Hugh Armstrong (1993). *The Double Ghetto,* Third Edition. Toronto: McClelland and Stewart. This book, which contains much Canadian as well as international data, demonstrates that the double burden is not simply a problem of women having too much work to do. It's also that "women's work" is not highly valued in either the marketplace or the domestic sphere.

2. Bell, Daniel (1973). *The Coming of Post-Industrial Society.* New York: Basic Books. This was the book that launched the debate on the nature of post-industrial societies. Twenty years later, it can also be read as an interesting case study in the field of social forecasting.

3. Sennett, R. and J. Cobb (1973). *The Hidden Injuries of Class.* New York: Vintage. The psychological costs of having a low status, menial job in a class-conscious society are examined in this book. The authors interviewed blue collar workers to find out their feelings about their own work and work in general.

4. Hamper, Ben (1992). *Rivethead: Tales From the Assembly Line.* New York: Warner Books. This lively, gritty, and often funny book is written by a man who spent several years working on a General Motors assembly line. He offers an insider's perspective on why this kind of work can be, at different times, boring, challenging, ridiculous, and tragic.

POPULATION

Introduction

The world's population increases through an excess of births (fertility) over deaths (mortality) and this excess is called *natural increase*. At present, the world's birth rate is about two percent higher than its death rate, which means that the population of the world is growing at two percent every year. If the world population continues to grow at this speed, it will double in less than 35 years. If that happens, the world will contain more than 8 billion people early in the next century.

Sooner or later, growth must stop. But when and how will growth come to an end? Will the change be sudden or gradual, chosen or forced upon us? Will it be accomplished by a drastic decline in childbearing or a rise in the number of deaths? There are only two ways for population growth to

slow (or stop): the fertility rate must fall and/or the mortality rate must rise. Which is it likely to be?

Malthusian Theory

This question has been the subject of a hot debate for the last two hundred years. The first to consider this question was Thomas Malthus (1766–1834), an English clergyman and economist. Malthus argued that population will always outgrow its food supply. That is because at best, Malthus claims, the food supply can increase only arithmetically, as in the series 1,2,3,4,5, but population will always increase geometrically, as in the series 1,2,4,8,16. The gap between these two series gets wider and wider, until finally a disaster occurs.

To illustrate this, consider a population of 1000 girls and 1000 boys. Now, assume that every female survives to adulthood, marries, has four children and dies. If all of the females survive to adulthood and bear four children each, then die, in the next generation there will be (roughly) 2000 women and 2000 men. If all of these women survive and bear four children, in the next generation there will be 4000 women and 4000 men; and in the generation after that, 8000 women and 8000 men, and so on.

It is easy to see that, with a constant pattern of four births per woman, the population doubles every generation — roughly thirty years. In four generations (a mere 120 years), the population will have grown from 2000 people to 32 000 people: a 16-fold increase. This is the power of exponential growth.

Can this really happen? Well, in fact, this is the current rate of population growth in southern and southeastern Asia, where 1.5 billion people live today. It is also the rate of growth in Latin America, where another half billion people live — so these kinds of calculations are not unrealistic.

Malthus doubted that food supplies could also increase 16-fold in 120 years. Increases in the food supply are only "additive" or "arithmetic," he said. Certainly, in 1800 when Malthus was writing, the growth of the food supply *was* severely limited by the amount of land available, the quality of the soil, and the level of agricultural technology — at that time, still fairly simple.

So, in Malthus's time, increase in the food supply *was* arithmetic and, in fact, fairly slow. And that's what led Malthus to believe there was a very real chance population growth would outstrip increases in the food supply. Said simply: in the long run, the human race is almost certain to starve.

Malthus saw that there were several ways out of the trap and we had to choose one of them, however unpleasant. In short, we had to settle for "preventive" or "positive" checks on population.

Positive checks limit population growth by increasing the death rate. They include war, famine, pestilence, and disease. *Preventive checks* limit population growth by limiting the numbers of births. These "preventive checks" include delaying marriage, using contraceptives, abortion, infanticide, and sexual abstinence. Of these two options, Malthus preferred the second, especially postponing marriage. Malthus simply couldn't recommend any of the other preventive checks (much less the positive checks). So people had a choice to make: either delay marrying, or face starvation, war, and epidemics.

Malthus painted a grim picture of the world's future, but was he right? Yes and no. Throughout the nineteenth and twentieth centuries, there have been famines and epidemics around the world; invariably, they have taken place where the population is poor, people marry young, and the birth rate is very high. Yet, amazingly, we haven't faced the kind of crisis Malthus predicted, for a number of reasons.

One reason was the opening of new land for food production in the nineteenth and twentieth centuries. Another reason is that our agricultural methods are better today than two centuries ago. Finally, we have shifted our economies from an agricultural to an industrial base, and industrialism produces more food *and* consumer goods than ever in history.

Since Malthus' time, it has been possible to increase the food supply more than arithmetically. It has also been possible to slow down the birth rate by using the preventive check Malthus couldn't support: contraception.

New Ways of Life Reduce Fertility

As England entered the twentieth century, the "Malthusian problem" of too many people seemed to take care of itself. The standard of living rose, yet people began bearing fewer children.

At some point people began to feel that they could plan and control the number of children they bear. They became "numerate" about family size, as van de Walle says in an excerpt in this section. It is far from clear how this new numeracy was related to economic development, or even if it was related at all. But it did happen, and is still happening today in less developed parts of the world.

Outside Europe, the decline in fertility has meant the breakdown of the extended family. Fertility begins to decline when extended families are replaced by nuclear families. Fertility also declines when children lose their economic value.

All of this means that many changes must take place for fertility to decline. People must become less worried about old-age security; the state takes care of that. They must become less concerned about their children surviving to adulthood; modern medicine takes care of that. And people must stop equating large families with wealth and blessings from heaven.

Other factors also play a part in lowering fertility. For example, higher educational and work aspirations lead women to limit their childbearing. When they do not have such aspirations, they are more likely to become teenage mothers, according to an excerpt in this section. Cheaper, safer, and easier contraception allows women to avoid or delay childbearing as much as they wish. And new individualistic values lead people to have fewer children as they become more prosperous — contrary to what Malthus had feared. These new values encourage people to enjoy their prosperity and leisure, not bear and raise a larger number of children. (On this, see the excerpt by van de Kaa on the "second demographic transition," in the last section of this book.)

In the less developed countries, a great many people still do not have enough food to eat. But many of the famines which have plagued Africa (for example) in recent years are not a result of overpopulation: they are due to poor land use and primitive technology. Sometimes, they are a result of civil war and other political factors. Whatever the cause, we are seeing an increase in international migration, as people flee from poorer to richer countries in hopes of a better life. Often, they meet with a cold, or even hostile reception.

In industrial countries, concerns about scarcity have shifted away from food to jobs and resources. With the collapse of communism in Eastern Europe and the recent world-wide recession, millions have come to Western Europe and elsewhere in hopes of a new start. Often, their presence has been resented: local people have accused the newcomers of taking scarce jobs and drawing on (already inadequate) social services. On this, see excerpt 9.4, which considers possible solutions to the problem of the "unstoppable immigrant."

Likewise, there have been repeated concerns voiced about a scarcity of resources — for example, energy and minerals — needed for industrial production. Unless they find new deposits, or ways of making synthetic copies of these non-renewable resources, people in the industrial world may face life-threatening scarcity at some time in the future. Having escaped the food shortage Malthus predicted, we may soon face a shortage of needed raw materials.

The Future

So, the Malthusian problem reasserts itself time and again. In the long run, how *is* the earth going to support a population that is growing faster than the resources it needs to survive? We are not out of the woods yet. Rates of fertility are still high in many parts of the world and positive checks — in the form of epidemics — are far from conquered, once and for all.

On the other hand, people are living longer than they did in Malthus's time. We begin this section with an excerpt on longevity and, in particular, the remarkable tales of longevity that have been coming out of the Russian Empire and Soviet Union for over a century.

REFERENCES

Malthus, T. R. (1958 [1798]). *Population: The First Essay*. Ann Arbor: University of Michigan Press.

9.1 Lea Keil Garson

Do People Live Longer in the Caucasus?

INTRODUCTION

People in our society have become very health-conscious in recent years. This befits a society which is aging and has, in historical and comparative terms, a very long average life span. Yet, for all the improvements in sanitation, medicine, nutrition, and public health care, our life expectancy still falls short of 100 years. In fact, it averages much closer to 75 or 80 years.

How, then, to account for the stories we have heard for nearly a century telling that, in certain parts of the world, it is not unusual for people to live to 100 years of age and older? Some writers even go on to describe the way of life that promotes such extreme longevity — a way of life that is very different from our own. Whatever the explanation, such extreme longevity is an advertisement for the society in which it is found: proof that better ways of living can be found outside capitalist, industrial, urban North America. (Perhaps in the kind of leisure-loving society described in excerpt 1.2, though there is no evidence of great longevity in Western Africa; quite the reverse.)

The next excerpt reveals certain peculiarities in the data which cause us to doubt the truth of these envied claims. In particular, Garson shows us that people seem to live longest where there is little certainty about people's actual birth-dates. More likely than not, the claims are unfounded and there is no heaven-on-earth in the Caucasus or anywhere else.

The Soviet Union, and the Russian Empire before it, have a long history of claims to extraordinary longevity, especially in the Caucasus region. Exceptionally high proportions of centenarians have been reported in the censuses, and much publicity has accompanied the announcements of "super-centenarians" living well beyond 150 years. Anthropologists, gerontologists, and others have conducted research on the "secrets" of Soviet longevity without adequately verifying that their subjects are actually as old as they purport to be. One anthropologist, for example, has stated: "It seems to be mere quibbling to discredit reports of longevity by questions about precise ages. If a person lives to 120 rather than 130 in health and vigour, the fact of old age is barely diminished."[1]

Garson, Lea Keil (1991). "The Centenarian Question: Old-Age Mortality in the Soviet Union, 1897–1970," *Population Studies*, 45, 265–278. Reprinted by permission.

Before debating whether yoghurt, mountain air, or the so-called simple life promote longevity, it is necessary to determine whether the centenarians studied are truly centenarians. In this paper I investigate the question whether the exceptionally high proportion of centenarians in the Soviet population, and the extraordinary ages that the centenarians are reported to have reached, are real phenomena, or rather a result of age overstatement in the census data.

Longevity and Age Overstatement: A Review of the Literature

The Soviet republics of the Caucasus — Georgia, Azerbaidzhan, and Armenia — have long been alleged to be centres of extreme longevity. Published accounts of Soviet centenarians are numerous. Take, for example, Medzhid Agayev, who at the age of 139 was the oldest resident of Azerbaidzhan in 1976. A collective farmer with 150 descendants, Agayev was assigned the "quieter job" of "herding cows" when he was 136 years old.[2] In 1970 the Novosti Press Agency reported that the oldest man in the Soviet Union was 165-year old Shirali Muslimov; at 195, Ashura Omarova qualified as the oldest woman.

Soviet slogan writers have heralded their country as the "State of Longevity." The U.S.S.R. claims to contain more centenarians than any other country in the world.[3] Soviet claims of extraordinary longevity follow a long-standing Russian tradition of similar claims. Tarkhnishvili reported that the 1819 Census of the Russian population included 1,789 centenarians, two of whom were reported as having reached the age of 160 years.[4] Russia "glorified in its centenarians and exceeded by five to six times the number of old people in the other countries of Europe," according to Tarkhnishvili, who also cautioned that age exaggeration might be a factor. Russian scientists studied longevity among the peoples of the Caucasus as early as 1811, and Soviet researchers today lead the world in terms of the quantity of longevity studies conducted.[5]

Soviet claims of extraordinary longevity are used to bolster the image of the U.S.S.R. at home and abroad, for exceptional numbers of centenarians are seen to reflect positively on the Soviet social system. The Soviet Union is not unique in this respect. One scholar has noted that: "Practically every culture for which there are records has made note of instances of exceptional human longevity. The claims have been used to emphasize the qualities of a particular locale, form of government, or other combinations of circumstances in which a community or a nation can take pride."[6]

Yet Soviet claims of extraordinary longevity are of special interest and merit close scrutiny due to their scope, their historical persistence, and because of the position of the U.S.S.R. on the world scene. The Soviet claims combine two elements: (1) exceptional numbers of centenarians, and (2) exceptional ages attained by Soviet centenarians. The official census tabulations appear to lend credence to both types of claims. Unlike census data for most countries, in which the oldest category is given as 100 years and over, the Soviet census age distributions for 1959 and 1970 continue to age 120. There were 219 men and 359 women reported to be aged 120 or older in 1959, and 110 men and 229 women in that category in 1970.

Available information on the limits of the human life span challenges the accuracy of reported ages in excess of 110–115. In Sweden, for example, where the age at death of every alleged centenarian is investigated, no deaths above age 110 have been verified.[7] The oldest authenticated centenarian in the world was an American woman, Mrs. Delina Filkins (née Ecker), who died in 1928 at the age of 113 years, 214 days.[8] [Editor's note: According to the most recent *Guinness Book of World Records*, the world's oldest person died in 1986 at the age of 120.]

Soviet claims of hundreds of citizens living to be over 120 years old have little credibility in light of the widely accepted view of 110 to 115 years as the maximum verified human life span at the present time. The fact that this element of the Soviet claims — the extraordinary ages attained by Soviet centenarians — is not credible, casts doubt on the other element of the claims as well, that is, the extremely high numbers of centenarians reported.

The unrealistically high incidence of alleged centenarians and the unbelievable ages which they are reported to have reached in all likelihood do not result from deliberate exaggeration on the part of the Soviet government. Rather, this phenomenon is caused by a virtually universal tendency of older census respondents to overstate their ages. Yet the Soviet government contributes to the perpetuation of a longevity "myth" by publishing, without qualification, an age distribution of centenarians that includes hundreds of persons aged 120 and over. Important evidence of age overstatement in many populations has accumulated over the years.[9]

The Soviet scientific literature on longevity is characterized both by a recognition that age exaggeration confounds census and survey data and by a failure to appreciate fully the effect of age exaggeration on estimates of life expectancy and the prevalence of centenarians. A statement made by the Soviet researcher Kolosova perhaps typifies the sometimes contradictory nature of Soviet researchers' attitudes toward age overstatement. Kolosova matter-of-factly refers to Shirali Muslimov, noting that at age 165 he was the oldest inhabitant of the Soviet Union according to the Census of 1970. No doubts are expressed about Muslimov's age despite Kolosova's earlier reference to the difficulty of obtaining accurate answers to the census question on age, and despite her discussion of the problem of age misstatement.[10]

In Soviet discussions of age overstatement, much emphasis is given to the fact that the 28,015 centenarians reported in the Census of 1959 were reduced to 21,708 after Soviet officials had made an effort to verify stated ages. However, it is significant that Soviet demographers and other researchers do not generally acknowledge that this adjusted figure itself is undoubtedly too high.[11] Demographic analysis by Western researchers such as Pressat[12] and Myers[13] strongly indicates that the verification procedures were not adequate to the task of eliminating all

TABLE 1 LIFE EXPECTANCY ABOVE AGE 100 ACCORDING TO THE
CENSUS-BASED LIFE TABLES WITH ZERO GROWTH RATE,
1959 AND 1970

	1959		1970	
Age	Males	Females	Males	Females
100	3.75	3.40	3.02	3.00
105	4.59	3.80	3.73	3.26
110	5.22	4.36	4.62	3.87
115	6.39	5.38	5.57	4.97
120	4.72	4.24	4.41	3.97

false centenarians from the roster. Bennett and Garson[14] analysed Soviet centenarian data from 1970 as well as 1959 and found additional evidence of age overstatement in the Soviet data.[15]

In this study I examine the available Soviet census and mortality data from 1959 and 1970 in order to assess Soviet claims of extraordinary numbers of centenarians.

Centenarians in 1959 and 1970

The 1959 and 1970 Soviet census publications provide a breakdown by age and sex of the population aged 100 and above. Using the additional data, life tables for the centenarian population were constructed by the census-based method. Table 1 shows the estimated life expectancies at ages 100 and above when a zero growth rate is assumed. Two patterns are apparent upon examining the table. First, the life expectancies for males and females in both census years *increase* from one age interval to the next between ages 100 and 115. Clearly this is not a believable trend.

Second, the age-specific life expectancies for both males and females are *lower* at every age in 1970 than in 1959. There has been a substantial increase in age-specific death rates for adult males in the Soviet Union since 1959,[16] but women's mortality has not risen comparably.[17] If mortality of both sexes had worsened significantly during the period 1959–1970, the diminished age-specific life expectancies could be accepted as an accurate reflection of reality. However, only mortality of men has been shown to have substantially increased, so the declining life expectancies cannot be explained simply by rising age-specific death rates. An alternative explanation is that the decrease in life expectancy for centenarians between 1959 and 1970 may be viewed as additional evidence of age overstatement in the two censuses, particularly in 1959.

An examination of the distribution of centenarians by republic in 1959 and 1970 (Table 2) reveals that the highest proportions of centenarians occur in the

TABLE 2   PROPORTION OF CENTENARIANS (AS PERCENTAGE OF
POPULATION OVER AGE 70), BY UNION REPUBLIC,
1959 AND 1970

	1959		1970	
	Males	Females	Males	Females
U.S.S.R.	0.21%	0.30%	0.13%	0.20%
Republic				
Armenia	0.81	0.94	0.62	0.82
Azerbaidzhan	2.05	2.28	1.20	1.56
Belorussia	0.19	0.35	0.11	0.24
Estonia	0.01	0.02	0.01	0.02
Georgia	0.90	1.07	0.66	0.86
Kazakhstan	0.19	0.39	0.13	0.25
Kirgizia	0.18	0.38	0.12	0.18
Latvia	0.02	0.07	0.03	0.05
Lithuania	0.19	0.44	0.09	0.22
Moldavia	0.14	0.26	0.09	0.15
R.S.F.S.R.	0.16	0.24	0.09	0.16
Tadzhikistan	0.24	0.47	0.19	0.34
Turkmenistan	0.13	0.38	0.16	0.34
Ukraine	0.07	0.17	0.04	0.12
Uzbekistan	0.17	0.38	0.14	0.24

republics of the Caucasus. Of the population over age 70 for the country as a whole, male centenarians constituted 0.21 percent and female centenarians 0.30 percent in 1959. In 1970 the figures were 0.13 and 0.20 percent, respectively. The figures for many of the republics of the Soviet Union do not deviate by much from these national averages. However, the proportion of centenarians in the Caucasian republics of Georgia, Armenia and Azerbaidzhan are in a class by themselves. The highest proportions are found in Azerbaidzhan, with over two percent of the population over age 70 in 1959 declared to be centenarians. In 1970, 1.20 percent of the males over age 70 and 1.56 percent of the females were reported to be centenarians. At the other end of the spectrum, the lowest proportion of centenarians in both 1959 and 1970 was found in the republic of Estonia, followed closely by Latvia.

The possibility that the exceptionally high proportions of centenarians in the Caucasus are a result of age overstatement must be considered. Several factors argue in favour of this interpretation. First, the Baltic republics of Estonia and Latvia are known for high standards of living and accurate data. Second, the fact that the Caucasus is renowned for longevity probably encourages age overstatement. Third, the age distribution of centenarians, examined by republic, lends credence to the age overstatement explanation.

No persons over age 110 were reported in Estonia, whereas a significant proportion of centenarians in the Caucasus region are reported as over age 120. Over five percent of the male Georgian centenarians in 1959 are reputed to have been over age 120, and in Azerbaidzhan nearly ten percent of the male centenarians in 1959 were listed as over age 120. The implausibly high proportions reported at ages above what is widely accepted as the limit of the human life span cast doubt on the entire centenarian age distribution. Furthermore, it is difficult to imagine how the centenarian data are to be considered accurate, when significant numbers of persons are included in a category of "centenarians of unknown age." This category was dropped in the Census of 1970.

Further evidence of the reduction in age overstatement between 1959 and 1970 is provided by the change in the proportionate age distribution of centenarians. In general, higher proportions were reported as younger centenarians in 1970 than in 1959, and there were fewer centenarians at the highest ages, although still too many to be believed.

The proportions of centenarians in the Soviet Union stand out glaringly in comparison with data for modern developed countries with low mortality and accurate age reporting. For example, according to data from the Census of 1926, the proportion of male centenarians in the population over age 70 was 35 times the proportion reported in Norway in 1980, and 45 times that in Sweden in 1980. The proportion of female centenarians is more than 16 times the Norwegian and 19 times the Swedish proportions.

The exaggeration in the Soviet figures is even more pronounced in comparison with Japanese data. The proportion of male centenarians reported in the Soviet Census of 1926 is 133 times the proportion of male Japanese centenarians in 1980. The proportion of female centenarians is over 42 times the Japanese proportion. Data from the Soviet Census of 1970 show a great reduction in the proportion of centenarians compared with the 1926 Census and a significant reduction since 1959 as well. Compared to Norway, Sweden and Japan, the exaggeration in the Soviet data is still quite apparent, however. The proportion of male centenarians reported in the Census of 1970 in the Soviet Union is over five times the proportion reported in Norway, nearly seven times the proportion in Sweden, and 20 times the proportion in Japan. The proportion of female Soviet centenarians in 1970 is almost four times the Norwegian, four times the Swedish, and over nine times the Japanese proportions.

Is the extraordinary longevity reported in the Soviet Union a real phenomenon or the result of inaccurate data? The evidence shows that the long history of longevity claims goes hand in hand with a long history of age overstatement in the census and mortality statistics. The extraordinary longevity observed is in all likelihood the result of that age overstatement.

ENDNOTES

1 Sula Benet, *How to Live to be 100: The Life-Style of the People of the Caucasus.* (New York, 1976).

2 G. Z. Pitskhelauri, M.D. *The Longliving of Soviet Georgia.* Translated and edited by Gari Lesnoff-Caravaglia. (New York, 1982), p. 53.

3 Pitskhelauri, *op. cit.* in fn. 2.

4 Cited by Pitskhelauri, *op. cit.* in fn. 2.

5 Pitskhelauri, *op. cit.* in fn. 2.

6 Joseph T. Freeman, "The old, old, very old Charlie Smith," *The Gerontologist* 22, 6 (1982), pp. 532–536.

7 Françoise Depoid, "La mortalité des grands vieillards," *Population* 28, 4–5 (1973), p. 780.

8 Norris McWhirter and Ross McWhirter. *Guinness Book of World Records* (New York, 1977), pp. 26–30.

9 See, for example: Robert J. Myers, "Validity of centenarian data in the 1960 census." *Demography* 3, 2 (1966), pp. 470–476; Robert J. Myers, "An investigation of the age of an alleged centenarian." *Demography* 15, 2 (1978), pp. 235–236; Zhores A. Medvedev, "Caucasus and Altay longevity: A biological or social problem?" *The Gerontologist* 14 (1974), pp. 381–387; I. I. Krupnik, "The Problem of Leadership in Abkhasian Social Organization from the Point of View of Longevity: Preliminary Observations," in *Proceedings of the First Joint US–USSR Symposium on Aging and Longevity.* (New York, 1980), pp. 76–84; Erdman B. Palmore, "Longevity in Abkhazia: A re-evaluation." *The Gerontologist* 24, 1 (1984), pp. 95–96; Richard B. Mazess and Sylvia H. Forman, "Longevity and age exaggeration in Vilcabamba, Ecuador." *Journal of Gerontology* 34, 1 (1979), pp. 94–98. These studies are discussed in Lea Keil Garson, *The Centenarian Question: Old-Age Mortality in the Soviet Union, 1897 to 1970.* Ph.D. dissertation, Princeton University (1986).

10 [G. I. Kolosova, *Sex, Age and Marital Status of the Population of the U.S.S.R.*], pp. 165–181 in [G. M. Maksimov, All-Union Census of the Population, 1970] (Moscow, 1976).

11 [M. S. Bednyi, Demographic Processes and Health Forecasts]. (Population, Moscow, 1972).

12 Roland Pressat, "Les premières tables de mortalité de l'Union Soviétique (1958–1959)." *Population* 18, 1 (1963), pp. 65–92.

13 Robert J. Myers, "Analysis of mortality in the Soviet Union according to 1958–59 life tables." *Transactions of the Society of Actuaries* 16 (1964), pp. 309–317.

14 Neil G. Bennett and Lea Keil Garson. "The centenarian question and old-age mortality in the Soviet Union, 1959–1970." *Demography* 20 (1983), pp. 587–606.

15 For a fuller discussion of the Soviet literature on longevity and age overstatement, see Garson, *op. cit.* in fn. 9.

16 John Dutton, Jr., "Changes in Soviet mortality patterns, 1959–77," *Population and Development Review* 2 (1979), pp. 267–291; Zhores A. Medvedev, "Negative trends in life expectancy in the USSR, 1964–1983," *The Gerontologist* 25, 2 (1985), pp. 201–208; R. H. Dinkel, "The seeming paradox of increasing mortality in a highly industrialized nation: The example of the Soviet Union," *Population Studies* 39 (1985), pp. 87–97.

17 The age-specific death rate for males aged 65–69 was 36.1 per 1,000 in 1958–59 and 41.2 in 1969–70. For females the rates were 20.8 and 21.1. For the 70+ age group, the death rates for males were 71.4 and 91.6 in 1958–59 and 1969–70, respectively. For females the death rates were 60.3 and 68.9 (Dutton, *loc. cit.* in fn. 16).

9.2 Etienne van de Walle

Numeracy, Conscious Choice, and the Lowering of Fertility in Africa

INTRODUCTION

Malthus was right to prefer preventive checks over positive checks like war, famine, and epidemic. Yet, in many parts of the world, people have been slow to adopt these preventive checks.

Why? We are ever less able to attribute this unwillingness to a lack of access to contraceptives, or even a lack of knowledge about what contraception can do. The answer offered in the next excerpt is that many people have not become accustomed to "numeracy" where children are concerned. The whole idea of choosing a limit on childbearing — a desired family size — and working to that limit, then stopping, remains foreign to them. (And, as we saw in the last excerpt, many people are also rather "innumerate" about their age and birthdate.)

The author van de Walle draws his data on this topic from West Africa and emphasizes that what is happening in Africa today is probably what happened in Europe a century earlier. There too, parents had to learn to imagine the size of family they wanted, and believe they could achieve it.

On the other hand, many Africans may be unmotivated to reduce their childbearing. Mali, for example, still has a low life expectancy, high infant mortality and low school enrollments. It may even be advantageous for women to bear many children, since they have no other claim to influence or security. Given these facts of life, Malians may be quite right to continue ignoring numeracy and producing children at a high rate. Read this excerpt and judge the evidence for yourself.

The term *numeracy about children* refers to a clear notion of what family size ought to be and to individuals' awareness of where they stand with respect to the norm. An analogy is the precise knowledge of one's age which is drilled into the memory of small children by most Western parents but is deemed irrelevant in many societies where there are otherwise clear notions of who is young or old. Age, for us, is an element of our personality. Similarly, our own family size and our number of children are defining characteristics; before numeracy in children had been attained, they were not important. Of course, women in a natural fertility

van de Walle, Etienne (1992). "Fertility Transition, Conscious Choice, and Numeracy," *Demography*, 29(4), November, 487–502. Reprinted by permission.

regime know how many children they have, but they do not generalize to other women, and they believe that their own family size is the result of happenstance (God's will), not design.

We find it difficult to accept that family size and the correlate notion that it can be manipulated by parents are not conceptualized universally, because the contemporary Western mind is obsessed with numeracy;[1] we define ourselves and other people by number of children or number of siblings.

Because the concept appears so obvious, we include questions on desired family size in fertility surveys. We are aware, of course, that the question may present problems, such as *a posteriori* rationalization. Nonetheless, the WFS or DHS think nothing of posing the following complex mental puzzle: "If you could go back to the time you did not have any children and could choose exactly the number of children to have in your whole life, how many would that be?" The question works in general, but not in certain contexts. In the 1987 DHS of Mali, for example, nonnumeric responses (such as "up to God") were given by 25 percent of the women. Matters were worse in earlier KAP surveys; it is likely that notions of family numeracy are gaining.

In a 1983–1984 survey in Ilori, Nigeria, more than 50 percent of the women gave a nonnumeric response. McCarthy and Oni (1987) believed that women who answer "up to God" to a question on the number of children wanted have not yet reached a first stage of the fertility transition, which includes awareness of family size and the possibility of influencing it. Only in the second stage may people act on the realization that their family is too big or too small, because they have a standard (ideal, or wanted family size) against which to measure it.

The Survey in Mali

Francine van de Walle conducted a small, intensive survey of women in Bamako, the capital of Mali, and tape-recorded their answers. The survey reflects the time when it was taken (1983); a clear "natural fertility" culture no longer may exist in that country today. The interviewers were given a series of topics to discuss (concerning children, postpartum behavior, and reproductive goals) but were left with a great deal of freedom on how they would phrase the questions. The goal was not so much comparability as insight, and the researchers thought that the interviewers' own approach would contribute an interesting point of view.

One of the topics was "ideal family size." In analyzing this material we distinguished two groups of women: the younger ones, whom the interviewers asked about a precise number of wanted children, and the older ones, who were asked about intentions to have more children.

Among the younger women represented in Figure 1, a common reaction was to refuse to state the number of children they wanted, other than "as many as God will send." In such instances, further probing sometimes elicited a preference. In the "no number" category, however, women were unwilling to respond, even when offered the option to negotiate with God.

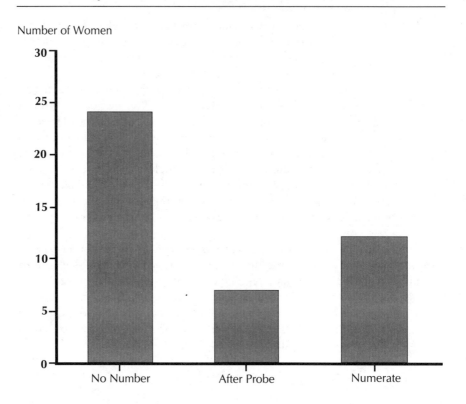

Number of Women

Age 28, Seven Children

Q. Maimouna, how many children would you like to have in your life?

A. Ah, what God gives me, that is it ... I cannot tell the number I will have in my life ... [Laughs.]

Q. It is true that God is the one who gives the child, but if God asked the number of children you wanted, how many would you say?

A. Oh, me, I cannot tell the number of children to God. What he gives me is good, that's enough. To say that I can stop and say the number, to tell God what to give me, I could not do so.

Q. Even if God asks you?

A. Even if He asks me, I cannot say it.

Q. Would you like to have many children, or not many?

A. Only what God gives me, that's what I want.

Q. Do you want more than those you have now?

A. What I say is that what God gives me, that's what I want.

Q. And if God gives you 12 children now?

A. Ah, if God gives me 12 children, then God created them.

Q. So you like that?

A. Ah, what God makes, that is that.

After probing, however, some women were willing to "suggest a number to God."

Age 19, 1 Child

A. How many children I want? How many [laughs] ... Can you know how many children there are in your blood?

Q. It is true that the number in your blood, nobody knows that. You are young, you had your first child. If God asks you how many children you want, what will you say?

A. If I could say ... if I could say, it would be six children.

And finally, a number of women adopted "modern" attitudes, and had clear notions of an ideal number of children:

Q. Sanou, you are young, 28 years old; you had four pregnancies but have only two children alive, how many would you like to have in your life?

A. I don't want to exceed four.

These women were willing to practice family limitation because they had a clear perception of a target.

Older women in the sample were asked whether they wanted to avoid another childbirth. For a substantial proportion, it was God's decision, or something that their husband controlled.

Although women in the next group acknowledged that God's will would prevail, they said they would prefer no more children. The following woman alluded to a weak preference for a number of children already exceeded, but would do nothing to avoid additional births:

Age 40, 10 Pregnancies

Q. Now you have had ten pregnancies. Do you want any more?

A. Truly, the number of children I wanted was four, but going on to ten was God's work.

Q. If it depended on you, would you like to stop?

A. Yes, this is what I would like.

[The interviewer starts discussing the subject of contraception.]

A. If God does not want it, it is impossible to stop pregnancies. It cannot succeed ...

Other women wanted no more children, but were not doing anything about it.

Age 41, 12 Children

Q. Why don't you go to the Planning?

A. I simply don't like it.

Q. Are there folk methods which prevent a women from becoming pregnant?

A. No, I don't know any.

Q. You had 12 deliveries, would you like to have more?

A. No.

Q. Why?

A. Because a delivery is difficult. Most of all, when the woman gets old, she becomes weaker and weaker.

Q. You want to stop at 12, is it also your husband's opinion?

A. It cannot be his opinion, but I want to stop at 12.

Q. Since you are not going to the Planning, what are you going to do not to have another child?

A. Eh! It all depends on God.

Q. But if it depended on you, what would you do?

A. I would do nothing.

We were surprised by women's passive attitudes towards spacing. It is well known that most respondents in sub-Saharan Africa are overwhelmingly in favor of well-spaced births, and they express strong reservations about short birth intervals. They are in favor of abstinence, and some eventually resort to refusing their husband as long as feasible. (In this respect, they do not differ from the English working-class women at the turn of the century who resorted to "staying up mending" after their husbands had gone to bed; Seccombe, 1990.) The long taboo on intercourse during breastfeeding is not practiced widely in Bamako; 40 days of abstinence after a birth comes closest to the norm.

If this society once knew a long taboo and has relinquished the custom recently, there would seem to be an ideal market for adoption of contraception. Even so, spacing seemed more an impossible ideal than a practical goal to the women in the sample. The large majority did not attempt to delay the next birth. They were not aware of the effect of prolonged nursing on delaying the resumption of menstruation; beyond the notion that a breast-feeding woman should avoid intercourse so that her child will not become sick (van de Walle and van de Walle, 1991), they mostly trusted their luck and did nothing to prevent conception once intercourse had resumed regularly.

Only a handful were contracepting to space the next child or stated that they intended to do so if they were pregnant. Many were opposed on principle, for religious reasons, or because they believed their husbands would not let them go to the family planning clinic, whose existence was known to a large majority of women in Bamako in 1983. Some were wary of contraceptives for health reasons.

Age 40, 10 Children

Q. Korotimi, according to you, how many years should a mother leave between her children?

A. The mother must leave several years between her children, but this depends on God ...

Q. Eh! Why does it depend on God. [Laughter.]

A. [Laughs.] We wait … we don't know at what time the child comes … What time there must be between one child and the next, one does not know … God only knows it.

Perhaps women were not motivated strongly enough to care. A number said they were willing to contracept, but did nothing.

Age Unknown, 9 Children

A. Ah! Truly, my children are spaced too closely, often I would like to go [to the Planning].

Q. And what prevents you from going?

A. [Laughs.] I say I am going to go, and then I forget.

This type of material allows us a clearer understanding of the preconditions of fertility decline. Means of control are not available; motivations are weak; but above all, the women lack the frame of mind and the clear numerical standard that would allow them to make sense of small families and the means to obtain them.

Did numeracy about children exist in Western countries before the transition, or is Africa exceptional in this respect? Of course, one cannot transpose the Malian reproductive views literally to historical Western Europe. Rather, we are trying to prove a negative, that is, the nonexistence of numeracy about children in the past, and we seek for constants of human psychology. The shreds of testimony for pretransition Europe — drawn from novels, biographies, and other literary forms — permit us to speculate that had it been possible to interrogate their authors aggressively, they would have been as indeterminate about ideal family size as were Maimouna and Korotimi. The circumstances in Mali and in Europe were different, but the pretransition psyches often seem remarkably similar.

Conclusion

On the basis of preliminary impressions, I hypothesize that numeracy about children and the norm of an ideal family size appeared not long before the fertility transition. A fertility decline is not very far away when people start conceptualizing their family size, and it cannot take place without such conceptualizing. Social scientists have largely assumed that family norms are bred into little children everywhere with basic socialization. I submit that in our own Western culture, the question was completely irrelevant before a certain date.

This is not a momentous discovery, with ponderous policy implications. Most populations now have become numerate about children; the event is interesting only in retrospect and has little bearing on the future. If the hypothesis is verified, however, it may provide a clue for reassessing the evidence on the fertility transition by dispelling a little of the cultural misunderstanding that separates different reproductive regimes.

ENDNOTES

[1] Cohen (1985) argues that a culture of numeracy appeared historically at specific times and in specific places. She defines the term, however, in a way that is unsuitable for the present argument, which is concerned about what we call "numeracy in children."

REFERENCES

Cohen, Patricia Cline (1985). *A Calculating People. The Spread of Numeracy in Early America.* Chicago: The University of Chicago Press.

McCarthy, James and Gbolahan A. Oni (1987). "Desired Family Size and its Determinants among Urban Nigerian Women: A Two-Stage Analysis," *Demography* 24(2):279–90.

Seccombe, Wally (1990). "Starting to Stop: Working-class Fertility Decline in Britain," *Past and Present* 126:151–88.

van de Walle, Etienne and F. van de Walle (1991). "Breastfeeding and Popular Aetiology in the Sahel," *Health Transition Review* 1(1):69–81.

9.3 Elise F. Jones et al.

Teenage Pregnancy in Comparative Perspective

INTRODUCTION

The last excerpt presented African women in a rather unfavourable light by Western standards, as being naive and fatalistic about their ability to control their own bodies and lives. But we don't have to go to Africa to find examples of naivete and fatalism.

Take the United States of America as another example. The United States has extremely high rates of teenage pregnancy, and many — demographers, policy-makers, and parents included — think this poses a problem. After all, many (most?) teenagers are scarcely able to take care of themselves, much less a baby. Usually, they lack the education and skills that would make them economically independent. Often, they have yet to establish stable relations with a mate. (Marriages between teenagers have notoriously high divorce rates.)

So let's assume, for the sake of argument, that teenaged childbearing is a bad idea; the question is, why is it so common in America?

Jones, Elise F. et al (eds.) (1986). Chapter 10, "Policy Implications for the United States," pp. 228–240. *Teenage Pregnancy in Industrial Countries.* © Yale University Press. Reprinted by permission of Yale University Press.

The answer provided by Jones and her collaborators is upsetting, but right in front of our eyes. Compared to other industrial countries, America does a poor job preparing young people for sexual activity and birth control.

One policy implication to come from this study is the discrediting of certain beliefs that have tended to paralyze efforts aimed at reducing the high rates of pregnancy experienced by American adolescents. What are those beliefs?

- Adolescent pregnancy rates are higher in the United States than in Europe mainly because of the high pregnancy rate among U.S. blacks
- American adolescents begin sex much earlier and more of them are sexually active than their counterparts in other developed countries
- Teenagers are too immature to use contraceptives effectively
- Unwed adolescents want to have babies in order to obtain welfare assistance
- Making abortions and contraceptives available and providing sex education only encourages promiscuity and, therefore, increases teenage pregnancy
- As long as there is no clear path for unemployed teenagers to improve their economic condition they will continue to have babies as one of the few sources of satisfaction and accomplishment available to them

None of these beliefs explains the differences between teenage pregnancy rates in the United States and other developed countries.

Lessons from the 37-Country Study

The study of 37 countries was restricted to an examination of the factors affecting teenage birthrates. Six factors were important in their effect on teenage fertility. Those associated with low teenage fertility rates are:

- High levels of socioeconomic modernization
- Openness about sex
- A relatively large proportion of household income distributed to the low-income population (important mainly for younger teenagers)
- A high minimum legal age at marriage (important for older teenagers only)

Factors associated with high teenage fertility are:
- Generous maternity leaves and benefits
- Overall pronatalist policies designed to raise fertility

Although it is one of the most highly developed countries, the United States has a teenage fertility rate much higher than the rates observed in countries that are comparably modernized, and considerably higher than the rates in a number of much less developed countries. The inconsonance applies particularly to fertility among younger teenagers, where the U.S. rate falls between that of Romania and

Hungary. The relatively high adolescent birthrate in the United States would suggest it has a pronatalist fertility policy (which it does not), high levels of maternity leaves and benefits, and a low minimum age at marriage. Maternity benefit policies on average are less liberal than those in most European countries (Kamerman, Kahn, and Kingston, 1983), and in most states women can marry on their own consent by age 18, an age similar to that in most of the countries studied.

The United States fits the pattern for high teenage fertility in that it is far less open about sexual matters than most countries with low teenage birthrates, and a smaller proportion of its income is distributed to families on the bottom rungs of the economic ladder. These findings suggest two factors are key to the United States' high teenage fertility: an ambivalent, sometimes puritanical attitude about sex, and the existence of a large, economically deprived underclass.

In the 37-country study, the United States does not appear to be more restrictive than low-fertility countries in the provision of contraceptive services to teenagers; however, comparable data could not be obtained on the provision of contraceptives free of charge or at very low cost — a factor that appears to be important in terms of accessibility in the case studies. In this respect, the United States is more restrictive than the other five countries studied in detail — all of which have much lower adolescent fertility and pregnancy rates than the United States. The very high levels of religiosity reported for the United States is probably one factor underlying the low rating of the United States on openness about sex. It is also noteworthy that the United States scores relatively low among the countries studied on the measures of availability of contraceptive education in the schools.

Intercountry differences in teenage fertility and in teenage pregnancy are *not* mainly due to the fact that these rates are much higher among U.S. black than white teenagers. The birthrates of white American teenagers are higher than those of teenagers in any Western European country (Westoff et al., 1983). Similarly, U.S. pregnancy rates for those young teenagers are higher than those in all developed countries for which there are data.[1]

The Six Country Case Studies

Two commonly held beliefs about teenage pregnancy are refuted in the case studies: teenagers are *not* precluded by their presumed immaturity from using contraceptives consistently and effectively; and teenagers in the United States are *not* more sexually experienced than adolescents in other countries with lower pregnancy rates.

With the possible exception of younger teenagers in Canada, national differences in the percentage of teenagers who have ever had intercourse appear to contribute little or nothing to the variations in teenage pregnancy rates.

In the five countries other than the United States, contraceptive use, particularly the pill, appears to be greater than in the United States — among younger as well as older teenagers. Physicians and clinics in these countries encourage pill use among teenagers, and in some of the countries, there have been active campaigns addressed to young men to encourage the use of condoms.

Does the availability of contraceptives, sex education, and abortion services in the United States encourage sexual promiscuity and thereby account for the higher teenage pregnancy rates in the United States? The findings suggest this cannot be the case, since availability is generally greater in countries with lower teenage pregnancy rates.

Abortions are available free of charge in England and Wales and in France. The cost to the woman is low in Canada and Sweden and is small enough in the Netherlands not to be prohibitive. In more than two-thirds of U.S. states, the full price of an abortion must be paid by the woman, whether or not she can afford it; and, because abortion services tend to be concentrated in populous metropolitan areas, costs can include not only the fee for the abortion itself, but travel and hotel expenses. Access to abortion in some of the countries studied, however, is more restrictive than in the United States with regard to parental consent, gestational age, required waiting period, legally required overnight hospital stays, and required approval by an additional doctor or doctors or a medical committee.

Sex and contraceptive education in the schools differs widely among the case-study countries. Sweden has by far the most extensive program. In the Netherlands, although there is little formal school sex education beyond the facts of reproduction, widespread public education via all the media is superior to that of any of the countries studied except, possibly, Sweden.

In short, teenagers living in countries where contraceptive services, sex education in and out of the schools, and abortion services are widely available have lower rates of adolescent pregnancy and do not have appreciably higher levels of sexual experience than do teenagers in the United States.

The findings from the 37-country study suggest generous maternity leaves and benefits are associated with higher fertility rates among older teenagers. The United States does not have generous policies compared to other countries, even when private programs, as well as public subsidy, are taken into account (Kamerman, Kahn, and Kingston, 1983). Nevertheless, it has been suggested that U.S. Aid to Families with Dependent Children — a benefit largely limited to single mothers, a very high proportion of whom are teenagers — encourages out-of-wedlock fertility in the United States.

All of the countries in the case studies have more generous health and welfare provisions for the general population and for mothers than does the United States; and several, like the United States, provide special financial assistance for single mothers. Yet these countries all have lower teenage fertility rates than the United States. Differences in welfare assistance to mothers, or to single mothers, does not explain the differentials in teenage birthrates between the United States and the other countries and they do not explain the differences in abortion rates.

Teenagers' prospects for economic improvement do not appear to be appreciably greater in the five case-study countries than in the United States; nor is the educational achievement of young people greater. However, more extensive health, welfare, and unemployment benefits in the other countries keep poverty from being as deep or as widespread as it is in the United States. The findings from the 37-country study suggest more equitable distribution of household income is associated with lower fertility among younger teenagers. The inequality of income distribution appears to be contributing to the differences between teenage birthrates in the United States and those in other developed countries.

To summarize, teenagers in these other countries apparently are *not* too immature to use contraceptives effectively; the availability of welfare services does *not* seem correlated with higher adolescent fertility; teenage pregnancy rates are *lower* in countries where there is *greater* availability of contraceptive and abortion services and of sex education; adolescent sexual activity in the United States is not very different from what it is in countries that have much *lower* teenage pregnancy rates; although the pregnancy rate of American blacks is much higher than that of whites, the white rate is still much higher than the teenage pregnancy rates in the other case-study countries; teenage unemployment appears to be at least as serious a problem in all the countries studied as it is in the United States, and American teenagers have at least as much schooling as those in most of the countries studied that have lower pregnancy rates. Because the other case-study countries have more extensive public health and welfare benefit systems, however, they do not have so extensive an economically deprived underclass as does the United States. However, the differences in teenage pregnancy rates would probably not be eliminated if socioeconomic status could be controlled.

By and large, Sweden has been the most active of the countries studied in developing programs and policies to reduce teenage pregnancy. Sweden has *lower* teenage pregnancy rates than have all of the countries examined, except for the Netherlands, although teenagers begin intercourse at earlier ages in Sweden.

None of the five case-study countries has developed government-sponsored programs designed to discourage teenagers from engaging in sexual relations — even at young ages — a program advocated in the United States and rewarded through government subsidies.

Possible Approaches

Several U.S. communities have instituted school-based health clinics that provide contraceptive services — usually in partnership with health, youth-serving, or other nonprofit agencies. In many cases, parental consent is required to enroll in the clinics (Dryfoos, 1985). Contraception, however, is only one of many health services offered, so the parent is not specifically informed when contraceptive services are being obtained.

A complementary approach would be to enhance the current family planning clinic system to provide free or low-cost contraceptive services to all teenagers who want them. In fact, however, although the high unmet need for family planning services among teenagers in the United States is well documented, federal subsidies in real dollars have declined. Moreover, in many communities family planning clinics tend to be stigmatized by teenagers who avoid them in the belief that they are restricted to very poor patients, that services are not confidential, that the surroundings are shabby and unclean, the services poor, and the treatment of patients disrespectful (Kisker et al., 1985). Advertising that portrays the clinic services as inviting, professional, confidential, and available to all segments of the community can counteract this negative image. In Planned Parenthood and some neighborhood health clinics, however, the trend toward charging a flat fee to all patients is likely to discourage teenage enrollment.

The growing reliance on health maintenance organizations (HMOs) to increase health coverage while reducing health costs provides another opportunity to extend family planning services to teenagers. There is no reason why HMOs cannot establish special adolescent clinics on the Swedish model to provide contraceptive services confidentially as part of a general health-care service.

The U.S. federal government does not mandate or encourage the inclusion of sex education courses in public schools. Although numerous public opinion polls show that American parents overwhelmingly approve of sex education in the schools, local school districts have tended to be timid about establishing courses because of fear of minority, but highly vocal, opposition. Although not all the countries studied put much emphasis on school sex education, the evidence from Sweden suggests comprehensive sex education programs can help reduce teenage pregnancy.

The federal and state governments are in a position to influence the development and establishment of school sex education courses. By asserting that sex education is desirable, they could help to legitimate the inclusion of sex education courses in the curricula. Congress, by providing subsidies for the development of curricula, for teacher-training programs, and perhaps for some demonstration programs could further encourage such instruction. State governments can promote sex education by offering selected subsidies, and providing practical help in curriculum development.

In the United States, sex is treated far less openly and is surrounded by more ambivalence than it is in most of the countries in the case studies. In virtually all of the countries examined, for example, information about contraception and sexuality is far more available through the media than it is in the United States; condoms are more widely distributed, and advertisements for contraceptives are far more ubiquitous.

The self-imposed restrictions on contraceptive advertising in the media are incongruous in an era when virtually every other product, including vaginal douches, sanitary napkins, and hemorrhoid preparations, is advertised everywhere and without protest. It seems likely that if the restrictions were lifted, some manufacturers would develop effective advertising campaigns.

There is also a need to disseminate more realistic information about the health risks of the pill (minimal for teenagers) and about its extensive benefits

(Ory et al., 1983). Most Americans are badly misinformed on this subject (Gallup, 1985). It is probable that the development of new methods more appropriate for teenagers who have episodic sex — such as a once-a-month pill — could greatly reduce teenage pregnancies in the United States. Yet funds for contraceptive development have declined in real terms in recent years in the United States and research into a monthly pill is further hampered by governmental restrictions on abortion-related expenditures.

In general, American teenagers have inherited the worst of all possible worlds insofar as their exposure to messages about sex are concerned: movies, music, radio, and television tell them nonmarital sex is romantic, exciting, and titillating; premarital sex and cohabitation are visible ways of life among the adults they see and hear about; their own parents or their parents' friends are likely to be divorced or separated but involved in sexual relationships. Yet, at the same time, young people get the message (now subsidized by the federal government) that good girls should say no. Little that teenagers see or hear about sex informs them about contraception or the consequences of sexual activity. Such mixed messages lead to the kind of ambivalence about sex that stifles communication between partners and exposes young people to increased risk of pregnancy. Increasing the legitimacy and availability of contraception and of sex education is likely to result in declining pregnancy rates, without raising teenage sexual activity rates to any great extent.

ENDNOTES

[1] Canada, Czechoslovakia, Denmark, England and Wales, Finland, France, Hungary, the Netherlands, New Zealand, Norway, Scotland, Sweden.

REFERENCES

Dryfoos, J. G. (1985). "School-based health clinics: A new approach to preventing adolescent pregnancy?" *Family Planning Perspectives,* 17, p. 70.

Gallup Organization, The (1985). "Attitudes towards contraception," unpublished report to the American College of Obstetricians and Gynecologists. Princeton, NJ.

Kamerman, S. B., A. J. Kahn, and P. Kingston (1983). *Income Transfers for Families with Children: An Eight-Country Study.* Philadelphia: Temple University Press.

Kisker, E. et al. (1985). "Teenagers talk about sex, pregnancy and contraception," *Family Planning Perspectives,* 17, p. 83.

Ory, H. W., J. D. Forrest, and R. Lincoln (1983). *Making Choices: Evaluating the Health Risks and Benefits of Birth Control Methods.* New York: Alan Guttmacher Institute.

Westoff, C. F., G. Calot, and A. D. Foster (1983). "Teenage fertility in developed nations, 1971–1980," *Family Planning Perspectives,* 15, p. 105.

9.4 Georges Photios Tapinos

The Unstoppable Immigrant

INTRODUCTION

One of the earliest theories in the demographic study of migration postulated that migration between two places increases as (1) the geographic distance between them decreases and (2) the amount of difference in opportunities increases. This theory is relevant today, as the transglobal migration of labour from poorer to richer countries grows, producing an anti-migrant backlash in the receiving countries. (This was alluded to in excerpt 5.4, on racial discrimination in Canada and Britain.)

Clearly, little can be done about the geographic distance between places: there is no way Italy can make itself more distant from Albania, Germany more distant from Turkey, or the United States more distant from Mexico. Nor is it likely that richer countries will be able to successfully enforce legal limits on immigration. Immigrants will continue to come, illegally if necessary; that's why the author calls them "unstoppable."

Unstoppable, that is, unless governments do the one thing in their power that — according to our theory — is likely to change immigrants' desires to leave their home country: namely, improve opportunities in their home country. From this standpoint, aid to poorer countries is not only a humanitarian gesture, it is a form of self-protection. By improving the economies of less-developed countries, richer nations may reduce the relative attractiveness of migration. Economically, staying at home becomes almost as attractive as leaving; socially and culturally, it remains much more attractive. But Tapinos doubts the success of even this strategy!

Since the mid-1970s, the more developed countries of Europe have closed their borders to the immigrants from the less-developed countries of Southern Europe, the Mediterranean and sub-Saharan Africa.[1] Restrictive policies were prompted by factors ranging from significant changes in labour market conditions and an economic slowdown to growing local resentment. These policies reflected the concerns of the receiving countries, with little or no consideration of the motives of the sending countries. Legal inflows were drastically reduced, although immigration was not stopped. Closings gave rise to new forms of entries, illegal immigrants, or refugees at a significant level.

Tapinos, Georges Photios (1990). "The Unstoppable Immigrant," *European Journal of International Affairs*, 10(4), 108–120.

The conflict between the declared intention of Europe not to reopen its borders and the existing and increasing labour-export pressure from the less-developed countries raises the question of the relevance of development assistance strategies as a means of decreasing this pressure and alleviating the North-South disequilibrium.

This article considers the following questions. Should one expect significant migrant supply pressure from the countries that formerly sent workers, as a result of their demographic, economic and labour market prospects? Have the European countries devised any development-assistance policy with the explicit intent of cutting down emigration from these countries? And would such a policy, if it existed, be efficient enough to decrease the incentives to migrate?

The anticipated pressure from the less-developed countries (LDCs) rests on two basic facts. In all the LDCs concerned — Yugoslavia, Turkey and the African countries — the expected demand for labor in the coming decades falls very short of the expected supply of labor. In the developed countries, however, the domestic demand for labor should be greater than the domestic supply after about the year 2000, when the "baby bust" will lead to reduced numbers entering the labor market. The conjunction of these two trends does not mean that migration will necessarily occur; it does mean that strong and increasing pressure will tend to be put on European countries to relax their restrictive policies.

A perusal of the demographic projections and development plans of the former sending countries pinpoints a disequilibrium between supply and demand for labor in the coming years. As a result of great improvements in life expectancy and the high level of fertility (though strongly declining in some cases), the sending countries' rate of population growth has been about three percent per year for the last 20 years; their supply of labor is thus expected to grow at a very high rate during the coming decades.[2]

Moreover, the prospects associated with the 1993 deadline seem to create more uncertainty and concern among potential emigrants from non-EEC countries. The fear is that unification of the respective national policies might do away with some of the advantages or privileges provided for in bilateral agreements that are based on historical links. In particular, the concern is that visa policies may end up being adjusted to match those of the country with the most restrictive legislation.

Gloomy Prospects

It is also feared that, because of the political unrest and gloomy prospects of most LDCs, particularly the African countries, private investors might be more strongly induced to take advantage of the facilities offered to them by the creation of a single market and keep their investments within the EEC.[3] In line with world-wide trends, the share of private investment accruing to LDCs has been strongly declining in the last decade and currently accounts for roughly 10 percent of total global private investment.[4] Moreover, former sending countries do not appear to be preferred recipients of either public or private international investments.

Finally, and most important, the entry of Greece, Spain, and Portugal into the EEC has greatly increased the concern of the Maghreb (Algeria, Morocco and Tunisia) trade partners, even though the financial and commercial protocols negotiated in 1986–1987 provide for privileged relations.

As to projected trends in Europe's labour force, the supply of labour, currently at a high level, is expected to decrease by the end of the century.[5] This is the expected outcome of the baby bust, reinforced by projected behavioural changes (more schooling, fewer hours worked, lower retirement age). In fact, the impact of the demographic deceleration of the 1970s on the working age population is already being felt. The phenomenon is particularly strong in countries like the Federal Republic of Germany where the decrease of fertility started earlier, (1.5 children per woman already in 1974), or in Italy where the decrease has been extremely rapid, (the total fertility rate went down from 1.69 in 1980 to 1.30 in 1986). The slowing down of the supply of labour is bound to accelerate in 1990–1995, and already the Federal Republic of Germany, the United Kingdom and Italy show an absolute decrease in the working population. Besides, contrary to what happened in the last two decades, the current and projected decline in the working age population is not expected to be compensated for by the increase in the women's participation rate.

On the demand side, the extensive discussions of the economic boom that is expected as a result of the establishment of a single market do not mention the necessary implications of emigration incentives in the third countries whose products will have to face a common external tariff.

In brief, whatever the projected increase in European economic growth and, consequently, in the increase in the demand for labour expected from the common market, the potential for emigration from North Africa, sub-Saharan Africa, non-EEC southern European countries (like Yugoslavia, or even Eastern European countries and Turkey), remains high and well above the absorption capacity of the EEC.

It would be unrealistic to believe it would be possible to cope with this issue merely or mainly by implementing restrictive immigration policies (such as extending visa obligations, reinforcing border control, and simplifying expulsion procedures). There is no reason to suppose market forces that have been relatively more significant than public policies in shaping migration flows and settlement in receiving countries before and after 1974 will not be at play in the future.[6] In this context, a case can be made for exploring the alternative strategy of decreasing the emigration incentive through increased development assistance.

More Aid, Less Immigrants?

The official development assistance from the EEC appears at two levels: overall assistance from the 12 countries, that is, the sum of official bilateral and multilateral aid from each country, plus assistance from the European Community. Total official development assistance from EEC countries ranks the EEC as the most important donor world-wide, contributing 31 percent of the aid received by the Third World. This amounted to 0.51 percent of the EEC countries' GNP in 1985–1986, compared with 0.23 percent for the United States.[7]

Relative to other major donors, like the United States and Japan, EEC assistance appears to be spread over a larger number of countries and, according to the official view, is "much less influenced by strategic or political consideration." This range is the result of the diversity of political concerns of the 12 countries involved. Sub-Saharan Africa is the major recipient of the EEC assistance; it gets 43.5 percent of European aid, which represents 59.2 percent of the total aid received by the region.

Basically, three sets of EEC development policies are relevant here: the generalized preference scheme, the ACP convention (LOME III),[8] and the Mediterranean policy. In one way or another, they all tend to enhance economic development in the less-developed countries. However, textiles and agricultural products — possibly critical sectors for growth and employment absorption in these countries — are subject to restrictive rules.

Consider, for instance, the bilateral agreements between the EEC and the Maghreb countries. Typically, they include a social component, which guarantees equal treatment for foreign and EEC workers, and include trade and financial components. Thus, the priority is put on food self-sufficiency, rural development, regional projects and technological transfer, all of which have an impact on the job-absorption capacity. For instance, the financial protocol with Yugoslavia favors the installation of small firms that would be set up by returning migrants. When migration is mentioned in the cooperation agreements, it falls into the social aspects category and deals exclusively with non-discriminatory policies concerning working conditions, remittances, pension rights, and so on, for workers and their families already resident in the EEC countries.

There are at least two explanations for this state of affairs. First, most of the bilateral agreements between the EEC and the LDCs go back to the mid-1970s, when the EEC had no competence and no concern in the area of migration. Second, and more important, following the closing of the borders, most sending countries showed a marked preference for resuming emigration rather than developing cooperative policies aimed at stabilizing the work force at home. The immediate financial and political benefits accruing from the export of surplus workers and the inflow of remittances outweighed by far the immediate benefits of alternative development strategies.

In fact, policies based on national interests and bilateral agreements have prevailed. There is no common European policy with regard to migration, apart from some very modest attempts. National institutions are still the major channels of public investments (Caisse Centrale de Coopération Économique in France, DES in the Federal Republic of Germany, Commonwealth Development Corporation in the United Kingdom). Few projects are comprehensive enough to meet significant job-creation requirements.

A final point needs to be underscored. It is precisely the countries of the southern Mediterranean — Italy, Greece, and Spain — which have been sending countries for decades, that are now the most exposed to illegal immigration. This reversal has been facilitated by their geographical position and their lack of institutional immigration controls — at least up to now — not to mention the absence of relevant data about immigration. Scattered evidence shows illegal migration — from the Arab world or Asia — is quite large and fuels migration flows toward the more developed countries of the EEC. The Southern Mediterranean countries thus play the role of first-entry countries. With growing awareness of these patterns, the southern Mediterranean countries have started implementing new institutional rules and expanding their development assistance to the Maghreb (Italy and Spain being the more active in this respect).

Emigration Incentives

Even though current development-assistance policies have failed to take into account job-creation and migration pressure, the issue remains and the economic rationale for such policies needs to be considered.

The success of these policies hinges on the extent to which they are likely to (a) foster a development process marked by an increase in income and employment, and (b) affect in a significant way and in the expected direction the determinants of the decision to migrate.

Past experiences suggest migration streams have emerged concomitant with the early stages of the development process (for example, in Spain and Greece) and that migration flows have remained steady during this process.

A comprehensive inquiry into the matter is beyond the scope of this article, but three points should be made here. First, if income differentials among groups in the sending areas and between potential sending and receiving countries are assumed to be the determinant of migration, the speed of growth that would be needed to close the gap in the foreseeable future is far beyond any domestic or international development strategy. A crude estimate of the magnitudes involved can be derived from World Bank data. In the most favorable case, countries like Algeria or Yugoslavia, with a current GNP per capita four to six times lower than that of the more developed EEC countries (assuming they maintain a one percent difference in their GNP per capita growth rate, i.e., 2.5 versus 1.5), would reach the French, Italian or Belgian levels in a century.

Second, the development-assistance policies, whatever their means (financial assistance, trade liberalization, or technological transfer) or their focus (rural development, food self-sufficiency) do not touch upon aspects of the development process that might prove crucial to job-absorption capacity and propensity to move, that is, institutional aspects. More generally, development-assistance policies cannot substitute for national development policies and have to fit the targets set by the developing country itself.

Finally, and most important, development policies that are expected to influence migration propensity have to take into account the determinants of the decision to migrate in the specific framework of an anticipated short-term migration. In fact, the *expected* duration of stay has strong implications for the decision to migrate and the age, family position, and occupational status of migrants who are more prone to move.[9]

Migration and economic development strategies can be viewed as two ways to improve household income. The difference is that migration reflects a microlevel strategy in which the outcome — that is, the expected increase in welfare — results directly from an individual's decision and not directly as a consequence of the national development process.

This individualistic strategy may have solid rational grounds such as the higher uncertainty of benefitting from a growth process and the shorter time needed to achieve the income target. In these respects, migration *is*, from an individual point of view, a risk-averting strategy or a substitute for development; however, at the same time, the development process affects the propensity to move and fosters migration.

The point is that these incentives are strongly reinforced in a situation where the possibility of an anticipated short-term move exists. Indeed, under such circumstances, the expected gain from migration does not only depend upon conditions that are given for the migrants, relative prices and relative incomes: they are the control variables that the potential migrant can manipulate to the extent that he himself decides on the savings and remittances rate and thus is able to maximize his welfare by taking advantage of the price differentials between the two countries. In fact, the possibility of an *ex-ante* short-term migration, whatever the *ex-post* effective duration of stay, may be a necessary condition for the move to be worthwhile.

The implication is that, though income differential remains a determinant, a reduction in the income gap between sending and receiving countries might be associated with an increase in the propensity to move, insofar as the possibility of an anticipated short-term stay makes migration feasible for some people who would not be able to do otherwise.

There are four major factors which are conducive to illegal migration: restrictive entry policies in all European countries, the importance of the networks created by past trends and the presence of large foreign communities, the easy access to European markets (thanks to low transportation cost), and the persistent demand for foreign labour in specific firms.

It is hard to expect development policies and restrictive measures to reverse the trend toward illegal migration. And this, as we have seen, for two reasons: first, because the restrictive policies implemented since 1974 have been significantly offset by the extension of parallel sources of entry (mainly refugees or illegal migrants); and second, because the comparative advantage of labour flows versus trade and capital flows is as strong today as in the 1960s.

Necessary and complementary as they are, restrictive immigration policies and development assistance strategies might not be sufficient to curtail immigration from LDCs to Europe.

ENDNOTES

1 The Federal Republic of Germany, France, Switzerland, the Benelux, and the United Kingdom have been the major recipient countries. More recently, traditional emigration countries such as Italy, Spain, or Greece became themselves immigration countries. At the same time, the tendency toward equalizing returns to factors resulting from free trade and factor movements among the EEC countries has decreased the incentive to migrate inside the EEC countries, the share of non-EEC nationals among foreign workers has tended to increase in these countries.

2 International Labor Office (ILO), *Economically Active Population 1950-2025,* Geneva, ILO 1986, 6 vols.

3 M. Pierini, "Relations entre la Communaulé Européenne et les pays en développement. Evolution et perspectives de la politique de Lomé," paper submitted at the First Congress of the Association Portugaise pour la Coopération Économique et le Développement (ELO), Lisbon, December 1988.

4 International Monetary Fund, *Balance of Payments Statistics,* 1988, vol. 39.

5 From a survey of national labour demand projections in France, Germany, Italy, Netherlands and the United Kingdom. R. M. Lindley concludes: "In none of the five countries studied does there occur to be any realistic prospect of achieving full employment before the end of the century." See R.M. Lindley, "Prospects for European Labor Demand," *European Journal of Population,* No. 3 (1987), pp. 383–410.

6 Tapinos, "European Migration Patterns."

7 Commission of the European Communities, *Official Development Assistance from the European Community and its Member States,* Brussels: European Community, May 1988.

8 The First Lomé Convention was signed in 1975 and covers the period April 1976–February 1980. The Second went until February 1985. The Third Lomé Convention (December 1984) concerns 66 ACP countries and adds 41.3 million people. It covered five years, until February 1990. Among other things, it aimed to facilitate "structural adjustment," and stressed the importance of small business in the development process. Putting aside sugar, bananas, rum, beef, and rice, the trade agreements were based on the principle of free access and non-reciprocity. Mention should be made also of STABEX (stabilization of export earnings from agricultural commodities).

9 Tapinos, *L'économic des migrations internationales,* Paris: Armand Colin, 1974.

QUESTIONS

DISCUSSION QUESTIONS

1. What is the ideological value of a long average life span or low rates of mortality?

2. "There's not much difference between pregnant teenagers in Mali and in Malibu." Discuss.

3. "It's better to be a poor migrant in a rich country than a not-quite-so-poor citizen of a poor country." Discuss.

4. Would we be likely to find teenage pregnancy in many industrial countries is much more common than we believe, if only we had more accurate statistics?

DATA COLLECTION EXERCISE

1. Collect data on longevity from two or three other parts of the world that are, socially, economically and politically, like the Caucasus region. Are centenarians common there?

2. Through interviews, collect some data in your community to determine (a) how conscious people are of their desired family size, (b) how many children they want to have, and (c) what they expect their children to do for them when they are old. What correlations do you find?

3. Collect data on the age and sex composition of international migrants. What "kinds of people" are most and least likely to migrate? How do you explain this pattern?

4. Collect some published data on trends in teenage pregnancy in Canada or the United States over the last 25 years. Make some systematic predictions about teenage pregnancies in 2020 and 2045.

WRITING EXERCISES

1. You are van de Walle or Jones. (You choose!) Write a brief speech explaining to major political leaders what they have to do to get women to reduce their childbearing.

2. "Changing cultural traditions is the most important, and difficult, thing a demographer can help to do." Write a brief essay evaluating this statement.

3. "Sex and death — that's mainly what demographers seem to think about." In a brief essay, indicate whether you agree or disagree, and the reasons why.

4. In your own words, explain briefly why the migration of poor people to rich countries is "unstoppable."

SUGGESTED READINGS

1. Chen, P. (1984). "China's other revolution: Findings from the One in 1,000 fertility survey," *International Family Planning Perspectives*, 10, 2, June, 48–57. This huge survey of Chinese women documents the amazing reductions in fertility that followed from official state policy to promote the idea of one child per woman.

2. Huth, Mary Jo (1986). "Population prospects for sub-Saharan Africa: Determinants, consequences and policy," *Journal of Contemporary African Studies*, 5, 1/2,

(April/October), 167–181. A comprehensive report on fertility planning and repro-ductive behaviour in sub-Saharan Africa, where many women still desire (and achieve) the world's highest levels of recorded childbearing.

3. Knodel, John and Etienne van de Walle (1979). "Lessons from the past: Policy im-plications of historical fertility studies," *Population and Development Review*, 5, 2, June, 217–245. A systematic attempt to use historical materials to understand why fertility fell in Europe when, where, and how it did. This paper can be read as a backdrop for the van de Walle excerpt in this section.

4. Ukaegbu, A. O. (1977). "Socio-cultural determination of fertility: A case study of rural Eastern Nigeria," *Journal of Comparative Family Studies*, 8, 1, Spring, 99–115. Based on a survey of Nigerian peasant women, this study gives us a clear idea of the cultural roots of African fertility — particularly, the high value Africans place on children as "gifts from God."

THE STATE AND GOVERNMENT

Introduction

Who makes the decisions that most shape the histories of countries and influence their futures? And do different societies have *similar* patterns of power distribution or *different* ones? Such questions have been central to sociology since its beginnings in the works of Karl Marx, Max Weber, and other scholars. This section presents selected studies that bear on these questions.

Sociologists have put forward two main theories to answer these questions for modern societies like Canada. One theory emphasizes the role of various *elites* that hold top positions in society's major institutions. This was the approach Max Weber took. The other theory looks for answers in the class structure. (See Section 4.) It locates power in the upper economic class, whose members typically inherited their wealth and influence from their parents. The first theory is called the "accommodating elite theory" and the other is the "capitalist class control theory." We will discuss each in turn.

Elites and the State

Let's begin with a few key definitions. An *elite* is a small group that holds power in society as a whole, or in a particular segment of society (for example, a large bureaucratic organization). The elite has legitimate (or proper) authority to make decisions that affect the lives and work of others.

As noted above, we find elite positions in economic organizations (for example, the highest ranking executive officers of the largest corporations), in government (for example, elected prime ministers or appointed deputy ministers), and in a variety of other organizations such as labour unions, universities, the church, and so on.

"The state" is a set of organizations concerned with maintaining and enforcing decisions that are binding upon all members of a particular society (Weber, 1946; Sinclair, 1991). Thus, the state includes the government and public bureaucracy, courts, police, and military. It follows, then, that the *state elite* includes the highest ranking members of state organizations.

Accommodating Elites

According to the "accommodating elite theory," elites in different sectors of society struggle to promote the goals of their own organizations. Each sector and each organization has some power in this struggle; but usually, no sector and no organization has *enough* power to prevail over all the others against their wishes. For that reason, any particular elite must usually work together with other elites. In the long run this will further the organizational interests of each elite.

Elites, whatever their locus of power, are fundamentally committed to keeping things as they are. They want to avoid upsetting the social order, which works to their advantage, and, often, they share a common set of values.

They hold common values because the elites interact with one another. Many of these people are acquaintances, friends, members of the same social class, with similar socialization experiences in the family and at schools. Sometimes, they are even kin. But even though they may be members of the same social class, elites fight to further their own organizations' interests.

Capitalist Class Control of the State

The other theory — capitalist class control theory — also assumes that dominant organizations are more likely to cooperate than they are to compete and conflict with one another. However, the theory argues that people in control of the economy — especially, the largest and wealthiest organizations like banks and other financial institutions — will control all other sectors of the economy. By controlling the economy, and through it all other organizations, they control all other elites. They even control the state's elected and appointed officials, all by controlling access to capital, the ultimate source of power.

The dominant economic elite is filled by people from the hereditary upper class and by a very few "new" capitalists. As a result, the elite structure of society simply duplicates the capitalist class structure. What *appears* to be elite accommodation is actually cooperation among capitalists and their agents.

The Competing Views Applied to Canada

John Porter's work has given the most sustained attention to the accommodating elite view in Canada. In *The Vertical Mosaic* (1965), Porter concludes that continuity and change in society are the product of acts, or failures to act, on the part of various elites. The average person has little chance to bring about social change except by working through organizations that may ultimately influence the behaviours of elites. Thus, organizations such as unions and lobby groups are essential weapons average people must use if they are to effect change.

In Porter's view, Canada is ruled by five collaborating elite groups. They consist of people in the top positions of each of five broad areas of Canadian society: the major economic corporations, political organizations, government bureaucracies, labour organizations, and ideological (church, educational, and media) organizations. Power is dispersed among elites because elite people are responsible to different large organizations, each with their own wealth, power, and goals.

Porter saw a plural set of elites, with two more powerful than the others. The economic (or "corporate") elite, according to Porter, has been the most successful of all in ensuring that its interests are served. In second place, by the same criterion, is the bureaucratic elite, made up of high-ranking civil servants — the so-called "mandarins" of government. Federal bureaucrats are the most powerful civil servants, but high-ranking personnel of provincial bureaucracies may also be members of this elite.

Why are the corporate and bureaucratic elites so powerful? It is because of the enormous economic resources each commands, and the fact that these two sectors employ large fractions of the Canadian working population. They also provide better-paying and more stable careers than politicians and labour leaders typically enjoy. That's why the corporate and bureaucratic sectors are able to recruit the most talented people for membership in their bureaucracies.

Despite much conflict between elites, Porter concluded that accommodation eventually holds sway. Cooperation between elites is facilitated by a sharing of values and interests, as we noted earlier. Each of the elites, Porter felt, has many members who subscribe to the idea that corporate capitalism is "for the common good," and they share in the "Western" values of democracy, nationalism, and Christianity. They come to these common views from similar social backgrounds and through similar social experiences: training in upper-class schools, interaction on boards of directors, memberships in the same clubs, and so on. These connections resemble "a web of kinship and lineage which provides cohesion to primitive life" (1965:304).

Porter stopped short of concluding that there is a dominant capitalist class. He rejected this possibility because, as he said, he found the Marxist theory of the state, according to which "the economic ... system is the master" (1965:206), too simplistic. Yet his evidence — for example, the paramount strength of the corporate elite, and the shared, entrenched values of the elite group — suggested otherwise. Porter remained impressed by the "counteracting power" (1965:522–23) of the other elites.

Not surprisingly, Porter's work has been most seriously criticized on the role of social class in the distribution of power. Many insist that the Canadian capitalist class exercises enormous control through the corporate elite and the state. In this alternative theory, the other elites are *forced* to accommodate or simply lose out. This is the view that Wallace Clement puts forward in his *The Canadian Corporate Elite* (1975) and *Continental Corporate Power* (1977). In Clement's view (1975:562),

> No matter what institution is the most powerful, a society reproduces itself through the production of means of living (food, clothes, shelter), and, therefore, the economy is always a fundamental activity, whether organized by religious, political, military, or business leaders. Those who control the economy are a powerful elite within any modern society.

Clement shows that the corporate elite is often tightly tied into the corporate elite of other countries, especially the United States. He finds it necessary, therefore, to distinguish between *comprador elites* and *indigenous elites* within the Canadian corporate elite. "Comprador elites" work for foreign-owned operations in Canada. They run these organizations as "branch plants," with most major policies originating in the foreign-based parent organization. By contrast, "indigenous elites" are people who control firms that are Canadian-owned.

Which Theory is Correct?

As you can see, sociologists do not agree on whether the accommodating elite theory or the class control theory best describes Canadian society. Perhaps there is a lot of truth to each theory. Undoubtedly, elite accommodation often occurs *and* the capitalist class, along with the state elite, is very influential. This is our view, based on the available evidence for Canada.

But what about other societies? Proponents of the accommodating elite and class control theories both believe their theories apply to all capitalist societies. But we should not simply extrapolate from Canada to other societies. This is an empirical question requiring study in a range of societies before a conclusive answer is possible.

We only begin to suggest an answer in the Section that follows. There, we look at selected studies of four different topics in four different settings. They include political control in Haiti, laws concerning the sexes in Switzerland, procedures for dealing with the poor in Britain, and the new men of power in Iran. To anticipate the readings, in each case the state elite commands with massive authority, giving priority to economic elite interests. The role of other elites, particularly the religious elite, varies greatly from one society to another.

REFERENCES

Clement, Wallace (1975). *The Canadian Corporate Elite: Economic Power in Canada.* Toronto: McClelland and Stewart.

—— (1977). *Continental Corporate Power: An Analysis of Economic Power.* Toronto: McClelland and Stewart.

Sinclair, Peter (1991). "Political and state institutions," in L. Tepperman and J. Richardson, eds., *The Social World,* Second Edition. Toronto: McGraw-Hill Ryerson.

Weber, Max (1946). *From Max Weber: Essays in Sociology,* trans. and edited by H. H. Gerth and C. W. Mills. New York: Oxford University Press.

10.1   Yolaine Armand

The Legacy of Anti-Democratic Traditions in Haiti

INTRODUCTION

In the next excerpt, Armand provides a historical overview of changes in the membership of the state elite in Haiti. Over a long sweep of time, various changes have taken place but the poor have benefited very little.

When the French ruled Haiti, whites held absolute power. After the French left Haiti, a ruling class of lighter-skinned, racially mixed people — the mulattoes — took over, and continued to exclude people from the elite on the basis of race. (Some of the reasons can be found in excerpt 1.4, on worldwide racial stratification.)

Under mulatto rule, many black Haitians actually became poorer. However, a black middle class eventually developed. Its climb to political power in the 1940s brought hope that things might improve for the masses of Haitian poor. This hope culminated in the election of a black president, Francois Duvalier, in 1957. But Duvalier became a ruthless dictator. His son Jean-Claude, who succeeded him, was equally corrupt. Things continued to get worse for the poor.

Duvalier was ousted in 1986, renewing hope of improvement in Haiti. But experiments with democracy and more equitable power sharing have all been short-lived. The black middle class oppresses the poor as much as the upper-class mulattoes did, and the poor have too few resources — too little power and organizational support — to do anything about it.

This paper examines Haiti's enduring political instability in terms of cultural and socio-historical variables. It examines the legacy of Haiti's political and economic past and an assortment of other obstructions that seriously impede the establishment of democracy in Haiti.

Political Obstacles

A Tradition of Political Autocracy

Political power in Haiti is highly centralized in a chief of state with lesser power delegated to a handful of friends. The latter in turn, control all other legal or political apparatus, including the Executive Branch, the Legislative, the Judiciary,

Armand, Yolaine (1989). "Democracy in Haiti: The Legacy of Anti-Democratic Political and Social Traditions," *International Journal of Politics, Culture and Society*, 2(4), Summer, 537–56. Reprinted by permission of Human Sciences Press, Inc.

the Armed Forces, all of which are rubber stamping institutions expressing the will of the supreme ruler. Once political power has been taken, most often by force or fraud, it becomes legitimized by its mere existence. The way it is usually challenged is again by violence.

For the Haitian people, it is so much easier to follow a familiar, undemocratic process. Attempts at changes are met with resistance, denials, skepticism, and a great deal of reticence. For example, when General Namphy regained political control last June 20 by ousting President Manigat, it was reported that people met the event with indifference. They went about their daily activities as if nothing significant had happened. The old pattern of favoritism and paternalism was so familiar that people seemed ready to fall back into it matter-of-factly. By the same token, General Avril's successful coup three months later seemed no less expected. A number of Haitians polled in New York reported only two general concerns: that the new ruler be "a good guy" and that he satisfy the demands set forth by the people after Duvalier's departure.

The Direct Legacy of 29 Years of Dictatorship

The long-awaited departure of former President Jean-Claude Duvalier in 1986 was greeted with elation among Haitians both in Haiti and abroad. The first few weeks after the overthrow saw a tremendous surge of relief and hope for a brighter future. People visiting the country reported seeing Haitians sweeping the sidewalks, disposing of long-accumulated garbage that defaced city streets and painting tree trunks with bright colors. Neighborhood community councils were spontaneously created to channel the ideas, needs, and suggestions of the people. All Haitians seemed willing to work together to defend their newly won freedom and to participate in the creation of a truly democratic system.

This euphoria was short-lived, however, for it soon became evident that twenty-nine years of absolute power had left the country with a burdensome political legacy that would impede the establishment of a democratic system.

The Remnants of an Anti-Democratic Political Structure

The Duvaliers created some peculiar institutions whose influences ran strongly counter to the democratic process:

A *unique party system akin to a "political mafia."* For many years, the only recognized (i.e., openly functioning) political party was the one represented by the ruling dictatorship. It is perhaps a misnomer to even call it a political party since it possessed neither a political platform open to discussion, nor any other democratic mechanisms responsive to the public. Adherents held membership cards identifying them as "Volunteers for National Security" (VSN), the official designation of the dreaded "Tontons Macoutes."[1]

An army dominated by Duvalier sympathizers. High army echelons and most officers were compelled by fear of reprisal to display loyalty to the system or at least to not demonstrate open opposition against it. Officers who were critical of the regime would be "retired" or went into exile. The rank and file expressed a similar loyalty for fear of denunciation by other soldiers or by the "tontons macoutes."

A cadre of undisciplined para-militaries (the "macoutes"). Some estimates place the number of "macoutes" as high as 100,000 at the time of Duvalier's departure. Since their purpose was to guarantee the security of the regime, the "macoutes" were left in disarray, with no recognized leadership. Many were armed, but afraid of popular vengeance.[2] Moreover, the upper to middle echelons were divided between the "old guard" attached to Francois Duvalier's rigid doctrine and the more liberal followers of Jean-Claude Duvalier.

An Inadequate Political Process

Although classifying itself as a "republic," Haiti has never had a tradition of institutions that could ensure the democratic process. The recent years of dictatorship have simply eliminated whatever embryo of democracy may have once existed in the country. Following are three major political obstacles left by the former regime.

Non-existence of key political institutions. No political institutions are sufficiently established to channel the demands and articulate the needs of the people. The Congress which traditionally rubber stamped presidential wishes had been abolished by Francois Duvalier. The press was heavily censored and local news of any significance was unilaterally broadcast by the biased government-owned media. The Constitution itself had no real weight since it had been routinely amended to reflect the many whims of ruling regimes.

Lack of alternatives in political leadership. Because it stifled all dissenting voices, the dictatorship left no real political leadership. Of those few opponents who managed to remain in the country, the most outspoken were in hiding most of the time and the remainder voiced only occasional timid protests. Except for the amorphous leadership of the Church, no effective political opposition existed. Shortly after Duvalier's departure, however, a flock of presidential candidates and political activists surged to the fore, several from abroad. As many as 20 odd political parties were created or came to action, many with undefined programs of government. The sudden surge of politicians caused people to divide their allegiance.

The controversial role of the Church in political leadership. When all dissenting voices were silenced, the Church-owned radio stations became the public voice, serving as the link both among the people and between the people and the government. Individuals and groups went to "Radio Soleil"[3] and "Radio Lumiere"[4] to report police brutality, riots, illegal arrests, murders, missing persons, and so forth. They used the Church sponsored radio stations to report hardships and to complain about poor public services.

Economic Obstacles

Widespread Poverty Hampering the Political Process

Haiti is among the poorest nations of the hemisphere, with a net per capita income currently at around $360 per year. The steady deterioration of rural farms due to years of unchecked land erosion, frequent hurricanes, the absence of governmental agricultural policy, the land workers' ignorance and lack of resources, and the dispossession of the farmers due to the corrupt political system all contributed to the steady impoverishment of the peasants and their exodus to urban areas.

This situation had worsened considerably during the Duvalier dictatorship. The last 30 years witnessed the neglect of the secondary towns, called "provinces." Under Duvalier, military — and therefore political — control was more easily maintained when all significant economic activities were centralized in the "Republic of Port-au-Prince." As a result, an estimated 20 percent of the total Haitian population (of about six million) is concentrated in the capital city of Port-au-Prince. As is usually the case in under-developed countries, there is a wide socio-economic gap between the few haves and the vast majority of have-nots.

The Political Elites

Political power has usually been seen as one means for gaining access to everything that can lead to the good life such as education, employment, and the countless lucrative forms of favoritism. Throughout Haitian history, each new political regime was expected to fire as many public employees as possible in order to replace them by a new hungry crowd. People pledged allegiance not to a political philosophy but solely to individuals who assured them of political favor, most often in the form of a salaried government position or other lucrative benefits.

Public political fund raising is not generally practiced. As a tradition, the financially well-to-do are able to "buy" potential voters by spending lavishly on food, money gifts, advertising, and anything else that will impress the public. By the same token, poor candidates are easily bought by private interest groups or wealthy industrialists who will finance their campaign in return for personal favors when elected. As a result, successful candidates for political power are often members of a privileged class bound by their own class interests, or have their hands tied by a powerful group whose interests they have pledged to support.

The Electorate

Haitians' widespread poverty is reinforced by a 75 percent rate of illiteracy. Illiteracy is another impediment to democracy. Ignorance of the political process and misconceptions about political issues, goals, and objectives make it easier for demagogy, intimidation, and sheer violence to take hold.

Socio-Cultural Obstacles

Political Implications of Class and Status in Haiti

The last three decades have brought significant changes in the social structure of Haiti. The previous two-class society in which income, education, occupation, skin color, and status were positively correlated has been modified. Research done by the author between 1981 and 1986 (Armand, 1988) found two patterns of social organization in Haitian cities: a system of *class* inequalities determined by the distribution of income, education, and occupation, and one of *status* inequalities based on such subjective factors as prestige, honor, and social recognition of worth.

A person's class, in turn, determines ownership of goods, patterns of consumption, areas and types of residence and general lifestyle.

Honor and prestige, which are more characteristic of *families* than of *individuals*, are based on such inherited attributes as family name, skin color, and wealth and occupation passed on by the family, as well as by such acquired distinctions as money, education, refined manners and tastes, and a mastery of the French language. The inherited or achieved sources of status further subdivides Haitian society into six status layers. These layers can be represented in descending order as follows:

- *White foreigners* who work with foreign or international agencies in Haiti.
- *The Higher Positive Status Group*, designated as "Elite," "Haute Bourgeoisie," or "bourgeoisie Traditionnelle." Consisting of upper class elites and a few black families, this group has some of the characteristics of a caste since membership is assigned at birth. Moreover, members retain their high prestige even if they lose (or fail to acquire) one or several of its identifying characteristics, such as education or occupation.
- *The Lower Positive Status Group*, known as "Bourgeoisie Noire," "Nouvelle Bourgeoisie," or "Nouveaux Riches."
- *The Neutral Status Group*, referred to as "Gens de Bien," "Honnetes Gens," "Bons Mounes" (Creole for "Good Folks").
- *The Negative Status Group*, identified as "La Masse" "Gens du Peuple," "Pitit So Yette," "Vagabonds," "Mounes Mone," "Gros Zoteye" (Creole for "Mountains Folks, Peasants").
- *The Lowest Negative Status Group*, considered as "Vauriens," or "Sans Zave" ("Good for Nothings, Trash").

Class, Status and Politics in Haiti

The dual pattern of class and status differentiation affects Haitian politics. Throughout the history of the country, the upper and middle classes have taken turns as the dominant political groups and have used politics as a means to strengthen their class positions, obtain new socio-economic gains, and acquire status. In the ongoing class and status competition, politics has become another battlefield.

For well over a century after independence, the economic upper class of mainly lighter skinned people entered politics as a way of sustaining or enhancing their status rather than to gain material privileges. The few well-educated dark-skinned persons of lesser economic rank also saw in politics a way to acquire status. The exercise of politics seemed to reflect the status conferred upon it by the upperclass, high-status group.

With President Magloire[5] and, to a greater extent, with the two Duvalier presidents, politics became the best avenue to intra-generational class mobility. Under the Duvalier regime, well-paid positions and all sorts of financial advantages could be obtained by allying oneself with the government. One entered politics not to espouse an ideology but to obtain power and material advantages. This helped to organize political practices and define political culture in a way that is antithetical to the principles of democracy.

As the traditional high status group was pushed out of politics by the black majority, they used their economic advantages to gain control of the business and industrial sector. The exercise of political power ceased to be a status symbol since it now belonged to those of lower status, but it remained the surest avenue of intragenerational class mobility. While the dark-skinned middle and lower classes used politics as a way of making status distinctions among themselves, the upper class now denied all such claims, regarding it as more prestigious to acquire wealth outside the arena of "dirty" and "shifty" politics.

Status and Political Leadership

The prevalence of status distinctions led to a tradition of political autocracy in Haiti. The authority of the president has been similar to that of a Patriarch. His authority was as undisputed as that of the old-fashioned husband and father over his family. The president expected to receive and was generally given respect and obedience, if not love and admiration. He centralized and epitomized the exercise of final authority, and was accepted as a legitimate ruler by a majority of people.

This authoritarian, paternalistic pattern has made the delegation of authority difficult in the country, imposed a heavy burden on higher-level administrators, and aroused temptations to abuse authority. Its consequence has been twofold: autocracy by those who hold power and dependency by those who do not.

Preeminence of Status as an Impediment to Democracy

Because of the predominance of status inequalities in Haitian society, the concept of equality that is inherent in democracy will be difficult to implement. The acceptance of inequality seems an integral part of Haitian culture and it conditions relationships among all groups and individuals. It is evident in the way people refer to and treat each other.

It is therefore not surprising that Haitians at different status levels attach different meanings to the idea of democracy. Both the upper class and the middle class welcome guarantees of human rights and freedom of expression, but are fearful of misinterpretations which could lead to "encroachment" and "invasion" by the lower class masses. With widespread illiteracy among the poor, it is assumed the latter will see democracy as unrestrained freedom to do and say what they please, with no self-restraint or respect for others. At the bottom levels of the society, even illiterate Haitians in Port-au-Prince understand democracy to mean the absence of arbitrary physical abuse and the freedom to vote without coercion or intimidation.

Conclusion

This paper has attempted to place Haiti's effort at democratization in its proper socio-cultural context. The Haitian case challenges the notion that in third-world countries with unstable political regimes, democracy needs only to be given a chance (i.e., to remove a dictator or a corrupt ruler) in order to be on its way. In their desperate efforts to survive and initiate socio-economic development, the less developed countries must often overcome age-old traditions and overwhelming internal constraints when political options are presented to them. As a case in point, Haiti's struggle for democracy is hampered by several serious obstacles whose origins are deep in the country's history. Besides widespread poverty and illiteracy, the country faces a tradition of autocracy and a pervasive acceptance of social inequalities which run counter the basic egalitarian principles of democracy. Class and status inequalities which permeate Haiti's social and political cultures and institutions, may prove to be one of the most serious roadblocks to the institutionalization of Haitian democracy.

ENDNOTES

[1] The term "Tontons Macoutes" refers to members of a civilian force appointed by Francois Duvalier to maintain his dictatorship. They often fulfilled their mission by threatening, intimidating, beating, jailing, torturing, and physically eliminating known opponents or people suspected to be non-sympathizers of the regime.

[2] There were widely publicized documented reports of a handful of incidents where angry mobs lynched or burned to death former Duvalier tortionaires in Port-au-Prince and in the countryside.

[3] "Radio Soleil," a regular broadcasting station sponsored by the Catholic clergy.

[4] "Radio Lumiere," the regular broadcasting station of the Protestant faith.

[5] Dumarsais Estime, a black politician, was elected President by a two-house Congress in 1946, and overthrown four years later, before the end of his six-year term, by Army General Paul Magloire who then became President from 1950 to his overthrow in 1956.

10.2 Patricia Schulz

Institutional Obstacles to Equality Between the Sexes

INTRODUCTION

According to the following excerpt by Schulz, one of the obstacles to equal power is that men, not women, make the laws. Women have been largely excluded from law-making activities of the state elite: indeed, from all types of activity in the state elite.

Even in the most progressive nations far less than half the members of parliament, judges, and civil service are women. Even countries that have had female heads-of-state are far from true gender equality. There is really no nation on earth with an equitable distribution of political power between the sexes.

In this excerpt Schulz shows that, until recently, many Swiss laws put women at a severe legal disadvantage compared to men. Marriage law explicitly defined domestic work and child-rearing as the sole responsibility of the wife. (This is not so different from the situation in Mexico described in excerpt 6.3.) Abortion was illegal and rape by a husband was not considered a crime. Violence in the privacy of the home was well tolerated.

However, Professor Schulz writes that "[t]his article [now] has historical, and not a present, value …. Very important changes that have taken place and/or are considered [include the following:] matrimonial law has become almost egalitarian; rape by a husband can be sued against under certain conditons; women now compose 15 percent of the federal parliament, and up to 35 percent of certain cantonal parliaments; the right [to] vote now exists in all cantons; there is an increasing number of women in cantonal and city governments …; a number of projects are under way to increase the number of women in all the state authorities (parliament, government, courts, civil service); a bill is being examined in the federal parliament to improve women's position in the field of employment and to fight gender discrimination." She concludes, "In general, there is a movement towards change that has been increased by the possible integration of Switzerland in the European community."

So much change in only ten years seems to show that institutional obstacles to gender equality can be cleared away in short order, if there is the political will to do so.

Today[1] Swiss law remains strongly influenced by nineteenth-century (and earlier) gender role traditions. The naturalist and sexist affirmation of man's superiority to woman, a superiority expressed countless times in laws,

Schulz, Patricia (1988). "Institutional Obstacles to Equality Between the Sexes," *Women's Studies International Forum*, 9(1), 5–11. Reprinted by permission.

parliamentary debates, government policies, court decisions, and jurisprudence, is equally influential.

Marriage law in particular is organised according to a strict division of labour between women and men, and it influences other fields such as social security and taxes. The basic model is that of the breadwinning husband who is chief of the conjugal community, and the housewife, who is legally responsible for housework and child-raising (articles 160 and 161 Swiss *Civil Code*). Only men are whole legal persons in Swiss law, their status not being dependent on another person.

Many people no longer respect this model. About 30 percent of women work outside the home in paid employment, as well as working in the home (Commission fédérale pour les questions féminines, 1982:37, hereafter CFQF). Women alone suffer from the double day, as most husbands consider they are entitled to the domestic work and raising of the children by their wives, who are legally required to undertake these tasks in exchange for being provided for by the husband (CFQF, 1982:40–44; Kellerhals et al., 1982:156–172).

As always in Switzerland changes are slow, under the influence of legislative modifications in other European countries, changes in the social and economic conditions in Switzerland, and feminist claims. A modification of marriage law is underway, implying less stereotyped roles for men and women without abandoning them altogether (Conseil fédéral, 1979).

Constitutional and Legislative Framework

The Constitution. Switzerland is a federal state comprising 23 *cantons* (member states, each with its constitution, government, parliament, court system, and so on). The present federal constitution dates back to 1874 and has been revised 106 times (as of 30 January, 1984), most of the amendments giving new rights and/or guarantees to the people. All amendments must be adopted in a ballot, by a double majority which is formed by the majority of the Swiss citizens participating in the ballot and the majority of the cantons (that is, 12 of the 23 cantons). Amendments can be proposed by the government, parliament, or by 100,000 citizens using the right of "initiative." Using this right, women launched an initiative for the equality of rights between men and women in 1975 and in somewhat modified form[2] the proposal was accepted on 14 June, 1981, becoming article 4, paragraph 2 of the *Constitution* (Chaponnière-Grandjean, 1983).

The equality rule. Since 1848, with the first federal *Constitution* (replaced in 1874), Swiss law has contained a basic principle:

> All Swiss are equal before the law. In Switzerland there are no privileges due to regions, birth, persons or family.

The interpretation of article 4 of the *Constitution* by the courts, in particular by the Federal Court, has been far-reaching. The rule can be invoked against a law or a decision by the courts or administration and is binding for all organs of the state on the federal, cantonal and communal level. It has been the basis of new constitutional rights that the Federal Court inferred despite the silence of the

Constitution — such as a right to a fair trial, protection against arbitrary state action (Aubert, 1967:124–125). But it has never been interpreted as a protection for women as women.

It took 133 years for women to gain the constitutional guarantee of equality in article 4, paragraph 2 of the *Constitution*,

> *Men and women have equal rights. Legislation shall provide equality, in particular in the fields of the family, education and work. Men and women have a right to equal pay for work of equal value.*

Contrary to article 4, paragraph 1 — which creates direct rights a citizen can claim in court — article 4, paragraph 2 is seen as creating only an obligation for parliament to change discriminatory laws (except in the case of equal pay which can be invoked directly in court (Bérenstein, 1980:193–200)).

The legislation. Federal laws are adopted by parliament and must be confirmed in a ballot if requested by 50,000 citizens. Under this threat, a compromise is generally reached by all the interested parties before the proposed law reaches the plenary session of parliament where it is seldom modified on important points.

Importance of the legal institutions for women. Although women gained the right to vote at the federal level in 1971 and have the right on the cantonal level in all but one canton, women are still excluded from the making of the law — in parliament and at the judicial level. Of 246 members of the federal parliament, 25 are women: there is an average of 10 percent of women in the cantonal parliaments; no women sits in the federal government; only one women is in the 23 cantonal governments; about four percent of women in the parliamentary and extra-parliamentary commissions; about two percent of women in the higher levels of the federal administration; and one woman among the 30 judges of the Federal Court (*Domaine public*, 1984; Germann, 1981:86–87, 198).

Even with article 4, paragraph 2 in the *Constitution*, difficulties remain — first, to define the meaning of the principle, and second, to implement equality. Additionally, women are faced with a double bind; as most laws determining the status of women and men are federal, it is necessary to accept new, still discriminatory laws, because they bring some improvements, without touching the fundamental discriminations, or to have them rejected in a referendum in the hope for a future, better law, but with the risk of remaining for decades with the present discriminatory laws.

With legislative modifications underway in marriage law and old age pensions, the relative value men give to the rule of equality when applied to women is evident. Cosmetic improvements are accepted, as long as basic male privileges remain untouched.[3] For example, the modification of the law on old age pensions — ostensibly to implement article 4, paragraph 2 — has been deprived of all meaning by the fact it is not supposed to cost anything.[4]

Additionally, there is a deeper problem. That is the relationship of women to the law as both a means of oppression *and* of liberation. It is necessary for women to look to the state that has oppressed us for an improvement in our situation: it is easier to influence the state than to influence the economy, that cannot be held accountable for women's situation. So women are faced with this contradiction, aggravated by the dichotomy of private and public realms, and all that has been built upon this division of the world.

The evolution of the private and public aspects of patriarchy does not mean freedom for us, even though we have passed gradually from total control by a man (father/husband), to a more diffuse power, defined by the state, and setting limits to the private power of our former owners. As women we still do not have control over our own lives; abortion is illegal in Switzerland, rape by a husband is not considered rape, and private violence against women — especially in the family — is well tolerated (CFQF, 1982:48–50). Women lose their name, nationality, domicile, individual rights to old age pension, individual status in tax matters, right to work outside the home in paid employment through marriage. In short, women are dependent and are denied autonomy by the state. Therefore freedom and the possibility to participate equally in power is denied (Castoriadis, 1982:26–32).

Control of the Constitutionality of Laws

Federal and Cantonal Laws Concerning Men and Women

As mentioned previously the major laws determining the status of men and women are federal. These laws give power to men over women under the guise of "protection."[5] They also influence cantonal laws. The economic and social status of women depends on the variations of their civil status (married, divorced, widowed, remarried). Marriage is the central institution because of the consequences federal laws attach to it (CFQF, 1980:2–31, 1982; Margolis and Margolis, 1981: 291–301). The criterion of sex thus influences our legal situation, and yet only the cantonal laws, having a more reduced importance, can be reviewed and struck down for unconstitutionality.

Lack of Control of the Constitutionality of Federal Laws

Due to a restrictive interpretation of the *Constitution*, the Federal Court has denied itself the right to control the constitutionality of federal laws (Aubert, 1967: 94–95, 173–179; Auer, 1983:68–70). Article 113, paragraph 3 of the *Constitution* simply states the Federal Court shall "apply" the laws passed by parliament, not that the Federal Court must *not* apply unconstitutional laws (Auer, 1980). It has been the consistent opinion of the Court that faced with a federal law that violates the *Constitution*, it must simply apply the law: otherwise, the judges would place themselves above the parliament and people. The primary consequence of this interpretation is that parliament can violate the *Constitution* freely, with no remedy for the individual suffering this violation (Auer, 1983:78–81). This means a law (adopted by parliament and the people) is superior to the *Constitution* (adopted by the people and cantons — that is, the most complicated procedure, supposed to guarantee its formal superiority over all others), and that parliament can violate the *Constitution* that gives it its very existence and power to pass laws.

It is often said that the democratic argument linked to the role of the people in the legislative process has won over the liberal argument of the protection of individual rights against state action (Auer, 1983:62–68 for a critical review). This reasoning opposes democracy and liberalism, equality and liberty as if one were not the condition of the other and vice versa, and it leaves the minorities with no protection against the power of the majority. I do not see how democracy is better respected by accepting violations of the *Constitution* than by giving the Federal Court the power to control federal as well as cantonal laws.

Even with its limits, the control of the constitutionality of cantonal laws has been very important, enabling the Federal Court to define constitutional rights, and to "create" some new ones. Indeed the fundamental rights of individual freedom, of freedom of opinion and of speech, of free assembly and the guarantee of the mother-tongue have all been created by the Federal Court, even though the written *Constitution* does not mention them. Auer has suggested this is possible thanks to the absence of control of federal laws, because the Federal Court could go ahead without being accused of interfering with the powers of parliament (Auer, 1983:104–105, 168–169, 220–222). As women we also benefit from these rights, but we must question the system and its logic: the Federal Court "invented" these rights because it found them necessary for a democracy to exist, in violation of the text of the *Constitution,* and of its rules on modifications; at the same time, the Federal Court refuses to control federal laws to avoid being above parliament, but does not hesitate to place itself above the organ normally competent to revise the *Constitution,* that is, the people and cantons!

So we have a progressive Federal Court which is increasing some constitutional rights but steadfastly refusing to accept that article 4 could also include women among the beneficiaries of the equality rule of "all Swiss are equal before the law" or of "all Swiss have the right to vote": in both cases the Federal Court decided the *Constitution* had to be explicitly modified to include women. It may then appear as a contradiction to advocate giving the Court the power to control federal laws in the hope it will protect women against discrimination, but at least it would create a forum and force the system, through court decisions, to make more explicit the unequal treatment to which it subjects women.

The Situation with Article 4, Paragraph 2 of the Constitution

Although most authors agree there are few unconstitutional laws in Switzerland, article 4, paragraph 2 rendered a great number of existing laws unconstitutional: all the laws making differences for "invalid" reasons between men and women should be changed by parliament. Yet, inequalities against women are watered down by male experts.

The federal government tried to advise the judges to overcome the contradiction of a clear, new constitutional rule of equality, and the impossibility of having it respected (Conseil Fédéral, 1980:134), but the system is blocked. The question is therefore to ask if a right without a remedy is really a right? The rule of equality between the sexes, although written in the federal *Constitution,* does not exist on the federal level — for lack of remedy.

Perhaps the best approach would be for women to launch a new constitutional initiative to modify article 113, paragraph 3, so the Federal Court would have to exercise control to ensure federal laws respect the *Constitution*. The absurdity of this situation and the double standard of the rule of equality (for only article 4, paragraph 1 creates direct rights, whereas article 4, paragraph 2 imposes a mandate on parliament to make equal laws — but when?) are generally not seen. This is because the unequal treatment of women as a group is not acknowledged; though, if the group of people with blue eyes were treated as women are, the male establishment might see the discrimination, because it would affect some of its members directly.

Conclusion

As a group, even with the constitutional "guarantee" of equality, women still do not receive like protection as men from the courts, because women cannot challenge the discriminatory laws. This is because the court system is biased against women by its very composition.

There is no escape from the fact that more rights for women will mean fewer privileges for men in certain fields, such as marriage law where men could lose the right to women's unpaid 30–60 hrs. of weekly domestic work, or the right to impose their name on wives and children. In other fields, more rights for women would mean more rights for all, such as the right for everyone to seek redress of all kinds of violations of the *Constitution*, were article 113, paragraph 3 modified.

More rights for women imply a redefinition of power, equality and liberty, and the acknowledgement that only by taking positive measures in favour of women will we overcome the history of discrimination that has been imposed on us.

ENDNOTES

[1] This article describes the situation as of *January 30, 1984*. Since then, the first woman in the Federal Government was elected and the revision of marriage law was accepted.

[2] Parliament can adopt a "counter proposal" when the people launch an initiative. Both texts are then submitted to the vote (and generally refused), unless the authors of the initiative withdraw their text in favour of the counter-proposal that has more chance of being accepted. This is what happened with article 4, paragraph 2.

[3] The revision aims at removing the most shocking and visible aspects of legal sexism, such as the definition of men as chief of the family and women as housewives, the power of husbands to prevent their wives from working outside the home in paid employment, the privileges of men in marital property rights, in questions of domicile, or in representation, and so on.

[4] Only men have an individual right to a pension according to what they have contributed into the system, whereas women's situations will vary according to their civil status; a divorce can thus make them lose the right to what they had previously paid into the system. Also, men's contributions create more rights for their family than the same contributions by women.

[5] For instance, marital property rights give the husband near entire control over his wife's property, the justification being that women are not experienced enough to deal with financial questions.

REFERENCES

Aubert, Jean-François (1967). *Traité de droit constitutionnel suisse,* 2 Vols. Ides et Calendes, Neuchâtel.

——— (1982). *Traité de droit constitutionnel suisse,* Supplément 1967–1982. Ides et Calendes, Neuchâtel.

Auer, Andreas (1980). "'… le Tribunal fédéral appliquera les lois votées par l'Assemblée fédérale …:' réflexions sur l'art." 113 al. 3 Cst. *Revue de droit suisse* 1980(I), 107–140.

——— (1983). *La juridiction constitutionnelle en Suisse.* Helbing & Lichtenhahn, Basel and Frankfurt.

Bérenstein, Alexandre (1980). "A propos de l'initiative pour l'égalité des droits entre hommes et femmes. Effet vertical ou effect horizontal?" *Schweiz. Zentbl. Staatsund Gemeindeverwaltung* 81, 193–200.

Castoriadis, Cornelius (1982). "Nature et valeur de l'égalité," in *L'exigence d'égalité.* XXXCIII ès Rencontres internationales de Genève. La Baconnière. Neuchâtel.

Chaponnière-Grandjean, Martine (1983). Histoire d'une initiative. *L'égalité des droits entre hommes et femmes.* Comité d'édition Egalité des droits. Genève-Zurich.

Commission fédérale pour les questions féminines (1980). *La situation de la femme en Suisse.* Troisième partie: Droit. Berne.

——— (1982). *La situation de la femme en Suisse.* Deuxième partie: Bibliographies et rôle. Berne.

Conseil fédéral (1979). Message concernant la révision du code civil suisse (effets généraux du mariage, régimes matrimoniaux et successions) du 11 juillet 1979. *Feuille fédérale* II(2), 1179–1405, Berne.

——— (1980). Message sur l'initiative populaire "pour l'égalité des droits entre hommes et femmes," du 14 novembre 1979. *Feuille fédérale* I(1), 73–155. Berne.

Domaine public (1984). La longue marche des femmes. No. 713. 12.1.1984.

Germann, Raimund E. (1981). *Ausserparlamentarische Kommissionen: Die Milizverwaltung des Bundes.* Verlag Paul Haupt, Bern und Stuttgart.

Kellerhals, Jean, J.-F. Petrin, G. Steinauer-Cresson, I. Voneche, and G. Wirth (1982). *Mariages au quotidien. Inégalités sociales, tensions culturelles et organisation familiale.* Favre, Lausanne.

Margolis, Clorinda and Joseph (1981). "The separation of marriage and family," in Vetterling-Braggin, Mary et al., eds. *Feminism and Philosophy.* Littlefield. Adams & Co., Totowa, New Jersey.

10.3   Peter Townsend

Why are the Many Poor in Britain?

INTRODUCTION

Some people believe the poor are to blame for their own troubles because they are unwilling to work. But Townsend, the author of the next excerpt, points out there are many unemployed people for every job vacancy in Britain. Unemployment is one of the main causes of poverty, Townsend argues. He sees this, and the government's economic policies, as the most important causes of recent increases in economic inequality.

Multinational corporations also worsen the problem, according to this author. These companies wield more power than many governments do, yet they are not responsible to any single country. They can always avoid attempts to limit their wealth by moving elsewhere, leaving massive unemployment in their wake.

Given this globalization of the economy, what steps should governments take to deal with poverty? The traditional anti-poverty approach taxes the rich to fund social programs for the poor. But this way of reducing inequality has failed: the rich resist paying high taxes. In fact, most people oppose paying higher benefits to welfare recipients, even though the existing benefits are too low for people to survive on. (Recall the problem of "downward jealousy" discussed in excerpt 4.3.) Townsend believes we need to rethink basic strategies for dealing with poverty.

The British government estimated there were, in 1981, 15 million people with very low incomes, including those with lower incomes than the state poverty line, those with incomes on that line, and those with incomes only marginally above.

The numbers in the categories I have described have doubled from seven and three-quarters of a million to 15 million in 20 years under successive governments, but have accelerated in the last five years. Between 1979 and 1981, the total increased from just over 11 million to 15 million — or by nearly four million — and there is no discernible halt to that trend. Since 1981 long-term unemployment has increased substantially. Instead of 15 million poor the total could now be 18 million.

Townsend, Peter (1986). "Why are the Many Poor?" *International Journal of Health Services*, 16(1), 1–32. Reprinted by permission of Baywood Publishing Company, Inc.

The recent increase in poverty in Britain is partly due to an increase in unemployment. In the early 1960s only about 250,000 people were in families with very low incomes because of unemployment which had lasted three months or longer. By the late 1970s the figure was in excess of one million. Between 1979 and 1981 the figure leapt to 2.6 million.[1]

But other categories of poor have also increased. Between 1971 and 1981 the number of one-parent families increased by 71 percent and now stands at nearly one million families. This is approximately one family in every seven with children. The long-standing inequality between the sexes in access to resources and the institutional bias in favor of conventionally married couples contribute to the poverty which lone parents and their children experience.

There have been fluctuations in the percentage of old people drawing supplementary benefit. During the last 25 years there has been a slight increase in the total proportion living on low incomes from around 60 percent to 68 percent. The actual number living *below* the state's standard has increased. Much of the poverty of the elderly has been "created" by the modern institutions of retirement and inadequate employer and state pensions. The total number of younger disabled people living on low incomes has stayed around the three-quarter million mark in the last ten years, but within that total the number below the poverty line has increased. Again, employment opportunities and access to social associations continue to be denied to many people with disabilities.

The number of low paid in poverty or on its margins has also increased. The tenth of wage earners with lowest earnings have a wage which has fallen to 64.1 percent of the median in the case of men, and 66.4 percent in the case of women (1983). Further evidence of the multiplication in number of low earners is to be found in the doubling in recent years of the numbers drawing Family Income Supplement.

Another method of getting closer to the structural causes of poverty is to examine changes in the distribution of incomes by age. A disproportionately large number of children and of old people, especially over 75, have incomes below or on the margins of the government's poverty line.[2] In middle life, between the ages of 45 and 60, disposable incomes tend on average to be nearly twice or more than twice the incomes available to the households in which young children and old people live.

The reasons for the growing inequality by age in the distribution of resources are several. Young people have been marrying younger and having their children younger than preceding generations. This means many couples in middle age do not have dependent children to support. More married women of this age are now taking paid employment and this means that for many households in middle life there are two wage earners rather than one at a time when there are no dependent children. More of the employed population are in nonmanual employment and therefore eligible for age increments in pay. "Seniority" payments among manual workers have also become more common. People who reach the most powerful managerial, professional, administrative and political positions are generally in this age group. Finally, the spread of owner-occupation means more people have high costs when raising a family and low housing costs when they have no dependent children.

What Causes Poverty?

A theory of poverty depends on a two-fold analysis. One strand shows how different institutions of economic and social management operate to distribute resources unequally. The other shows how the terms of social membership are continually revised by new laws, new housing, new transport systems, new environments and modes of living. This explains what individual members of society *need* to do at any time and what resources they require to minimally fulfil their obligations as citizens.

Control of poverty therefore lies not just in controlling the allocation of resources but controlling the construction and reproduction of those institutions which govern social behavior.

Institutional Causes of Poverty

Jobs and Wages

The problem arises first and foremost in the institutions of employment and the wage structure. The growth in influence and power of the large corporation has been succeeded by the crucial phenomenon of the multinational corporation. Because of their flexibility to enter and leave international markets, multinational companies are overcoming the restraints imposed on them by some national governments. Threats of nationalization, for example, can be met by shifting production to other countries or by separating production into stages, so denying any single country access to control of all the stages of production.

For workers and representative trade unions this means a weakening of bargaining powers. It is felt that concessions have to be made to management in order to preserve jobs. For management, there is a less widely discussed problem. Loyalties to family concerns, work groups and local communities are replaced by the uncertain disciplines of international camaraderie within big organizations. There is bound to be loss of national as well as local affiliation, and certainly among some a growth of social cynicism which knows few geographical roots and depends more and more upon the advancement of self-interest.

It is disinvestment and the relocation of employment overseas, and not just world recession, which has brought about mass unemployment in the 1980s. An example is Scotland. The authors of one study describe the disinvestments of Singer, Chrysler-Peugot, Hoover, NCR, Honeywell and Goodyear and the resulting loss of 45,000 jobs between 1976 and 1981.[3] To the problem in Britain of disinvestment and relocation of industry overseas have to be added the increasing use by management of the threats of robotics, computerization and privatization to suborn and reduce labor forces. The politics of wage control is being replaced by the politics of redundancy.

The internationalization of finance is a parallel trend. Those in charge of insurance companies, unit trusts, pension funds, and other institutions have been transferring money overseas. This means the health of the British economy is of lesser importance than it used to be to those in leading positions in the city of London. The financial viability and profits of concerns and individuals is more and more dependent on developments overseas rather than at home.

The growth of corporations and multinational companies as well as international agencies has also had its effect on augmenting pay at the top, introducing more grades of pay and lowering the pay of subordinate groups like temporary staff and wholly or partly dependent subsidiaries. On June 3, 1984, the *Sunday Times* listed the salaries, as far as they are known, of the leading 100 public company directors. They varied from £82,000 to £522,000 a year.

"Many a highly paid director's salary is of course dwarfed by the earnings of his super salesmen or vital executives. At Grand Met, for example, the chairman, Stanley Grinstead, earns £111,000 — but two of his top casino executives, Max Kingsley and Philip Isaacs, earn nearly £400,000 apiece.... But then, for many a chairman or highly paid director, his salary is simply the loose change in his pocket. Tiny Rowland earned over £4m in the final Lonrho dividend in his £56m stake in the Company, compared to a mere £265,000 salary in 1983."[4]

The Unfair Tax System

The gains to the rich since 1979 have been in profitability to companies, as partly engineered and encouraged by the government. Some salaries include bonuses for additional profits. But they have also come from deliberate redistribution. Of a total of £4.17 billion cuts in income taxes since 1979 the richest one percent receive 44 percent and the poorest 25 percent, only three percent. The average reduction in income tax for those earning over £50,000 is £11,700, but for those earning under £5,000 is £20.[5]

Fringe benefits have not figured prominently in the debates about tax allowances and tax rates. During the 1960s and 1970s inequality was therefore made out by different interest groups to be diminishing when in fact it was increasing.

Tax allowances have made a mockery of the personal income tax system. Because of their existence the tax base is narrow.[6] Tax is now collected on less than half gross declared income and perhaps only a third of total real income. Chartered accountants working on behalf of the rich can save their clients huge sums of money. "For the rich," concluded one recent review, "Britain has become a fiscal paradise."[7] Wealth taxes in Britain (Capital Gains, Estate Duty, and Capital Transfer Taxes) have never been very consequential but have declined in value and percentage of total taxes since 1975. They accounted for 7.5 percent of total Inland Revenue taxes in the early 1970s but only for 2.5 percent by 1983–84, and had declined, expressed as a percentage of GNP, from 1.2 to 0.5 percent. The tax structure has become far less progressive. Higher tax rates on higher incomes were reduced and the thresholds raised. In 1984 it was estimated that only three percent of tax units are paying tax above the standard rate of 30 percent. At 650,000, their numbers are half what they were in the late 1970s.

The government's analysis of income distribution (see Endnote 1 for source) shows a shrinkage since 1975–76 and especially since 1978–79 in the share of disposable income of the poorest 20 percent and a substantial increase in the share of the top 20 percent of taxable units. The figures are summarized in Table 1.

Engineered Dependency

Just as the tax structure became less egalitarian, the dependent population increased — in largest measure "artificially" through unemployment and premature retirement, and some postponement of the completion of education. Between 1973 and 1983 the number of men aged 55 to 59 who are economically active fell from 94 percent to 85 percent and, at ages 60 to 64, from 85 to 63 percent. There were corresponding reductions among divorced and other single women in these two age groups from 69 percent to 53 percent, and 34 percent to 17 percent. This increase in dependency at such youthful ages is nationally self-destructive. The need to finance this increase in dependency has brought the tax threshold down and caused taxes to be increased on the goods purchased by the mass of the population.

Cuts In Government Benefits

The Thatcher Government is seeking change by drastically reducing public expenditure and ensuring that more of it is paid for by the poor. Taxation has been

TABLE 1   SHARES OF INCOME AFTER TAX

	1975–76	1978–79	1981–82
Top 10 percent	23.1	23.4	25.6
Top 20 percent	39.0	39.7	42.0
21–40 percent	24.8	24.8	24.0
41–60 percent	17.3	17.0	16.1
61–80 percent	11.6	11.5	11.5
Bottom 20 percent	7.3	7.0	6.4

Estimated Average Real Income at 1981–82 Prices

	1975–76	1978–79	1981–82	Gain or loss 1978–79 1981–82
Top 10 percent	£10,638	£11,295	£12,851	+£1,557
Top 20 percent	£8,980	£9,572	£10,542	+£970
Bottom 20 percent	£1,681	£1,688	£1,606	–£82

Source: Central Statistical Office, *Economic Trends*.

introduced for unemployment benefit. Changes in regulations have stopped some groups of unemployed getting any supplementary benefit at all and have stopped others from getting as much as their former entitlement. Earnings related supplement has been abolished. The activities of the Special Claims Control Teams to identify fraud have been stepped up. As a percentage both of earnings and of the benefits received by long-term claimants, other than the unemployed, the unemployed person's weekly benefit has declined. Unemployment benefit is at its lowest level relative to earnings since the early 1960s. Housing benefit is now payable by local authorities. The transfer of its administration, like the reorganization of supplementary benefit beforehand, has involved reductions in weekly income for hundreds of thousands of recipients, as conceded by Government Ministers.

Summary: *Thatcherism as Class Warfare*

The government is following a policy of "get tough with the poor." This is its major *raison d'être* and far more important in fact than its well-advertised neo-monetarism. It is a covert form of class warfare.

The government is aiming to lower prices first by lowering already low levels of pay; (We can cite decisions in public sector industries, on wages councils and the history of the Youth Training Scheme.) second, by refusing to set principled limits on the extent or growth of unemployment; and third, as we have seen, by lowering benefits in order to make lower pay acceptable. It is a downward spiral whereby the government fails to recognize the ultimate destination — the establishment of Third World wages and Third World social conditions in an otherwise rich country for more than a third of its people.

For the first time since the war a majority of the British Cabinet seem prepared to allow conditions of life for a large minority of the people to deteriorate in the mistaken belief that conditions for the rest of the population will thereby be improved. That is a departure from the consensus politics of post-war Britain. But there is a worse implication still. For the first time Government Ministers seem prepared to depart even from the most tenuous principles of one nation and consider seriously that certain sections of the British population are beyond redemption, have to be taught some rough lessons, and are expendable.

ENDNOTES

1 *Economic Trends,* July, 1984.

2 Townsend, P. *Fewer Children, More Poverty: An Incomes Plan.* University of Bristol, England, 1984.

3 Hood, N. and S. Young. *Multi-nationals in Retreat, the Scottish Experience.* Edinburgh University Press, Scotland, 1982.

4 Beresford, P. "Boom at the top." *Sunday Times* (London), June 3, 1984.

5 *Hansard,* April 4, 1984.

6 Report by the Board of Inland Revenue, Table 1–5, London, 1983.

7 Bellini, J. "The tax avoidance boom." *The Listener,* April 5, 1984.

10.4   Ahmad Ashraf

Charisma and State Power in Iran

INTRODUCTION

Ayatollah Khomeini took power over the state in Iran in 1979 through the revolutionary overthrow of the Shah and his government. Khomeini ruled until his death in 1989.

The author of the next excerpt, Ashraf, emphasizes that Khomeini's power and authority were very much of the "charismatic" type. ("Charismatic authority" refers to authority based on the belief that the leader possesses extraordinary personal qualities that should be admired and deferred to, independent of any bureaucratic office the leader may or may not hold.) But once in power, Khomeini ended up also exercising strong bureaucratic or "rational-legal" control of the state.

The author argues that because of the economic interests of the state Khomeini had to modify his anti-economic and anti-bureaucratic views. The Ayatolah's views carried great force because of his charisma and near-absolute authority, so they had integrative consequences for Iran. However, since his death, it has been difficult for the new leadership to rule with the same effect, the author explains.

The current leadership of the state lacks charismatic authority of the sort Khomeini had, but this should not be surprising. Because charismatic authority is rooted in the person, it generally cannot be passed on to others, or inherited. The new men of power (they are all men in Iran) must rely even more heavily on bureaucratic control of the state, economy, and religion than their predecessor did.

A yatollah Ruhollah Khomeini's prophetic mein, the manner of his rise to power, the overwhelming commemoration of his death, and the edifice of a shrine which was erected over his graveyard leave little doubt that his leadership warrants the attribution, "charismatic." Genuine charisma is a rare historical circumstance, deriving from a conviction that an individual possesses a mysterious and supernatural gift of grace — a belief which the person and his disciples share collectively. Even though the phenomenon of pure charisma is universal, it is often most evident in the religious realm, and it thrives with particular abundance in the fertile soil of the Shi'ite culture.

Ashraf, Ahmad (1990). "Theocracy and Charisma: New Men of Power in Iran," *International Journal of Politics, Culture and Society*, 4(1), 113–153. Reprinted by permission of Human Sciences Press, Inc.

Television has rarely shown more astonishing sights than the crowds in Tehran literally ripping the shroud from Ayatollah Khomeini. It was a scene from the Age of Belief: mourners flagellating themselves and crushing one another as they grabbed at a helicopter bearing aloft the Imam's coffin. What may also have fed the crowd's awesome grief was awareness that the Ayatollah's authority was unique, that this was the last act of drama expiring with its dominating character (NYT, editorial, June 8, 1989:A30).

Khomeini exemplified in his own person the presence of a multiple charisma in the course of his ascendance, first, to the position of the highest Shi'ite authority and, later, to the theocratic position of the national political leadership. Both positions were achieved through his leadership of rebellious movements. Khomeini's multiple charisma led to the creation of a number of contradictory positions.

First, and above all else, he was the most emotional and inventive charismatic leader of recent times; the radius of his charisma spread beyond the boundaries of Iran to reach millions of Muslims all over the world. Khomeini was endowed with a number of character traits that could easily appeal to the hearts and minds of Muslims in the times of crisis, including the will to power, cunning, an innovating orientation, youthfulness, asceticism, militancy, and radicalism. Khomeini gave the masses a sense of personal integrity, collective identity, historical rootedness, and feelings of pride and superiority.

Second, Khomeini acquired an "office charisma," a religious office with traditional charismatic authority, i.e., the well-established traditional office of the Shi'ite source of emulation which granted him the religious authority and entitled him to receive religious charities and financial obligations, including the tithe as the share of the Hidden Imam. Third, Khomeini introduced the new theocratic institution of the divine commission of the jurisconsult to assume political authority and sovereignty as the vicegerent of the Hidden Imam. Fourth, Khomeini assumed the position of the supreme leader and commander in chief of the armed forces of a modernizing state apparatus, while as a supreme theocratic ruler he transcended the constitutional constraints of an apparently legal-rational order. Finally, Khomeini assumed the title of the Imam, the position exclusively reserved in the Iranian Shi'ite community for the twelve infallible Imams.

For Weber (1968:1115) the prototype of the charismatic leader is a person who "in a revolutionary and sovereign manner ... transforms all values and breaks all traditional and rational norms." Such a person says to his disciples, "It is written ..., but I say onto you ..." — a claim that clearly challenges the authority of the established order, without regard for whether it is traditional or legal-rational. He is not bound by administrative organs, rules of conduct or legal wisdom oriented to judicial precedent. Charismatic leadership is prophetic; the leader demands obedience from his disciples and followers on the basis of the mission he feels called upon to perform. The genuine prophet, Weber (1968:243) says, "demands *new* obligations — most typically by virtue of revelation, oracle, inspiration, or of his own will."

Khomeini's Charisma and Power

Khomeini's rise to the theocratic leadership of the bureaucratic apparatus of a modern state with a sizable "surplus producing" economic sector confronted him with a very complex situation in the period of 1979–89. He found himself caught between the pressures coming from the major conflicting forces in the state and civil society. He had to modify his personal and traditional arenas of leadership and adapt himself to the new situation. In doing so he had to cope with three basic challenges: (1) to modify his antibureaucratic orientation; (2) to alter his antieconomic stance; and (3) to adopt a radical stand that deviated significantly from conservative Islamic jurisprudence.

Genuine charisma is antibureaucratic — it does not get along with officials. Khomeini, therefore, was faced with a number of problems in the process of transforming his inexperienced clerical and lay disciples into the officials of the bureaucratic state: of bringing under his control a large number of modernized officials and state managers; of leading a huge and complicated state apparatus; and of bridging the hiatus between the two inherently contradictory political entities of theocracy and modern republican democracy.

The men of power who emerged had to learn through trial and error and a sort of an in-service-training how to run the modern state. The confidants of the leader were superimposed upon major revolutionary and ordinary bureaucratic agencies. A mode of democratic centralism was developed in which the elected representatives, councilmen, and officials of the state could express their views and even stand against the will of the leader, but the final voice in the key decisions was that of the leader. At the same time the constitution gave the supreme charismatic leader the authority to appoint the members of the Council of Guardians of the Constitution who had veto power over legislations passed by the Majlis. When he became dissatisfied with the conservative and traditional stance of the guardianship Council in vetoing several radical bills, Khomeini did not hesitate to institute a Discretionary Council to overrule the veto power of the former council.

Economic factors were even more significant and pressing in shaping the behavior of the new men of power and privilege than were the workings of the bureaucracy. The economics of charismatic revolution, as an independent variable, directs the process of transformation (Weber, 1968:254).

Khomeini was fairly successful in revolutionizing Shi'ite world views but he was limited by the requirements of the modern state and its economic base. Thus, he succeeded in making a revolution in Qom because in "traditionalistic periods charisma is the great revolutionary force," but he was forced to modify his attitude and assume an adaptive orientation in Tehran because of overwhelming bureaucratic and economic constraints. In the end, Khomeini became an ardent advocate of the central state and its superordination over the civil society. He also accepted the principles of rationality, efficiency and profitability in administering the public bureaucracy and state owned capitalist enterprises.

Khomeini exemplified, apparently, a rare case of a genuine charisma in the modern time. Most modern charismatic figures, including Lenin, Mao, Castro, and

Nkrumah, argue Bensman and Givani (1975:599–604), do not have genuine charisma. They are at best pseudocharismatics. Their charisma is non-personal and rational, it was fabricated by rational planning, by mediation of the impersonal mass media, by the propaganda machine of a bureaucratic mass society. By operating in the modern world, Khomeini's genuine charisma was thus contaminated by rationality, by impersonality, and by accommodation to the modern bureaucratic and economic order.

He combined, however, tradition and modernity, personal relation of *gemeinschaft* with impersonal relations of *gesellschaft*. He increasingly used the mass media, particularly television, for communicating with the masses. As a matter of fact, the mass appeal of his charisma emerged at this stage through the use of newspapers, cassettes, radio, and later, television. Furthermore, tens of thousands of believers who were seduced by the regime's propaganda officers and the mass media were brain-washed and dispatched to the war front for suicide missions and martyrdom.

Most observers of modern charisma recognize the central role of the mass media in the making of modern charismatic politics. Bendix (1971:172) notes that "modern means of publicity can give such leadership all the appearance of charisma." Loewenstein (1966:86) observed that "mass media can produce a reinforcement and deepening of an originally spurious but artificially promoted charisma attributed to the ruler." Bensman and Givani (1975:604,606) say that

> Modern charisma ... rests upon the conscious selection of themes, appeals, slogans, and imagery that is based upon the systematic study of audiences, target populations, constituencies, and strategic public.... Modern charismatic leaders may rationally select irrational themes, motifs, and values to personify those themes and values and a sense of pseudo-Gemeinschaft to distant publics."

Khomeini's charisma, as a typical case, was also a dramaturgical phenomenon. It was created by symbolic representations in the Shi'ite community and involved selective and purposive activities in terms of mobilization of human, physical, and financial resources as well as manipulation of tools and strategies of a rhetorical nature. The drama and the passion play of Hossein, the commemoration of his death, and the notion of martyrdom in Shi'ite culture were manipulated for the purpose of political mobilization of the masses. These rhetorical symbols served as significant *cultural resources* for the purpose of mass mobilization.

Furthermore to appeal to the intelligentsia, Khomeini's disciples adopted an innovative modern political discourse as early as 1960. By mastering three contradictory discourses of the traditional elitist language of Islamic law, the popular rhetorical sermons and passion plays focused on the drama of Hossein, and the modern political discourse of the intellectuals, Khomeini's group succeeded in manipulating and deceiving individuals from all walks of life.

Khomeini's charismatic revolution in Iran was the culmination of the recent Islamic revivalist movements and provided them with a new perspective and hope. Khomeini's movement was, at the same time, an Iranian national movement. It was a religious revolution which served, though tragically and at a great human cost, the arena of political development and nation building. It has led to an expansion of national identity which goes beyond loyalty to small groups. The *Protestant reformation* occurred in the West much earlier than the processes of *industrialization* and *nation building* began. All these three major processes of our time have occurred, argues Ernest Gellner (1985:1–3), simultaneously in the Islamic society in the recent time. The combination of these giant processes has profoundly affected and complicated the processes and goals of the Islamic movements; it has constituted the heart of "the Islamic dilemmas."

A significant consequence of Khomeini's charismatic revolution has been the process of further integration of the state through mass participation in the course of rebellious activities and particularly via the mass mobilization of hundreds of thousands of villagers, tribesmen, and urbanites to fight in the eight-year war. Even though the motives for fighting in the war were a mixture of patriotism and a religious duty to wage a holy war, it led to the intensification of feelings of both national identity and political participation.

Unintended consequences of what Ali Banuazizi (1988) has called the "democratization of martyrdom" may lead to further the national identity and even to enhance democratic processes. A shift in the primary loyalty of individuals from their village, tribe, clan, neighborhood, status group, class or profession to that of the Islamic state seems to have taken place. Furthermore, the revolution had advanced the level of political awareness and the political maturity of major social classes and groups and brought them to the arena of national politics. Thus, it is fair to say that the charismatic revolution has led to further political integration and that the process of national integration has, to some extent, reduced the intra-societal tensions and led to further cultural-ideological consensus.

Khomeini's charismatic revolution was, however, a double-edged sword. It also led to the exacerbation of a number of salient internal tensions, which could potentially lead to instability of the regime and deter the progressive integration of the state. One major area of tension and conflict is the genuine arational charismatic pursuit of a futile war abroad and an oppressive policy at home with grave human cost and destructive physical effects. Almost all major leaders of the regime spelled out their grievances due to the directives of the supreme leader on major issues on the occasion of the commemoration of the tenth anniversary of the revolution on February 11, 1989. They believe, for example, that they "had to make an effort to prevent war to break out," from the beginning or at least "to refrain from prolonging the war after the retreat of Iraqi forces from Khorramshahr" (*Iran Times*, 17 February, 1989).

A major event with disintegrative effects has been the mass exodus of hundreds of thousands of well-educated and prosperous members of the new middle classes. This has created a brain drain at home and a sizable hostile Iranian community in exile of about two million abroad. Together with those members of the middle classes who still reside in Iran, they constitute a threat to political integration and the stability of the regime.

Another source of conflict is the status of religious minorities in a predominantly Shi'ite theocratic state. Armenians, Jews, Zoroastrians, and Baha'is have been increasingly excluded from the public domain, alienated from the society, purged from offices, persecuted and even executed in postrevolutionary Iran.

A more severe area of strife and antagonism is the problem of ethnolinguistic groups that may cost the very geographical integrity of the nation state. The ambivalent attitude of the theocratic regime toward the question of Iranian nationalism and Islamic internationalism has, ironically, fanned the nationalist feelings of both Persian speaking Iranians as well as other ethnolinguistic groups. The intelligentsia of the former group have increasingly resorted to their pre-Islamic historical roots and mythologies. Azaris, Kurds, Turkomans, Baluchis, and Arabs who have been alienated from the Islamic state have been encouraged by the Islamic internationalist ideology to denounce the overarching Iranian nationalism, on the one hand, and to resort to their own secessionist local chauvinism under the oppressive measures and ambiguous signals of nationalism/internationalism of the Islamic state, on the other. This tendency has been particularly enhanced as they have become the targets of mounting propaganda campaigns by neighboring states with claims over these groups.

Above all, the major disintegrative legacies of Khomeini's charisma are the exacerbation of internal strife within the religious hierarchy, the factional politics within the regime, and increasing antagonism between the state and the civil society. The split and antagonism between the state and the Shi'ite establishment emerged from the beginning of the post-Khomeini era; the regime is separated from the source of emulation and thus its theocratic basis of legitimation is under question.

The split among the followers of Khomeini in supporting two sources of emulation, the Grand Ayatollah Mohammad Reza Golpayegani and the prominent Ayatollah Mohammad Ali Araki, marks the beginning of a long road of strife and antagonism within the regime. This conflict is exacerbated by the antagonism between the state and the bazaar-mosque alliance. The core elements within the regime have supported Ayatollah Araki, whereas the traditional marginal force of the bazaar-mosque alliance has supported Ayatollah Golpayegani. The roots of some of these tensions, with disintegrative potential, could be traced into the very politics of Khomeini's charismatic revolution and the symbolic manipulation of the rhetoric of the Shi'ite movement on the one hand and the canopy of his leadership that temporarily united conflicting social forces against the old regime on the other.

In this way, Khomeini's charismatic revolution has had both integrative and disintegrative effects, both constructive and immensely destructive consequences on modern state building in Iran. Thus it seems premature to overestimate the integrative effects of the revolution or to characterize the charismatic movement of Khomeini as simply "the turban for the crown."

Both international and internal developments which have occurred in the late 1980s and at the turn of 1990s are likely to lead to a more moderate regime in Iran. The sweeping changes which have rolled the socialist world and the new relations which have developed between the West and the Eastern block have drastically altered the old geopolitical role of Iran as a buffer state. Iran has already lost most of its capability for playing a militant role in the region and is likely to follow a more moderate foreign policy in the future. Furthermore, the failure of state socialism will lead to demoralization of the radical groups within the regime — the groups who have preached an Islamic variant of state socialism for Iran — and will strengthen the position of more moderate groups.

As a result, those who are succeeding Khomeini are far less preoccupied with his charismatic mission. They are men who are concerned mainly with the day-to-day problems of the country. Their goal is not to change the world, but to accommodate themselves to it. As Weber (1968:1120) noted:

> Every charisma is on the road from a turbulently emotional life that knows no economic rationality to slow death by suffocation under the weight of material interests: every hour of its existence brings it nearer to its end.

Conclusion

Yet, the shadow of Khomeini's charismatic revolution and the bolstering of the sense of self-esteem, collective identity, and historical rootedness that it gave to the masses, with all its productive and destructive repercussions, seems to remain in Iran and the world of Islam in the future.

REFERENCES

Banuazizi, A. (1988). "Martyrdom in Revolutionary Iran," a lecture delivered at the Iranian Studies Seminar, Columbia University.

Bendix, R. (1977). *Max Weber: an Intellectual Portrait.* Berkeley: University of California Press.

Bendix, R. and G. Roth (1971). *Scholarship and Partisanship: Essays on Max Weber.* Berkeley: University of California Press.

Bensman, J. and M. Givani. "Charisma and Modernity: The Use and Abuse of a Concept," in *Social Research,* Vol. 2, No. 4, pp. 570–614.

Gelner, E. (1985). "Introduction," in *The Islamic Dilemma.* Berlin: Mouton Publishers.

Loewenstein, K. (1966). *Max Weber: Political Ideas in the Perspective of Our Time.* Amherst: The University of Massachusetts Press.

Weber, M. (1968). *Economy and Society.* Translated by G. Roth and C. Wittich. New York: Bedminister Press.

QUESTIONS

DISCUSSION QUESTIONS

1. "Elites" and "upper classes" (see also the material in Section 4) are related, but they are also quite different. Contrast the two and think of some good examples that show the importance of distinguishing between them.

2. In your view, which theory best describes the distribution of power in Canada: the accommodating elites theory or the capitalist class control theory? Indicate why you think so.

3. In your view, which of the above two theories would do the best job explaining the details presented in the four excerpts in this Section? Why do you think so?

4. Schulz argues that because males, not females, tend to make laws, the interests of women are rarely well served. Discuss three or four examples of laws in Canada that favour men over women. Can you find any that favour women over men?

DATA COLLECTION EXERCISES

1. Armand describes the role of race in conflicts over power and leadership in Haiti. Gather some library information on the role of race or ethnicity in power and leadership in Canada.

2. Collect some information on the proportions of women and men in the top positions in government and law in Canada, to parallel Schulz's analysis for Switzerland. How far from representative are the results (that is, compared with the proportions of women and men in the society) in the labour force?

3. For Canada or another society of your choice, find out the number of job vacancies and the number of unemployed people in some recent period. Would you draw the same conclusions from these data as Townsend did from his data?

4. Khomeini exercised "charismatic" authority within bureaucratic state organizations in Iran. Gather some data from library sources on one or two other examples of a religious-political leader who had strong charismatic authority in a country of your choice. Say a few words in defense of your type of evidence on charisma — i.e., defend your way of measuring charisma.

WRITING EXERCISES

1. "The patterns of power in society seldom change very much." Write a brief essay agreeing or disagreeing with this view, drawing on the selections in this section where appropriate.

2. Write a brief speculative piece on which laws might be different if female politicians and lawyers had largely made them instead of male politicians and lawyers.

3. In a brief essay, explain why you agree or disagree with Townsend's answers to "why are the many poor?"

4. Prepare a short essay in which you spell out what the average citizen can learn about decision-making from the four excerpts in this Section.

SUGGESTED READINGS

1. Lane, David (1989). *The End of Social Inequality? Class, Status and Power Under State Socialism.* London: Allen and Unwin. A detailed analysis of the relationship of state power to patterns of inequality in socialist regimes.

2. Laxer, Gordon (1989). *Open for Business.* Toronto: Oxford University Press. The author uses a comparative approach to examine the role of government and the state in shaping historical patterns of foreign ownership in the Canadian economy.

3. Michels, Robert (1962). *Political Parties.* New York: Harcourt Brace. A classic study that argues that for any organization (political or otherwise) to be successful as it grows in size and complexity it must become bureaucratized. As a result, even democratically inclined leaders of democratic parties come to focus their attention on keeping power.

4. Weber, Max (1946). *From Max Weber: Essays in Sociology* (H. Gerth and C. W. Mills, eds. and trans.). New York: Oxford University Press. Also, Weber, Max (1947). *The Theory of Social and Economic Organization* (T. Parsons, ed. and trans.) New York: The Free Press. One gets the impression that Weber was *not* an elegant writer. But what he lacks in grace he more than makes up for with encyclopedic knowledge, unquenchable curiosity, and an amazing ability to find connections between political, legal, social, economic, and religious changes.

IDEOLOGY AND PROTEST

Introduction

Ideologies

We saw in Section 1 of this volume that cultures include, among other things, values and beliefs. Often, these combine to form what sociologists call "ideologies." *Ideologies* are emotionally charged values and beliefs that "explain" how society is organized. They are very important in understanding society because they influence the distribution of power and control. Sometimes they help contain social protest and social change; other times, they facilitate change. In Canada, we are accustomed to ideological debates on political and economic topics. This Section focuses on ideologies and their role in promoting protest and change.

One main ideological element of our culture is the idea that winners deserve to win and losers deserve to lose. This becomes clear in a study by Smith and Stone (1989), who asked 200 Texan adults why some people are poor and other people are rich. They found people's answers fell into two main groupings, or clusters, which Smith and Stone called "individualism" and "structuralism."

A respondent with "individualistic views" about poverty thinks poor people are poor because they are not motivated to succeed. That is because they can get welfare without any trouble, and because they lack drive and perseverance, have loose morals, abuse drugs and alcohol, are not thrifty, and are lazy. A respondent with individualistic views also thinks that rich people are rich because they have more drive and perseverance than other people, are more willing to take risks, are harder-working, and are thrifty.

These are "individualistic" views because they explain success and failure in terms of the personal characteristics of the rich or poor individual. Only the individual is to blame, or be praised, for success and failure.

On the other hand, a respondent with "structuralist" views focuses on the situation in which an individual finds him- or herself. So, a structuralist explains poverty by saying that poor people lack contacts or pull, are victims of discrimination in hiring, promotions and wages, are taken advantage of by the rich, are forced to attend bad schools, and are ignored by an insensitive government.

Likewise, a person with a structuralist explanation of wealth notes that rich people have a lot of pull or contacts, attend good schools, inherit lots of money, are favoured in hiring, wages, and promotions, receive special treatment from the government, sacrifice their families for their careers, and take advantage of the poor.

Smith and Stone found the most common outlook in Texas was "individualism," especially in explaining poverty. Perhaps most interesting of all, the researchers found no connection between the respondent's own characteristics — sex, race, age, income, or educational attainment — and his or her explanation of wealth and poverty.

This means that poor people are just as ready to attribute poverty to personal failure, and wealth to personal virtue, as rich people are. This state of mind — self-blame, even self-hatred on the part of the poor, self-congratulation on the part of the rich — creates a powerful force against changes in the direction of more equality.

But this is not the sum total of ideology in our society. Questions of ideology arise in widely varying areas of life: for example, in debates about whether

- Canada should admit more refugees
- Crown corporations should be privatized
- a fetus is a person entitled to legal rights
- Canada owes a moral, legal, and economic debt to its native peoples
- we need affirmative action to correct past discrimination against women and racial minorities

and so on. A review of articles in our newspapers will remind us of many areas of intense ideological debate.

Ideologies are Vehicles of Social Control and Protest

We must distinguish between two broad types of ideology. *Reformist and radical ideologies* rally the forces of change, while *dominant ideologies* support existing social arrangements, or the status quo (Parkin, 1971; Abercrombie et al., 1980; Marchak, 1988).

Reformist ideologies call for changes without challenging the basic ground rules. This is what happened when medicare, welfare, and unemployment insurance were established in Canada. They helped people but failed to eliminate the unequal distribution of wealth between owners of capital and workers, or to challenge the principle of private property that underlies our economic order.

By contrast, *radical ideologies* call for a fundamental restructuring of society or one of its institutions. This is what the Co-operative Commonwealth Federation (CCF, the predecessor of today's New Democratic Party) did at the time of its founding in the 1930s. The Regina Manifesto, adopted by the CCF at its founding convention in 1933, declared, "No CCF government will rest content until it has eradicated capitalism and put into operation the full programme of socialized planning which will lead to the establishment in Canada of the co-operative commonwealth."

Another radical ideology is the proposed reform to medicare, which would eliminate its universal coverage, on the grounds that universal health care is too costly for taxpayers. Underlying this belief is the view that people should assume more of the cost of their own care, as they once did.

A second type of ideology is called *dominant ideology*, to emphasize its role in domination. Ideologies can be "dominant" in either of two senses. On the one hand, they may be dominant in the sense that most people endorse them. Or they may be dominant in the sense that the most powerful groups in society sponsor them, whether or not most people agree, and they reflect the way society is run.

The "belief in private property" is an example of ideology that is dominant in both respects in our society. Other dominant ideologies are sexism, which justifies the unequal treatment of women and men, and racism, which justifies the unequal treatment of visible minorities.

The reform and radical ideologies we find in any society are *counter-ideologies*. They are "counter" in the sense that they challenge the assumptions and beliefs of dominant ideologies. The purpose of counter-ideology is to expose the interests that dominant ideologies serve and to offer an alternative vision of society.

Acquiring Ideologies

In acquiring ideologies, individuals are often unaware of the learning process, or that they have "acquired" anything at all. Over our lifetimes, we are exposed to ideological beliefs and values in many subtle ways. We begin to learn ideology during early family socialization, where we are taught the values and beliefs of our parents. This learning extends to socialization through education and interaction with friends and workmates. As well, the media reflect the ideologies of government and business, so they are central to the teaching of ideology.

Counter-ideologies often are responses to people's experiences with unequal treatment. Counter-ideologies call the status quo to account and, at least to some extent, threaten to delegitimize customary ways of treating people. So, for example, feminism is a counter-ideology that undermines sexist ideology and traditional ways of treating men and women.

Similarly, the ideas that support human rights commissions and the Charter of Rights in Canada are counter-ideologies which attack various forms of discrimination. Organizations which promote counter-ideology get their message out to people in various ways, particularly through public meetings and the media.

As we have noted, the media also promote dominant ideologies. So does the educational system. For example, Bowles and Gintis (1976) have shown that, by attending school year after year, students acquire a conception of social structure and their place in it, which helps support the status quo. By learning to passively take notes and directions from teachers, they learn a way of submitting to authority that they will continue in the workplace. They learn to work for grades, certificates, degrees, and the approval of their teachers. In so doing, they learn to work for *extrinsic* reasons and rewards, rather than for *intrinsic* rewards such as the joy of learning.

McDonald's (1978) analysis of the development of education in mid-nineteenth-century Ontario illustrates further some of the ideological effects of education. Egerton Ryerson designed Ontario's school system. He wanted to ensure that young people would remain loyal to the Crown, would never participate in the kind of rebellion that had been put down in Upper Canada in 1837, and would learn to cooperate with others, regardless of their social class background.

Ryerson believed that a successful educational system would persuade the working classes that "their interests were also those of the middle and upper classes, and that, as a collectivity, there was a 'common' or 'public' good towards which all must work" (McDonald, 1978:96–97). In short, Ryerson was aiming at social control through education.

Ideology and Empowerment

Yet sometimes ideology has the effect of *empowering* people in subordinate positions in society. "Empowerment" refers to ideology's effect on people's greater self-esteem and higher sense of power, and to people's better understanding of their position in the social structure. Once they have knowledge and confidence, they willingly express their views and argue for them. Conversely, people who do not have knowledge and confidence are not likely to pursue their interests.

For example, counter-ideologies equip members of racial minorities to question what happens to them, understand changes in race relations and, perhaps, even anticipate significant changes in their social status. As we have said, counter-ideology is a source of self-esteem, as in "black is beautiful." It motivates members of minority groups to push for their own personal and collective advancement.

Consciousness-raising refers to a process of empowerment that occurs as people come to understand their own subordination and the "deceptions" dominant ideology use to mask that subordination. This empowerment helps minority people to survive in the face of unequal treatment.

Ideologies and Social Change

Often, social change emerges from the clash of competing ideologies that are embodied in political parties, interest groups and social movements. Social change is rarely the victory of one ideological perspective over other perspectives. Usually, it involves some uneasy compromise between interest groups. The recent political struggle around revisions to the Canadian constitution illustrated one such attempt at compromise. These struggles continue, of course, and the direction of further change is still unclear.

The excerpts in this section will give still other examples — all from other cultures — of ideologies that maintain the status quo or call for change, and of the social conflicts between their proponents.

REFERENCES

Abercrombie, Nicholas, Stephen Hill, and Bryan S. Turner (1980). *The Dominant Ideology Thesis.* London: Allen and Unwin.

Bowles, S. and H. Gintis (1976). *Schooling in Capitalist America.* New York: Basic Books.

Marchak, Patricia M. (1988). *Ideological Perceptions on Canada,* Third edition. Toronto: McGraw-Hill Ryerson.

McDonald, N. (1978). "Egerton Ryerson and the School as an Agent of political socialization," in N. McDonald and A. Chaiton, eds., *Egerton Ryerson and His Time.* Toronto: Macmillian.

Parkin, Frank (1971). *Class, Inequality and Political Order.* London: McGibbon and Kee.

11.1   Carol Andreas

People's Kitchens and Radical Organizing in Peru

INTRODUCTION

The People's Kitchens of Lima (Peru) described in the next excerpt by Andreas are "cooperative kitchens," operated and supplied by some 20 to 25 households. Families contribute labour and money and receive meals from the kitchen.

These kitchens are a collective response by the urban poor to the hunger caused by severe and unpredictable economic conditions. The realization that working together can make a difference has given the people (mainly women) who manage the kitchens more self-esteem and a new sense of power. Feminists have used them as a springboard for women's agendas. For example, women who work in the cooperatives can leave their houses without their husbands asking where they are going. This is a significant step forward for some Peruvian women.

People's Kitchens are vehicles for counter ideology in Peru and centres of protest by the disadvantaged. They show poor people they can overcome the obstacles to community organization. The success of the People's Kitchens also legitimizes women's critique of public policies relating to reproductive rights, marital issues, and violence against women.

Finally, they serve as an interesting contrast to the "People's Kitchens" we have in North America: namely, hostels and food banks for the desperately poor. Unlike our food banks, Lima's serve a political and educational purpose that should not be ignored.

There seems to be a breaking point in semi-colonial situations where unemployed or underemployed poor outnumber the employed so much that new conditions for class struggle come into existence. Distribution of goods and services becomes such an acute problem that issues of exploitation *per se* take second place to issues of survival or reproduction. The crisis in the family and community reaches a point of no return. Those who are excluded from regular wage work play an increasingly important role in defining political agendas, paving the way for the revolutionary transformation of daily life, not only in the production of goods and services, but also in the relations among women, men, and children in their communities.

Andreas, Carol (1989). "People's Kitchens and Radical Organizing in Lima, Peru," *Monthly Review*, November, 12–21. Copyright © 1989 by Monthly Review Inc. Reprinted by permission of Monthly Review Foundation.

Issues such as sanitation, public health, transportation, childcare, education, food, and housing are essentially reproductive concerns that are particularly acute in cities where massive migration from the countryside occurs. New community structures generated out of these concerns prepare the poor to take collective responsibility for their lives.

A decade of economic crisis in Peru has spawned many such structures. The most notable of these are the People's Kitchens established by the urban poor. At least 1500 existed in Lima alone by the end of 1988. In each of these some 20 to 25 families pool resources and work cooperatively to help maintain family members and others who may be temporarily or permanently without a stable source of income.

Because most of those involved in the administration of People's Kitchens are women, the growing importance of these organizations has given women a new source of political power, a new sense of self-esteem, and the experience of radical praxis in political struggle against the state.

Background and Development

The People's Kitchens in Lima have their roots in the *olla común* (common pot), prepared during fiestas and community work projects in native communities in the countryside. The *olla común* is also traditionally prepared in support of striking workers in mines and factories, especially when families accompany workers on *marchas de sacrificio*, in which workers walk for days or weeks to confront government officials with their demands.

Another antecedent of the People's Kitchens can be found in the Mothers' Clubs established by the government and the Catholic Church (using surplus commodities from the United States). Some of these date from the 1950s and the 1960s. The Clubs were established to gain the political support of women and to establish a relationship of what Peruvians call *asistencialismo* — welfare clientelism. These programs "corraled" women with the enticement of individual allotments of basic food supplies such as cooking oil and flour, as well as certain sought-after items such as nylon hose, plastic kitchenware, and sewing supplies. In the 1970s, some Mothers' Clubs escaped the bounds of *asistencialismo* and became centers for grassroots organizing efforts aided by progressive nuns influenced by the Popular Church movement and feminism.

The first People's Kitchens in the *barriada* of Comas (Lima) were organized in 1979. Some women were able to utilize food allotments provided by Caritas, a Catholic relief service, even though collective utilization of Caritas' assistance was prohibited in other places by conservative church officials. Since the husbands of many women were hostile to the idea at first, and mothers were reluctant to be away from their homes for extended periods, the program operated out of individual homes. Families donated big cooking pots and other supplies, and women prepared meals for each neighborhood entirely on the basis of rotating labor. Those who were *socios*, or members of the program, came by to receive prepared food and carry it to their own homes.

Weekly meetings of those responsible for the planning, shopping, and cooking for People's Kitchens, and less frequent meetings of the entire membership, determined how much labor and/or money participants owed and on what basis free food and other assistance could be provided to the elderly, orphans, or others who couldn't contribute to the program for whatever reason. As the program expanded and became more centralized at the district level, and eventually at the city-wide level, those who planned menus were required to attend seminars in nutrition given by local health professionals. Savings were also effected, where possible, by organizing *almacenes* or food warehouses so that extra costs due to price speculation by individual businesses or market vendors could be avoided.

The Organization and Politics of People's Kitchens

People's Kitchens are often organized in buildings or rooms that previously served some other purpose, such as a clinic or school. Several women serve as "permanent staff" for a period of time and receive four or five portions of free meals for their families each day in return for their efforts. Others pay either by the meal or in advance. In some cases, outsiders such as workers from nearby factories come to eat at the People's Kitchen regularly and pay a higher price than *socios*. On weekends the locale is used by individuals or groups to serve meals to the general public as a way of earning money for neighborhood causes or personal needs.

Young people support the People's Kitchens through volunteer labor and through helping connect the organization with other neighborhood programs such as literacy classes and political education.

While in most cases leaders of the People's Kitchens bring to these organizations years of neighborhood organizing experience and a certain amount of political sophistication, many *socios* are shy at first about speaking at meetings or taking initiative or responsibility. Over the years, such women have been transformed by their participation in the People's Kitchens. Not only have they come to be outspoken and self-confident, they are critical of those who used the Kitchens for personal profit and of those who attempted to manipulate the community's neediness to promote outside interests.

Fernando Belaúnde, who preceded Alán García as president of Peru, received U.S. government support in setting up official versions of the People's Kitchens, where inexpensive meals would be provided under government auspices. There was much fanfare over the establishment of several government-sponsored *comedores* (eating places). However, this token effort did not undermine the People's Kitchen movement but instead encouraged the women to demand government support of their own efforts.

The existence of People's Kitchens that were not subservient to the central government was important in the success of another *barriada* program, initiated by the Left Unity mayor of Lima in 1984. Alfonso Barrantes secured foreign assistance (but not from the United States) in order to provide a glass of milk daily for children and nursing mothers in the *barriadas*. Local women's committees were set up to administer the program, which was centralized in an overall Emergency Plan. This caused chaos in the *barriadas*, as many party men resisted turning local power over to the women's committees, which were thought to be insufficiently loyal to Left Unity. In many cases, committee membership overlapped with that of the *comedores populares* or People's Kitchens. When Barrantes was no longer mayor, the Glass of Milk Committees struggled to retain autonomy from the ruling APRA party and still receive powdered milk allotments.

More often than not, food assistance from the Church and/or the government has been cut off whenever People's Kitchens begin to show solidarity with other causes by sheltering political refugees or organizing marches to make demands on the government. It is this process, more than anything else, that radicalized many members. In the end, most Kitchens have been forced to "go it alone." In Villa El Salvador, 156 such *comedores* became the core of the Popular Women's Federation of the *barriada*. Nearly half the *socios* were the sole support of their families (that is, single mothers). The People's Kitchens helped free these women to work outside their homes.

In 1985, when the female-based organizations of Villa El Salvador and other *barriadas* of Lima attempted to get official recognition from the city-wide Federation of New Towns (*barriadas*), organized primarily by the Left Unity electoral coalition, they were told to go home.[1] The women persisted, however, and female political party members eventually found it necessary to work within the People's Kitchens in order to legitimize themselves as political leaders. The myriad of political parties of the left attempting to win support among the *socios* of the People's Kitchens gave rise to political debates about the function of these Kitchens beyond the provision of low-cost food for the families who benefited from them. Thus, the process of centralization further radicalized some of the women who were involved in organizing People's Kitchens, even as it gave rise to internal conflicts.

By 1987, the People's Kitchens were experiencing a leadership crisis. Centralization of the movement was resulting in disputes over who were the legitimate representatives of the coordinating bodies. Some were accused of being "terrorists" (in this case, Shining Path guerrillas). Others were accused of being conciliatory with APRA. Women sympathetic to Shining Path had been slow to involve themselves in the People's Kitchen movement. However, as Church and government participation became marginal or nonexistent within the movement, women who had been influenced by Shining Path began to take part in the organizations and to work to redirect them away from any remaining forms of *asistencialismo*.

Feminists were active in seeing the People's Kitchen movement through its initial political crises. Their involvement has been most effective when feminists are *pobladores* themselves, which is not as unusual in Peru today as it would have been even six or eight years ago. Feminists began to see the People's Kitchen movement as a potential springboard for women's agendas, ranging from a critique of public policies relating to reproductive rights, marital issues, and issues of violence toward women, to the legitimizing of collective domestic work.

In August 1988, the Peruvian government reinitiated a temporary work program that had been forced to close down earlier because of scandalous misappropriation of funds. Critics had also charged that workers were used to break unions and to engage in activities specifically in support of APRA. The recreated temporary work program is modeled after OFASA, a work-relief program for *barriada* women administered by the Seventh-Day Adventist Church. (As in the case of Caritas, this program enjoys the support of the U.S. government.) According to grassroots leaders in the *barriadas*, these programs are aimed primarily at disrupting non-governmental programs such as the People's Kitchen movement. Over 80 percent of those employed by the government work programs are female. Because these women work mainly cleaning up garbage dumps in the *barriadas*, they are unusually susceptible to bacterial infections. *Socios* of the Kitchens complain that by the time women have finished working in government programs they are so sick they can't help with the work in the *comedores populares*, yet are in need of the services these provide.

During the past two years the coordinating bodies of the People's Kitchens, Glass of Milk Committees, and Mothers' Clubs in Lima have waged periodic campaigns to demand that their programs be financed, at least in part, directly from government coffers. The demands were at first met with defiance and repression on the part of the government. However, a new National Program for Food Assistance has been implemented. It is based in part on the issuance of food stamps for the "truly needy." Thousands of other women have also been attracted to newly-established *comedores* sponsored directly by APRA, and *apristas* have taken over many *comedores* which used to be considered autonomous.

Electoral politics in 1989 has turned many People's Kitchens into centers for the organization of conservative forces. Welfare clientelism is rampant. But other forces are also at work.

As the food crisis continues in the cities, some urban migrants are returning to rural areas. Noncommercial avenues of food distribution and the "requisitioning" of trucks carrying food products to urban markets are reportedly increasing.

Organizations born in the *barriadas* are more than a reflection of workplace struggles. I think it is more useful to view them as direct expressions of popular discontent over issues of reproduction rather than production. These expressions bring into the political arena new social forces, predominantly female rather than male, and a new kind of revolutionary vision, not necessarily less radical than that of the urban work force.

It has often been assumed that the primary locus for revolutionary change is at the point of production, among those who work for wages in strategic industries. Political economists have also tended to take as given an ever-increasing demand for labor in an expanding economy.

The inexorable expansion of industry provides the main basis for working-class political power, even as periodic recessions are necessary for economic readjustment in capitalist societies. But conditions in debt-ridden "developing" countries are quite different. While workers on strike are a constant threat to stability, both government repression and efforts at "pacification" are often centered in working-class neighborhoods rather than at the workplace. In the neighborhoods, popular organization is facilitated by geographic concentration of the poor. Students, housewives, and unemployed workers are more active politically on a regular basis than are those employed in urban industries. The interests of these groups are also identified more closely with the interests of the rural poor. This is especially true in countries like Peru, where recent arrivals to the city are discriminated against as Indians. All these factors are important in assessing the significance of People's Kitchens in Peru and elsewhere.

It should be emphasized that the development of People's Kitchens in Peru has not been "spontaneous." Obstacles encountered by the women involved — from husbands, from political parties of both the left and the right, and even from within their own ranks as charges of opportunism and betrayal threatened to destroy their movement — have been at times overwhelming. However, many leaders have been able to resist cooptation and repression. Where women have succumbed to external or internal pressures, or retired from active involvement, often others have emerged to replace them.

Conclusion

In Peru, as People's Kitchens have assumed an ever more visible role in maintaining the physical well-being and promoting the collective strength of *pobladores*, the recognition of women's importance as political actors has been immeasurably advanced. And the possibility of a democratically-based revolution encompassing the larger concerns of families in their homes and communities as well as workers in the wage economy has also come into clearer focus.

ENDNOTES

[1] Cecelia Blondet, *Muchas Vidas Construyendo una Identidad: Mujeres Pobladoras de un Barrio Limeño,* Documento de Trabajo No. 9 (Lima: Instituto de Estudios Peruanos (IEP), January, 1986), p. 61.

11.2   Benedict Kerkvliet

Everyday Resistance to Injustice in a Philippine Village

INTRODUCTION

People deal with their lack of power in many ways, ranging from resistance and protest, to crime, acquiescence and retreat. We saw all of these responses in excerpt 4.4 on the black underclass in America.

The words "resistance" and "protest" conjure up images of organized groups fighting against injustice. However, resistance and protest are not always organized or easily visible. Kerkvliet, the author of the next excerpt, believes unorganized, individual acts of resistance can also be effective forms of protest. In the Philippine village of San Ricardo, he finds individual "everyday resistance" to be common.

"Everyday resistance" is anything people do to express anger or opposition to what they regard as unfair treatment by people who hold power over their lives. This definition allows for a wide variety of acts: singing derogatory songs about the boss when he isn't around, "foot-dragging" on the job, even sabotaging the farm machinery of a miserly employer. What all acts of everyday resistance have in common is that they are unorganized.

Why this response? In the rural Philippines, poor people are uncertain about how to press for a better livelihood and more dignity. More important, they are afraid of government reprisals against protestors. In this kind of atmosphere, everyday resistance may be the only way the poor can demand a fairer share of rewards.

While studying in a Philippine village named San Ricardo for eleven months in 1978–79, I tried to be aware of various ways people might indicate discontent with their conditions.[1]

I tried to discover the bases upon which people justify to themselves and possibly to others the hostile, angry, or indignant reactions they have to what other people or institutions do to them.

Reprinted by permission from the second issue volume thirteen of *The Journal of Peasant Studies*, published by Frank Cass and Company Limited, 11 Gainsborough Road, London EII, England. Copyright Frank Cass and Co. Ltd.

Everyday Resistance: A Definition

"Everyday resistance" refers to what people do short of organised confrontation that reveals disgust, anger, indignation, or opposition to what they regard as unjust or unfair actions by others more wealthy or powerful than they. Through such resistance people struggle to affirm what they regard as just or fair — or less unjust, less unfair — treatment and conditions. They are expressions of people who perceive injustice but for various reasons are unable or unwilling to push for improvements in an organised, direct manner.

This definition only includes acts against or at the expense of individuals, groups, or institutions of or symbolic of better off or more powerful classes than those who are resisting.

By definition, everyday resistance is done by individuals and small groups with little leadership. Resistance that involves co-ordination among large numbers of people and a set of leaders is not "everyday."

What is resisted are often specific individuals or institutions such as a certain moneylender, landowner, government official, or governmental agency, but it can also be a general condition. To the extent the target is rather specific, those who resist imagine their actions would not be condoned by the target.

Two contending values for which there is evidence from several parts of the Philippines are that people are entitled to be treated with dignity and entitled to livelihood. I shall refer to these as entitlement norms.

These entitlement norms are ambiguous. What exactly constitutes livelihood, dignity, and bringing them together, livelihood with dignity? The better-off should help the poor but what constitutes help? There is considerable room for interpretation. In political terms, this means probing, testing, and struggle among those with alternative, often conflicting sets of values and interpretations about how values should be practiced. Here we can find everyday resistance.

Background for Everyday Resistance

In order to appreciate the context in which everyday resistance occurs, I shall highlight six points. First, society in San Ricardo has become much more complex than it was one or two generations ago. Economic diversity, competition for scarce work, and frequent moving in and out of the village has made such community customs as mutual aid and exchange labour difficult to sustain.

Second, paternalistic relationships that once characterised relations between large landowners (landlords) and share tenants are nearly gone. Share tenancy is now the exception rather than the rule. Most tenant farmers in San Ricardo and vicinity are leasehold (*namumuwisan*). Rather than giving the landowner a certain percentage of the harvest as share tenants did, leasehold tenants pay a fixed amount (in cash or *palay*). This means landlords can make no claims on tenants (other than the rent), but it also means that, unlike before, tenants can make no claims on them.

Third, within the last decade, new hybrid varieties of rice have almost completely displaced previous seeds. The new varieties require enormous amounts of cash (especially for chemical fertilisers and insecticides). But capital is scarce, and interest rates from moneylenders are high.

Fourth, poverty is widespread. About 30 percent of San Ricardo's households live virtually hand-to-mouth. Another 60 percent usually have enough rice and vegetables to avoid hunger and frequently have cash to meet small necessities. For big expenditures or emergencies, they need to borrow. Only about ten percent of the households have ample food, well-constructed homes, and otherwise enjoy some comforts of life. A few here are very wealthy even by urban standards.

Fifth, San Ricardo was in the thick of unrest that grew in the 1930s as peasants protested against landlords who changed the terms of tenancy and against the government for supporting the landlords. This evolved into the Huk rebellion, which dominated politics in the region between the mid-1940s and mid-1950s (Kerkvliet, 1977).

Sixth, although no soldiers or police are in San Ricardo and its vicinity, people know that the central government can swiftly react to visible, organised signs of discontent. And, villages generally hold, the government is run by and for the benefit of well-to-do sectors of society.

The significance of these points is that even though the need for better living conditions is great, it is not clear to people where and how claims to livelihood with dignity can be made. Many previous customs helping to assure at least subsistence have disappeared with the demise of paternalist relations with landowners and the increased complexity of society. Moreover, because cash and capital have become necessities, sheer subsistence is often inadequate for one's livelihood. The Huk legacy remains an inspiration to many villagers, as a period when "little people" organised against oppression, but it was easier then to identify the oppressors — unscrupulous landlords, vicious soldiers, the police. Now it is often unclear who or what to blame for impoverishment and degradation. Besides, during the rebellion many died and suffered tremendous hardship. The price for standing up was high and would undoubtedly be so again were villagers to attempt to organise today.

Entitlement Norms

Generally, it is to one's advantage to have a favourable reputation among people with less means. Otherwise, in the words of one middle-aged tenant farmer, "that stingy fellow [who has means] is likely to be picked on, stolen from, even hurt by the poor people."

For instance, two Tinio families, large landowners who evicted numerous tenant families in the 1950s–60s in order to mechanise farming operations and whom many in San Ricardo regard as the epitome of selfishness and insensitivity, no longer live in the village but maintain large houses where family members stay while visiting their hacienda. But they will not remain in the area after dusk because, as some villagers said, "they wouldn't dare," or as one Tinio member told me, "it's too dangerous." This man also said that unless the family hires guards (usually not from the area) during harvests, San Ricardo people "rob us blind," sneaking into the vast fields at night to harvest. Confirming this to me, several villagers explained that they are not stealing; they are "just taking" a little rice because "we have none ourselves" and because the landowning family "is so mean."

Loans of money or rice with interest rates that are "too high" are, as one elderly tenant said wryly, the kind that "don't deserve to be paid back." One local moneylender went broke because, in her words, "ungrateful borrowers" never repaid several thousand pesos she had loaned. She received little sympathy from others who tended to say that she deserves her fate because the interest rate she charged was extremely high.

Another example of what a reputation can mean for better off people involves the quality of *miryenda* (snacks). When a landholder arranges through a *kabisilya* (labour recruiter and foreman) for planters, miryenda is not part of the agreement. But it is customary for the landholder to provide it at mid-morning and mid-afternoon. What the landholder serves is her choice. If the *miryenda* is cheap, planters may grumble, especially if they believe the landholder can afford to "be a little generous." In 1979, complaining planters in a couple of fields went so far as to refuse to resume planting the fields of stingy landholders and marched to the fields of owners who were giving tasty *miryenda*.

There are, of course, limits. Transplanters who drag their feet when working for a landholder serving lousy miryendas might be replaced next time with others more desperate for work. And if no planters in the vicinity are to a landholder's liking, others might be imported from distant villages. The same goes for harvesters and other landless workers. Landholders, though, who ignore landless villagers can expect to hear about unflattering names that they are called or even to discover one morning that part of their field was harvested during the night.

Struggle involving entitlement norms is also reflected in other problems between transplanters and landholders. Landholders sometimes become careless about how they speak to transplanters, calling them lazy, stupid, or worse (for example, devils, animals). Or they might harshly criticise some workmanship. Transplanters often respond to such rudeness by purposefully planting sloppily or slowing down. There are also instances of planters abruptly leaving and refusing to return until the landholder apologises. The same thing can occur in other work settings such as distant construction sites where San Ricardo residents are sometimes hired.

Entitlement norms are also expressed in controversies regarding land use. The two haciendas from which many tenants were evicted in the 1950s–60s have lately gone unplanted or only partially planted with sugar cane rather than *palay*.[2] The strong sentiment in San Ricardo is that "it's not right" for land to sit idle while "so many here are landless," reduced, as many say, "to living like chickens" scratching about for kernels. Twice in recent years fires have occurred in the sugar cane field. Arsonists did it, claim the Tinios. Some residents indicate arson is a possibility because people are angry at the inconsiderate and greedy (*matakaw*) Tinios.[3]

By custom, pasturing one's goats and carabao, foraging for edible wild plants and shellfish, and gleaning after harvest are permissible in any unplanted field, no matter who owns it. Sometimes landowners try to interfere and say that people are "trespassing" or are "destroying the dikes." Frequently people will leave but later, when the owner is not around, return to forage or pasture their animals. "It is not right to keep me out," complained one lady who had defiantly returned to a field she had previously been told to leave. "My family needs something to eat."

Entitlement is also expressed in justifications poor people have for taking from the better off. This "taking" can be a way for people both to assert their right to a livelihood and to blame better off people for their impoverishment. Landlords and former tenants alike tell about how tenants used to take grain surreptitiously from fields prior to the actual harvest. Tenants justify this on grounds that their shares were too small or the landlord was too strict and lacked consideration. They also defend their deed by saying the landholder "can afford" to lose a little grain.

Another expression of the entitlement norm are reasons people sometimes have for not paying certain debts, rents, and fees. An illustration concerns several *Masagana*-99 borrowers. Started in the mid-1970s, Masagana-99 is a government programme to extend loans to peasants who cannot otherwise qualify for bank loans because they lack collateral. In the first year or two of the programme, about 30 landholders from San Ricardo had Masagana-99 loans. By 1979, however, only eight continued to qualify. The others no longer did because they had not fully repaid previous loans. Their reasons were that due to poor crops or extraordinary family expenses (usually large medical bills), they had considerably less income to meet family needs and to pay all claimants.

Expecting that many households throughout the province would be unable to pay, villagers surmised — correctly — that the banking and governmental offices lacked adequate staffs to track down most delinquents. Possibly Masagana-99 itself would collapse, as so many governmental programmes have. Some borrowers also thought the government might or *should* give them consideration and not demand repayment. Especially important to many is their low regard for the Rural Bank through which they had received their loans. Besides having to wait weeks and make numerous trips to the bank before actually receiving the loan, they had to purchase the required fertiliser and other chemicals from a store owned by the bank's managing family, an illegal arrangement about which people felt powerless to do anything directly. Not repaying loans, so long as no repercussions came down on them, was a way to get back at the bank and the fertiliser store.

Significantly, people did not cut their family expenditures to bare bones subsistence in an attempt to meet all claims on their income. Some probably could have reduced expenses without going hungry had they wanted to pay their Masagana-99 loans. But they did not reduce drastically. They seem to be saying they are entitled to what they have and maybe even a little more. They will not forego that in order to pay everything that was claimed of them.

The view that a family is entitled to more than subsistence and that claims should be somewhat flexible is a view of justice. It asserts that people have a right to live like human beings, not animals, and this means having enough resources in order to live with dignity.

Conclusion

In San Ricardo, there is a friction due to entitlement norms rubbing abrasively against values that encourage individuals and families to scramble to accumulate material goods and wealth. Most villagers experience conflicting values within themselves and may attempt to act according to both. It would be incorrect to say that the better off hold the acquisitive values while only the poorer ones have entitlement norms. The everyday resistance discussed in this article, however, reflects poorer residents' efforts, based on entitlement norms, to qualify and shape their relations with those who are better off.

Practising entitlement ideas has been more difficult in recent years. A generation ago share tenants had a right to help from their landlords. That system of land tenure is gone, however, and no longer do share tenants compose the bulk of society. Earlier, socio-economic divisions within the village and surrounding area were sharper, mainly between the numerous poor share tenants and the few prosperous landlords. Now distinctions are more gradual and complex. Hence, struggles involving entitlement norms frequently occur in unfamiliar contexts and among people whose socio-economic differences are less pronounced.

Entitlement norms come from the past. But then, so do rival ideas reinforcing self-enrichment and success. The meaning of entitlement has not remained constant. Its content and how and where it should be practised are changing with new influences. Villagers have been attempting not only to maintain a standard of subsistence that was appropriate for an earlier period but to reach beyond it to some of what other sectors of society take for granted. The idea that education, sturdy housing, sanitation, and regular income are necessities — something the dominant classes have long enjoyed — has worked its way into San Ricardo people's thinking and is beginning to be expressed in entitlement terms when villagers associate these with human dignity and decent livelihood.

Everyday resistance often brings important gains to the poor. The miserably paid workers' acts of defiance often help them to assert their humanity and put rice on the table. Second, the cumulative effects of everyday resistance can thwart the plans of those with more power and status. A small example from San Ricardo is that individuals' persistent day-by-day opposition to landowners who try to keep them from pasturing, gleaning, and foraging in fallow land has sustained these practices. Finally, everyday resistance may help to nurture ideas of justice that can be the basis for far-reaching visions and protest movements in another time under different conditions.

ENDNOTES

[1] Names of people are fictitious. San Ricardo is located in Nueva Ecija province, about 150 kilometres north of Manila.

[2] The two families have other businesses and investments that are more lucrative, engaging, and, as they say, "less headache" than their haciendas. In addition, siblings in one family are quarrelling about whether to farm or sell the 200-hectare hacienda and how to divide either the land's harvests or the land itself.

[3] Signs of discontent became serious enough in 1978–79 to prompt village officials to petition the Ministry of Agrarian Reform to subject the haciendas to land reform. Some in San Ricardo are hopeful this will succeed. More, however, doubt it will ever happen.

REFERENCES

Kerkvliet, Benedict J. (1977). *The Huk Rebellion.* Berkeley: University of California Press.

11.3   Daniel Bart-Tal

Delegitimization: Ideologies of Conflict and Ethnocentrism

INTRODUCTION

Stereotyping and discrimination are commonplace when groups interact. In fact, they are among the most basic strategies powerful groups use to discredit the less powerful. For this reason, disadvantaged groups often must debunk the false assumptions that perpetuate stereotypes and "rationalize" discrimination, to make their case for a better lot in life.

In the next excerpt, Daniel Bar-Tal drives home these points by analyzing international examples of extreme stereotyping and discrimination. The author shows how powerful groups use a process of "delegitimization" against others. Through this process, the powerful ingroup comes to see the outgroup as less than fully human: deserving of social exclusion and, even, aggressive attack. This is what the outgroup is up against in its efforts to protest and promote change.

Drawing on theories of conflict and ethnocentrism (the idea that one's own group is superior), the author shows cases of delegitimization always begin with perceptions of threat to

Bart-Tal, Daniel (1990). "Causes and Consequences of Delegitimization: Models of Conflict and Ethnocentrism," *Journal of Social Issues*, 46(1), 65–81. Reprinted by permission.

the ingroup from the outgroup. Delegitimization tends to intensify this sense of threat, rather than weaken it. That is because any acts that strengthen group cohesion by drawing clearer group boundaries also strengthen the sense of distance and separation from other groups.

Put another way, the search for spies, witches, or devils in our midst will certainly find (and punish) enemies, however imaginary. It will also arouse intense fear of retribution.

The concept, *delegitimization,* describes *categorization of a group or groups into extremely negative social categories that are excluded from the realm of acceptable norms and/or values* (Bar-Tal, 1988, 1989a). Delegitimization permits moral exclusion. The most common means of delegitimization, which are not mutually exclusive, are:

1. *Dehumanization:* labeling a group as inhuman by characterizing members as different from the human race — using either categories of subhuman creatures, such as "inferior races" and animals, or categories of negatively valued superhuman creatures, such as demons, monsters, and satans.

2. *Trait characterization:* describing a group as possessing extremely negative traits such as aggressors, idiots, or parasites.

3. *Outcasting:* categorizing members of a group as transgressors of such pivotal social norms that they should be excluded from society and/or institutionalized — e.g., murderers, thieves, psychopaths, or maniacs.

4. *Use of political labels:* describing a group as a political entity that threatens the basic values of the given society — e.g., Nazis, fascists, communists, or imperialists.

5. *Group comparison:* labeling with the name of a group that is negatively perceived, such as "Vandals" or "Huns."

Delegitimization (a) utilizes extremely negative, salient, and atypical bases for categorization, (b) denies the humanity of the delegitimized group, (c) is accompanied by intense, negative emotions of rejection, (d) implies the delegitimized group has the potential to endanger one's own group, and (e) implies the delegitimized group does not deserve human treatment and therefore harming it is justified.

The present paper explores the phenomenon of delegitimization by analyzing its causes and consequences. Two models are described —the conflict model and the ethnocentric model.

The Conflict Model

Every intergroup conflict begins with the perception that one group's goals are incompatible with the goals of another group (Bar-Tal, Kruglanski, and Klar, 1989; Pruitt and Rubin, 1986). The perception that a conflict exists means a group finds itself blocked because the attainment of its goal or goals is precluded by another group.

FIGURE 1   CONFLICT MODEL: FAR-REACHING
INCOMPATIBILITY OF GOALS

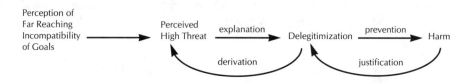

Two conditions in a conflict most frequently incite delegitimization: perception of the outgroup's goals as contradictory, far-reaching, and sinister; and the occurrence of extreme violence.

Threat and Delegitimization

An ingroup experiences threat when it perceives it cannot easily achieve its goals because of outgroup opposition. (See Figure 1.) The crucial questions in explaining the appearance of delegitimization in the early phase of conflict are: (a) How are the goals of the opponent perceived? (b) What is the nature of one's own goals that are perceived as blocked?

The first proposition is that *when a group perceives that the negating goal(s) of an outgroup is (are) far-reaching, especially unjustified, and threatening to the basic goals of the ingroup, then the ingroup uses delegitimization to explain the conflict.* These aspects are linked; when the goals of the outgroup are perceived as outrageous, farfetched, irrational, and malevolent, they are also seen as negating fundamental ingroup goals and therefore as threatening.

Usually this is a zero-sum type of conflict. The perception that the outgroup will achieve its goals poses a danger to the very existence of the ingroup. The danger can be economic, political, or military.

Threat perception in general is accompanied by stress, uncertainty, vulnerability, and fear. These feelings arouse the need to understand and structure the situation quickly, thus allowing explanation and prediction (Y. Bar-Tal, 1989). Delegitimization fulfills this function. It explains why the other group threatens and predicts what the other group will do in the future. (See Figure 1.)

Figure 1 illustrates this situation where the ingroup uses delegitimization to explain the outgroup's enraging aspirations and demands. As examples, delegitimizing labels provide an explanation to Poles about why German Nazis decided to occupy their country, or to Americans about why the Soviet Union strives to dominate the world. Who else would do such things other than a group that is imperialistic, satanic, or fascistic?

Once employed, delegitimization leads to inferences of threat from the delegitimizing category. (See Figure 1.) Thus, the labels "aggressive," "ruthless," "devious," or "oppressive" indicate the outgroup is capable of destruction, violence, or brutality, and this further disrupts the ingroup's sense of security. In this way, the perception of severe threat and delegitimization feed each other.

Delegitimization and Harm

In most serious conflicts, delegitimization leads to harm. Once the ingroup delegitimizes the outgroup with labels that imply threat and evil — "imperialists," "fascists," "terrorists" — acts for preventing danger usually follow. Because the outgroup is delegitimized, preventive measures can be severe, for delegitimized groups are perceived as not deserving human treatment. Deportations, destruction, and mass killings of civil populations are not unusual in these cases. An example of this phenomenon was provided in an insightful statement by an American soldier in the Vietnam War:

> When you go into basic training you are taught that the Vietnamese are not people. You are taught they are gooks, and all you hear is "gook, gook, gook, gook...." The Asian serviceman in Vietnam is the brunt of the same racism because the GIs over there do not distinguish one Asian from another.... You are trained "gook, gook, gook" and once the military has got the idea implanted in your mind that these people are not humans, they are subhuman, it makes it a little bit easier to kill 'em. (Boyle, 1972, p. 141)

Exceptionally violent and harmful actions by the ingroup augment the delegitimization because they seem to justify further actions that exceed normative behavior. (See Figure 1.) The more violent the behavior, the more delegitimization occurs because more justification is needed to explain the harm done. In addition, violent acts of the delegitimized group during confrontation reinforce delegitimization because they explain the deviant and extreme behavior of the delegitimizing group. Thus, the second proposition states that *a violent conflict leads to delegitimization to justify and explain it*.

A current example of delegitimization based on far-reaching incompatibility of goals exists in the Middle East. Israeli Jews and Palestinians persistently delegitimize each other to explain the threat that each group poses to the other and to justify the harm they inflict on each other (Bar-Tal, 1988, in press a). Both groups have struggled for the same land over the present century, and today, despite attempts to bridge the irreconcilable goals, the conflict continues.

The protracted conflict intensified the perception of threat and caused mutual attempts to exclude the other group from the community of nations through delegitimization. The continuing mutual harm and violence has strengthened the delegitimization process. The Palestinians label Israeli Jews as "colonialists," "racists," "aggressors," "Nazis," "imperialists," "fascists," and "oppressors." They call them "Zionists," and consider Zionism a "colonialist movement in its inception, aggressive and expansionist in its goals, racist and segregationist in its configurations, and fascist in its means and aims" (Article 19 in the National Covenant of the Palestine Liberation Organization (PLO) — Harkabi, 1979).

The Israeli Jews, from the beginning of their encounters with Palestinians, viewed them as primitive, bandits, cruel mobs, and failed to recognize their national identity. Later, with the eruption of violence, they delegitimized

FIGURE 2   CONFLICT MODEL: DETERIORATION

FIGURE 3   ETHNOCENTRIC MODEL

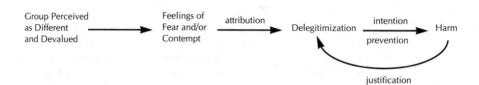

Palestinians with labels such as "robbers," "criminals," "gangs," "anti-Semites," "terrorists," and "neo-Nazis." In the last decades, special efforts have been made to delegitimize members and sympathizers of the PLO, which represents the national aspirations of the Palestinians. On September 1, 1977, the Knesset of Israel adopted a resolution by a vote of 92–4 saying

> The organization called the PLO aspires, as stated in its Covenant, to destroy and ex-terminate the State of Israel. The murder of women and children, and terror, are part of this organization's ideology, which it is implementing in practice.

Not all conflicts begin with far-reaching incompatibility between the goals of the parties involved. Conflicts may also begin with less incompatibility that does not involve a high level of threat. Although such a situation can continue as a stalemate for a long time, this can also escalate into violent confrontation.

As Figure 2 shows, delegitimization emerges from violence because an ingroup needs to justify and explain harm perpetrated by its members, as well as explain similar acts performed by the members of the outgroup.

The Ethnocentric Model

Delegitimization does not occur only in conflict. A group may also attribute dele-gitimizing labels to another group as a result of ethnocentrism. Ethnocentrism, a term introduced by Sumner (1906), denotes a tendency to accept the ingroup and reject outgroups. Delegitimization can serve this tendency. Using delegitimization, ingroup members see themselves as virtuous and superior, and the outgroup as contemptible and inferior (LeVine and Campbell, 1972).

Figure 3 illustrates how the ethnocentric tendency can foster delegitimization. Nevertheless, a necessary mediating condition for delegitimization is fear and/or contempt toward the outgroup. Subsequently, delegitimization can engender harm when the ingroup attempts to prevent the danger implied by the delegitimizing label, or to treat the outgroup inhumanely, "as deserved."

Ethnocentrism and Delegitimization

Delegitimization is used in extreme cases of ethnocentrism because it maximizes intergroup differences and totally excludes the delegitimized group from commonly accepted groups, implying a total superiority of the ingroup. It denies the humanity of the outgroup.

A mere perception of difference and devaluation does not lead necessarily to exclusion, for arousal of fear and/or contempt for the outgroup is also necessary. (See Figure 3.) The third proposition states *delegitimization is used when a group perceives another group as different and devalued, and feels fear of it and/or contempt for it.*

The more the two groups differ, the easier it is to delegitimize. The most salient differences are based on physical appearance because they enable a clear distinction and an easy identification. Thus, skin color, physiognomic features, hair color, body structure, or even dress permit unmistakable differentiation between groups. Throughout history, these differences were most often the bases for differentiation and delegitimization. People also differentiate and delegitimize on the basis of religion or ideology. In these cases, however, external identification may be impossible.

In addition to intergroup differences, devaluation is necessary for delegitimization to occur. Devaluation results from the ethnocentric tendency (Brewer and Campbell, 1976) for ingroup members to feel positive about their own group and attribute favorable characteristics to it, while feeling antipathy toward outgroups and attributing unfavorable characteristics to them. (See Adorno, Frenkel-Brunswik, Levinson, and Sanford, 1950.)

The final necessary condition, which not only evokes delegitimization but causes it, is fear and/or contempt. Fear is elicited when the different and devalued group presents a threat or a mysterious aspect. In this case, the ingroup uses delegitimization to explain their fear. (See Figure 3.) Feelings of contempt emerge when the outgroup is perceived as absolutely inferior, based on perceived cultural, economic, military, scientific, and/or political achievements.

There are two main reasons for ethnocentric delegitimization: first, the desire to completely differentiate the outgroup from the ingroup in order to exclude it from humanity; second, the desire to exploit the outgroup. These two reasons do not necessarily appear together.

A prime example of delegitimization used to rationalize exploitation is the enslavement of black people by white people. Delegitimization was, perhaps, the most important justification for slavery. Otherwise, how could the moral, deeply religious, and gallant Southerners have treated these people so inhumanely? Black people differed from whites in physical appearance, folkways and mores, religion, language, and culture, and these characteristics were also greatly devalued, so that black people were a perfect target for exploitation.

Stampp (1956) pointed to three beliefs that undergirded slavery: (a) the "all wise Creator" had designed black people for labor in the South; (b) being inferior in intellect and having a particular temperament, blacks were the natural slaves of white people; and (c) black people were barbarians who needed rigid discipline and control. These perceptions legitimized slavery in the Southern states.

The Intention and Justification of Harm

Once invoked, delegitimization can open the way to harm. Delegitimizing labels may indicate either that the delegitimized group is inhuman and therefore harming it is allowed, or that it is threatening and therefore, to prevent the danger, harm should be carried out. In addition, delegitimization may lead to intergroup conflicts. The goals of the ingroup and the outgroup may clash because of the superior and imperialistic feelings of the ingroup. Then, when harms are committed, delegitimization serves to justify inhumane treatment of the outgroup. (See Figure 3.)

The delegitimization of the American Indians facilitated cruel behavior toward them. Once they were labeled "savages," "inferior," or "animals," it was but a short distance to harm. Because "inferior" and "savage" men do not deserve human treatment, Europeans did not hesitate to destroy, to enslave, to drive them away, or to kill them.

The strengthening of delegitimization after harming others is illustrated in the development of defenses by white people to justify their enslavement of black people. Doctors, scientists, and phrenologists in the South searched for physiological differences to substantiate the assumed temperamental and intellectual differences:

> Dr. Samuel W. Cartwright of Louisiana argued that the visible difference in skin pigmentation is also extended to "the membranes, the muscles, the tendons, and ... [to] all the fluids and secretions. Even the negro's brain and nerves, the chyle and all the humors, are tinctured with a shade of the pervading darkness," and Dr. Josiah C. Nott of Mobile proposed that negroes and whites do not belong to the same species. (Stampp, 1956, p. 8)

One striking case of ethnocentric delegitimization that led to tragic consequences is the treatment of Jews in Germany between 1933–1945.

Between 1933 and 1945, Jews in Europe were subjected to exclusion, deportation, expropriation, expulsion, pogroms, mass killings, and ultimately genocide. During 1939–1945, about six million Jews perished as a consequence of starvation, deadly epidemics, mass executions, and systematic gassing. There is little doubt that as these actions were carried out, Germans justified them with delegitimizing beliefs, which first encouraged the atrocities and later supported and reinforced them.

Delegitimization, the exclusion of an outgroup and denial of its humanity, is a phenomenon with cognitive, affective, and behavioral aspects. On the cognitive level, delegitimization organizes "reality" by providing an explanation for the perceived characteristics and behaviors of the outgroup and a prediction of potential future events. On the emotional level, delegitimization is a reaction to feelings of fear, threat, or contempt stimulated by another group. Its occurrence not only strengthens these feelings, but also may provoke new negative emotions. On the behavioral level, delegitimization leads to an array of behaviors including malevolent treatment and preventive steps to avert potential danger to the ingroup. Delegitimization is also a consequence of brutal and cruel behavior because it serves as a justification mechanism.

Delegitimization, as an extreme case of stereotyping and prejudice, is a widespread phenomenon. Two related models of the process have focused on situations that elicit delegitimization: conflict and ethnocentrism. Delegitimization occurs in conflicts that involve a perception of far-reaching, outrageous, and incompatible goals between groups and/or a high level of brutal violence. Delegitimization occurs in ethnocentrism when an outgroup is perceived as very different and is devalued.

REFERENCES

Adorno, W., E. Frenkel-Brunswik, D. J. Levinson, and R. N. Sanford (1950). *The authoritarian personality*. New York: Harper & Row.

Bar-Tal, D. (1988). "Delegitimizing relations between Israeli Jews and Palestinians: A social psychological analysis," in J. Hofman (Ed.), *Arab-Jewish relations in Israel: A quest in human understanding* (pp. 217–248). Bristol, IN: Wyndham Hall.

——— (1989a). "Delegitimization: The extreme case of stereotyping and prejudice," in D. Bar-Tal, C. Graumann, A. W. Kruglanski, and W. Stroebe (Eds.), *Stereotyping and prejudice: Changing conceptions* (pp. 169–188). New York: Springer-Verlag.

——— (in press a). "Israeli-Palestinian conflict: A cognitive analysis," *International Journal of Intercultural Relations*.

Bar-Tal, D., A. W. Kruglanski, and Y. Klar, (1989). "Conflict termination: An epistemological analysis of international cases," *Political Psychology, 10,* 233–255.

Boyle, R. (1972). *The flower of the dragon: The breakdown of the U.S. Army in Vietnam*. San Francisco: Ramparts.

Brewer, M. B. and D. T. Campbell (1976). *Ethnocentrism and intergroup attitudes: East African evidence*. New York: Halsted.

LeVine, R. A. and D. T. Campbell (1972). *Ethnocentrism: Theories of conflict, ethnic attitudes and group behavior*. New York: Wiley.

Lieberman, E. J. (1964). "Threat and assurance in the conduct of conflict," in R. Fisher (Ed.), *International conflict and behavioral science* (pp. 110–122). New York: Basic Books.

Pruitt, D. G. and J. Z. Rubin (1986). *Social conflict*. New York: Random House.

Stampp, K. M. (1956). *The peculiar institution: Slavery in the ante-bellum South*. New York: Vintage.

Sumner, W. G. (1906). *Folkways*. New York: Ginn.

11.4   James Petras

Social Movements in Latin America

INTRODUCTION

If we think only of examples from within our own society, we might conclude that strong political protest movements occur rarely. After all, there are only so many political movements to consider in our society's history.

However, when we look at other societies, we find many examples of strong and successful protest movements. This is one of the lessons of the next selection by Petras.

In a sweeping comparison of Latin American countries over the last three decades, the author shows that political protest movements are very widespread; in fact, they are the norm rather than the exception. Moreover, this is true of several societies with repressive political regimes, where one might expect protest to be prevented by fear of the regime. The movements occur in part because of state repression and terrorism, Petras says. He goes on to enumerate a list of other reasons for the high level of political protest.

As you read this, you may want to think back to the excerpts on narco-terrorism in Latin America (excerpt 3.3) and political repression in Haiti (excerpt 10.1). All three excerpts, including the present one, show a political climate which, historically, has been characterized by violent repression, violent protest, and violent efforts by criminals to capture the state.

Т he most striking fact about revolutionary politics in Latin America is that its only socialist revolutions were not organized by political parties but by political movements. Neither the Communist Party of Cuba nor that of Nicaragua played a significant role in the making of these revolutions: the July 26th movement in Cuba and the Sandinista National Liberation Front in Nicaragua were the organizational forms through which the revolutionary forces were able to mobilize mass support, overthrow dictatorships, and consolidate the new revolutionary states.

The Latin American experience and history thus challenge the orthodoxy that a revolutionary party is essential to revolution. Nowhere in Latin America has the European/Soviet model of a party built around factory-based trade unions been successful in gaining mass hegemony and challenging the capitalist state.

Petras, James (1989). "State Terror and Social Movements in Latin America," *International Journal of Politics, Culture and Society*, 3(2), Winter, 179–212. Reprinted by permission.

The reasons for this have to do with the patterns of Latin American economic development, the nature of the social structure, the relationship between social movements and political class, and the new ideological currents which have emerged over the past three decades.

The Political Class

The political class is made up of those individuals who have a vocation for politics, particularly electoral politics. They are largely made up of professionals — lawyers, professors, business people, etc. — who engage in negotiations and transactions within established political institutions. Their shared norms of reciprocity and loyalties compromise their vertical ties with extraparliamentary groups.

The political class cuts across the social class structure, including in some cases trade union or popular leaders, but mainly upper and lower middle-class individuals. Entrance into the political class usually means entering the political culture of ministries, party bureaucracies, and state-private sector collaboration; as a corollary, it means abandoning the politics of mass organizing, social confrontation, and political rupture. For those individuals who rise from the social movements and retain ties to them, entering the political class creates serious and continuing tensions between the conflicting demands, styles of politics, norms of political practice, and class/institutional interests. There is no single factor that can explain the centrality of movements to revolutionary politics: their importance is the result of multiple determinations that have their origins in the socio-economic patterns and structures which are subsequently mediated by political-ideological relationships and processes. These different but interrelated factors must all be taken into account, otherwise we cannot explain why some movements develop with greater dynamism in different regions and times, and why some movements become the basis of revolutionary politics while others do not.

While there are significant variations in movement politics, practically all of the significant political changes that took place in Latin America in the 1960s and 1970s were the result of massive social movements and not of electoral processes or militarized guerrilla movements.

Movements of the 1960s to 1980s

Over the past 30 years social movements have been a major political force in Latin American politics, both as agents of social transformations and as objects of unprecedented violence. The dynamic qualities that have led movements to build vast networks of activists are the same as those that provoke the deep-seated hostility and opposition from the dominant classes. The striking contrast of our times is that Latin America, to an unprecedented degree, has experienced both the extension of popular democratic participation and the most systematic state repression since the Conquest.

The connection between popular democracy and state terror is not fortuitous. The deepening of movement-based popular democracy is linked to the erosion of bourgeois hegemony. This constitutes a challenge to the dominant role of the military-civilian political class. Movement politics reconstruct and strengthen civil society against the state. They strengthen horizontal social solidarity and challenge vertically structured markets. They counterpose direct political representation, and debate against indirect elite representation by the professional political class. Because movement politics resonate among the poor and cut so deeply against the grain of so many fundamental elite interests, they evoke the pathological violence of elites and the cohesion of the masses.

The growth of movement politics is not linear nor is it immune to influence by nonmovement political processes. Movements have risen in Chile (between 1965–1973), have been destroyed (1973–1982), have risen again (1983–1986), and ebbed (1986–1989). While the trajectory of the movements is not linear, there is a considerable accumulation of experience that is retained by opinion leaders and in the collective consciousness enabling movement action to be reconstructed at almost any time. Movements do not consistently advance forward and upward, but civilian and military regimes have been unable to impose enduring constraints on them. Neither the populists nor the liberals have been successful in incorporating them into their political machinery. At best, there are conjunctural convergences between the political class and the movements punctuated by tensions and countervailing claims, followed by cleavages and political divergences.

The determinant factor leading to all major societal transformations in Latin America over the past 30 years has been, directly or indirectly, the sociopolitical movements. The Nicaraguan and the Cuban *social revolutions* were led by movements (the July 26th Movement and the Sandinista Front for National Liberation), not by parties or by politicians from the electoral political class. The major *agrarian reforms* undertaken in Latin America — in Chile during the Frei-Allende period and in Peru — were preceded by an unprecedented degree of mass mobilization and direct action by non-parliamentary movements. The *displacement* of the region's *military rulers* was largely the product of mass popular movements, i.e., the *Cordobazo* and related uprisings in Argentina during 1969–1973, the mass popular struggles in Brazil during the early 1980s, the general strikes in Peru in the mid to late-1970s.

The *creation* of *new civil organizations* that have politicized previously uninvolved poor people has been largely the product of the social movements: in Colombia, with a rate of up to 65 percent of voter abstention from national elections, the social movements have created a massive network of local membership organizations that include many of the abstainers: in El Salvador and Guatemala, peasants and Indians overlooked or excluded by the electoral political class were deeply engaged in movement activity. The social movements have their own *autonomous political culture* that draws on diverse ideological traditions including liberation theology, movement Marxism, and classical democratic theory. Elite efforts to impose corporatist structures have been unsuccessful, undermined by democratic popular movements that exist side-by-side with authoritarian statist institutions. The *democratization* of Latin American *civil society has proceeded far in advance of the democratization of the state*.

The electoral regimes embedded in authoritarian states have generally been hostile to the movements, occasionally responsive to specific pressures and seldom in accordance with its strategic aims. The construction of civil society through the diverse movement organizations and actions has stimulated a tradition of popular participation, assemblies and elections without the limitations, and authoritarian constraints and elite alliances that characterize the transition to electoral regimes.

Recent examples of turns to electoral politics in Latin America are not complete transitions and are probably temporary. The class orientation of the electoral regimes with their commitments to the overseas bankers and local rich has been associated with a close working relationship with the military. The electoral class has initiated a process of militarization of politics to counteract the rising social movements, thus radicalizing political conflict. The neoliberal and reformist-nationalist policies have failed to stem both the economic decline and growing social polarization. As a consequence, the electoral regimes have been unable to consolidate power and establish hegemony over civil society.

On the other hand, it is clear that the defeats of the social movements over the past decade were conjunctural, not historic: the movements have not been destroyed, nor the populace atomized. In the late 1980s, the social movements are on the ascendancy everywhere, but at an uneven pace and with disparate political-economic characteristics in different countries.

In Chile and Mexico, the movements are demanding social and political democratization and attacking both the military and party dictatorships. The massive defeat of Pinochet in the plebescite and the exposure of the fraudulent victory of Salinas de Gortari in Mexico are the work of movement mobilization. The social movements are strong at the grassroots level but weaker at the national level, making them subject to manipulation by the political class in the immediate present. Both the ex-PRI leaders, grouped around Cárdenas in Mexico, and the Christian Democrats in Chile, offer limited opportunities for consolidating movement power. Nevertheless, the movements are playing a major role in undermining the existing political monopolies and are likely in the new electoral situation to reassert their socioeconomic demands against the political class.

In Argentina, Colombia, Guatemala, and Bolivia, the labor movements, civic organizations, and, in some cases, peasant movements have reemerged and have focused on "defensive economic struggles," trying to stem the decline in living standards, stop the privatization of industry, prevent the closing of public enterprises, and halt state encroachments on basic human rights.

In Brazil the movements are moving beyond "defensive" to offensive positions, challenging the power and prerogatives of the governing party and supporting radical political alternatives (PT, PTB) that promise to be responsive to movement demands for social-economic transformations. The limits of the electoral leadership of these parties, however, and their tendency to become "crisis managers," suggests that the "offensive" phase of movement politics may lead them to look for other than electoral solutions or revert to defensive struggles against their "own" elected representatives.

In El Salvador and Peru the popular movements are clearly on the offensive. The military power and political support of the FMLN in El Salvador have created a dual power structure challenging the disintegrating Christian Democratic party and the military rulers. In Peru, the social movements dominate major sectors of the society, including the main plazas and downtown streets, and are firmly entrenched in the urban slums and rural villages. The guerrillas are growing in numbers, have extended their network to the major cities, and openly appear at major public demonstrations: the regime and state are under "siege." In both countries conditions exist for a popular challenge to state power or the launching of a massive and bloody counter-reaction by the military and the dominant classes.

The movements thus occupy a central place in democratization processes and in the redefinition of the relationship between state and society. The movements have introduced a new tradition of political practice. We are now in the age of popular ideologies that classless politics cannot suppress or silence with slogans. It has been reinvigorated and found new sites for struggle, new forms of organization.

QUESTIONS

DISCUSSION QUESTIONS

1. Compare "dominant ideologies" and "counter ideologies" using examples chosen from the selections in this Section. Can you find any other examples in earlier sections?

2. By what means may counter-ideologies succeed in replacing dominant ideologies? Can you think of any examples?

3. Looking back to the material in Section 1, show how ideologies are aspects of "culture" but not identical to culture. What are the main differences between "culture" and "ideology?" Discuss using specific examples.

4. Define and discuss "delegitimization" following Bar-Tal's use of the term. Under what conditions might this strategy be used against alien life forms from outer space, and under what conditions might it not be used?

DATA COLLECTION EXERCISES

1. Using newspaper articles, identify some particular aspect of "counter ideology" in your society and indicate how the counter ideology calls for changes from existing

ways of doing things. Then, show how the ideology is presented in the articles; for example, is the treatment by the newspaper a fair and balanced one? Are any of the main ideas distorted in the articles?

2. Do the same exercise as in question #1, but for a "dominant ideology." Indicate how these ideas, and newspaper presentations of them, help support existing social arrangements.

3. Interview some of the administrators of any organization serving the poor in your community or region. Identify how the organization "empowers" the poor, if it does. Indicate ways of increasing empowerment.

4. Kerkvliet does not present much data to substantiate the idea that unorganized, individual acts of protest can be *effective* forms of resistance. Indicate how he (or you) could test this view.

WRITING EXERCISES

1. In Canada and the United States, "people's kitchens" are not at all common. Write a brief essay speculating on the reasons this form of social organization has not developed in North America.

2. Kerkvliet thinks "everyday resistance" is different from "deviance," as discussed in Section 3. Write a brief essay in which you indicate whether you agree or disagree, and why.

3. Choose any disadvantaged group in your society (e.g., the poor or lower classes, women, a minority racial or ethnic group, or the aged). Write a brief essay on ways they have been "delegitimatized."

4. Choose a political protest movement from Canada or elsewhere. Describe in a brief essay the social sources or explanations for the movement. Are the explanations similar to Petras' for Latin American protest movements?

SUGGESTED READINGS

1. Abercrombie, Nicholas, Stephen Hill, and Bryan S. Turner (1980). *The Dominant Ideology Thesis.* London: Allen and Unwin. A detailed analysis of theories on the role of ideology in supporting social inequalities, and in promoting social change.

2. Curtis, James, Edward Grabb, and Neil Guppy, eds. (1993). *Social Inequality in Canada: Patterns, Problems and Policies,* Second Edition. Scarborough: Prentice-Hall. Contains a series of articles that show how patterns of social inequality are rooted in ideological supports (including the law) and that changes in an egalitarian direction have usually required political struggles between have-nots and haves.

3. Hartz, Louis (1964). *The Founding of New Societies.* New York: Harcourt, Brace and World. Presents a theory about the origins of dominant political ideologies in

the United States, Canada, and other "new nations." These societies are said to be based on "fragments" of ideological approaches brought from Europe. The local elites drew on the traditional political philosophies in modified forms.

4. Parkin, Frank (1971). *Class, Inequality and Political Order.* London: McGibbon and Kee. A highly readable analysis of counter ideologies and dominant ideologies, their social roles, and their relationships to social class.

SOCIAL CHANGE

Introduction

Social change has become, as the twentieth century wanes, a conspicuous fact of life all around the world. Everywhere, it seems, the barriers to change are crumbling, albeit at differing rates and in differing ways, in response to differing pressures from one society to another. Because social change is so widespread (and so important), sociologists have taken pains to try to understand it.

Dimensions of Social Change

Social change obviously has many dimensions — ideological, cultural, economic, technological, political, and demographic. So one question sociologists ask is: how do these different dimensions interact with one another? How, for example, does technological change influence economic change? How does ideological change affect politics and vice versa? How do cultural changes lead to demographic changes? And so on.

The fact that these different aspects of social change are inter-related raises a tantalizing possibility in the minds of many would-be social reformers: the possibility that social change can be consciously manipulated by altering just a few "key" characteristics of the social structure. If change occurs in chain reactions, then maybe big improvements can be sparked by relatively small initial efforts.

This kind of thinking prompted, for example, the American economist W. I. Rostow to theorize in 1960 that economic development consists of "Five Stages of Growth." He said these comprise a traditional stage followed by a pre-takeoff stage, a take-off stage, a maturing stage, and finally by a stage of high mass consumption. Western societies such as Canada are in the last stage, by this formulation.

Rostow's advice was clear: to achieve affluence, first establish the pre-conditions necessary for economic take-off and then let economic forces do the rest. Part of the appeal of theories like Rostow's is that they make the task of development seem suddenly less daunting. In particular, such optimism fit the can-do mood of the 1960s, when many Third World countries were just embarking on their independence. If Rostow was right it was no longer necessary to contemplate closing the huge gap between affluent societies and poor ones overnight. It would simply happen in due course.

The immediate task was to get the process started, to reach the next stage of growth. And once take-off had occurred (at a relatively low level of affluence) eventual success — that is, a high consumption economy — was only a matter of time.

Theories such as Rostow's that look for the keys, catalysts, or levers of social change abound, but there is little consensus on whether a single prescription for producing social change in all (or most) societies even exists. Is the engine of economic growth started by different types of keys in different types of societies, or do all economies respond pretty much alike to the same treatment? That is the unanswered question!

This debate often surfaces when, for example, the International Monetary Fund (IMF) sends its experts in to advise a financially strapped nation on how to get its finances back in order. The IMF experts tend to prescribe economic remedies that have worked elsewhere while the host countries tend to seek more individualized remedies that are "sensitive to local conditions."

Nathan Keyfitz's excerpt in this section lends some support to the idea that there are keys to social change which work essentially the same way everywhere. He argues that one key factor in economic development is the universal desire for more and more, better and better material possessions. Once people anywhere have tasted even a little middle class affluence, they will undoubtedly hunger for more and evermore, Keyfitz believes. And so, this endless desire for more material wealth becomes the fuel that drives an economy, transforming it from a traditional society to a modern, mass consumption society.

Measuring Social Change

Since material affluence is universally sought, the best indicator of development (or progress) in theories like Keyfitz's is the amount of material wealth already amassed. The more cars, stereos, telephones, and refrigerators people have, the further along the development process a society has moved. There is a problem, though. The desire for material things is a key to stimulating economic growth but it is not, according to Keyfitz, an easily manipulated key. Once the key is turned, unexpected things can happen.

Sometimes, for example, the desire for material goods generates unrealistic attitudes and an impatience and greed that are not conducive to sound economic decision-making. The desire for middle class affluence is only the key that turns on the economic engine. It doesn't guarantee that the economy will be driven in the "right" direction — that is, that wealth will be distributed in a fair, sensible, or profitable manner.

The dynamism and often unpredictable nature of social change provide a backdrop for the second excerpt in this section. Melikan and Al-Easa's excerpt is about the way oil revenues are transforming the traditional Arab societies of the Persian Gulf. The excerpt raises another fundamentally important question about social change: once it starts, to what extent can social change be controlled, shaped, regulated, and directed? Given that the dimensions of social change are inter-related, is it realistic to expect that a society can pick and choose which aspects of change it will accept and which it will reject? Said another way, is being a "little bit modern" about as realistic as being a "little bit pregnant?"

This dilemma of how to separate the wanted and unwanted aspects of social change is not just a problem for traditional societies that are beginning to modernize. It is a problem for all societies.

Consider, for example, the decision by communist governments in Eastern Europe during the 1980s to make a few "minor" adjustments to their system, such as introducing some market forces into their economies and showing a greater tolerance for unorthodox, dissenting, and foreign viewpoints. Those governments soon found those "minor" adjustments snow-balling into a major social revolution that swept all the communist governments in Europe from power.

In our own society too, we are forever grappling with the issue of how to separate the undesirable aspects of social change from the desirable ones. For example, is it possible to enjoy big city sophistication without big city crime? Is it possible to achieve a growth in industrial output without causing an increase in industrial pollution? Is hate literature bound to proliferate with a greater tolerance for free speech?

Ousting an Established World View or Paradigm

Once social change does take hold, however, it usually sets down deep roots. New ideas that seem useful are rarely confined to a single application. Science and reason, for example, are held in high esteem in our society. But their relevance affects the way we do much more than just science. All our social institutions are expected to be organized on a rational basis. And we even try to employ reason and factual evidence in our personal decision-making. It is understood and taken for granted in our society that one should not behave "irrationally" or voice "unscientific" beliefs.

When beliefs become as deeply entrenched as the belief in science and reason are in our society, alternative viewpoints have a hard time getting a serious hearing. Calls to "radically rethink" a basic tenet of the society's beliefs usually fall on deaf ears. Because "radical rethinking" seems inherently odd to the majority of people, it tends to be dismissed as something only the lunatic fringe would advocate.

Still, the very belief in people's rational nature makes would-be reformers keep looking for key insights that could be used to persuade society of the need for reform. This is the school of thought that says ideas are, in and of themselves, a powerful tool for affecting change. The third excerpt in this section, by Eisler and Loye, is one example of an attempt to argue that recognizing one key truth would have major and positive consequences for the whole society (or in this case, for the whole planet).

The End of Social Change?

Finally, it should be said that social change is probably an endless process. That may seem like an obvious statement now but it hasn't always been obvious. The assumption that change has an end-point is embedded in the terms that have been used to describe social change. Consider, for example, the practice of calling nations "under-developed," "developing," or "developed." What is the term for a developed country that continues to change? There isn't one.

Social commentators have had to scramble to coin new terms like "post-modern" and "post-industrial" to describe changes that occurred after the process was expected to end. The fourth excerpt in this section, by Dirk van de Kaa, deals with one such social change that caught many social scientists by surprise. It's about Europe's "second demographic transition," which is occurring about 60 years after the "final" demographic transition ended. No doubt this latest demographic phenomenom will spark still further changes in European society.

12.1 Nathan Keyfitz

Development and the Elimination of Poverty

INTRODUCTION

The consumer society is often criticized for being wasteful and harmful to the environment and for promoting shallow, materialistic values. Such criticisms are often heard in affluent Western societies. But how does consumerism look to people living in poorer countries?

According to the next excerpt by Nathan Keyfitz, the consumer society still looks pretty appealing to them. Keyfitz argues that the desire for a middle-class lifestyle and standard of living is becoming universal. People everywhere, he says, want automobiles, refrigerators, and the other comforts associated with affluence. This desire for material possessions has begun to fuel economic development. To get the money to buy such goods, people work harder or borrow money. Both activities stimulate the economy and expand the middle class. The bigger the middle class gets, the more entrenched middle class values become.

Keyfitz thinks people's desire for a middle class lifestyle and standard of living can also have counter-productive economic consequences. For example, the civil service might be expanded just to increase the supply of desirable white-collar jobs. But those jobs aren't productive and are therefore a drain on the public purse. Similarly, the middle class tends to be urban and to have little interest in agriculture or rural development. So the agricultural sector might suffer from neglect if middle class priorities start influencing government policies.

The influence of the middle class in determining the course and type of development is strong even in those countries in which there is full democracy and in which the peasants are by far the largest part of the electorate.

The middle class has access to education and can understand the issues, is aware of its interests and able to act politically to further them. Schooling and influence enable it to pass its status to its young, and so it tends to be hereditary. It recruits from the peasantry through the process of urbanization, in highly selective fashion. Its initial task is to break the rural landholding class; once that is accomplished its influence is decisive, for the dispersed, uneducated peasantry are no match for it.

Keyfitz, Nathan (1982). "Development and the Elimination of Poverty," *Economic Development and Cultural Change*, 30(3), 649–670. Reprinted by permission of the University of Chicago Press and Nathan Keyfitz.

Diffusion of the Modern Culture

Development may be seen as the diffusion of a certain culture and the dominance of a new class that carries that culture. This article is complementary to, rather than inconsistent with, the view of development as rising average income per head; it attempts to place the economics of development in a social and cultural framework.

The Modern Way of Life

The middle-class style has been taught to the Third World by the United States and Europe. It consists of centrally heated and cooled homes equipped with television sets and refrigerators, transport by automobile, and procurement of foodstuffs and other supplies in self-service supermarkets. It is found typically in cities with paved streets, the countryside between those cities being laced with a network of paved roads and another network of air transport. Literacy is essential to it, and the daily press and monthly magazines are conspicuous, along with television. The content of its media has remarkable similarity worldwide: local, national, and world politics; urban crime; and the cost of living.

Economists have written on one aspect of this modern conception of how to live and work, calling it the demonstration effect. People learn from films and other media to want a level of consumption that is for the moment beyond the capacity of their national productive apparatus to support. Such wishes cause premature spending and impedes the saving and investment that would bring such benefits within the scope of national production and trade. But in fact the demonstration effect has not had a large impact on economics. It should be taken seriously, both in its negative aspects, and positively as the motor of development.

Measuring the Poor and the Middle Class

In the United States it is easier to measure poverty and take the middle class as a residual; in other countries it is on the whole easier to measure the middle class, the minority, and take the poor as the residual.

The U.S. Department of Agriculture designed a 1961 Economy Food Plan that forms the basis for the calculation of poverty income thresholds, recognizing family size, sex, and age of the family head, number of children under 18, and farm-nonfarm residence. Annual adjustments are made on the basis of the Consumer Price Index, but the consumption levels continue to be those established for the base year 1963.[1] The number of families that fall below the poverty line in the United States was just under 40 million in the late 1950s, and had dropped to 25 million by 1977.[2]

The figures, extrapolated to 1980, show 24 million poor, 196 million middle class, for a total population of 220 million. Our task is to find how this can be extended to the world.

The middle class can be traced broadly through statistics of ownership of certain artifacts. An automobile is one indicator, and we have statistics of automobile ownership for 75 countries. Counting two persons per automobile, the American standard, is a first approximation.

The *United Nations Statistical Yearbook* gives 271,620,000 passenger vehicles in the world in 1976, of which 109,003,000 were in the United States. Using this ratio to bring the U.S. middle class of 196 million to a world total gives us 196 x 271,620/109,003 = 488 million. But because automobiles are less used elsewhere by people who could afford them than they are in the United States, this is a low figure. It is also low insofar as families elsewhere are larger than in the United States. A figure of 2.5 or 3 middle-class persons per vehicle would bring us closer.

Energy consumed is one indicator. The total in million tons of coal equivalent for the world in 1976 was 8,318, and for the United States it was 2,485.[3] This ratio would bring us to 656 million middle-class people in the world. Better than automobiles, but still probably too low; the American burns more energy than middle-class people elsewhere.

The problem is distribution is not the same in all countries and is difficult to measure. We note the total for the market economies of the world in 1976 at 5,426 billion, and the United States in that year at 1,695 billion.[4] The ratio used crudely gives us 627 million people above the poverty line. To it would have to be added the middle class in nonmarket economies — on the order of 150 million. (The United Nations calculates for the centrally planned a weight of 0.196 in the world economy.)[5]

On the basis of such evidence, the number of middle class in the world in 1980 might be 700–800 million.

A similar calculation gives 200 million for the middle class of 1950. The entry of Europe and Japan, plus some progress in the Third World, brought the total to 800 million by 1980.[6]

Production

Being middle class is not a matter of consumption alone; certain kinds of work are middle class and other kinds are not. Office work at a salary that permits owning a car and an adequately equipped house is the ideal; if the salary does not permit buying a car, then obtaining one as a perquisite of office will do. The boundary of the middle class does not coincide with that of nonmanual workers. Wages converge so that all can aspire to middle-class style.

Middle-class workers seek to avoid the hazards of entrepreneurship. Much better is the job of senior administrator, working according to fixed rules within a framework of law, with no personal capital at stake. Next in desirability to a job in government, and paying better, is being hired by a multinational corporation. The multinationals have access nearly everywhere, partly because their kind of operation is understandable and gratifying.

The entry of such cultural preferences into the work world creates a difficulty. The kind of work people like to do, and which they get jobs doing, diverges from the kind of work that produces the goods on which collectively they want to spend their salaries. The government employee may be engaged in the collection of taxes, or the organization of cooperatives, or the country's foreign policy. These activities make little contribution to producing the groceries he seeks to buy at the supermarket or the plumbing fixtures for his new house.

Relief of Poverty versus a New Culture

Growth in the form of an expanding middle class is consistent with an increasing number of poor. Of course the middle-class way by itself is relief of poverty for some. Yet this relief of poverty seems incidental. For if adequate food and clothing, basic medical services, and literacy were the main objectives of development it would go on in a very different way from that now pursued. Brazil's national income per capita of $1,400 could provide these amenities for every one of its inhabitants. Yet in fact, the majority of its inhabitants lack these altogether, while others have them and much more. After 30 years of formal development effort in 75 countries, we can infer the objective of the process from actual observation. As much as anything it is the diffusion of the artifacts that support a certain way of life, and in a poor country only a minority can benefit.

While the particular culture of the middle class belongs to the second half of the twentieth century, the idea of an urban industrial group with incomes far higher than their rural contemporaries goes back much farther. Adam Smith saw development as taking place in the measure in which material capital accumulated in cities. With each increment of city capital some jobs would be created. A new factory or mill could offer wages high enough to attract people from the countryside. Until the call to city employment came, the peasant would remain in his ancestral village.

Incentives to Rural-Urban Migration

Whatever expands city facilities, or lowers the price of foodstuffs, increases the size of the city. We can even suggest a positive feedback that results from legislation and administrative action. The price of rice is, in many countries, fixed well below the world market, and a law requires peasants to deliver part of their crop at this price. Officials go into the countryside to execute the procurement. The unpleasantness and actual loss contribute to causing some peasants to leave and go to the city. That increases the need for foodstuffs in the city, so the procurement activity is intensified.

One might think there would be an equilibrium point in migration. When enough have left, the living should be equal to what migrants could get by going to the city, and at that point migration should stop. One reason it does not, as Alfred Marshall pointed out (quoted by Lipton), is that there is selection on who comes to the city; on the whole those who come are better educated, and have more initiative.[7] Thus their departure does not make things better but worse.

We can imagine policies that would discourage internal migration. For one, taxes to provide urban services could be levied on urban real estate rather than coming out of the national budget. Inputs to agriculture could be subsidized. An effect similar to subsidies would be obtained by better prices for farm outputs.

The elite cannot make the city better for themselves without making it better for the newcomers, and so encouraging further newcomers. They could forcibly prevent migration, or expel existing migrants, and this has been tried in Moscow, Jakarta, and elsewhere, but by and large has not been successful.

The masses in the capital city are physically close enough to the government to communicate their wishes, as those of Cairo did two years ago when they forced the government to cancel its increase of food prices. Such an increase would have helped the peasant and discouraged migration, but the political forces did not permit it. Governments cannot always resist the reasonable demands of the protected segment of the labor force for decent places to live. Government often builds houses with funds that could have gone to rural investment.

Local transport within the city is often government run. The costs of the buses it imports, and the fares it charges, are public matters, and very much the business of administrators and legislators. They do not always set the fares high enough for even their low-cost imported buses, and when the bus operations make a loss it is covered from general revenues, which means in some part from the rural sector.

Other public utilities run by government at a loss even more clearly favor the middle class. Electricity is largely used by them. The view has been that industry needs protection more than agriculture, that manufactured exports are better than farm exports, that agriculture's decreasing returns justify removing resources to help industries giving increasing returns.

The need for food supplies to permit the town people to engage in manufacturing was accepted by all the classics: thus Smith says, "it is the surplus produce of the country only, or what is over and above the maintenance of the cultivators, that constitutes the subsistence of the town, which can therefore increase only with the increase of the surplus produce."[8]

Holding the price of grain down is not the way to increase the supply. Investment in agriculture is called for. Szcaepanik shows that the gross marginal capital/output ratios for 1960–65 are much higher for nonagricultural than for agricultural investment. On the whole the capital required to produce a given amount of income is more than double in industry what it is in agriculture.

Some of these points are now being recognized, and efforts are being made on behalf of agricultural output. The Mexican government is investing in modernization and stressing the use of machinery. The man with the bullock is to be replaced by a tractor operator, with backing by soil chemists, agronomists, irrigation specialists, and bankers ready to advance rural credit. All this will indeed provide employment, but for specialists and not for the masses in the countryside. Indeed, it could accelerate the move to the city.

Here much depends on the patterns of consumption and residence of the new classes in the rural areas. If the tractor operator and the soil chemist live in the city and commute to the rural area, or if they live in the village but use their new incomes on city goods, then unemployment in the countryside will be greater than ever, and cityward migration will continue and even accelerate.

In few fields does the middle-class urban bias reveal itself as clearly as in education. Most schools above the primary level are in cities, and the ordinary peasant's children stand little chance of attending. The disparity in numbers of secondary schools between rural and urban areas is matched by some disparity in the quality of instruction. Moreover, the primary schools that are now attended at least long enough for most peasant children to learn to read and write, have little to do with peasant life. Rather than being planned to make better farmers, they serve as a selection device, by which ability is discovered and sent to secondary school, usually in the city.

Explanation Rather Than Policy Guidance

The present paper stands back from development and refrains from offering policy advice, at the same time that it tries to look at it from a point of view of the citizen undergoing the process. The citizen of poor countries sees development as the advent of goods that make possible a modern style of life. The goods are above all symbols that one has attained a certain status.

This wish for middle-class status is an engine of development — it can induce acceptance of the hard work and abstinence that development requires. Yet it is not a readily manipulated policy variable, like a tariff or the rate of interest. The object of this paper is not to reveal some easy way by which development can be brought about but to make it look as difficult on paper as it is in reality. I have tried to show why excellent policy advice is disregarded. Thus, reaching for middle-class status is an explanatory rather than a policy variable. It tells us why government has grown, why cities have expanded, why poor countries aim to produce automobiles rather than bicycles, why the import of consumption goods is everywhere so large an element in the balance of payments.

Within each of the poor countries is an expanding middle-class enclave. We need to observe more closely the social mechanisms that cause the spread of the middle class to take precedence over the alleviation of poverty.

ENDNOTES

[1] U.S. Bureau of the Census, *Statistical Abstract* (Washington, D.C.: Government Printing Office, 1978), p. 438.

[2] Ibid., p. 465.

[3] United Nations, *United Nations Statistical Handbook* (New York: United Nations Department of International Economic and Social Affairs, 1978), p. 389.

[4] Ibid., p. 748.

[5] Ibid., p. 10.

[6] Ibid.

[7] Michael Lipton, *Why Poor People Stay Poor: Urban Bias in World Development* (Cambridge, Mass.: Harvard University Press, 1977), p. 376.

[8] Lipton, p. 94.

12.2

L. H. Melikian and J. S. Al-Easa

Oil and Social Change in the Persian Gulf

INTRODUCTION

The following excerpt is about receptivity to one aspect of social change in a society that, until recently, hadn't seen much social change. More specifically it is about the receptivity to new ideas on marriage among a group of male and female students at a university in Qatar, a Persian Gulf oil-exporting state.

Before oil revenues transformed the country, starting in the 1950s, Qatar had been poor and shut off from outside influences. But the study found that college women have recently embraced non-traditional ideas about marriage more fully than men have. For example, women are more open to marrying outside their tribe and are more inclined to see marriage as an equal partnership. The women also want fewer children than the men do and believe that women should marry at an older age than is traditional.

In one sense it is surprising that women are the "progressive" ones in this study, since Qatari culture does not encourage women to become independent, unconventional thinkers. Self-interest could explain part of the women's new-found intellectual independence. Perhaps their displeasure with traditional marriage outweighs their reluctance to disagree with the menfolk. Could exposure to Western ideas through a university education be another factor? And is one change (in access to education) begetting others (by creating more assertive women)?

Melikian, L. H. and J. S. Al-Easa (1981). "Oil and Social Change in the Gulf," *Journal of Arab Affairs,* 1(1), October, 79–98. Reprinted by permission.

*T*he objective of this study is to report the findings of a survey conducted between 1974 and 1978 among Qatari college men and women students.

The State of Qatar is situated on the west coast of the Arabian Gulf. The indigeneous population is of pure Arab stock. It consists mainly of nomadic tribesmen who became sedentarized and settled along the coast. The annual rate in the increase of the indigenous population is estimated at eight percent. This is attributed to an increase in the birth rate as well as to a liberal policy of naturalization whereby Arabs from the surrounding Gulf areas could take up Qatari citizenship. The increase in the number of expatriates, estimated to be 8.1 percent, was mainly due to the increasing demands for experts, professionals, teachers, laborers and others needed for its development and industrialization programs. Though Qatar was never isolated from other cultures the present contact with foreigners is higher than at any other period of its history.

Since the early fifties Qatar has been enjoying a boom economy because of the spiraling increase in oil revenues. These revenues are utilized to provide a free education up to the university level, free medical services, free electricity and water, low cost housing as well as opportunities for work with a regular income. The present industrialization program is aimed at the diversification of the economy. All of these developments influence the structure and function of the family.

In Qatar, the tribe, clan and family (extended) represent the three levels of the kinship system. Kinship shapes almost all the individual and group patterns of behavior. The net of relationships extends to many generations and connects each tribe with its branches outside of Qatar. The family remains the primary institution for economic and social control as well as for the protection of the rights of its members. It retains the traditional characteristics of being patriarchal, extended, patrilineal, patrilocal, endogamous, and occasionally polygamous.

The large extended family was the dominant type. It consisted of grandfather, grandmother, their married sons with their wives and children, and their unmarried children all living under the same roof. Other relatives may also have lived in the same household.

Extended families living near each other generally belong to the same lineage, clan or tribe. Prior to the oil era, almost 50 percent of the families living close to each other were related. This figure had dropped to 37 percent by 1975.[1] The tendency for proximal living of relatives is still reflected in the residential areas of the capital which are named after the clans or tribes which originally lived, or still reside, in them. The residential pattern of the extended family has somewhat changed. Whereas previously all members lived under one roof, the grandfather and each of his married sons now live in separate dwellings within one compound. They still share a common kitchen and a common *majlis* or guest room. The classical extended family is, however, on the decline with the nuclear family slowly replacing it as the dominant type.

Role and status are traditionally determined by age and sex. Men are considered superior to women and older people command more respect than younger ones. At the wider social level education and wealth have begun to assume a greater role in determining status. The husband is responsible for the economic affairs of the family, while the wife is expected to take care of all domestic affairs. Among the more conservative sections of the population all shopping is made by the husband or an older son. Women are not supposed to go to the market place or leave their house unless accompanied by their husband or son. The role differentiation is reinforced by the segregation of the sexes at age ten. However, variations from this strict code are slowly becoming more common.

Relationships between husband and wife, parents and children, and between siblings themselves, are hierarchical. The young are expected to obey the old and females are expected to obey males. A study conducted by Melikian in Saudi Arabia found that among university students who had lived outside of Saudi Arabia for a minimum of one year or more, the mother shared the peak of the power hierarchy with the father and the eldest son.

These findings indicate the concentration of power — power being defined as obeying others least — is in the hands of the father and the eldest son in the traditional families while among the exposed families — those who have resided abroad — the mother's position is equal to that of the father and to that of the eldest son. The position of the eldest son may have been enhanced by his level of education which far exceeds that of his father. Most fathers in this study did not have more than three years of schooling.[2]

The father not only controls the money, but decides who his sons and daughters are to marry, who they can mix with and when to change their place of residence. The mother exercises authority over her daughters-in-law, her unmarried daughters and grandchildren. But most students of the Arab family feel the wife wields more authority over husband and children than is commonly recognized.

The Qatari family plays a major role in socialization. Strong emphasis is placed on training a child to conform to the patterns laid down by his elders. Corporal punishment is employed as well as withdrawal of privilege. Fathers become active in bringing up their sons between the ages of five and seven. At that time the father starts taking his son along to the *majlis*, the guest room, in which the elders and men of the family and their male guests congregate in the evenings. The father also takes his sons to the mosque to join other men in prayers. Here the child experiences a sense of a community which extends beyond the confines of the family. As the boy grows older he is encouraged to participate in communal activities but mainly with children from the same family and clan. As the boy grows up he may accompany his father to work.

The mother sees to it that her daughter grows into an adult who can play the role prescribed by society. By age seven she is given simple household duties, which progressively become more difficult. She is told she will have to serve and respect not only her husband, but her in-laws and other kin living in the same house.

Even though no definite studies have been made on the socialization of the Qatari child it can be said that the process instills conformity and docility. In addition religious injunctions teach that obedience to parents and grandparents comes second to obedience towards God and the Prophet.

Marriages tend to be arranged by the parents when the son is able to support a wife and expresses his desire for marriage. The girl does not initiate this procedure but is given a chance to reject her suitor. Early marriages, especially for girls, are common. On average women marry men 5 to 10 years older than they are.

Preference is given first to marriages contracted within the extended family, next to a marriage within the lineage followed by marriage within the tribe. Marrying from within the family insures the principle or condition of equal descent is fulfilled. Thus a man ought to marry one of equal descent status, but if no such suitable spouse is available he may marry a woman of lower descent. Such a marriage is allowed because the children will take the descent status of their father. A woman, however, is never allowed to marry a man of a lower descent though she may marry someone of a higher status. Descent takes precedence over wealth. A man chooses a wife from a series of possible spouses graded in order of preference ranging from his patrilineal parallel cousin, father's brother's daughter, to any other woman within the stratum. Preference for marriage from within the descent group is not, however, a religious injunction and even before the oil era paternal-cousin marriage was not prevalent.

Qatari college students perceive marriage as inevitable. Most men are practical about it while the women idealize it. More men than women see it as restricting their freedom. More men than women appear concerned with its sexual and procreative aspects. Almost all expect to get married and remain monogamous.

The same group was asked the age at which they expected to get married. The men expect to get married at an average of 25.9 and the women at 23.4 years.

How endogamous are they in their preferences? Sixty-four men and 34 women students were asked to indicate which one they preferred to marry: paternal cousin, a close relative, from the same clan, from Qatar, from the other Gulf States, from other Arab countries, or a non-Arab.

The results show that 61 percent of the men preferred to marry either a paternal cousin, or someone from the same lineage or clan while the remaining 39 percent preferred to marry an outsider. By comparison only 24 percent of the women preferred to marry a relative while the remaining 76 percent opted for an exogamous marriage.

Assuming the respondents marry the partner of their choice, what are the personal qualities they would like this person to have? To answer this, the same group of men and women were asked to rank three personal qualities in order of preference.

Some interesting differences appear. A larger proportion of women than men preferred companionship and a pleasant disposition in their spouses. Secondly, over twice as many men want their future wives to share in their beliefs and opinions. The same proportions of men and women rank intelligence and common sense first. Over half the women emphasized pleasant disposition and companionship in a husband.

TABLE 1

387

Oil and Social Change in the Persian Gulf

	Men	Women
	Percentage	
1. (a) A man should feel closer to his wife.	63	87
(b) A man should feel closer to his family (father & mother)	37	13
2. (a) A wife should be allowed to make decisions on her own even though she disagrees with her husband.	21	71
(b) A good wife obeys her husband always.	79	29

The traditional attitudes of the men were further confirmed when the subjects were asked to choose one of two alternative questions seen in Table 1.

Both men and women wanted fewer children than they expected to have. Men also appear to want and expect more children than women. Both men and women also appear to expect and want more boys than girls with the trend being more marked in the case of the men. Qatari college students neither expect nor want as many children as their parents had. Seventy-nine percent of the men and 82 percent of the women in this study indicated they favor limiting the number of children.

A Summary of the Findings

The findings are summarized as follows:

1. More men than women see marriage as a practical and inevitable event that restricts their freedom. While women also see the inevitability of marriage, more of them idealize it as a mutual bond, a companionship, which contributes to the security of the couple.

2. Men prefer to marry at the same age as their fathers did. The age of the women they prefer to marry is less than the age at which women prefer to get married.

3. Most of the men prefer to marry a relative, from within the tribe, who shares their opinions and ideas, while most of the women prefer to marry a non-relative, from outside the tribe, who has a "pleasant disposition" and who will be a "good companion."

4. Both men and women expect to have more children than they would like to have. Men want more children than women.

5. Most of the attitudes of the women are less traditional than those held by the men. College women appear to press for a more egalitarian status with the men — at least within the family.

The Future

What does the future hold for the family in Qatar? Here are some projections:

1. The extended family will be replaced by the nuclear family.

2. Most young men would upon marriage live in separate households. The trend for proximal living will, however, continue.

3. Both young men and women will insist on getting to know each other before getting married.

4. Polygamous marriages will continue to decrease.

5. The age differences between husband and wife will decrease, with women marrying at an older age than their mothers did.

6. There will be fewer paternal-cousin marriages and fewer marriages from within the same lineage. The shift will be towards marrying within one's tribe and country.

7. Couples will have fewer children than their parents did.

8. Women will strive for a more egalitarian partnership in the family.

ENDNOTES

1 Juhaina S. Al-Easa, "Acculturation and the Changing Family Structure in Qatar," unpublished Master's Degree Thesis (Cairo: Cairo University, 1975).

2 Levon H. Melikian, "Modernization and the Perception of the Power Structure in the Saudi Arab Family," paper presented at the International Congress of Applied Psychology, Munich, 1978.

12.3 Riane Eisler and David Loye

New Ways to Value the Undervalued

INTRODUCTION

The scope and breadth of social change varies widely. For example, passing fads are a form of social change. Social change can occur on a much broader scale too; but very rarely do entire civilizations undergo social transformation. Historians who believe in "the power of ideas" to

Eisler, Riane and David Loye (1983). "The Hidden Future: A Global View from Another Paradigm", *World-Futures*, 19(1–2), October, 123–136. Reprinted by permission of Gordon and Breach Science Publishers.

cause social changes have linked these rare historic transformations to shifts in world view, or "paradigms." Thus, the European Christians who designed and lived in the feudal society of the Middle Ages are thought to have been inspired by a different paradigm than the one that had inspired the ancient world. Another major shift in paradigms occurred during the Scientific Revolution of the seventeenth century.

Each paradigm shift presents a few initial insights that are touted as very important keys to further knowledge. For example, the key insight of the medieval Christian paradigm might be summarized as: people have souls that can be saved by following the tenets of Christianity. And in the Scientific Revolution, the key initial insight was: human reason is capable of understanding the physical universe and using that knowledge to improve human life. Massive social changes flowed from believing in those initial insights. That's why some social reformers see the search for new paradigms as useful.

The following excerpt is an attempt to find a new paradigm that could spur social reforms. It offers the insight that sexual inequality is at the root of many of the world's problems.

We have a mounting body of data from national and international agencies, as well as from the social sciences, indicating that, when viewed in systems terms, sexual inequality and equality are central to the better understanding and eventual solution of the world problematique.

At first glance this may seem absurd. But study after study documents the power of perceptual blindness induced by the prevailing social and ideological organization. Of such ideologically induced blindness, none has been as powerful as that relating to the social facts about sexual inequality, so taken for granted that they are invisible.

Emile Durkheim observed how social facts are like the air we breathe.[1] Just as we take air for granted until it is not there for us to breathe, so social facts only become visible as we become aware of their presence through social change. In the contemporary laboratory of social change, sexual inequality has become increasingly visible. But what is only gradually becoming visible is the all-pervasive effect of sexual inequality in the ideological sphere, where it acts as a kind of filter, distorting and obscuring perception, invisibilizing the obvious, and blocking appropriate actions.

Despite the urgent necessity for global population control, almost everywhere on our planet religious and secular ideologies defining women primarily in terms of reproduction-related functions prevent the formulation and implementation of the necessary policies. That this is *not* a function of lack of knowledge is evidenced not only by the masses of readily available reports on the necessity for policies vigorously promoting reproductive freedom of choice and other fundamental changes in the status of women.[2] It is also explicit in statements by people like Robert F. McNamara, President of the World Bank, on how "greater economic opportunity for women and the greater educational opportunity that undergirds it would substantially reduce fertility," and how, in cost-effective dollars and cents terms, this would be "a very good buy."[3]

To further illustrate how the problem is ideology let us move on to two additional aspects of the world problematique. The first is the growing problem of global poverty and hunger, with all its ramifications for global economic development and global security, where once again we encounter the deleterious policy effects of the prevailing world view which trivializes and/or invisibilizes "women's issues." Were it not for these ideological dynamics, policy makers could not speak of economic development and the elimination of poverty and hunger while ignoring the mounting data indicating that the female half of humanity and the children primarily dependent on their mothers for sustenance are the poorest of the world's poor and the hungriest of the world's hungry.

Reports are explicitly documenting how there is little likelihood that economic development and foreign aid programs will ever achieve their aims as long as the people who need this aid the most — women — are systematically excluded from financial aid, from land grants, from loans, from training, from education for modernization.[4] Nevertheless, these programs continue to be based on the premise that the economic development of men will automatically result in economic development for women and children. And instead of paying particular attention to women and children, these programs continue to be almost exclusively geared to men.[5]

But perhaps nowhere is our ideologically-induced blindness as potentially lethal as in relation to the danger of nuclear war. For if we look at war, as some social scientists do, as basically a function of demographic factors — of population pressures which create conflicts over scarce resources — we again come back to the issue of population control: the need for policies where women are not only given free access to birth control technologies but are also no longer barred from non-breeding life and work roles. And if we look at war, as other social scientists do, as a direct derivative of the socialization of men to be tough and warlike, we once again come face to face with a so-called women's issue — stereotypical sexual socialization.

This link between sexual inequality and warfare is being increasingly examined and the result has been a growing body of studies indicating significant statistical correlations. For example, in a 1976 study, anthropologists Divale and Harris found a significant correlation between the extent to which a tribe or society engaged in warfare and measures of its sexual inequality.[6] A 1978 study by Arkin and Dobrofsky focused on how the he-man, conquest-oriented male stereotype and male-dominance over women is central to the way the military teaches soldiers to kill.[7]

Even more significantly, these kinds of correlations have been found to extend to social violence in general. For example, using a randomly selected sample of primitive cultures, McConahay and McConahay in 1977 observed a statistically significant relationship between violence and rigid male-female stereotypes; societies with more pronounced sexual inequality had a higher degree of social violence, ranging from punitive violence in child-rearing to rape, wife-beating, and blood vengeance within the group, and a higher incidence of violence against other groups in the form of raids and wars.[8]

Anthropologist Geoffry Gorer has suggested a key element in societies characterized by low social violence is a lack of concern for having males learn adult sex-role definitions idealizing aggressiveness, as well as a general indifference about which sex fills the important roles in the society.[9] Summarizing the statistically significant behavioral characteristics associated with primitive societies which rigidly restrict women's freedom of reproductive choice by severely punishing abortions, anthropologist R. B. Textor found that such societies tended also to practice slavery and polygyny, to kill, torture, and mutilate enemies captured in war, to be generally sexually repressive, and to be patrilineal rather than matrilineal. In primitive societies which did not have such restrictions, there was a statistically significant converse relationship.[10]

There is also a growing number of studies indicating that societies where there is marked male-dominance, tend to be authoritarian and that a central component of what psychologists call the authoritarian personality type is a rigid internalization of stereotypical sex roles. One of the studies in this area is *The Authoritarian Personality*, in which a group of scientists, alarmed by the threat of fascism, conducted extensive research into the kind of personality that would tend to support and comfortably function in such a system.[11] The co-principal investigator Else Frenkel-Brunswik, found that individuals high in prejudice, and with such potentially violent and explosive personality traits as a high degree of repressed anger and hostility and inordinate difficulties in forming satisfactory love relationships, characteristically saw women and men in terms of rigidly stereotypical masculine-feminine roles.[12]

New Findings from History and Prehistory

Such data present startling implications. And yet, if we think about it, it is not so strange that societies which see women and men primarily in terms of ranking rather than linkage should also see humanity in general in such terms. And so, it is not so strange that, as historians are beginning to look at social configurations from the perspective of what happens when there is movement toward sexual equality, they are finding there is movement away from authoritarianism and social violence.

Some of the most interesting data are from studies of the early Christian movement. Scholars are now able to reconstruct a picture of the group dynamics of some of the early Christian communities, where women and men lived in sexual equality. Here, Christians not only preached Jesus' teachings of equality — that we must work for a moral order where there shall be no master and no slave, no male or female — but actually lived that way, with women taking leading roles as teachers, and the Deity was seen as both Mother and Father. They also lived and preached nonviolence, until they themselves fell victim to the authoritarian Church structure that later evolved, which hunted them down as heretics and burned and expunged their writings from the Holy Scriptures — writings like the 52 Gnostic Gospels recently discovered after being buried for over 1600 years in Egypt.[13]

One final area which is, perhaps to some, providing the greatest shock of all, is the new data from prehistory.

We now know civilization was not, as we have been taught, born in Sumer about 5,000 years ago, but that there were a number of cradles of civilization, all of them thousands of years older.[14] For example, in Europe there is now evidence of stable Neolithic societies where the arts flourished, where people peacefully tilled the soil, traded, and engaged in crafts, and where there seems to have been a written script predating Sumerian writing by 2,000 years.[15]

In these societies, the social organization was basically egalitarian. Differences in status and in wealth were not marked. Moreover, women priestesses, women craftspeople, and the supreme deity conceptualized as female are all indications that these were *not* male dominated societies. Likewise, these societies do not seem to have had wars. Throughout the digs revealing this ancient culture from Europe into Asia, there is a general absence of fortifications, as well as an absence in their extensive art of the glorification of warriors and wars.

These findings are meeting with a great deal of resistance, both by lay people and academicians, because they are truly heretical. In short, it is information that is being met much the way the information that the world is round was once met, because that, too, went against Holy Scripture and against everything people *knew* to be the truth.

There is, of course, always resistance to anything new and unfamiliar — although, this actually is *not* unfamiliar information. We are familiar with it, from many ancient stories about a more innocent time when humanity lived in a garden (as these people did because they were the first farmers), a time before woman was (as the Biblical story has it) condemned by a male god to henceforth be forever subservient to man. We have all, in fact, heard of these prehistoric societies through our most ancient texts: not only the Bible, but Chinese texts, Sumerian texts, and Greek texts. They are referred to in the works of the Greek poet Hesiod, who wrote just before Homer, and who told of an earlier and nobler golden race who also lived in a garden and did not make war,[16] and in legends of Atlantis, now believed to be a garbled memory of Minoan Crete, where this type of social organization prevailed.[17]

Pertinent Questions and Effective Solutions

The importance of the increasing number of studies that are focusing on the hitherto invisible women's issues lies in what they tell us about sexual equality and inequality in systems terms.

Viewed in this context, the data surveyed here can serve to stimulate thinking so that we may begin to ask whether and how, at this juncture in global history, sexual equality might be a key to the creation of a more peaceful, more egalitarian world.

One such question might be whether it is merely coincidental that those who are trying to push women back into so-called traditional male-dominated roles in the home are at the same time ideologically committed to a social order run by a small male elite, with little respect for the civil and economic rights of the mass of not only women but men.

We might further ask whether it can be coincidental that the great modern surge toward sexual equality should come at a time when our world desperately needs a new way of running human affairs.

And we might conclude all this is *not* just coincidental, and that what we are seeing today in the struggle over sexual equality is the struggle of two very different ways of living.

One, the way based on sexual inequality, is the idea of ranking as the primary organizational principle in human affairs. This way has led not only to the subordination of women, but also to the conquest of one nation by another, and to man's so-called conquest of nature, a conquest against which nature herself is now rebelling in countless ways. It is the way of strong-man rule that has led to authoritarianism, totalitarianism, racism and colonialism.[18]

The other way seems to have been the original path for our species, from which we have undergone a 5,000 year detour. It is a way based on linkage rather than ranking in human relations, and it is the way that is beginning to re-assert itself, not only in the partnership as equals between women and men, but also in the general movement toward egalitarianism and democracy and in our growing understanding of the necessity of finding a more peaceful way of living on this Earth.

Which of these two ways will be the way of the future still hangs in the balance. What is here suggested is that at its most fundamental level, the much discussed shift in paradigm generally recognized as a pre-requisite to a better future is a shift in our paradigm (or world view) about the relationship between the individuals associated with femininity and masculinity.

ENDNOTES

[1] E. Durkheim, *The Rules of Sociological Method* (Free Press, New York, 1964).

[2] See e.g. *Draper World Population Fund Report, no. 9: Improving the Status of Women,* October 1980.

[3] R. McNamara, *Accelerating Population Stabilization through Social and Economic Progress,* (Development Paper 24, Overseas Development Council, Washington D.C. 1977).

[4] P. Huston, *Third World Women Speak Out* (Praeger, New York, 1979); H. Loutfi, *Rural Women: Unequal Partners in Development* (International Labour Organization, Geneva, 1980); M. Rihani, *Development As If Women Mattered* (Occasional Paper no. 10, Overseas Development Council, Washington D.C., 1978).

[5] See e.g. E. Boserup, *Woman's Role in Economic Development* (Allen and Unwin, London, 1970); B. Rogers, *The Domestication of Women* (St. Martin's Press, New York, 1980).

[6] W. F. Divale and M. Harris, "Population, Warfare, and the Male Supremacist Complex," *Am. Anthropologist* 78, 521–538 (1976).

[7] W. Arkin and L. Dobrofsky, "Military Socialization and Masculinity," *Journal of Social Issues* 34, 1, 151–168 (1978).

[8] S. McConahay and J. McConahay, "Sexual Permissiveness, Sex-Role Rigidity and Violence Across Cultures," *J. of Social Issues* 33, 2, 143–143 (1977).

[9] G. Gorer, "Man Has No Killer Instinct," in A. Montagu, *Man and Aggression,* First edition (Oxford University Press, New York, 1968).

[10] R. B. Textor, *A Cross Cultural Summary* (HRAF Press, New Haven, Conn., 1967).

[11] T. W. Adorno et al., *The Authoritarian Personality* (Harper and Row, New York, 1950).

[12] Ibid, Part II.

[13] See e.g., E. Pagels, *The Gnostic Gospels* (Random House, New York, 1979).

[14] See e.g., J. Mellaart, *The Neolithic of the Near East* (Scribner, New York, 1975).

[15] See e.g. M. Gimbutas, *Goddesses and Gods of Old Europe* (University of California Press, Los Angeles, 1982).

[16] Hesiod, *Works and Days,* in J. M. Robinson, *An Introduction to Early Greek Philosophy* (Houghton-Mifflin, Boston, 1968), pp. 12–17.

[17] See e.g. J. V. Luce, *The End of Atlantis* (Thames and Hudson, London, 1969).

[18] R. Eisler, *The Blade and The Chalice,* work in progress.

12.4   Dirk van de Kaa

Europe's Second Demographic Transition

INTRODUCTION

Once upon a time, not long ago, Europe's population trend seemed clear. The widely accepted demographic transition theory predicted that birth rates and death rates would become balanced, leaving the continent with zero population growth for some time. That didn't happen. Instead, birth rates have plunged below the level needed to replace the population. Some European countries have already seen their population sizes decline; others will experience the same trend soon. What happened? Why are European women having so few babies?

In this excerpt, Dirk van de Kaa explains this "second demographic transition" in terms of a shift in values. He argues that in the last 30 years more and more Europeans have become concerned with the "opportunity costs" of having children. People are now more likely to see children putting a crimp in their lifestyle and strain on their marriage. In short, parents are no longer as willing as they once were to sacrifice their own enjoyment for the sake of having children.

van de Kaa, Dirk (1987). "Europe's Second Demographic Transition," *Population Bulletin,* 42(1), March, 1–57. (Washington, D.C., Population Reference Bureau, Inc.) Reprinted by permission.

A second factor in the dropping birth rates, according to van de Kaa, is that today's Europeans feel freer than Europeans did in the past to make choices about using contraceptives, having abortions or remaining childless. And they are exercising their right to choose. As a result, unwanted babies are far less likely to be born in Europe now than in the past.

According to current United Nations medium projections, Europe's population will increase a scant six percent between 1985 and 2025, from 492 to 524 million, while the world's population nearly doubles, from 4.5 to 8.2 billion, and nearly one in every five Europeans in 2025 will be pensioners aged 65 and over.

The new stage in Europe's demographic history might be called its "second demographic transition." Europe's first demographic transition began with a gradual decline in death rates dating from the early 19th century, followed by fertility decline beginning around 1880 in most countries, though earlier in France. By the 1930s, both birth and death rates were at low levels.

The start of the second transition can arbitrarily be set at 1965. In the interim had come World War II and the baby boom that followed it. The principal demographic feature of the second transition is the decline in fertility from somewhat above the "replacement" level of 2.1 births per woman, which ensures that births and deaths will stay in balance and population remain stationary over the long run, to a level well below replacement.

If fertility stabilizes below replacement, as seems likely in Europe, and barring immigration, population numbers will sooner or later decline, as had begun already by 1985 in four countries (Austria, Denmark, the Federal Republic of Germany, and Hungary). Changes in mortality and migration — the other two variables that shape changes in population numbers — have had relatively little impact in the second transition.

Early theories about the demographic transition, based on Europe's experience to the 1930s, usually ended with the stage of "zero" population growth. The stage of long-term population decline, now imminent in Europe, has since been called "beyond the demographic transition," but its special features in Europe seem to merit the label "second demographic transition." This *Bulletin* describes the broad features of this second demographic transition as it has evolved among Europe's some 30 heterogeneous countries.

Second Demographic Transition: The Background

Two keywords characterize the norms and attitudes behind the first and second demographic transitions and highlight the contrasts between them: *altruistic* and *individualistic*. The first transition to low fertility was dominated by concerns for family and offspring, but the second emphasizes the rights and self-fulfillment of individuals. Demographers Ron Lesthaeghe and Christopher Wilson argue convincingly that industrialization, urbanization, and secularization were the indirect determinants of the first transition.[1] The shift from family-based production to wage-paid labor that accompanied industrialization and urbanization reduced the economic utility of children. Moreover, a large number of children could mean the dissipation of family assets like land after the parents' death, so birth control became a sound strategy. Secularization reduced the influence of the churches and increased couples' willingness to practice family planning.

Demographically, the first transition reflected the disappearance of the Malthusian pattern of family formation. Couples no longer had to delay marriage until they acquired a separate means of existence by succeeding their parents. The age at marriage declined and so did the number of people who remained permanently single. Within marriage, the number of children was controlled; quality replaced quantity.

The indirect determinants of the second transition cannot be summed up so neatly.

In these societies, one's standard of living is largely determined by one's level and quality of education, degree of commitment to societal goals, and motivation to develop and use one's talents. This holds for women as well as men; both sexes tend to strive to earn a personal income. Getting married and/or having children may involve considerable opportunity costs.

For a couple, children involve not only direct expenditures, but also their utility has declined even further. They are no longer either expected or legally required to support their parents in old age or help with family finances. The emotional satisfactions of parenthood can be achieved most economically by having one or perhaps two children.

Beyond the simple calculation of economic utilities, social and cultural changes play a role in people's move away from marriage and parenthood in postindustrial societies. The forces behind these changes have been described in various ways.

I have argued that most European societies have shifted remarkably toward greater progressiveness in the postwar period and this helps explain many demographic changes. Philosophically, "progressiveness" characterizes a tendency to embrace the new, look critically at the present, and largely disregard the past.

A Sequence of Events in Family Formation

An interesting perspective on recent population change in Europe is to see the changes that have occurred in factors bearing on family formation as a sequence through which all countries pass. The timing and speed of the sequence have differed substantially between Eastern and Western Europe and within these regions, but there is strong evidence of a logical ordering. Each step taken seems to have led to the next; each option chosen made a further choice possible. Looking back, the sequence of events that led to today's low fertility seems both logical and understandable. One wonders why it was not predicted! Reflecting the shift to progressiveness and individualism, the sequence involves shifts from marriage toward cohabitation, from children to the adult couple as the focus of a family, from contraception to prevent unwanted births to deliberate, self-fulfilling choices whether and when to conceive a child, and from uniform to widely diversified families and households. Let us sketch the sequence as it has progressed to completion in a "standard" European country.

To trace the story, one must begin with the great impact of World War II. Virtually all European countries were involved in the fighting, suffered from occupation and shortages, and experienced the uncertainties and sorrows that war brings. Many young men saw military service and became familiar with techniques to prevent conception and venereal disease. Retrospective surveys document a steady increase from cohort to cohort in the proportions of adults who have experienced premarital intercourse and a sharp postwar decline in the age at which such sexual relations begin. Geeraert, citing a long list of research in Western European countries since 1900, concludes that among young women in particular, both students and working women, premarital intercourse is increasingly common.[2]

Social attitudes regarding premarital or extramarital sexual relations did not change so rapidly. Most couples therefore sought official sanction through marriage. This was also the solution in the case of an out-of-wedlock pregnancy.

Besides official sanction to live together, most couples who married in the early 1950s also wanted and were economically ready to start a family. The average age at first marriage declined, the interval between marriage and the first birth remained short, and birth rates for lower-order births began to rise. The increase in fertility in the early childbearing ages more than made up for the decline in higher-order births, so that the total fertility rate increased — at least to the mid-1960s.

The decline in higher-order births reflected general acceptance of birth control as a means to limit family size. This was the tail end of the first demographic transition in which birth control was used not for spacing but to bring completed family size down from seven or eight children in the 1880s to two or three some 50–60 years later. But the contraceptives available before the mid-1960s were not very effective or suitable for inexperienced couples and many "unwanted" children were no doubt born.

The decline in age at first marriage loosened the link between marriage and the start of childbearing. Marriage was still desired to earn official approval of sexual relations (certainly by a couple's parents), but for many young couples it no longer marked a readiness to have children. Parents anxious to help their just-married children avoid the burdens of an immediate birth may well have introduced them to family planning. Family planning organization enrollments soared. Membership in the Dutch organization (Netherlands Association for Sexual Reform, NVSH) more than doubled from 97,000 in 1955 to a peak of 206,000 in 1965 (and now has almost evaporated). As contraception became more popular for avoiding births early in married life, the age at marriage could decline further. Young married couples could accumulate assets together before deciding to take on the care of children.

Just about that time, in the mid-1960s, the effective, as well as safe, pills and IUDs came on the market. They were readily adopted. First and second birth intervals lengthened, and there were somewhat fewer lower-order births. Doubtless due also to further reductions in family-size norms, fertility above age 30 plummeted and the birth of fourth, fifth, and later children became an exception. The proportion of unwanted births — conceived out of marriage or too late in marriage — declined.

By the early 1970s, changes in abortion law made it possible to terminate unintended premarital pregnancies safely, so the frequency of unwanted first births declined further. The gradual disappearance of "forced marriages" slowed the decline in age at first marriage and this age began to climb.

Abortion could, of course, also be used to avert unwanted births among married women — high-order births, risky and socially unacceptable births to older women, and, if so desired, births conceived extramaritally. Increased adoption of sterilization to control fertility after couples had all the children they wanted further cut the number of higher-order births in the early 1970s. Fertility fell below replacement level.

Once it was generally accepted that sexual relations in marriage were not solely or primarily aimed at procreation and contraceptives of high quality had become available, a further step was taken. Law changes had already increased the frequency of divorce and legal separation. Divorce and separation were also occurring at earlier ages and sooner after marriage. Since young people now married with the intention of delaying childbearing for several years, it is understandable that the need to seek a seal of approval for such an arrangement was questioned. Why not start living together and marry only when children were wanted or on the way? Stable unions were formed, differing from early marriage mainly in that they were "paperless." The first marriage rate began to decline and the age at first marriage went up.

The proportions ever-marrying declined markedly; age at first marriage rose further. Remarriages became much less common. A rise in out-of-wedlock fertility became noticeable, particularly among somewhat older women. Some of these women deliberately chose to bear a child without having a stable relationship with a male partner. The proportions of out-of-wedlock births legitimated by marriage or the male partner declined. In addition, voluntary childlessness was no longer solely an option for men and women who elected not to marry. Being married or living in a stable union no longer differentiated people strongly with regard either to having children or desired family size. Fertility seemed to stabilize well below replacement level.

This "standard" sequence of changes in family formation is obviously impossible to trace in detail for all 30 of Europe's heterogeneous countries and the sequence itself is likely to be different as it evolves among them. However, the countries can be grouped roughly according to their place in the sequence as it has evolved so far and fairly simple period data available for a reasonable number of the countries demonstrate the basic features of the second transition to low fertility. These features involve four related shifts:

1. Shift from the *golden age of marriage* to the *dawn of cohabitation;*
2. Shift from the era of the *king-child with parents* to that of the *king-pair with a child;*
3. Shift from *preventive contraception* to *self-fulfilling conception;*
4. Shift from *uniform* to *pluralistic families and households*.

Where Countries are in the Sequence

Only two European countries appear to have experienced the full sequence of changes in family formation that have led to very low fertility — Denmark and Sweden. Even here there have been deviations from the "standard" sequence described above. However, in these two countries the proportion of out-of-wedlock births has risen from about 10 percent in 1956–60 to well over 40 percent currently. And the tremendously changed social significance of the "married" status probably best demonstrates the transition toward greater individualism.

The following four groups indicate where European countries now are in the standard sequence.

First Group. In addition to Denmark and Sweden, this group includes the Northern and Western European countries which appear to be following close in their tracks. The birth rates of these countries as of the mid-1980s generally fall between 10 and 12 per 1,000 population and the rate of natural increase (births minus deaths) is no more than 0.4 percentage points above zero or actually negative. Finland, Norway, the United Kingdom, Austria, Belgium, France, the Federal Republic of Germany, the Netherlands, Switzerland, and Italy (in Southern Europe) all qualify for this group. Here the second demographic transition is well advanced.

Second Group. This group includes Greece, Malta, Portugal, Spain, and Yugoslavia in Southern Europe. The fertility decline has been less marked in these countries; they follow the first group at a distance. Current birth rates range from 12 to 16 per 1,000 population and the rate of natural increase usually exceeds 0.4 percent. The second transition is late, but there is little doubt that it has begun and will be completed.

Third Group. The six Eastern European countries make up this group: Bulgaria, Czechoslovakia, the German Democratic Republic, Hungary, Poland, and Romania. Here the postwar trend toward greater sexual freedom appears to be less pronounced. In reaction to forcible attempts to change the structure and norms of society after the political change, many people have clung tenaciously to traditional mores in their personal lives. On the other hand, legal abortion became available in these countries earlier than in most other European countries, while government intervention to raise birth rates has had some impact on fertility trends. Current birth rates are close to 14 per 1,000 population, except for Hungary (12.2 in 1985) and Poland (18.2).

Fourth Group. This group covers the remaining countries which, for a variety of cultural and historical reasons, are all late in completing the *first* demographic transition. It includes Iceland and Ireland in Northern Europe and Albania and Turkey in Southern Europe. Even parts of the USSR belong to this group. Whether or when they will begin the second demographic transition is not easy to predict. Their current birth rates tend to be high by European standards and rates of natural increase range from about 0.9 percent in Iceland and Ireland to 2.1 percent in Turkey.

Making the Gift of a Baby to the Pension Funds?

In 1986 the influential Germany weekly *Der Spiegel* ran a series of articles under the heading *Den Alterskassen ein Baby schenken?*, which translates roughly as above. It sums up Europe's demographic dilemma well. Collective and individual interests do not seem to coincide. The transition to individualism appears to have led to an extended period of below-replacement-level fertility, population decline, and an age structure that will in the long run make full funding of old-age pensions virtually impossible. Yet it is difficult to imagine people having babies to please the pension funds, and economic incentives, even at the level offered in France and some Eastern European countries, appear incapable of overcoming individualistic desires and raising fertility to replacement level. Relying on immigration to adjust age structures is practically out of the question. All countries of immigration have taken effective measures to end the influx and increasingly aim at rapid integration of the current minorities.

What then is the answer to the predicament? Most countries will probably follow the old maxim: If in doubt, do nothing; wait and see.

Another approach is to try out new, more imaginative measures to raise fertility and have them ready when needed. Thinking in this direction is developing rapidly. So far no serious proposal seems to be compatible with the shift to individualistic values. But a recent proposition by demographer Paul Demeny is certainly imaginative.[3] He proposes to relink fertility behavior and economic security in old age. The pronatalist institution he sees would earmark a socially agreed-upon fraction of the compulsory contribution from earnings that flow into the common pool from which pay-as-you-go national social security schemes are now financed and transfer that fraction to individual contributors' live parents as an additional entitlement."

It is easy to make a long list of reasons why this proposal has no chance in the world of being implemented. But then, in demographic matters the unexpected sometimes happens.

ENDNOTES

[1] Lesthaeghe, R. and C. Wilson. *Modes of Production, Secularisation, and the Pace of the Fertility Decline in Western Europe, 1870–1930,* working paper, Brussels, 1978.

[2] Geeraert, A. *Sexualiteit bij jongeren* (Sexuality among Young People) (Brussels: De Sikkel, 1977), p. 27.

[3] Demeny, P. *Population Note No. 57* (New York: The Population Council, December 1, 1986).

QUESTIONS

DISCUSSION QUESTIONS

1. Is the history of the way the West developed a useful and relevant guide for understanding and planning the development of today's poorest countries?

2. Many social problems are talked about more openly now than in the past (for example, incest or wife battering). Do societies have significantly more (or worse) problems today or do we just talk about them more?

3. How has the feminist movement changed Canadian society in the twentieth century?

4. The term "progress" is sometimes used to mean change that is positive or desirable. Discuss some recent social trends and see whether your group reaches any consensus about which trends are "progressive."

DATA COLLECTION EXERCISES

1. How many years of formal education did a person need 50 years ago to be in the top five percent of Canada's population, in terms of educational achievement? How many years of schooling would a person need to achieve the same ranking today?

2. Interview a small sample of people who are enthusiastic about one form of social innovation. For example, they might be computer hackers or trend setters in fashion. Try to determine whether they tend to be interested in innovation in general or just within their own narrow field. Do you think some personality types are more receptive to change than others?

3. The rate of increase in urbanization can be used as one measure of how fast social change is occurring. Find out what percentage of the world's population lived in urban areas in 1950 and what percentage lives in such areas now. If urbanization continues to rise at the same rate as in the past, how many years will it take before the world as a whole reaches Canada's current level of urbanization?

4. Traditionally, each generation of Canadians has been financially better off than their parents' generation. Is this still true today? What would be the best empirical way of answering this question?

WRITING EXERCISES

1. Some groups in modern society (such as the Amish) have successfully resisted the temptation to adopt modern lifestyles. Do some research on one such group and write a brief essay explaining why the group opposes modern lifestyles.

2. Write a brief essay explaining how and why rapid social change can lead to intergenerational conflict.

3. You are Minister of the Environment in a provincial government. Your job is to

find the best way of getting people to leave their cars at home and take public transit to work. Some advisors say banning single-passenger cars from city streets is the best idea. Others say more public education is the best approach; and so on. Decide what you are going to do and defend your decision in a brief memo to your Premier.

4. Write a brief scenario outlining some events that could cause European birth rates to go up again.

SUGGESTED READINGS

1. Chirot, Daniel (1977). *Social Change in the Twentieth Century.* New York: Harcourt Brace Jovanovich. This book attempts to show how the prospects of an individual country depend on how it fits into the world system of "core" and "peripheral" countries. It calls attention to the fact that, for all countries, social change takes place within a "small world."

2. Inkeles, Alex and David H. Smith (1974). *Becoming Modern: Individual Change in Six Developing Countries.* London: Heinemann. The impact of industrialization on people's traditional ideas, attitudes, and social customs is explored in this book, using survey data from six nations around the world. In particular, it explores the effect of people's interactions with new technology.

3. Rifkin, Jeremy with Ted Howard (1980). *Entropy: A New World View.* New York: Bantam. This book seeks to change society by changing basic assumptions about the natural world. The authors believe that by changing those basic assumptions we will begin to see the need for a major reorganization of society.

4. Toffler, Alvin (1970). *Future Shock* New York: Bantam. This book has sold millions of copies. Its theme is the difficulty of trying to cope with the accelerated pace of social change in modern societies. You, for example, may experience such shock when you read a book like this one, or the daily newspaper (for that matter).

GLOSSARY

achieved status — a social status based on characteristics over which the individual exerts *some* control, such as educational attainment, marital status, or type of employment.

accommodating elites theory — an approach that holds that there are several elite groups in society that compete and compromise in pursuing their respective interests.

affirmative action — a type of legislation (particularly related to recruitment, hiring and promotion practices) aimed at ensuring that certain types of people (whether women, racial minorities, or otherwise) who have previously been excluded will enjoy a slight advantage over competitors in the future.

age-ism — a prejudiced attitude and/or willingness to discriminate against people of a particular age, especially elderly people.

agents of socialization — social settings and groups in which socialization takes place, the most important of which are the family, school, peer group, and mass media.

anticipatory socialization — training in preparation for a future role which the person hopes or expects to enter.

anti-feminism — beliefs and values opposed to feminist doctrine; see *feminism* below.

ascribed status — a social status based on the position into which an individual is born, or on characteristics (like sex) over which he or she exerts *no* control. (Contrast with *achieved status* above.)

authoritarianism — a point of view or style of organization which places the greatest importance on obedience to people in positions of superior authority. Often associated with unbending (rigid) rules and a preference for conventional behaviour.

authority — the ability of an individual or group to issue commands and have them obeyed because their control is perceived as legitimate.

biological determinism — the view that differences among individuals or cultures exist because nature has selected for them; any genetic explanation of behaviour.

black underclass — refers to urban blacks in the United States who are persistently very poor; "underclass" can be applied to other examples of persistent poverty among racial or ethnic groups as well (e.g., among native peoples in Canada).

bourgeoisie — in Marxist terminology, the group of people who own the means of production: capitalists. Sometimes also used to refer to the middle class in a capitalist society. The bourgeoisie employ the *proletariat*, who own none of the means of production and sell their own labour power.

brown racism — refers to prejudice among "brown-skinned" groups toward darker or "black-skinned" groups. "Brown" is used here to refer to people of the Third World who are neither whites nor blacks.

bureaucracy — a hierarchically organized type of formal organization featuring written rules and offices (interrelated positions). Recruitment and careers are based on performances, not ascribed statuses.

bureaucratic authority — the rational-legal authority typically found in bureaucracies and modern legal systems; authority rooted in formal, written rules and procedures.

capitalist class control theory — an approach that holds that the dominant group in society is the capitalist class; this class is said to prevail by controlling capital and the state.

caste system — a hierarchy of groups separated from each other by rules of ritual purity and prevented from intermarrying, changing castes through mobility, or holding certain jobs.

charismatic authority — a type of authority which gains its legitimacy from *charisma*, an exceptional ability to inspire devotion and enthusiasm among followers.

class system — a hierarchy of groups with different market conditions, work situations, and life chances. In Marxist theory, classes stand in different relations to the means of production.

cohabitation — a stable sexual union in which two people live together without marrying.

commensalism (or commensality) — the practice of eating together or (literally) sharing the same table. Often this act both symbolizes and reinforces the boundaries of a status group.

comprador elite — an elite made up of people who run corporations located in Canada but owned or controlled by foreigners.

confirmation bias — the process whereby people tend to look for evidence that confirms their attitudes and ignore evidence that does not.

conflict theory — a theoretical perspective that emphasizes conflict and change as the regular and permanent features of society, because society is made up of various groups who wield varying amounts of power.

consciousness-raising — the process of making a group aware of its interests, so that they may better pursue these interests; often takes place through social movements and the use of the mass media, meetings, and rallies led by the leaders of such groups.

conspicuous consumption — consumption (of material goods) that is for show alone, to establish the boundaries of a status group (especially, a wealthy "leisure class") and keep others out.

counter ideologies — reform and radical ideologies that challenge current social arrangements and call for social change.

crude divorce rate — divorces in a given year, per 100 000 people in the total population.

delegitimization — the process whereby powerful ingroups come to define some outgroup(s) as less than fully human and, therefore, as deserving of social exclusion, or even aggressive attacks.

differentiation — the process whereby various sets of activities are divided up and performed by a number of separate institutions. A complementary process is *integration*, whereby various elements of a society are combined to form a unified whole.

disability — the reduction of a person's life chances, often because the person has been convinced that he or she cannot succeed in a particular type of activity.

discrimination — the denial of access to opportunities that would be available to equally qualified members of the dominant group.

dominant ideologies — emotionally charged beliefs that offer explanations and justifications for existing social arrangements.

domination — the exercise of control over an individual or group who must submit to that person's power. (See also *submission*.)

double day (or second shift) — the way many women have to work at two "jobs" each day — one involving paid work in the labour market, and the other being unpaid domestic work in the household.

downward jealousy — where one group, or class, resents the gains of other less-advantaged groups.

elite — a small group that has power or influence over others and is regarded as being superior in some way. (See also *power elite* below.)

empowerment — any act or process which gives a disadvantaged group or individual more control over its life chances.

ethnocentrism — a tendency to view social life from the point of view of one's own culture, which enters into both common thought and also social research.

everyday resistance — what people do, as individuals, to express anger or opposition to unfair treatment by people who exert power over their lives; not organized or group resistance, but (often spontaneous) individual resistance.

exploitation — the gaining of unjustified profit as a result of someone else's work.

family life cycle — the sequential stages of family change and development.

feminism — a doctrine that argues women are systematically disadvantaged, compared to men, and they should be guaranteed opportunities that are equal to men's.

feminization of poverty — the growing tendency of poor people to be women, due to lone parenthood or impoverished old age.

functional theory (or structural functionalism) — a theoretical perspective that emphasizes the way each part of a society functions to fulfill the needs of society as a whole. In relation to inequality, it argues that unequal rewards are needed to ensure society is supplied with highly trained, highly motivated workers.

gemeinschaft — a sentiment found in relatively small close-knit communities or organizations, where commitment to tradition, intimate social interaction, and feelings of group solidarity are all prominant. (Compare with *gesellschaft*.)

gender — the socially (or culturally) constructed idea of what attributes and behaviours are appropriate to a given sex.

gender differences — socially defined roles for females and males, calling for different behaviours from the two sexes, and attributing different traits to the two sexes.

gender inequality — male/female differences in opportunities for obtaining power, status (prestige), and income and wealth; females are generally disadvantaged compared to males in each respect.

gender stereotypes — assumptions made about the abilities of people based on their sex; males are often seen as more able than females.

generalized other — a person's general idea of how the society, or surrounding social group, expects him or her to behave.

genocide — the state-planned and systematic murder of people who belong to a particular ethnic, racial, or religious group.

gesellschaft — a sentiment found in relatively large communities or organizations where there is a limited commitment to tradition, little intimate interaction, and weak feelings of group solidarity. (Compare with *gemeinschaft*.)

hegemony — the power exercised by one social group over another; especially, the ideological or cultural domination of one class by another.

ideologies — emotionally charged beliefs that either explain and justify existing social arrangements, or in the case of *counter ideologies*, call for and justify alternative ways of doing things.

indigenous elite — the top decision-makers in Canadian-owned corporations.

inequality of condition — an inequality in the distribution of social goods (food, housing, health, wealth, respect, authority, power, and so on) in society.

inequality of opportunity — an inequality in the chances that individuals or groups have to increase their social goods relative to other individuals or groups. (*See also* inequality of condition.)

infanticide — the purposeful killing of infant children.

labour power — the human capacity to work which is sold as a commodity to capitalists for wages.

legitimacy — a willing acceptance of existing social arrangements (especially, inequalities of condition or opportunity, or existing authority relations).

leisure — any time or activity which is under control of the people who are participating in the activity.

leisure class — the class of people who have inherited wealth and use their time in non-work (often, frivolous and wasteful) activities.

looking-glass self — a sense of self formed through interaction with others, by assessing others' opinions about oneself.

Marxist approach — an approach to sociological analysis which follows in the path of Karl Marx in emphasizing the importance of class relations to understanding social inequality, conflict, and change.

means of production — the machines, buildings, land and materials used in the production of goods and services by the bourgeoisie or capitalist class.

multiculturalism — a policy intended to help maintain ethnic group differences or uniqueness in culture, or lifestyle.

merit principle (or meritocracy) — a view that society is, or should be, organized in a way that rewards the most "meritorious" (or most socially useful and valuable) people most highly.

modernization (also, industrialization and socioeconomic development) — the process by which a society becomes industrialized, urbanized, and Westernized.

occupational prestige — the prestige, or respect, members of a society commonly attach to a particular occupation or occupational group (e.g., doctors, assembly-line workers).

occupational segregation — concentrations of members of a particular group in a relatively few occupations, where they greatly outnumber others, as with the concentration of women in some occupations and men in other ones.

oligarchy — control of members of the society by a few elite members; rule by a power elite.

one-child policy — a campaign begun in China in the early 1970s to attempt to restrict young couples to having only one child; it included the widespread distribution of birth control information and technology.

people's kitchens — cooperative kitchens operated and supplied by the pooled resources of several poor households; the participating families contribute labour and money, and receive meals from the kitchens.

personal troubles (vs. public issues) — difficulties we are having that we think are due to our own failings. Often they are really public issues in disguise. Many people have the same troubles for the same reasons, and political action is needed to solve the problem.

petite bourgeoisie — self-employed people who own their own businesses, get the productive labour for these businesses from themselves and family members, and do not employ others.

poverty (absolute) — a condition that occurs when people do not have enough of the basic necessities (food, shelter, and medicine, for example) for physical survival. (Compare with *relative poverty.*)

poverty (relative) — a condition defined by the general living standards of the society or social group; a low standard of living compared to most in the society or group. (Compare with *absolute poverty.*)

power — the ability to prevail over others (i.e., exercise one's will) despite resistance. In Marxist theory, power is the capacity of one class to realize its interests in opposition to other classes.

power elite — that group in a society which rules by controlling the dominant social organizations.

prejudice — a negative or hostile attitude toward members of a particular group simply because they belong to that group, based on untested assumptions about their characteristics.

prestige — the enjoyment of social honor and treatment with respect, a dimension of stratification that is separate from income, authority, or class position.

primary socialization — the early socialization of children, much of which takes place in a family setting.

proletariat — see *bourgeoisie.*

public issues — issues of importance in many people's everyday lives which have become part of political debate. (Compare with *personal troubles.*)

race — a group whose members are socially defined as sharing the same physical characteristics. The term is used as a biological concept, rather than a cultural one.

racism — the belief that one's own race is superior to all others.

radical feminism — the view that the oppression of women by men is the longest-lasting, most pervasive, most harmful, and most basic form of all social inequality.

radical ideologies — beliefs favouring the fundamental reconstruction of society.

rational-legal authority — a type of authority which gains its legitimacy through appeals to reason, legal contract, and concerns with efficiency.

reformist ideologies — beliefs favouring changes in society without calling for a fundamental reconstruction of society.

resocialization — the process of learning new roles in response to changes in life circumstances.

residential segregation — the geographic setting apart of two or more different groups (especially, racial or ethnic groups, or social classes) within a single city, state, or country.

second demographic transition — a second round of changes in family life and childbearing in developed countries, beginning in the 1960s; unlike the first transition, this one is motivated by individualistic values and attitudes.

secondary socialization — the ongoing and lifelong process of socialization, including accumulated learning in adolescence and adulthood.

sex (biological) differences — the physiological or biological differences between females and males.

sexism — a prejudiced attitude and/or willingness to discriminate against people of a particular sex, especially women.

social distance — reserve in social interaction between people who belong to groups ranked as superior and inferior in status.

socialization — the social learning process through which an individual becomes a capable member of society.

social mobility — the movement of individuals among different levels of the social hierarchy, defined occupationally. Movement may be vertical or horizontal, intergenerational or intragenerational.

social (protest) movements — forms of collective action aimed at protesting some existing arrangements in society and calling for social change.

social status — people's "standing" in the community, as measured by the amount of respect, deference or prestige they are granted.

socially constructed reality — behaviours or interactions that result from a shared perception or belief (for example, belief in the inferiority of women or non-white people).

socioeconomic status (SES) — a method of social ranking which combines measures of wealth, authority (or power), and prestige.

split labour market model — a theoretical approach to the study of work which argues that only people with certain characteristics are eligible for certain kinds of opportunities and benefits. The result is a two-tiered job system, in which one tier lacks high rewards, job security, good working conditions, and respect.

(the) state — a set of organizations concerned with enforcing decisions in society, making them binding on society's members; includes government and public bureaucracies, courts, police, and military.

state elites — the highest ranking members of the organization comprising the state. (See *state*.)

status group — a group that shares certain key social characteristics (e.g., ethnic or class origins), forms an identity based on these characteristics, and promotes interaction mainly among group members.

status inequality — inequality in access to desired social goods based on exclusion from a status group and/or low *social status*. (See definition above.) Based on the distribution of symbolic resources.

stereotype — a fixed mental image embracing all that is believed to be typical of members of a given group.

stratification system — a system of inequality that integrates class, status, and domination with other forms of differentiation, such as gender, race, and ethnicity.

subculture — a group in society that shares some of the cultural traits of the larger society but also has its own distinctive values, beliefs, norms, style of dress, and behaviour.

submission — subjection to control by another group or individual whose power is based on a higher class position or higher status position.

symbol (of domination) — a sign — for example, a gesture, artifact or word — that can meaningfully represent the superiority (or control) of one individual over another.

symbolic interactionism — a theoretical perspective that studies the process by which individuals interpret and respond to the actions of others, and that conceives of society as the product of their continuous face-to-face interaction.

symbolization — a process that represents social reality in an abstract or indirect form. For example, having women walk behind their husbands, or stay silent in their presence unless addressed directly, *symbolizes* the submission of women to men.

systematic (or institutional) discrimination — the unintended denial of opportunities to members of particular groups because of certain physical or cultural characteristics.

traditional authority — a type of authority which gains its legitimacy through appeals to custom and time-honoured tradition.

untouchability — a traditional distinction between certain Indian castes which forbids any kind of social contact.

Weberian approach — an approach to sociological analysis which follows in the path of Max Weber in emphasizing the importance of status relations to understanding social inequality, conflict, and change.